'EDMONTON'S FIRST STREET CAR. OCT 29th 08.
BROWN PHOTO 150¼

THE STORY OF
THE EDMONTON TRANSIT SYSTEM

Ride of the Century

Ken Tingley

Library and Archives Canada Cataloguing in Publication

Tingley, Kenneth W. (Kenneth Wayne), 1947–

Ride of the century : the story of the Edmonton Transit System / Ken Tingley.

Includes bibliographical references and index.

ISBN 978-0-9809275-0-4

1. Edmonton Transit System—History. 2. Urban transportation—Alberta— Edmonton—History. I. Edmonton Transit System II. Title. III. Title: Story of the Edmonton Transit System.

HE4509 E35 T56 2010   338.4097123'34   C2010-904903-9

Acknowledgements

Edmonton Transit acknowledges the generous financial assistance of Alberta Culture and Community Spirit in the production of this book.

Editing and production by Full Court Press.

Design by Boldface Technologies Inc.

Printed in China.

Cover and dust jacket photos:
Front cover: *Niall Fitzgerald*
Back cover: *Provincial Archives of Alberta A2246*
Spine top: *Glenbow Archives NA-1328-64585* bottom: *ETS*
Front flap top: *Provincial Archives of Alberta A1387* bottom: *ETS*
Back flap: *City of Edmonton*

Author's Acknowledgements

Many people cooperated during the preparation of the centennial history of Edmonton Transit. Pat Church initiated the project, while Margaret Dorey coordinated its many components. Dennis Nowicki and Lorna Stewart also placed priority on the history project and encouraged it at important junctures during its preparation. Jason Baxter, Jeff Stuart and Suzanne Lewis provided additional research and support. Denis Pigeon advised on and created several images used in the book, also providing the images for the inside front and back covers, and Niall Fitzgerald created the front jacket design.

Carolina Roemmich deserves special thanks for her tireless fact checking and the preparation of the invaluable fleet list included in the publication. Michael Payne, City of Edmonton Archivist, located many photographs and other resources, while the City of Edmonton Archives staff provided these to the project in usable format. The Provincial Archives of Alberta and the Glenbow Archives also were extremely helpful sources of photographic images. The Edmonton Radial Railway Society took a special interest in the book project and made available their resources. Doug Cowan shared not only his memories, but his unique collection of early images of trolleys, many of which appear in this book.

Early operators like Gordon Oleschuk and Kathleen Andrews, and early riders like Jessie Nichols, shared their memories. Such interviews added an otherwise unavailable dimension to the research. For that reason special thanks are due to: Olive Ainsley, Ernie Bastide, Glen Benson, Allan Bolstad, Bob Boutilier, Bernie Budney, Wes Brodhead, Terry Cavanagh, Norm Corness, Dave Geake, Dean Kulhavy, Greg Latham, Wayne Mandryk, Brian Mason, Arlene Meldrum, Rick Millican, Rick Paul, Cec Purves, Armin Preiksaitis, John Reid, Marion Robinson, Hans Ryffel, Don Scafe, John Sirovyak, Bill Smith, Jim Stewart, Charles Stolte, Ken Strachan, and Ken Thomas.

Several early sources were of special assistance during the initial research for this history. These include Colin Hatcher and Tom Schwarzkopf's *Edmonton's Electric Transit: The Story of Edmonton's Streetcars and Trolley Buses*; Colin Hatcher's *Edmonton's Light Rail Transit, the First 25 Years, 1978-2003*; and George H. Buck's thesis "A Technological History of Municipally Owned Public Transportation in Edmonton: 1893-1981."

As always Sheila Tingley provided real assistance in the planning and organization of the project.

ETS Acknowledgement

The process of coaxing this book from the germ of an idea to the finished creation you now hold has been a labour of love, a prolonged test of patience, and a journey through the telling of our story, via the mysterious and often confusing world of book publishing.

This legacy project has been possible only through the unwavering commitment, passion, and contributions of many people who have supported and encouraged the development of our historical story throughout its many steps and stages.

A book celebrating a centennial obviously comes along infrequently. With most of us not planning to be here for the bi-centennial, there were many cooks trying to add their own ingredients and play with the recipe. Of special note among the cooks, ETS is especially indebted to Jacquie Morris, Ken Tingley, and Dennis Johnson. Their contributions and guidance have been invaluable, their support and patience endless, and their dedication to our vision the foundation upon which this book has been built.

To all of them, the past and present employees of Edmonton Transit, and the many more unsung heroes in this project, our deepest thanks.

In Memoriam

Olive Marjorie Ainslie
Book Contributor, ERR Conductorette
March 31, 2011

Dennis Johnson
Editor and Friend
January 10, 2011

Arlene Meldrum
Book Contributor, Longtime ETS Customer, Transit Advocate
October 8, 2010

1908-2008
ETS celebrates **100** years

Design by Shelby Briggs

Contents

1908-2008
ETS celebrates **100** years

Design by Shelby Briggs

Message from Honourable Ed Stelmach
Premier of Alberta

On behalf of the Government of Alberta, I would like to congratulate the Edmonton Transit System on its 100th anniversary.

Edmonton has experienced tremendous growth over the past century and Edmonton Transit System has always stepped up to the challenge. One hundred years ago, Edmonton Transit System was able to serve a new city with just four streetcars. Many technological advances later, Edmonton Transit System continues to meet the needs of a growing, vibrant community.

Edmonton Transit System has been a provincial leader in creating a sustainable, fully-accessible, environmentally-friendly transportation option for Edmontonians. I know the Edmonton Transit System will continue to make significant contributions to our community that will help build a stronger Alberta for current and future generations. Everyone with the Edmonton Transit System should be proud of their history and be excited about the future.

I commend the Edmonton Transit System for a century of great accomplishments and extend my best wishes for many more years of success.

Ed Stelmach

Ed Stelmach

2008

Office of the Premier, Legislature Building, Edmonton, Alberta, Canada T5K 2B6
Telephone (780) 427-2251 Fax (780) 427-1349

Message from His Worship Mayor Stephen Mandel

On behalf of City Council and the people of Edmonton, Alberta's Capital City, I extend sincere congratulations to the Edmonton Transit team as you celebrate 100 years of public transit in our city.

A successful public transportation system comes from visionary civic leaders like John A. McDougall, Mayor of Edmonton in 1908. That year 18,500 people called Edmonton home and the Edmonton Radial Railway began providing public transportation with four streetcars that travelled up and down 21 kilometres of track. Those were exciting times, as we were the first prairie city with a public streetcar system!

"The Ride of the Century" tells the story of Edmonton's first century of public transit. This enlightening book showcases the people and the events that shaped the system that serves Edmontonians today. You'll read about transit's contribution to our economic growth, and you'll learn how public transit enhances the quality of life for seniors and persons with disabilities. This book showcases the pivotal role that Edmonton Transit has played in hosting major special events, like the 1978 Commonwealth Games for which we built the first leg of the LRT.

Today, over one million people live, work and play in the Edmonton region, and unprecedented growth is on the horizon. We need to get back to the levels of ridership on public transit that existed when Edmonton launched its streetcar system, when everyone took transit to work, to shop, to live their lives. Reflecting on our history through this book helps us build a bridge to the future. Our future is fully integrating transit plans with overall land-use plans to make a more walkable city and region, to reduce people's need to use personal vehicles.

Congratulations to everyone who contributed to "The Ride of the Century." Publishing this book helps record this important aspect of Edmonton's heritage, preserving it for future generations. This will be an enjoyable read for many years to come!

Yours truly,

Stephen Mandel

Stephen Mandel
Mayor

*Edmonton,
proud home of the
University of Alberta for 100 years.*

1908-2008

ETS celebrates 100 years

Design by Shelby Briggs

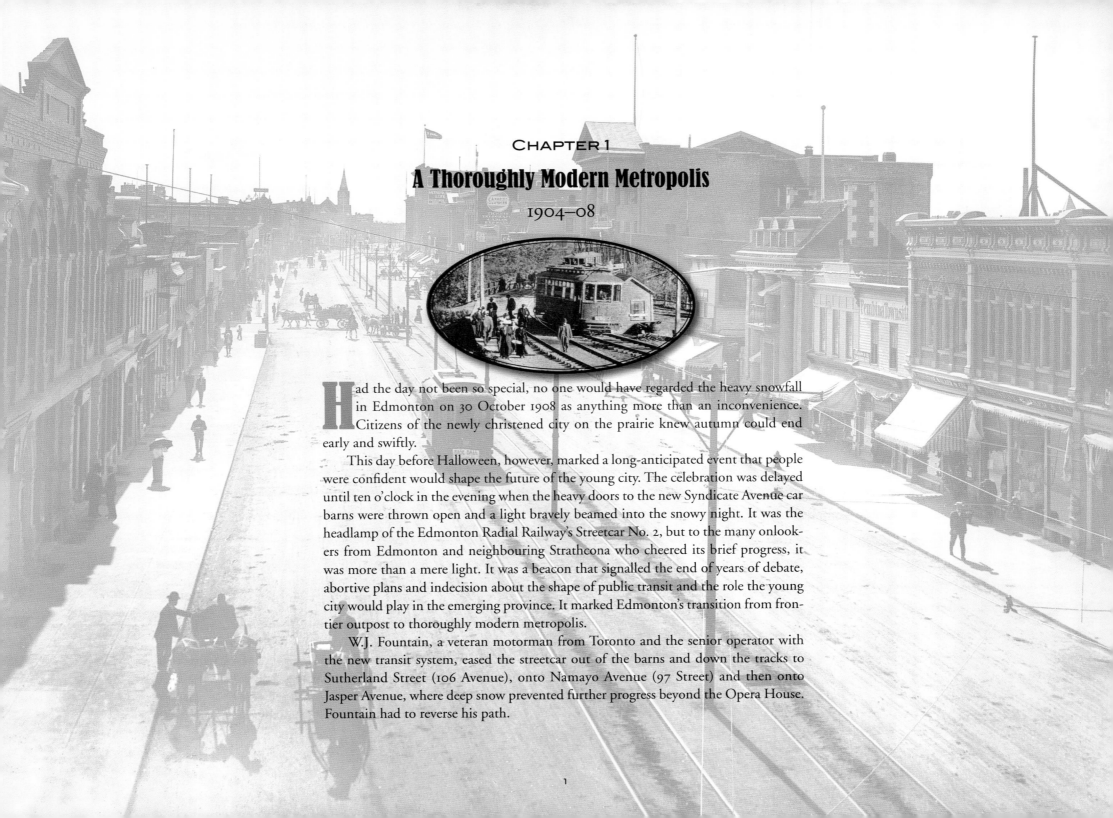

Chapter 1

A Thoroughly Modern Metropolis

1904–08

Had the day not been so special, no one would have regarded the heavy snowfall in Edmonton on 30 October 1908 as anything more than an inconvenience. Citizens of the newly christened city on the prairie knew autumn could end early and swiftly.

This day before Halloween, however, marked a long-anticipated event that people were confident would shape the future of the young city. The celebration was delayed until ten o'clock in the evening when the heavy doors to the new Syndicate Avenue car barns were thrown open and a light bravely beamed into the snowy night. It was the headlamp of the Edmonton Radial Railway's Streetcar No. 2, but to the many onlookers from Edmonton and neighbouring Strathcona who cheered its brief progress, it was more than a mere light. It was a beacon that signalled the end of years of debate, abortive plans and indecision about the shape of public transit and the role the young city would play in the emerging province. It marked Edmonton's transition from frontier outpost to thoroughly modern metropolis.

W.J. Fountain, a veteran motorman from Toronto and the senior operator with the new transit system, eased the streetcar out of the barns and down the tracks to Sutherland Street (106 Avenue), onto Namayo Avenue (97 Street) and then onto Jasper Avenue, where deep snow prevented further progress beyond the Opera House. Fountain had to reverse his path.

1

Edmonton Radial Railway's first streetcar travels past Norwood School on the first day of regular service, 9 November 1908.
(Provincial Archives of Alberta A2246)

No matter. The late start and wintry scene did nothing to dampen the crowd's enthusiasm. They raised their hands and voices in the frozen air. Then a blown fuse interrupted No. 2's progress altogether. After repair, the streetcar began another run back at Sutherland Avenue on the instruction of Edmonton Radial Railway (ERR) Superintendent Charles Taylor. Carrying a group of boisterous young women, Car No. 2 experienced another problem when a disconnected trolley pole halted progress and threw it into darkness. The festivities continued undaunted. Thus did a new city take its first hesitant steps into the modern age of urban transportation and electricity.

The first short test run of the Edmonton Radial Railway (ERR) had occurred the day before the inaugural public run and only three days before the deadline imposed by the City for the launch of the Edmonton Radial Railway. This wasn't the first time an increasingly frustrated citizenry had

watched plans go awry, and City Council was determined to inaugurate service on time. On Halloween the streetcar conveyed a delegation of city representatives across the river to Strathcona to officially link the two cities in a single streetcar network. The cities took immense pride in their new urban railway, the only example in Canada between Winnipeg and Vancouver, and the most northerly streetcar system in North America.

Streetcar No. 2 was used for the inaugural run because the cars were numbered during production at the Ottawa Car Company, and No. 1 arrived in Edmonton after No. 2. In a contest of rival railways, the Canadian Northern Railway shipped Car No. 1 west, while the Canadian Pacific Railway transported Car No. 2. The Canadian Northern's route lacked two important rail links across northern Ontario, and its progress was slowed further when freight had to be shipped by boat across Lakes Huron and Superior. The CPR

Streetcar No. 2 on its test run.
(Provincial Archives of Alberta B 5797)

BROWN PHOTO. (506)

EDMONTON'S FIRST STREETCAR
(OCT. 29. 1908)

won the contest when Car No. 2 arrived in Strathcona on 24 October and was transferred across the Low Level Bridge to Edmonton for final assembly at the Canadian Northern yards downtown. No. 1 arrived on Halloween; a week later, the same day No. 2 took its first run.

Regular streetcar service began in Edmonton at 7:00 AM 9 November 1908. Cars No. 1 and 2 operated out of the Syndicate Avenue car barns, running as far as 121 Street until midnight. The first day of operation brought in $150 in receipts at a nickel a ride, 3,000 rides in all. Within two weeks, four cars were operating on the line. The start that had been made was hampered by a critical power shortage, lack of an adequate fleet to meet demand and no final confirmation that the Low Level Bridge could be used to cross the river. The ERR cautiously chose to hold no official ceremony to launch the service.

Edmonton Radial Railway Track Map 1908

Railway workers adjust the electric pole in preparation for the Edmonton Radial Railway's first test run. *(Provincial Archives of Alberta B 5785a)*

Edmonton Radial Railway track, 1908. *(ETS)*

Charles E. Taylor, First Superintendent of the Edmonton Radial Railway

A wire from the Fort McMurray RCMP constable on 18 July 1921 brought the shocking news to Edmonton that Charles E. Taylor, first superintendent of the Edmonton Radial Railway and a local business leader, had shot himself in the head with his automatic pistol while aboard the steamboat *McMurray* on the Athabasca River. He had died the previous day in the presence of his horrified travelling companion, Dr. H.L. McInnis, who reported at the court of inquiry held aboard the *McMurray* that Taylor had suddenly begun acting erratically.

Charles Taylor's life had been the epitome of business and social success. Born and raised in Ottawa, he became a civil, mechanical and electrical engineer. Before arriving in Edmonton in 1900, Taylor served as superintendent of the street railway system in Hull, Quebec. He was hired to oversee the construction of the Edmonton Radial Railway and then served as superintendent for four years. Later, he worked for Crafts, Lee and Gallinger to develop the Tofield coalfields east of the city, and then became a consulting engineer for Fairchilds, Jones and Taylor from 1914 to 1917. In 1916 he was appointed superintendent of the Alliance Power Company, which operated the municipal power plant.

Taylor was influential in attracting the Imperial Oil Company to western Canadian oil exploration and was responsible for the ambitious geological survey conducted in northern Alberta in 1917. He worked for Imperial Oil from this time until his death, becoming a consulting engineer and western Canadian manager for the company's production department.

Taylor gained local notoriety in January 1921 when he coordinated the legendary Wop May's experimental cross-continental flight in an Imperial Oil Ltd aircraft. "In making this flight across country, the boys have done just the kind of work that will be needed in the North," Taylor announced after the big plane touched down at Edmonton's Blatchford Field. Taylor left Edmonton in May 1921 to travel for Imperial Oil and was making his way home when he took his life.

Funeral services for Taylor were held at First Presbyterian with pallbearers representing the city's business and professional elites: the Hon. Frank Oliver, A.B. Campbell, W.T. Henry, H.H. Hyndman, J.P. McMillan and Dr. H.L McInnis. What private anguish drove the public man of storied accomplishment to suicide remains a mystery *(Edmonton Journal; Edmonton Bulletin).*

Charles E. Taylor (back row centre), H. Myers (back row right), G.W. Gorman (front row left), "Wop" May (front row centre) pose in front of an Imperial Oil Ltd. Junker F-13 in 1921.
(City of Edmonton Archives EA-10-3181-13-4)

A new century driven by the wonder of electricity presented Edmontonians new transportation and communication technologies. In 1904, Joe Morris had brought the first automobile to the city. That same year, Edmonton established Canada's first municipally owned telephone system followed in 1908 by the nation's first automatic telephone service. Reginald Hunt amazed Edmontonians on Labour Day 1909 when he piloted his experimental flying machine on the first powered flight in western Canada, heralding the role the city would play in the development of northern aviation. In 1912, the eventful year of the amalgamation of Edmonton and Strathcona, the high point in Edmonton's boundless ambition was marked by a mammoth Hudson's Bay Company land sale that attracted long queues of excited speculators betting on a future of exuberant growth.

Just over 100 years before the fledgling Radial Railways' first run, Edmonton sprang up on the north bank of the North Saskatchewan River outside the walls of the last in a series of Hudson's Bay Company fur-trading forts of the same name. South Edmonton, as Strathcona was known until 1899, developed on the opposite side of the river. Together, they marked the western terminus of the Carlton Trail, the principal overland route over which Red River carts transported trade goods into the region before returning east laden with furs. When settlement of the fertile land of the Parkland Region began in earnest in the late nineteenth century, Edmonton and Strathcona became important agricultural supply centres.

Edmonton became a city on 8 October 1904 with a population of 8,350. During the next decade,

The first car in Edmonton, driven by Joe H. Morris, with Vernon Barford, centre back, and Mrs. Morris beside him on the right, in 1904. *(City of Edmonton Archives EA-10-2781)*

Pioneering aviatrix Katherine Stinson piloted Alberta's first airmail flight from Calgary to Edmonton on 9 July 1918, signalling yet another early commercialization of the airplane in Western Canada. *(City of Edmonton Archives EA-10-1246)*

The first automobile in Edmonton driving behind another car on Groat Estate, c. 1903. *(Provincial Archives of Alberta B 4784)*

the city's population swelled eightfold as settlers, entrepreneurs, professionals and workers descended on the "last best West" holding out its golden promise of wealth to those with initiative and vision. By 1906 Edmonton had grown to 14,088, and by 1914, Greater Edmonton, newly amalgamated with Strathcona, boasted 72,516 residents. Fire-zone bylaws encouraged the replacement of the hastily constructed first generation of wooden commercial structures with more impressive brick buildings felt appropriate for a booming city. Edmonton was transformed almost overnight from a city of temporary timber to one of permanent brick.

On 1 September 1905, the Province of Alberta was proclaimed amid heated debate over the location of the new capital. Both Edmonton and Calgary vied determinedly for the honour. The rivalry between the two cities dated to the 1880s when the Canadian Pacific Railway (CPR) built its transcontinental line through the southern settlement rather than the generally preferred northern Yellowhead Route through Edmonton. From 1891 to 1905,

Edmonton's access to continental transportation depended on the Calgary and Edmonton Railway (later acquired by the CPR) and its tiny connector line, the grandiosely named Edmonton, Yukon and Pacific Railway, which crossed the river on the Low Level Bridge in 1902 but terminated within a few kilometres of the city. Desperately needing improved links to commerce and travel, Edmontonians rose up in indignation and frustration, with Frank Oliver, an Edmonton native and the federal government's new Minister of the Interior, becoming the city's foremost champion of transportation.

Oliver's unbending diligence and influence over the next two decades gave Edmonton the prize. On 15 March 1906, the first session of the provincial legislature convened at the Thistle Roller and Ice Rink because the young province did not yet have a permanent legislature building. Two months later, legislative sessions moved to the more distinguished McKay Avenue School. Only another three months passed before the last spike for the Canadian Northern Railway was driven in the city, providing Edmonton with its own rail connection to the Ontario lakehead and international markets. A second railway, the Grand Trunk Pacific, arrived in 1909, and by 1915 the Grand Trunk had opened its landmark Hotel Macdonald. In 1908 the University of Alberta opened in Strathcona, and when Strathcona amalgamated with Edmonton in 1912, Edmonton inherited the title of provincial University City in addition to Capital City.

Wheat sheaves being laid on the decorative arch on Jasper Avenue west of 100 Street to commemorate the proclamation of the new Province of Alberta. In three years, streetcar tracks would appear at this location. (Glenbow Archives NA-2251-8)

As the capital of the new province, Edmonton faced expectations beyond constructing a permanent legislature. It needed the infrastructure of a thoroughly modern metropolis. Although the Edmonton Radial Railway met its first deadline of establishing service by 1 November 1908, the minor electrical problem experienced during the first run augured things to come when electrical shortages would hinder the development of the ERR and frustrate Edmontonians. Contributing to the problem were conditions dating back to 1869–70 when the Dominion of Canada purchased the North-West Territories from the Hudson's Bay Company (HBC). At the time of the Radial Railway's construction, the HBC still retained control of a large land reserve in central Edmonton that forced the first settlement beyond its boundaries into what is now 101 Street to the east and 121 Street to the west, the North Saskatchewan River to the south and 122 Avenue to the north.

The ERR was tasked with connecting the resulting far-flung business and residential districts along Jasper and Namayo avenues with the working-class districts isolated in the river valley pockets of Gallagher, Walter and Fraser Flats, where much industrial and residential activity had been concentrated since the early days of the fur trade posts. For years the only means of transportation from the flats to the top of the river valley was by foot or horse-drawn bus. To serve districts scattered below the escarpment, the ERR had to cope with the steep banks of the valley, a physical obstacle that would challenge development of the streetcar system for years (*Strathcona Plaindealer*).

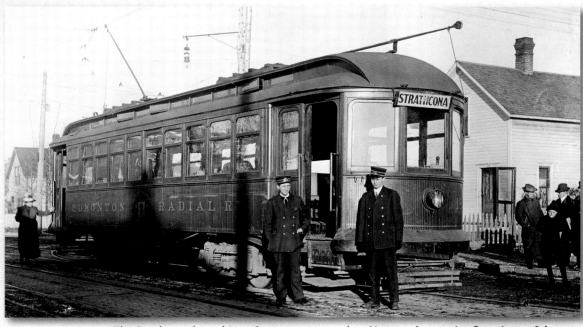

The Strathcona-bound No. 18 streetcar stopped on Namayo Avenue (97 Street) at 106 Avenue around the time of the Edmonton–Strathcona amalgamation. *(Glenbow Archives NA-55-1)*

Looking west along Whyte Avenue from Main Street (104 Street) prior to the building of the first trolley line. *(Canadian Pacific Railway Archives #1884)*

Even more challenging was crossing the deep escarpment of the North Saskatchewan River to link the City of Strathcona with Edmonton. Strathcona had become a centre of development when the Calgary and Edmonton Railway terminated on the south side of the North Saskatchewan River in 1891. "One of the greatest obstacles to the progress not only of these towns but of the whole district has been removed," opined the *Alberta Plaindealer* upon completion of the Low Level Bridge that connected the two communities in 1900. Two years later, the tiny Edmonton, Yukon and Pacific Railway made its first crossing of the bridge (*Alberta Plaindealer*).

In 1868, under terms of the Rupert's Land Act, the Government of Canada purchased the vast western lands that had been owned for 200 years by the Hudson's Bay Company under deed from the British Crown. Following the land transfer, transportation systems developed rapidly to serve settlers flooding into the Edmonton district. The steamboat *Northcote* launched service in 1875, providing an important link to the mouth of the Saskatchewan River and Lake Winnipeg. Stagecoaches running on the Calgary and Edmonton Trail, blazed in 1873, linked Edmonton and

Strathcona with Calgary and then with the Canadian Pacific Railway after its arrival in 1883. Supply cart trails north of Edmonton to Athabasca Landing supplied a vital link to the northern fur trade.

Between 1891, when the railway terminus was established across the river from Edmonton, until the advent of the radial railway, private horse-drawn buses transported passengers and freight across the river on two ferries that remained in operation until shortly after the opening of the Low Level Bridge. "The two lines now running divide the time so that a bus can be caught for either town at almost any hour in the day," the *Alberta Plaindealer* boasted in 1901. Three more horse-drawn buses were soon added, and in October 1902, D.E. Cameron, located at the Mallette Barn on West Railway Street in Strathcona, and N. Leclerc added another bus service (*Alberta Plaindealer*). Leclerc advertised daily service leaving Edmonton for Strathcona at 7:00 AM and 9:30 AM, 1:30 PM and 3:30 PM.

When the Calgary and Edmonton Railway (C & E) reached South Edmonton (soon to be called Strathcona) in the summer of 1891, Edmonton recognized the immediate need to link up with this new freight and

The Low Level Bridge in about 1906, two years before it became an important link in the Edmonton Radial Railway. Gallagher Flats is visible on the south bank of the North Saskatchewan River. *(Glenbow Archives NA-303-31)*

John Walter's Ferry in 1892, a year after the Calgary and Edmonton Railway arrived in South Edmonton. Ferries provided the only cross-river transport until the Low Level Bridge opened. *(Glenbow Archives NA-2801-3)*

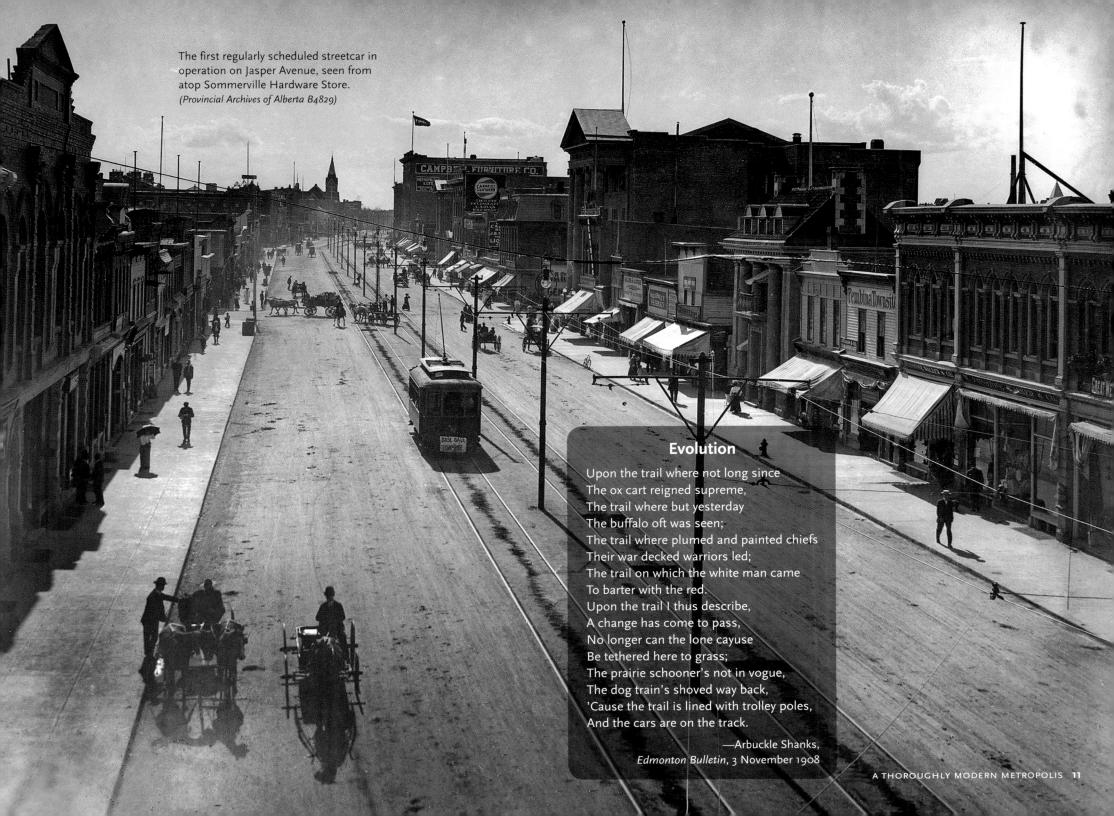

The first regularly scheduled streetcar in operation on Jasper Avenue, seen from atop Sommerville Hardware Store.
(Provincial Archives of Alberta B4829)

Evolution

Upon the trail where not long since
The ox cart reigned supreme,
The trail where but yesterday
The buffalo oft was seen;
The trail where plumed and painted chiefs
Their war decked warriors led;
The trail on which the white man came
To barter with the red.
Upon the trail I thus describe,
A change has come to pass,
No longer can the lone cayuse
Be tethered here to grass;
The prairie schooner's not in vogue,
The dog train's shoved way back,
'Cause the trail is lined with trolley poles,
And the cars are on the track.

—Arbuckle Shanks,
Edmonton Bulletin, 3 November 1908

passenger terminal frustratingly located just across the North Saskatchewan River's deep valley. With incorporation in February 1892, the first Town of Edmonton council looked for a solution in the interurban railways proliferating in central Canada and the United States.

Edmonton's first public transit initiative was launched a year later when *An Ordinance to Empower the Municipality of the Town of Edmonton to Construct and Operate a Tramway* was assented to by the North-West Territories Council. Ordinance No. 32 (1893) Section 8 laid down a number of essential provisions. Edmonton was authorized to build either a single- or double-track tramway, a term borrowed from the British transit systems. The ordinance extended up to eight kilometres outside Edmonton's municipal limits to allow the tramway to connect with the newly established Calgary and Edmonton railhead in South Edmonton. Any form of motive power was permitted except steam, presumably to forestall the formation of a little railway empire on the north bank of the river. Edmonton could also build a ferry across the North Saskatchewan "expedient for the use of the tramway during the summer and may lay a track across the Saskatchewan [River] upon

Transit coaches climbing Ross Street Hill in 1906 with passengers from the south side.
(Glenbow Archives NA-1328-60495)

Ferries continued in use after the Low Level Bridge opened, but they soon disappeared from the scene. *(City of Edmonton Archives EA-9-1)*

the ice during the winter if the same is deemed expedient" (*An Ordinance to Empower the Municipality of the Town of Edmonton to Construct and Operate a Tramway*).

Despite the Town Council's enthusiasm, lack of federal commitment and a slow economy prevented the enactment of the ordinance by the Canadian federal government. The plan would lie dormant for the next 15 years. Although the original 1893 ordinance established the framework for a municipally owned transit system, the intervening years brought repeated debate over the merits of public ownership, and the plan failed to gain traction because of concern that the town's investment would not be recovered through transit revenue.

When early public initiatives languished for lack of vision or funding, private investors and developers quickly attempted to fill the void, which beckoned invitingly with promises of quick profits. In 1903 William G. Tretheway, a Montreal real estate agent, proposed the first privately financed urban transit system to Edmonton Town Council. Tretheway purchased the franchise rights for the existing radial railway scheme from the City for $10,000 as a component in his overall plan for a residential development in the west end of the city. The bylaw approving the plan committed Tretheway to completion in 1905, but the plan was derailed when he failed to deliver on his promises.

Edmonton City Council returned to planning a publicly owned model, but their renewed interest seemed to be fuelled more by pique than vision as the high-flying Tretheway forfeited his bond and packed his bags for Montreal. By 1907, however, an ambitious street-paving program demanded an immediate decision on the fate of the radial railway. City Council would face public condemnation if they paved the streets one day only to tear them up the next. Streetcar rails, it was decided, would be simultaneously laid with paving. A public ownership model had been finally and firmly adopted.

The completion of the C & E Railway led to the rapid decline of the stagecoach service between Calgary and Edmonton, though coaches like these, shown in 1910, continued in service for some time.
(City of Edmonton Archives EA-10-1272)

Across the river, South Edmonton also recognized the need for an electric railway, and in 1895 the *South Edmonton News* fired the first shot in its editorial campaign for such a system. R.P. "Parm" Pettipiece, the energetic founding editor, informed south-side readers that one Professor Jennings was soon to arrive from Toronto to investigate the possibilities of a franchise to connect South Edmonton and "North Edmonton," as he insisted on calling the community on the other side of the river. "We find upon investigation that there has been enough freight transported from here to North Edmonton, by drays, to pay the interest on $80,000, the sum which will be required to build an electric railway," he reported, going on to claim that "there is an immense amount of freight exported every season from here, a large portion of which comes from across the river. Every day there are passengers including commercial men and others going to and from North Edmonton. If there was an easier and cheaper way for the farmers north of the river to send their grain across the valley to our flour and oatmeal mills they would certainly ship it here from North Edmonton by that means. . . . Then there is another thing to our advantage. South Edmonton would become a railway centre which in the near future would be regarded as Northern Alberta's commercial centre" (*South Edmonton News*).

The first South Edmonton railway plan also ended in failure, but the seed of an idea had been planted that would grow into a better-planned and -financed project within a decade when the Strathcona Radial Tramway Company was formed by a group of Edmonton, Strathcona and Fort Saskatchewan investors. The hopeful venture was authorized to connect the renamed Strathcona with Fort Saskatchewan, Morinville and other communities within 130 kilometres of Strathcona's boundaries. The company was obligated by the ordinance to build at least 24 kilometres of track within three years (*Strathcona Plaindealer*). The plan proved exaggeratedly ambitious, and the company abandoned the goal of building branch lines into district communities in favour a more manageable street railway plan for Strathcona alone (Hatcher and Schwarzkopf).

In January 1905, the Calgary and Edmonton Railway announced its intention to make application to the next parliamentary session for an act empowering the company to construct the High Level Bridge with the purpose of connecting Strathcona Station with Edmonton. A new bridge to augment the existing Low Level Bridge brought added

PLOWING JASPER AVE   Brown 103W
WITH A STEAMROLLER
FOR TRACTION

Clearing a grade on Jasper Avenue to lay streetcar tracks.
(Provincial Archives of Alberta B1133)

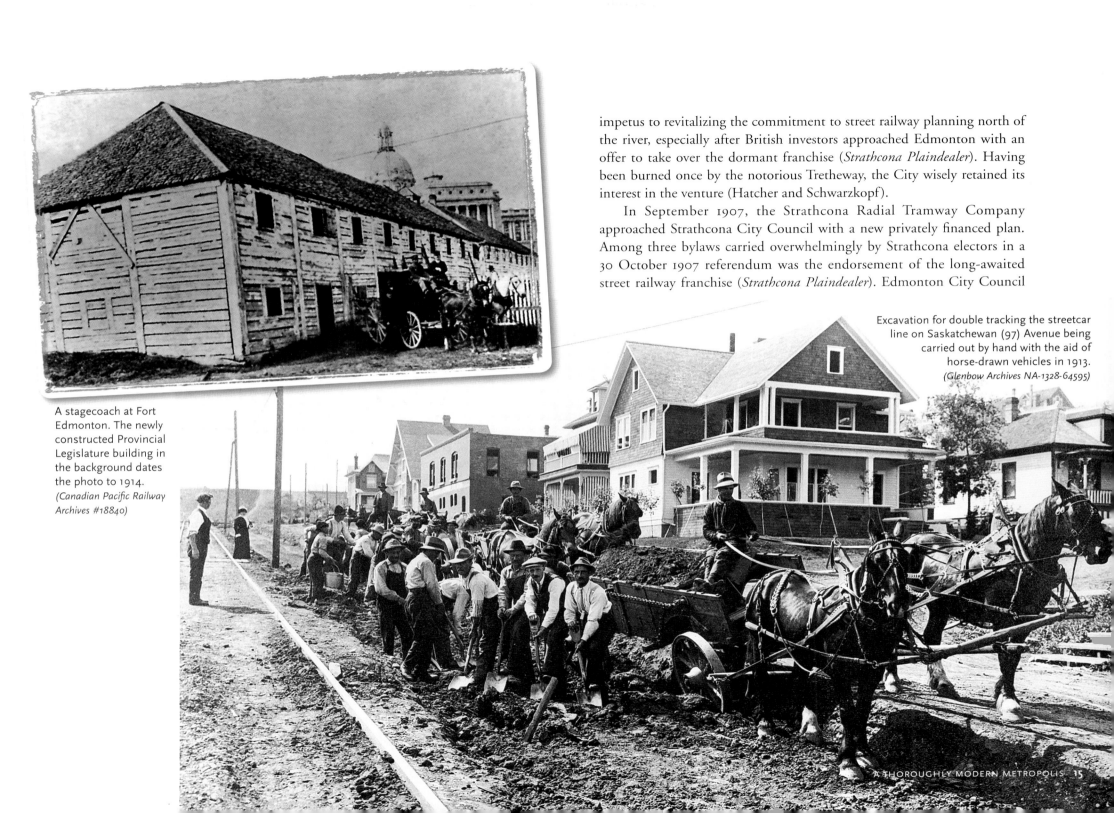

impetus to revitalizing the commitment to street railway planning north of the river, especially after British investors approached Edmonton with an offer to take over the dormant franchise (*Strathcona Plaindealer*). Having been burned once by the notorious Tretheway, the City wisely retained its interest in the venture (Hatcher and Schwarzkopf).

In September 1907, the Strathcona Radial Tramway Company approached Strathcona City Council with a new privately financed plan. Among three bylaws carried overwhelmingly by Strathcona electors in a 30 October 1907 referendum was the endorsement of the long-awaited street railway franchise (*Strathcona Plaindealer*). Edmonton City Council

Excavation for double tracking the streetcar line on Saskatchewan (97) Avenue being carried out by hand with the aid of horse-drawn vehicles in 1913.
(Glenbow Archives NA-1328-64595)

A stagecoach at Fort Edmonton. The newly constructed Provincial Legislature building in the background dates the photo to 1914.
(Canadian Pacific Railway Archives #18840)

swiftly dispatched a committee including Mayor W.A. Griesbach, Alderman Robert J. Manson (soon to be appointed Chairman of the Public Works Committee) and Alderman Wilfrid Gariepy to meet with the Strathcona City Council. The committee advocated a cooperative venture with Edmonton purchasing the Strathcona radial railway franchise. The *Strathcona Plaindealer* wryly observed that there was "no doubt that the great anxiety of Mayor Griesbach and his council to defeat the by-law did a great deal to carry it" (*Strathcona Plaindealer*).

The Strathcona street railway bylaw committed the company to begin work by 1 August 1908 and to have track laid by 1 November 1909, a tight schedule that perhaps reflected the impatience of the city fathers to finally get their radial railway. No doubt beating Edmonton to the punch also contributed to the urgency. The street railway plan, however, was developed during a difficult financial period. Panic gripped international capital markets on

22 October 1907 when a run on New York banks spread financial alarm throughout the North American economy. The panic was curbed only when industrial magnate and financier J.P. Morgan provided an immense infusion of cash, but its after effects lingered in the United States and Canada for some months, casting a pall over investment. Entrepreneurial optimism nevertheless returned quickly to western Canada, and by 1908 the boom cycle was gathering momentum again.

Meanwhile, across the river, Edmonton City Council continued to cast an envious eye on transit plans in Strathcona. Surveys conducted in April 1907 by the Edmonton Engineering Department located "a very favourable grade for the proposed street railway" through the river valley. It was felt that a line could be constructed from the corner of Jasper Avenue and Ninth Street, on the north side, to the Strathcona CPR station on the south side at an estimated cost of $77,000. This seemed to be an obvious commuter connector in any developing interurban transit system. When passengers on the

Hotel buses and taxis await the arrival of the train from Calgary near the station in Strathcona in 1906. *(City of Edmonton Archives EA-10-1273)*

CPR train arrived at the station, it was important to have modern transportation to carry them to their hotels and commercial destinations on both sides of the river. "The proposed railway will be utilized as a belt line with the High Level Bridge," the *Edmonton Bulletin* reported, "should a traffic section be constructed in connection with the latter, and the commissioners are of the opinion that it would be a good paying proposition. An exclusive franchise would not be asked, but only the privilege of laying tracks on streets of the southern city" (*Edmonton Bulletin*).

The *Edmonton Bulletin* expressed the optimistic view that a streetcar line would connect Edmonton and Strathcona by the summer of 1907. The fact that the twin cities had just agreed to share the new Strowger automatic telephone system suggested that a similar friendly cooperation on the radial railway would follow suit. The Bulletin explained to readers that the "opinion generally was in favor of granting a franchise of the proposed line for the purpose of serving [Edmonton] as a whole. . . . It is generally understood, however, that the Edmonton commissioners and council would consider favorably building the line along Whyte Avenue to the terminus of the proposed High Level Bridge to make the belt line on the completion of that structure. . ." (*Edmonton Bulletin*).

Alderman William A. Griesbach in 1906, the year before becoming mayor of Edmonton.
(*Loyal Edmonton Regiment Museum*)

Streetcar tracks being laid on Jasper Avenue at 104 Street on 1 June 1907.
(*Provincial Archives of Alberta B5791*)

The debate concerning amalgamating the separate rail network plans on opposite sides of the river continued until 29 July 1908 when Edmonton purchased the Strathcona Radial Tramway Company the day before the private developer was pledged to begin construction. Though Strathcona had led the way in radial railway planning, it would ultimately have its dream fulfilled by its neighbour to the north. Charles E. Taylor was hired as the first Superintendent of Construction for the new transit system, to be named the Edmonton Radial Railway. The agreement was ratified by Bylaws 184 and 185, passed hurriedly on 4 August 1908 to authorize the funds to purchase lands and equipment and commence construction (Hatcher and Schwarzkopf).

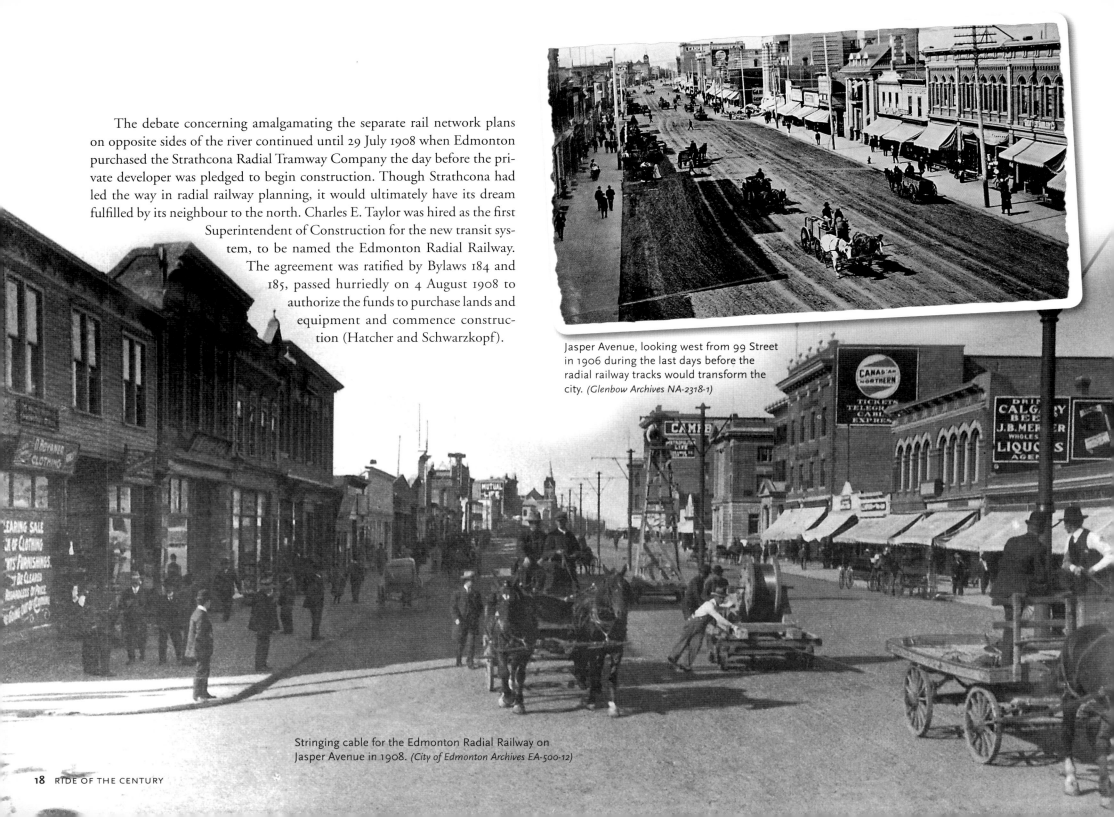

Jasper Avenue, looking west from 99 Street in 1906 during the last days before the radial railway tracks would transform the city. *(Glenbow Archives NA-2318-1)*

Stringing cable for the Edmonton Radial Railway on Jasper Avenue in 1908. *(City of Edmonton Archives EA-500-12)*

Radial railway planning, after languishing for 15 years, was suddenly in motion, and the city fathers moved with a compelling sense of urgency. Though having previously favoured a beltline system encircling commercial districts and residential neighbourhoods, they reversed themselves in a matter of days to approve a radial system at the City Council meeting of 1 September 1908. The radial model, sometimes known as the out-and-back system, was designed with rail lines radiating from the urban centre into outlying districts, where the cars reversed direction and returned to the centre, providing a sort of shuttle service.

Laying radial railway tracks on Jasper in 1908.
(City of Edmonton Archives EA-500-13)

The Albany Avenue (110 Avenue) car displaying its Pay-As-You-Enter sign at front immediately above the trucks. *(Glenbow Archives NA-1328-593)*

The plan called for the one radial line to run west along Jasper Avenue from Namayo Avenue (97 Street) to Twenty-First Street (121 Street), connecting the principal commercial centre with the long strip of businesses and rapidly growing residential districts along Jasper Avenue. Another line connected Namayo Avenue's important commercial strip with Sutherland Street (106 Avenue), where it jogged east to connect with Syndicate Avenue (95 Street). The route then followed Syndicate to Norwood Boulevard, part of 111 Avenue, before moving up Kirkness Street (95 Street) to Alberta Avenue (118 Avenue). The route to Strathcona followed Ninth Street (109 Street) from Jasper Avenue to Saskatchewan Avenue (97 Avenue), where it turned north to Curry Street (100 Street) and then down to the Low Level Bridge and across to Strathcona. The initial network of radial routes would prove a significant factor in the expansion of greater Edmonton, fostering and encouraging growth, and in turn being pressed to expand as the city grew beyond the end of lines.

The decision to adopt the radial railway model determined the types of streetcars to be purchased, and by 1908, manufacturers offered a large variety of suitable models. To connect the downtown with the west end, river valley flats and Strathcona, the Edmonton Radial Railway required a dual-control, reversible car, and the first seven were purchased immediately from the Ottawa Car Manufacturing Company Ltd. The cars were of wood construction reinforced by steel and had controls and trolley poles located at each end. When an Ottawa car reached the end of its line, the motorman fastened down the rear trolley pole, attached the fore pole and moved to the other end of the car with the reverse key and controller handle. The first cars manufactured in the national capital were numbered 1 to 7 and painted two shades of brown with the "Edmonton Radial Railway" proudly painted in gold on both sides.

The minor electrical faults on the first memorable run of Halloween 1908 were but a foretaste of problems to come as the new streetcar system placed an additional burden on an electrical system already struggling to supply the needs of a population of

Streetcar No. 4, a double-ended Ottawa car with two overhead poles. *(Provincial Archives of Alberta B5787)*

about 23,000. The seven streetcars in the fleet were just one short of the maximum number the electrical system could accommodate. When an explosion at the gas plant limited power production only days after Car No. 2 made its maiden voyage, the launch of Strathcona service had to be delayed until 4 December. Later that winter, when Edmontonians kept their electrical pumps running continuously to prevent water pipes from freezing, the drain on the power plant forced the ERR to grind to a complete halt at 4:00 PM on one memorable afternoon.

In spite of early problems, the first year of Edmonton Radial Railway operations drew to a close in the cities of Edmonton and Strathcona amid unprecedented growth and optimism in the future. The cities had joined the ranks of North American metropolitan centres with thoroughly modern public transportation systems. Only a cynic would have forecast that the five years of continued rapid development to follow would challenge the transit system on every front and provoke further the debate over the costs and benefits of public transit.

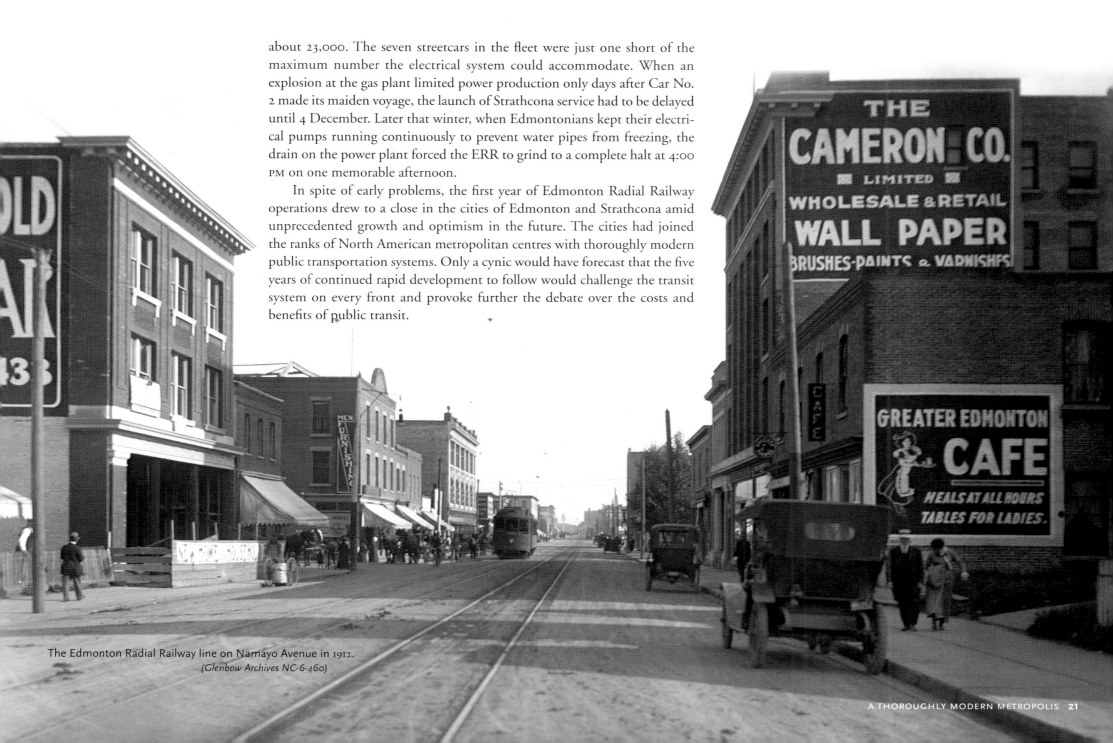

The Edmonton Radial Railway line on Namayo Avenue in 1912.
(Glenbow Archives NC-6-460)

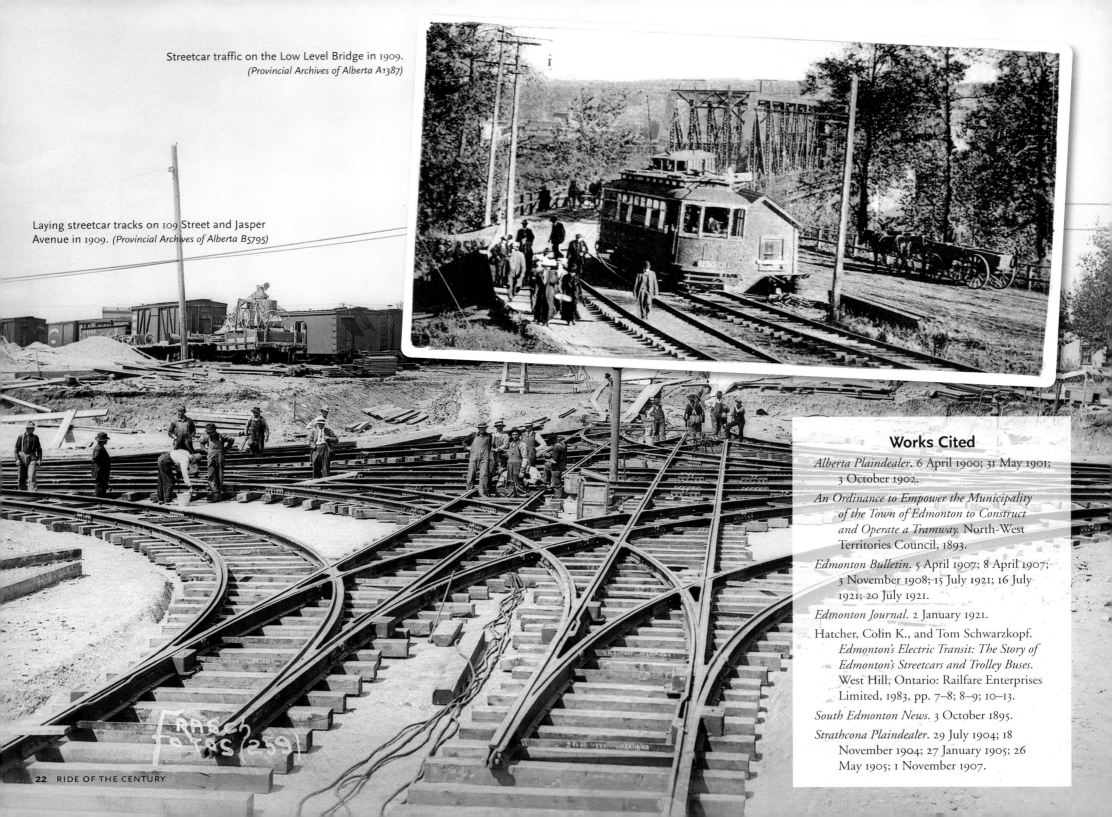

Streetcar traffic on the Low Level Bridge in 1909.
(*Provincial Archives of Alberta A1387*)

Laying streetcar tracks on 109 Street and Jasper Avenue in 1909. (*Provincial Archives of Alberta B5795*)

Works Cited

Alberta Plaindealer. 6 April 1900; 31 May 1901; 3 October 1902.

An Ordinance to Empower the Municipality of the Town of Edmonton to Construct and Operate a Tramway. North-West Territories Council, 1893.

Edmonton Bulletin. 5 April 1907; 8 April 1907; 3 November 1908; 15 July 1921; 16 July 1921; 20 July 1921.

Edmonton Journal. 2 January 1921.

Hatcher, Colin K., and Tom Schwarzkopf. *Edmonton's Electric Transit: The Story of Edmonton's Streetcars and Trolley Buses.* West Hill, Ontario: Railfare Enterprises Limited, 1983, pp. 7–8; 8–9; 10–13.

South Edmonton News. 3 October 1895.

Strathcona Plaindealer. 29 July 1904; 18 November 1904; 27 January 1905; 26 May 1905; 1 November 1907.

CHAPTER 2

Boom-Time Growing Pains

1909–13

In 1912–13 the Hudson's Bay Company divested itself of some of its lands in and around Edmonton in two of the greatest land sales in Canadian history. Edmontonians and newly arrived land speculators and settlers converged on the land sales centre, many sleeping overnight on the street to keep a coveted place in the queue. Waiting for them were members of the Edmonton Real Estate Exchange, which had grown in a few short years from 60 members to over 300. All were eagerly profiting from the sale of lots in many of the 274 new subdivisions laid out in Edmonton in just over a decade. The hopeful throngs buying and selling exemplified the enthusiasm and optimism of the period from 1909–13.

The Edmonton Radial Railway entered its second year of operation already struggling to keep abreast of growth. Within two years of the first streetcar rolling down the first 21 kilometres of track, the cities of Edmonton and Strathcona had grown by 15 percent, leaving every part of the system from routes to rolling stock, from electrical systems to maintenance, in dire need of immediate upgrading and expansion. Not every demand could be satisfied with limited financial resources, and political controversy dogged the ERR's efforts to satisfy the competing claims of emerging neighbourhoods. Even those that could be met required the ERR to run the system at a loss, igniting renewed debate over whether expansion should be funded by taxes or transit fares, or even whether urban transit should be owned by public or private interests.

After basking in an outpouring of praise as the first streetcars rolled down the tracks in November 1908, the fledgling ERR quickly plummeted in Edmontonians' esteem when service disruptions highlighted the system's inability to cope with severe winter weather and the demand for expanded service from a growing population. The ERR learned quickly that the wood-block paving on which tracks were hurriedly laid to meet the service launch deadline did not hold up under winter conditions. Frost heaving in the first month of operation pushed rails out of alignment and caused derailments. When frost coming out of the ground in spring brought a return of

the problem, much of the wood paving along Jasper, Namayo and Whyte avenues, the principal commercial corridors in the two cities, had to be hastily taken up and temporarily replaced with gravel and ash.

Before launching the radial railway in 1908, the City had purchased a Westinghouse motor generator to convert the gas plant's alternating current to the direct current the streetcars required, but growing demand in 1909 required the installation of two additional dedicated generators to serve the radial railway exclusively. New electrical capacity allowed more than eight cars to run, but power outages and shortages still continued to disrupt service.

A long queue of eager buyers lined up around several city blocks to purchase land from the Hudson's Bay Company in 1912.
(City of Edmonton Archives EA-10-2929)

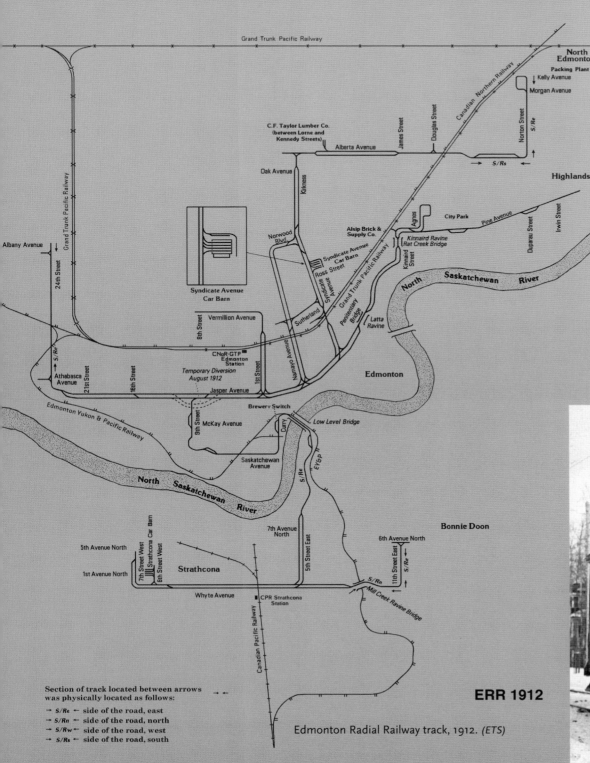

Grand Trunk Pacific Railway

North Edmonton

Packing Plant
Kelly Avenue
Morgan Avenue

C.F. Taylor Lumber Co.
(between Lorne and
Kennedy Streets)

Alberta Avenue

James Street
Douglas Street
Norton Street
S/Re

S/Rs

Highlands

Oak Avenue

Kikness

City Park
Pine Avenue
Duparau Street
Irwin Street

Alsip Brick &
Supply Co.

Agnes
Kinnaird Ravine
Rat Creek Bridge

Norwood Blvd.

Syndicate Avenue
Car Barn

Ross Street

Kinnaird Street

North Saskatchewan River

Albany Avenue

Grand Trunk Pacific Railway

24th Street

Syndicate Avenue
Car Barn

Sutherland

Namayo Avenue

Grand Trunk Pacific Railway

Penitentiary Bridge

Latta Ravine

Vermillion Avenue

8th Street

CNoR-GTP
Edmonton Station

Temporary Diversion
August 1912

1st Street

Edmonton

S/Re

Athabasca Avenue

21st Street
16th Street

Jasper Avenue

Brewery Switch

Edmonton Yukon & Pacific Railway

5th Street
McKay Avenue

Curry
EV5rP

Low Level Bridge

Saskatchewan Avenue

North Saskatchewan River

S/Re

EV5rP

Bonnie Doon

7th Avenue North

6th Avenue North

5th Avenue North

1st Avenue North

7th Street West
6th Street West
Strathcona Car Barn

Strathcona

5th Street East

11th Street East

S/Re

Whyte Avenue

CPR Strathcona Station

S/Rn

Mill Creek Ravine Bridge

Canadian Pacific Railway

ERR 1912

Section of track located between arrows
was physically located as follows:

→ S/Re ← side of the road, east
→ S/Rn ← side of the road, north
→ S/Rw ← side of the road, west
→ S/Rs ← side of the road, south

Edmonton Radial Railway track, 1912. *(ETS)*

So great was the risk of power failure in the early years that streetcars carried lanterns to be lit in an emergency to warn approaching streetcars of their presence. Another new generator had to be brought on line before the 1912 Edmonton Exhibition. The cost of electricity was enormous, accounting for more than wages and salaries during the Edmonton Radial Railway's first two years of operation.

For many Edmontonians and Strathconians, the honeymoon was over. Writing in the Edmonton *News-Plaindealer,* Clarence Stout encapsulated the limitation to expansion: "So long as we are confronted with an annual shortage of power and equipment, it is useless to hope for the construction of these important radial systems," he concluded. Nevertheless, he urged that "no effort can wisely be spared in saving every franchise right for the subsequent use of the city" (*News-Plaindealer*).

Soon, local newspapers began taking almost droll pleasure in reporting the frequency of service delays and mishaps. "The wet weather has had the usual disastrous effect upon the street railway service, and derailed cars during the past two days have

No. 6, the Syndicate Avenue car, carries a lantern for night safety.
(Glenbow Archives NA-55-3 GM)

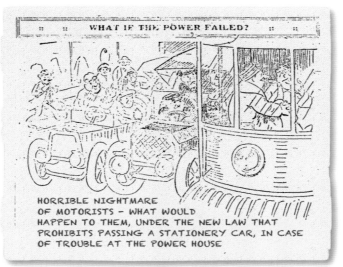

been frequent happenings," the *Strathcona News-Plaindealer* harangued in July 1912. "On Whyte Avenue West considerable difficulty was experienced through mishaps of this kind" (*Strathcona News-Plaindealer*). More serious were accidents, especially on the Low Level Bridge, where streetcars shared the road with horse-drawn traffic. When the tracks were coated with frost, as occurred on a September night in 1911, motormen could not always brake quickly enough to avoid a collision. On this occasion, a streetcar struck a democrat and team owned by south-side farmer John Moravic, and damages were awarded to Mrs. Moravic for injuries. In July 1912, Car No. 8 struck and killed a horse hauling an Edmonton City Dairy wagon on Jasper Avenue and Second Street. Such incidents were common during the ERR's early years, though few resulted in serious injury.

The first Ottawa streetcars arrived with a flanger mechanism on the forward edge of the trucks to clear snow from the tracks, but the equipment proved no match for Edmonton winters. The ERR was obliged to order its first purpose-built snow sweeper from Chicago, another city familiar with heavy snow. The McGuire-Cummings sweeper was powered by a heavy-duty electric motor driving robust rattan brooms that cleared the tracks very efficiently. Sweeper E-17, the first of three required over the years, came into service during the winter of 1909–10 and served the city for years.

Sweeper E-17, the first purchased by the ERR. *(City of Edmonton Archives EA-10-1374)*

Edmonton photographer Hubert Hollingsworth's wintry scene shows a sweeper working to clear the intersection at 97 Street and 111 Avenue in 1938. *(City of Edmonton Archives EA-160-1452)*

New residential and industrial development drove ERR expansion during the boom years preceding the First World War, and few development plans failed to provoke public dissention. The first hullabaloo flared up in 1909 between the North Edmonton "Packing Town" community that was growing up around the J.Y. Griffith Packing Plant, later Swift, and miners who were working farther east along Jasper Avenue in the river valley coal mines. Both expanding work forces demanded that streetcar service be extended for them immediately, although their destinations demanded separate routes. The issue was bitterly contested in a day when the streetcar represented the only economical alternative to horse-drawn taxis that were prohibitively expensive for workers. Instead of extending the streetcar line east along Jasper Avenue to the mines and then north to the packing plant, Superintendent Charles Taylor chose a more northerly route along Alberta Avenue (118 Avenue) that ran east only as far as Norton Street (66 Street), some distance from the mines, before turning north to the Packing Town community and its huge plant at 124 Avenue. Superintendent Taylor's decision seems to have been based largely on the greater revenue potential from the larger residential development contiguous with his preferred route.

The meatpackers' win was the miners' loss. The Alberta Avenue extension was but one early example of competing interests locking horns over public transit planning.

The Highlands on the east side of Edmonton and Glenora on the west were other notable examples of residential developments courting streetcar expansion. The Highlands was an exclusive district on the outskirts of the city developed by the Magrath-Holgate Company beginning in 1910. A building covenant restricted construction to homes of more than $2,500 in value, two to three times the cost of the average working class home. Magrath–Holgate marketed the development as a natural paradise of refined, graceful homes situated above the scenic North Saskatchewan River valley.

While isolation may have appealed to those who valued exclusivity, the Highlands community nevertheless desired streetcar service, and the developer went about achieving his aim in a way that foreshadowed contemporary

A clean, progressive view of the industrial development planned around the Swift packing plant. (*Glenbow Archives NC-6-1065*)

The S-1 street sprinkler, the first in service, cleans Jasper Avenue in Edmonton's west end near 121 Street in 1909. The attractive little structure to the left is an early example of a passenger shelter. (*Provincial Archives of Alberta EA-10-1387*)

public–private partnerships. On 29 August 1911, Magrath–Holgate proposed to pay for construction and cover any losses for the first 18 months of streetcar operation if the City supervised and administered bringing service to the isolated district. The cash-strapped city fathers accepted the offer a week later. In just 10 months, the line was running from the boundary of East City Park (renamed Borden Park after Prime Minister Robert Borden visited Edmonton in 1914) along Pine Avenue (112 Avenue) to Irwin Street (63 Street). The line was soon extended two blocks farther east.

The extension of the line in the district of Glenora ran less smoothly. Less than a week after the west-end streetcars began running in 1913, Glenora ratepayers mounted a vitriolic protest to complain that it took an hour to travel from McDougall Avenue (100 Street) to 124 Street in the downtown.

Car No. 11 ending its run at City Park (Borden Park) in the summer of 1913. *(Glenbow Archives NA-1328-64585)*

H.W. Heathcote and F.J. Lorimer, "the principal protestants . . . complained of the most chaotic arrangement of the west end street car service." Slow service, especially during Sunday church rush hour, provided seemingly endless annoyance to the dissatisfied Glenora residents. "Frequently," the *Edmonton Journal* reported, "cars stand on a siding on Twenty-fourth Street, and when they do get started on their journey toward the downtown district that the empty cars pass by a corner where seven and eight people are standing and deliberately stop to pick up a single passenger at the next corner (*Edmonton Journal*)."

Other than the extensions to Highlands and Glenora, the main track work between 1909–12 consisted of double-tracking a number of the more heavily used routes to speed service. On the north side these included Jasper Avenue east from Syndicate Avenue (95 Street) to the Penitentiary Bridge over Latta Ravine, then to the Rat Creek Bridge across Kinnaird Ravine; north on Syndicate Avenue from Jasper Avenue to the Grand Trunk Pacific Railway level crossing, then north to Ross Street (108A Avenue); and east on Whyte Avenue from Fifth Street East (99 Street) to Seventh Street East (97 Street). By the end of 1912, ERR service had reached the most significant commercial and residential districts (*News-Plaindealer*; Hatcher and Schwarzkopf).

To service new routes and add capacity to existing lines, the ERR purchased new cars. Within weeks of launching service with the original seven streetcars, four new streetcars were ordered from the Preston Car and Coach Company of Preston, Ontario. The first Prestons, arriving in May 1909, introduced the first official ERR colour scheme of red above the windowsills and green beneath. The City of Edmonton coat of arms with its motto of "Industry, Energy, Enterprise" along with the abbreviated railway's name, "Edmonton Radial Ry," appeared in gold lettering on the sides the new streetcars.

The Prestons featured improved air brakes essential for the steep grades of the cross-river routes. Other safety features included window bars to prevent gawking passengers from sticking their heads out the windows and being decapitated on power poles located close to the tracks. Retractable steps allowed motormen to control passenger entry and exit to the correct side of the car rather than into traffic.

Streetcar interior.
(Provincial Archives of Alberta B10488)

Preston streetcar No. 14 heading east on Jasper Avenue near 96 Street. The Alberta Hotel, its flag flying high, is visible in the background.
(Provincial Archives of Alberta B5788)

Other innovative features on the new Prestons included a more efficient Pay-As-You-Enter system based on the model introduced by the Montreal Street Railway three years previously. Conductors and drivers now sported new dark blue uniforms with gold braid. A strict dress code governed that they be worn with the military panache favoured in the Edwardian age.

The Prestons set a high standard of luxury with their rosewood and mahogany interiors, and convenient push-button signals for passengers to indicate that they wished to disembark at the next stop. Unfortunately, similar to previously purchased streetcars, their electric heaters were ill equipped for Edmonton winters. In January 1911, the first Peter Smith coal heater was installed as a test. The new heater, which used an electrically powered fan to circulate heated air through ducts at floor level, provided improved comfort for riders and was much cheaper to operate, a benefit to a system plagued with an inadequate power supply. Soon Peter Smith heaters were installed in all ERR cars. The "smoke jack required by this type of heater became a hallmark of streetcars on Canada's prairie transit systems during winter months" (Hatcher and Schwarzkopf).

In 1910 the ERR also began a transition from double- to single-ended streetcars in the interest of efficiency. With the order for the first single-end cars in that year, the ERR installed wyes, which allowed the cars to turn around at the end of their routes. The *wye*, a term in use since about 1857, referred to a track that branches from a main line to create a loop for reversing streetcars' direction.

In the few short years between 1908 and 1913, the ERR built its fleet from eight streetcars to a total of 83 pieces of rolling stock. The expansion included service cars such as a Preston sprinkler and McGuire-Cummings baggage car-sweeper purchased in 1909; an Ottawa Car Company horse-drawn tower wagon added in 1910; an Ottawa sand car in 1911; a McGuire-Cummings flatcar in 1912; three more service cars in 1913; as well as another dump car manufactured by Canadian Car and Foundry Company, a line car made by the ERR and another sprinkler delivered from McGuire-Cummings. Eight double-ended streetcars built by the Ottawa Car Company launched the service in 1908, with four more double-enders from the Preston Car and Coach Company added in 1909. Six Ottawa cars were added in 1910,

Employees of the ERR, including motormen and conductors, outside the Syndicate Avenue barns in 1910 or 1911. *(Provincial Archives of Alberta B7297)*

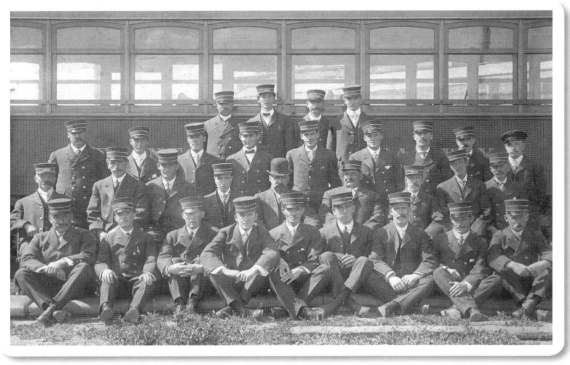

ERR conductors in their first uniforms. *(City of Edmonton Archives EA-10-11)*

Nos. 1 and 3, double-ended Ottawa cars, stopped at the Calgary and Edmonton Railway level crossing on Whyte Avenue. (Provincial Archives of Alberta A3001)

with 10 more Ottawas and four Prestons joining the fleet in 1911 (all single-end). Fifteen St. Louis double-end cars, soon to be rebuilt as single-enders, arrived in 1912, and 28 more Preston single-end cars were added in 1913. (See Fleet List in Appendix.)

Two bus barns serviced the Edmonton Radial Railway cars in its early days. A downtown barn was located on Syndicate Avenue (95 Street) and 109A Avenue. When it closed in 1913, operations were moved to the new Cromdale Garage located at 80 Street and 116 Avenue. A south-side car barn at 6 Street West (110 Street) and 1 Avenue North (83 Avenue) became operational in 1909, and an addition was constructed in 1912. The barn was declared surplus in 1921 when all services were transferred to the Cromdale Garage (Hatcher and Schwarzkopf).

ERR personnel pose beside a Preston car in 1910. The retractable steps are visible. (City of Edmonton Archives EA-10-1384)

No. 26, a single-ended Ottawa streetcar, passing the *Edmonton Journal* Building on 101 Street in 1913. (Provincial Archives of Alberta B4952)

An ERR tower wagon crew stringing overhead wire in 1913.
(Provincial Archives of Alberta A4707)

In the spring of 1913, the Canadian Pacific Railway completed construction of the High Level Bridge to provide a full rail link to downtown Edmonton via its subsidiary, the Calgary and Edmonton Railway. The first passenger train crossed at the beginning of June, and the first streetcar followed on 11 August amid much fanfare. This direct streetcar connection to the university made for more rapid connections to the emerging new campus, and connected the commercial centres of the newly amalgamated cities of Strathcona and Edmonton. The design of the impressive bridge is attributed to the CPR's Engineer of Bridges, P.B. Motley, a designer of national importance. In its early years, the High Level was the only bridge in western Canada to accommodate trains, streetcars, automobiles and pedestrians, a dubious distinction to some because of the congestion caused.

In November 1913, with new tracks in place, Superintendent W.T. Woodroofe unveiled a new 15-minute schedule that was heralded by the *Edmonton Journal* as one that would finally "give satisfaction to every citizen, whether he lives in the north, south, east or west end of the city." Using the ERR's 37 cars to their maximum efficiency, the average speed increased significantly to 9.25 miles per hour.

The Syndicate Avenue car barn in 1910.
(City of Edmonton Archives EA-267-166)

The new Cromdale car barns in 1913.
(Glenbow Archives NA-1328-2087)

The Strathcona car barn, a replica of which was later constructed at Fort Edmonton Park by the Edmonton Radial Railway Society.
(Glenbow Archives NA-1328-2100)

Interior views of the Cromdale barns in 1913.
(Glenbow Archives NA-1328-2089, NA-1328-2098, NA-1328-2247)

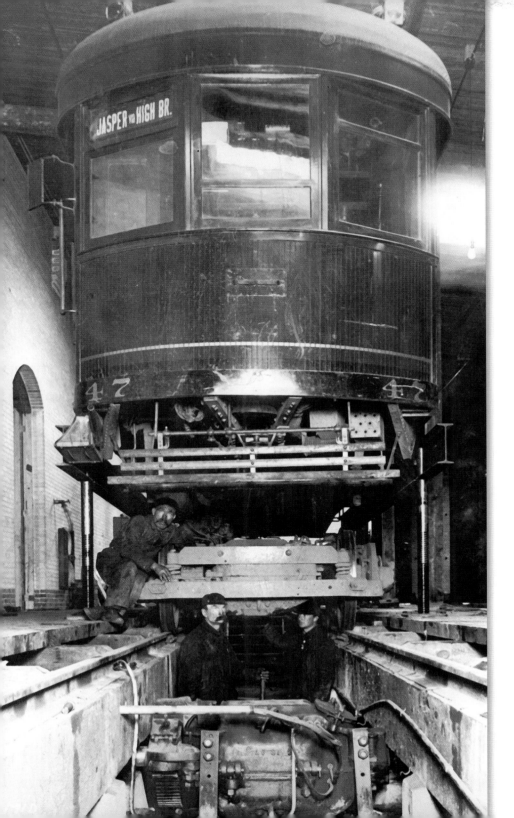

City Council, at the recommendation of City Commissioners, made an early decision to support the Edmonton Radial Railway system expansion through deficit spending. Short-term pain, it was reasoned, would result in long-term gain when increased ridership on new extensions pushed operations into the black. In the meantime, the little ERR turned to freight and recreation services to provide new revenue streams to reduce financial shortfalls. Meat delivery service to retail outlets was launched even before the new line to the J.Y. Griffith meatpacking plant was completed. With streetcars in short supply, a new track cleaner did double duty as the railway's first freight delivery car. As the construction boom caused Edmonton to mushroom between 1909 and 1913, the ERR delivered construction supplies from companies such as the Alsip Brick and Supply Company on the Canadian Northern Railway tracks at Pine Avenue (112 Avenue) and Kinnaird Street (82 Street). Alsip, one of the city's major manufacturers before the First World War, made 90,000 sand-lime bricks daily in two 10-hour shifts employing up to 52 men.

The Edwardian Age in Edmonton was the grand era of sociability when virtually everyone participated in public events, and the ERR routed cars from regular schedules to transport recreation users to lectures, concerts, parties, balls, exhibitions, picnics and sporting events. Every New Year's Day, thousands attended the annual holiday hockey game between Edmonton and Strathcona, and when the Loyal Orange Lodge held its annual meeting in either city, visitors flocked to the event. The most attended event of the year was the agricultural exhibition week, and the ERR was sorely pressed to serve the increase in ridership. During the 1912 exhibition, every car in the fleet was on the streets as the ERR broke all previous records in carrying 327,696 passengers, roughly six rides for each of Edmonton's 53,611 residents.

In 1913, to further bolster recreation revenue, the ERR extended Strathcona's Main Street line south to McKernan Lake to provide skating excursions that became a popular part of Edmonton's cultural life for decades. Local residents quickly became sentimental about this sparsely populated route and named it the Toonerville Trolley after the comic strip *Toonerville Folks*, created by Fontaine Fox. The cartoon featured a dilapidated trolley driven with gusto by the ancient Skipper and peopled by the Terrible-Tempered Mr. Bang, the Powerful Katrinka, Little Woo-Woo Wortle, Aunt Eppie Hogg, Mickey McGuire, the town bully, and others. The characters quickly won the hearts of North Americans who could relate to the archetypal personalities and situations (Hatcher and Schwarzkopf).

The ERR also turned early to advertising as source of additional revenue. Almost from the start, streetcar windows displayed advertisements for products such as Elk cigars and Kodak cameras.

For all the ERR's efforts to expand service and bolster revenue, Edmonton and Strathcona were growing so rapidly, and the demands were so unrelenting, that the little transit system was forced to struggle mightily to catch up. The public clamoured continuously for more service while objecting to increased fare prices on the one hand and mounting deficits on the other. The Edmonton City Auditor's report for 1910 commended the Electric Light and Power Department for its $10,948.10 surplus while casting a jaundiced eye on the ERR's $29,269.74 deficit, a sum roughly equal to $3.5 million in today's dollars. This would have been a bitter pill to swallow, since many of the ERR's service complaints stemmed from uncertain and inadequate electrical supply and much of its deficit was caused by the high cost of electricity.

The ERR finally turned a profit 1912. After years of almost daily pummelling in City Council and the press, the ERR may justifiably have felt vindicated in the knowledge that it was traffic over new extensions that finally took it into the black, at least for a short while (*News-Plaindealer*).

A by-product of the pressures on the ERR to grow with limited financial means in the early years was the revolving door of superintendents who attempted to steer the system through troubled waters. Superintendent Charles Taylor, appointed in 1908, resigned effective 1 June 1910. "When Taylor left, the system was operating at peak capacity and was in need of more rolling stock," writes historian Colin Hatcher, "both to keep up to passenger demand and to allow enough of a surplus so that cars could be cycled into the shop for much-needed repairs." Inadequate civic funding doubtless frustrated Taylor. After a brief interregnum under Commissioner A.V. Bouillon, C.V. Biswanger became superintendent on 21 June. Biswanger held the position long enough to launch service to the newly relocated exhibition grounds before being replaced by Robert Knight in January 1911. Knight lasted only until July 1912 when W.T. Woodroofe of Vancouver took the helm to "take charge of the much-maligned utility of traffic" (Hatcher and Schwarzkopf).

Trains and streetcars shared the upper deck of the High Level Bridge, sometimes to the dismay of the ERR passengers. *(City of Edmonton Archives EA-10-1289)*

Edmonton Radial Railway tracks under construction on the upper deck of the High Level Bridge in 1913. The new Legislature Building and the final incarnation of Fort Edmonton can be seen on the north bank of the North Saskatchewan River. *(City of Edmonton Archives EA-24-10)*

Streetcar tracks under construction on Saskatchewan Avenue, 1913. *(Glenbow Archives NA-1328-64602)*

Car No. 25 crossing the upper deck of the High Level Bridge in August 1913, one of the first ERR cars to make what some passengers found an unnerving journey high above the North Saskatchewan River valley. *(Provincial Archives of Alberta B3299)*

Woodroofe's immediate challenge was to prepare the system for the influx of riders during the annual Edmonton Exhibition, a regular test for the ERR. A new generator from the Canadian Westinghouse Company was expected to be in operation by the time of the fair, and Woodroofe promised that the full transit fleet would be in operation for the occasion. Later in August, Woodroofe installed 75 new P-A-Y-E (Pay-as-You-Enter) fare boxes to ensure that every nickel was retained by the ERR. He later announced that he intended to have a fleet of 80 cars ready for Exhibition week the following year (*News-Plaindealer*).

In the autumn of 1912, just as the ERR was getting its financial house in order, political pressure began to mount to develop more ambitious plans for new beltline routes, an idea rejected in earlier planning. Alderman Charles May put a motion before City Council that a committee be appointed to work with Superintendent Woodroofe and the City Commissioners on a plan to extend the deadlines or undertake some of the building programs authorized by the original Edmonton Radial Tramway Act of 1908.

No. S-5, a freight car, dumps bricks for the Alsip Brick and Supply Company in 1912. *(Glenbow Archives NC-6-284)*

Bricks being loaded onto the S-5 at the Alsip brickyard in 1912. *(Glenbow Archives NC-6-285)*

McKernan Lake, shown here in 1913, provided for skating and tobogganing (the run is on the right). Edmontonians boarded the Toonerville Trolley, visible in the background on the left, to get to this popular location. *(Provincial Archives of Alberta B6363)*

A jubilant Edmonton Exhibition parade followed the First World War.
(Glenbow Archives NC-6-11269)

ERR streetcars were to be found wherever crowds gathered.
(City of Edmonton Archives EA-373-1)

William Turton Woodroofe, Fourth Superintendent of the Edmonton Radial Railway

William Turton Woodroofe was born on 10 August 1880 in Wallasey, Cheshire, England, and served two years in the 1st Cheshire Artillery before immigrating to Canada. When the First World War broke out, Woodroofe joined the 101st Regiment, a militia unit, where he was able to train while continuing his duties with the ERR. He was a corporal in this Regiment for six months before enlisting in the Canadian Expeditionary Force at Edmonton on 28 August 1915.

The dashing red-haired soldier-superintendent died in action on 17 September 1916 while serving with the 24th Battalion CEF (Quebec Regiment). He is buried at Pas de Calais, at the Vimy Ridge Memorial. W.J. Cunningham, another Cheshire man, would serve as superintendent after him.

Church Service Versus Transit Service

The Lord's Day Alliance of Canada, a lay organization founded in 1888 by the Presbyterian Church, opposed the secularization of the Sabbath. "In the early phases of Canada's industrialization and urbanization," historian Sharon Meen writes, "Sunday was usually the only day of rest: the issue was whether that day should be a holy day or a holiday." The Alliance became one of the most powerful political lobbies of the early twentieth century, gaining support of the French-Canadian Catholic church and organized labour "with its promise of a legislated weekly rest day" (Meen).

In 1906 the federal parliament introduced the Lord's Day Act, and the Alberta government followed with legislation that prohibited the operation of streetcars on Sundays. However, the act permitted municipalities to hold a referendum to decide whether service would be allowed locally. A plebiscite held in June 1909 endorsed Sunday service overwhelmingly in Edmonton, while Strathcona voters narrowly rejected a similar proposal that December. The decision was overturned in a second referendum only days later, and Sunday service was extended to Strathcona on 20 December 1910.

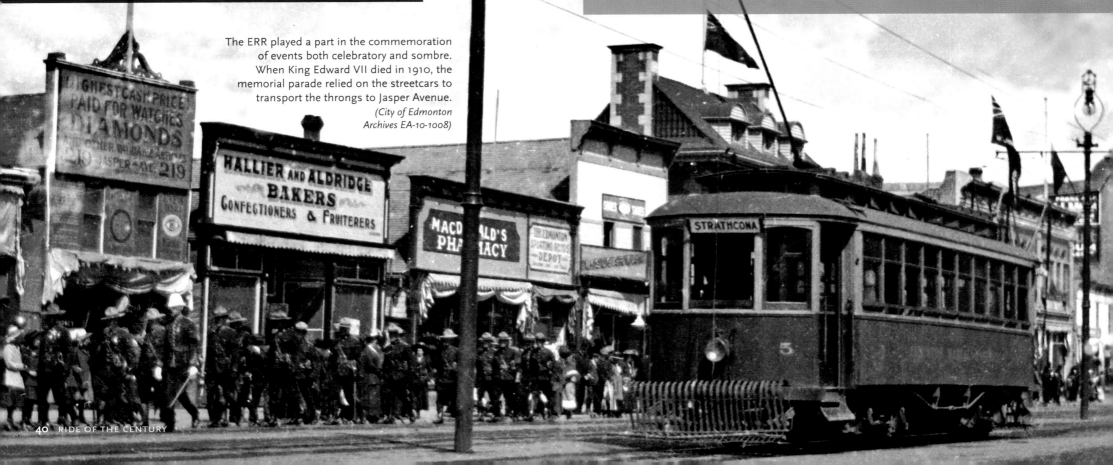

The ERR played a part in the commemoration of events both celebratory and sombre. When King Edward VII died in 1910, the memorial parade relied on the streetcars to transport the throngs to Jasper Avenue.
(City of Edmonton Archives EA-10-1008)

The act had granted the City the five-year authority to build lines to Stony Plain, White Whale Lake (now Lake Wabamun), Lac Ste. Anne, Morinville, Edison, Namayo, Athabasca Landing, Fort Saskatchewan, Lacombe, Daysland and other locations within a 130-kilometre radius of the city. Though some rights had been extended to seven years by a 1909 amendment that allowed more flexibility in financing, Alderman May warned that many provisions would expire in a matter of months.

By early October, the City, likely in response to May's pressure, was considering an extension of the radial railway network to St. Albert. The Edmonton *News-Plaindealer* reminded City Hall that "about two years ago a private company succeeded in obtaining a government franchise for tramway construction in this same direction. How the difficulties that must exist have been settled remains to be explained" (*News-Plaindealer*).

Ambitious plans for a total of 19 intersecting beltline routes were developed, although they would never be built. These circular routes challenged the fundamental concept of the radial streetcar system on which routes radiated from a central point with cars reversing direction and returning along the same route. The proposed Route 1 beltline, for example, would have begun at First Street, run north to Alberta Avenue, west to Twenty-fourth Street, south to Jasper Avenue and finally back to First Street. Along the way it

The Fighting Fusiliers

Superintendent Woodroofe's success during the 1912 Exhibition would no doubt have helped dim the civic recollection of a near riot involving the Edmonton Radial Railway and his own 101st Regiment.

The young city of Edmonton saw the establishment of the 101st Regiment of Infantry in 1908, shortly thereafter renamed the 101st Edmonton Fusiliers. Major W.F.W. Carstairs was among the founders of the unit. Carstairs thought it useful to organize "a little outing which would combine instruction and amusement." The first took place at Cooking Lake in 1910, and sessions at the Sarcee Camp at Calgary soon followed.

Circumstances combined to create something of a sensation as the Fusiliers were returning from the Sarcee summer camp on 30 June 1912. The men were on parade, marching up McDougall Hill on their way back to their armoury from the south-side CPR railway depot. The line of march had just turned onto Jasper Avenue when an eastbound streetcar approached. Apparently, it stopped when Motorman Elliott noticed that "the redcoats were approaching," according to the next day's headline story in the *Edmonton Bulletin*.

William Frederick Wallace Carstairs.
(Glenbow Archives ND-200-32)

Elliott waited until the band and the first company had passed before attempting to drive through a gap in the parade.

Colonel Carstairs, mounted and leading the parade, rode back and ordered the car to stop, but the motorman seemed to have disregarded the order. The car moved ahead and "almost struck the Colonel's horse." Enraged, Carstairs then smashed in a window with his riding crop.

William Frederick Wallace Carstairs was a man of commanding presence and military bearing, not to say self-importance. The scion of a prominent Kingston family, he served with the North-West Mounted Police during the Riel Rebellion and later with the Royal Nigerian Constabulary, where he took part in several colonial punitive expeditions.

Carstairs placed Conductor Henry Stark, Motorman Arthur Elliott and Inspector Thomas Ferrier under arrest and had them dragged from the car. "Following this a number of members of the regiment proceeded to smash up the car with the aid of the butts of their guns," reported the *Bulletin*. "Most of the windows were smashed, likewise the headlight."

At this time, Constable Vize rushed up to investigate the excitement, which was gathering a substantial crowd, and sized up the situation. If the crew was arrested and marched away by Constable Vize, the entire street railway system would grind to a halt almost immediately, so the constable instead guaranteed that the culprits would appear in court the following Tuesday morning. Carstairs reluctantly accepted this development, and "a carload of indignant and wrathful passengers proceeded on their interrupted journey."

When the miscreants appeared before North Side Police Magistrate F.D. Byers, they were charged with having obstructed Her Majesty's Militia. E.B. Williams, Carstairs' lawyer, asked that only a nominal fine of one dollar and costs be levied. The ERR men were convicted, paid their fine and costs, and conditions returned to peaceful orderliness on the streets of Edmonton.

would cross other routes at transfer points. The interconnected beltways were designed to allow more efficient travel outward from the city centre and to improve commuting times by keeping cars in continuous movement without having to stand idle at the ends of the radial lines. Beltways accommodated the existing central core network while serving what was already becoming an incipient urban sprawl on both sides of the river.

City Commissioner Harrison optimistically forecast in the Edmonton *News-Plaindealer* that the impressive plan to develop a large number of beltways in the immediate future "should do for the next fifty years of Edmonton's growth, with only possibly a few more extensions in the outlying districts." Harrison may have been essentially correct, but his predicted timing missed the reality of transit development by decades.

Route expansion plans switched into high gear when the long-debated amalgamation between Edmonton and Strathcona became a reality in 1912, although they would continue to adhere to the existing radial grid. In a single stroke, the population of the newly amalgamated Greater Edmonton grew by over 70 percent to 53,611.

The Edmonton Interurban No. 1 Streetcar in October 1913.
(Provincial Archives of Alberta, Missionary Oblates, Grandin Collection, OB1953)

A work crew poses by an Edmonton Interurban streetcar.
(Glenbow Archives NA-1328-1883)

The Edmonton to St. Albert Interurban Railway

The interurban railway model of public transit had passed through its frantic heyday in North America by the time the ERR was launched, but the Edmonton district nevertheless got its own proud example when the Edmonton Interurban Railway made its short-lived appearance on the scene. Operating from Edmonton to St. Albert with a tiny fleet of gasoline-powered streetcars, the Interurban suffered a devastating fire in its car barn on 1 April 1914 and suspended operations, never to resume. Some track was leased and later sold to the Edmonton Radial Railway, and the rest was torn up in 1916–17, the steel recycled for wartime uses.

The *Edmonton-Strathcona Amalgamation Act,* assented in the provincial legislature on 20 December 1911, specified certain guarantees to insure that all future ERR development would be standardized and equitable between the two centres. The legislation required four Strathcona extensions to be completed by the end of 1914, including a line connecting Whyte Avenue with the growing University of Alberta campus. In negotiating the merger, Strathcona was insistent that service to its flagship institution be appropriately direct and convenient for varsity students. Strathcona also demanded an eastern extension connecting Whyte Avenue's Fifth Street (99 Avenue) intersection with the community's eastern boundary at Bonnie Doon. A third extension was to run south from the central intersection at Whyte Avenue and Main Street (104 Street) as far as Sixth Avenue South (76 Avenue). From this point a fourth extension was to be constructed west along a line to be determined at a later date. The legislation also stipulated half-hour service south from Whyte Avenue to the Low Level Bridge and back, acknowledging the importance of the industrial developments and working-class residential areas in the east Strathcona districts and Gallagher Flats (*Edmonton–Strathcona Amalgamation Act*). By the close of 1912, the line brought students within a short walk of the new brick halls of learning. The east boundary of Strathcona was accessible via the Mill Creek Bridge and a northern route up 11 Street East to a wye on 6 Avenue North. The southern routes would have to wait, however, and their development would be largely eclipsed by economic decline in 1913.

Though the Edmonton Radial Railway was tasked with providing streetcar service on both sides of the North Saskatchewan River, the agreement through which Strathcona came into the ERR called for the sharing of revenue, and both cities jealously guarded the right to collect transit fares in their environs. Passengers boarding in Strathcona thus paid five cents to ride to the river and then another five cents to cross the Low Level Bridge into Edmonton. If they desired to travel farther north on Namayo Avenue (97 Street) beyond the Canadian Northern Railway tracks or west on Jasper Avenue beyond 109 Street, a third nickel had to be paid. Conductors certainly earned their pay keeping track of fares from irate riders who keenly objected to what they saw as inequities based upon the location of their residence and place of business or work.

To address some consumer complaints, the transit transfer was introduced on the north side of the river on 1 April 1909 in the new Preston cars, though a nickel still had to be shelled out at the Low Level Bridge connecting the two cities. Still, a nickel saved was a nickel earned. Only after amalgamation could the ERR replace the controversial duplicate fares with a single five-cent fare. Although the ERR lost revenue in the short term, it nevertheless celebrated the union by running a specially decorated streetcar through the streets with "Boost Greater Edmonton" emblazoned on both sides in electric lights along the roofline.

Amidst all the hoopla of amalgamation, the ERR was not immune to volatile labour relations and scandal. Just before Christmas 1912, a minor dispute concerning a motorman's refusal to take out an east-end car lacking a fender quickly escalated into threats of a full strike. The offender, Motorman Covey, apologized to Superintendent Woodroofe and, according to the *News-Plaindealer,* the matter was resolved to the satisfaction of all. The reporter noted, tongue-in-cheek, that Covey "fell upon Supt. Woodroofe's ample neck and the spirit of peace and good will [for the future] has been gracefully anticipated by the officials and employees of the Radial Railway" (*News-Plaindealer*).

A brilliantly lit and decorated car ran throughout Greater Edmonton to celebrate the amalgamation of Edmonton and Strathcona in 1912. *(City of Edmonton Archives EA-10-1383)*

Boosting Greater Edmonton was the sentiment of the day, as this decorated streetcar attests. L–R: Gus Connelly, Chief Inspector John Moir, Superintendent Robert Knight, Inspector Thomas Ferrier, Commissioner John Chalmers, Commissioner A.G. Harrison, Mayor George S. Armstrong and Commissioner S.W. Candy. *(City of Edmonton Archives EA-10-1382)*

Streetcar tracks looking east along Whyte Ave at 105 Street, 1913. *(Glenbow Archives NA-1328-64604)*

The ERR became embroiled in its first real political scandal in November 1912 when a provisional plan for the proposed beltway system, prepared for City Council by Chief Inspector Moir, was leaked to the press and printed in both daily newspapers. "The plan is very comprehensive," reported the *News-Plaindealer*, "and is calculated to meet the demands of the greater city for many years to come." Alderman Joe Clarke, later notorious as Mayor "Fightin' Joe" Clarke, announced publicly that even before the proposed new route map had been leaked to the newspapers "certain firms with mysterious advance information had been purchasing options [on properties adjacent to the planned lines] for the past two weeks" (*News-Plaindealer*). Advance knowledge of the proposed route extension was potentially of significant financial value to real estate developers, and suspicion fell on the P.M. Schubert real estate development company that was publicly advertising Richmond Park properties (located near the present Ritchie and Hazeldean neighbourhoods) with the promise of street car service "in the near future." The charge of insider knowledge was never validated, and, in fact, when streetcar service to east Strathcona commenced in 1912 via the Mill Creek Bridge, it was some distance from Richmond Park. Few of the particulars of the 1912 Moir plan, with its 15 beltways, would ever be realized as economic decline and global war overtook them. Nevertheless, many were whipped up through Joe Clarke's rhetoric and still believed there had been corruption in the halls of power. The seeds of Moir's later dismissal by Clarke probably were sown at this time (*News-Plaindealer*; Hatcher and Schwarzkopf).

With more streetcars and routes in operation by 1912, better car signage was needed to help riders identify routes, especially those sharing portions of the same track. Illuminated signs featuring white lettering on a black background were installed on the front, rear and sides of all streetcars, replacing the previous signboards. Coloured route markers that would characterize the system for many years also were affixed to the roof corners. These markers were unique in Canada and appear to have been unique in North America. At first there were three routes: blue markers identified the route between Namayo Avenue and Albany Avenue (110 Avenue), red markers indicated the Strathcona route and green markers signalled the route between Syndicate Avenue (95 Street) and Athabasca Avenue (102 Avenue). The new route running from East End City Park to the posh new Highlands development was designated the white route. Colour-coded signage was doubly important to passengers because the implementation of the new post-amalgamation street numbering system was delayed until well after the outbreak of the First World War.

As Christmas 1913 approached, over 250 members of the Street Railway Men's Association and their guests met for their annual gathering in the new Cromdale Garage to "talk over the business of the year and above all have a good time" (*Edmonton Journal*). The members provided their own musical entertainment and recitations following the dinner with emphasis on humorous and sentimental subjects. Superintendent Woodroofe, Alf Farmilo, president of the Edmonton Trades and Labour Council, aldermen and other dignitaries also attended the smoker. Though the great settlement boom that had buoyed the Canadian West was slowing, their spirits were high. They could look back with pride on what had been accomplished in so short a time. No one talked of the ominous storm clouds growing over Europe. Soon the world would be at war, and the Edmonton Radial Railway, which had finally started to catch up to the booming city, would face familiar problems from new sources.

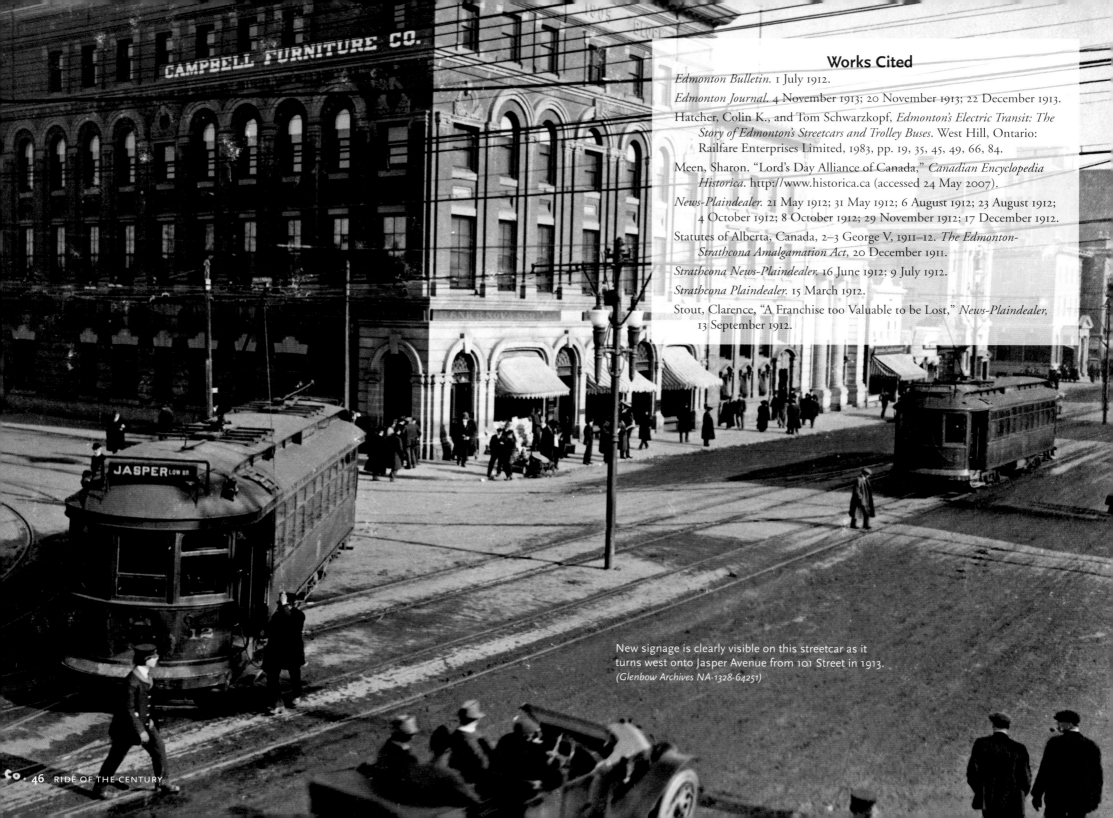

Works Cited

Edmonton Bulletin. 1 July 1912.

Edmonton Journal. 4 November 1913; 20 November 1913; 22 December 1913.

Hatcher, Colin K., and Tom Schwarzkopf, *Edmonton's Electric Transit: The Story of Edmonton's Streetcars and Trolley Buses*. West Hill, Ontario: Railfare Enterprises Limited, 1983, pp. 19, 35, 45, 49, 66, 84.

Meen, Sharon. "Lord's Day Alliance of Canada," *Canadian Encyclopedia Historica*. http://www.historica.ca (accessed 24 May 2007).

News-Plaindealer. 21 May 1912; 31 May 1912; 6 August 1912; 23 August 1912; 4 October 1912; 8 October 1912; 29 November 1912; 17 December 1912.

Statutes of Alberta, Canada, 2–3 George V, 1911–12. *The Edmonton-Strathcona Amalgamation Act*, 20 December 1911.

Strathcona News-Plaindealer. 16 June 1912; 9 July 1912.

Strathcona Plaindealer. 15 March 1912.

Stout, Clarence, "A Franchise too Valuable to be Lost," *News-Plaindealer*, 13 September 1912.

New signage is clearly visible on this streetcar as it turns west onto Jasper Avenue from 101 Street in 1913.
(Glenbow Archives NA-1328-64251)

CHAPTER 3

Casualties of War

1914–18

The enormous building boom in Edmonton reached its peak in 1912 with new buildings, bridges and construction projects dotting the urban landscape. Rutherford House, the majestic home of the first premier, Alexander Rutherford, had been completed in Strathcona in 1911. The impressive dome of the new Legislature Building rose above the riverbank at the north end of the new High Level Bridge. The McLeod Block, located in the downtown core, was declared the tallest building in the Canadian West in 1913, and on Christmas Day of that year, the first hockey game was played in the imposing new Edmonton Exhibition Arena (later to be redubbed the Edmonton Gardens), which would host many more unforgettable games. The magnificent Princess Theatre and Hotel Macdonald both opened in 1915, their sumptuously appointed features a source of pride for the whole city despite the pall of war.

These were the final monuments to the prosperity of Edmonton's first decade as a city. The next decade tried the character and determination of its people as the First World War placed enormous demands on the country, province and city. By its end, some 600,000 Canadians would serve in Europe, and Edmonton, like other Canadian cities, contributed heavily to the cause. The Edmonton Radial Railway once again struggled to meet the continuing challenge of providing the transit benefits expected by Edmontonians. While ERR had strained to keep pace with rapid urban growth in the twin cities during its first decade, the war would bring substantially increased ridership even as wartime shortages of funds and the availability of cars and parts hindered service expansion.

This view, looking west down Jasper Avenue from 99 Street, taken in 1912–13, shows the city's growth during the preceding decade. *(Provincial Archives of Alberta B4848)*

Building Ridership the Hard Way

Despite the growing tensions in Europe just before the outbreak of war, the ERR was party to a life-affirming event that would become one of Edmonton's enduring urban legends. On this occasion, the Edmonton Radial Railway played stork. Years later, the participants shared their story with *Edmonton Journal* reporter Bob Shields on the occasion of the final streetcar run:

"Move over, Mr. Mayor. And you too, Mr. Alderman, please. And, Commissioner, would you make room? Here's a citizen who should be sitting beside you when the last street car makes its last run in Edmonton Saturday night.

"Meet Peter Budnyk. He's 37 years, two months and 13 days old. And he had his first street car ride 37 years, two months and 13 days ago. He was born on Car No. 42.

"The blessed event—it must be unique in E.T.S. annals—occurred at 7:30 pm June 19, 1914, near the corner of Kirkness Street and Alberta Avenue.

"The story, as pieced together from a talk with Mr. Budnyk and from a newspaper report dated June 20, 1914, goes like this:

"Peter's mother, who still lives here . . . is Mrs. Alexander Budnyk. On the day of the fateful event, she had been working at her job downtown all day and was making her way home on car No. 42 when the 'unexpected-expected' happened. Near Norwood Boulevard, she went to the front of the car, and whispered something into the ear of the conductor, a Mr. Skiffinton. The conductor blushed, glanced at his carload of passengers, and hastily assured Mrs. Budnyk he would hurry the car along to the doctor's office as fast as possible.

"It probably is no reflection on car No. 42, but the car and Conductor Skiffinton lost the race. Little Peter arrived sooner than expected.

"When the car reached Kirkness and Alberta Avenue, two helpful women carried the mother and the new baby into the street railway's waiting room there. The doctor rushed to the scene, but by the time he arrived there was little need for his services.

"The city ambulance was called, and Peter and his mother were rushed to hospital.

"Mrs. Budnyk was the mother of a healthy 10-pound baby boy. Peter obviously never suffered from his experience for today he is a happily married man with his own family of one. He has lived in Edmonton nearly all his life [and] is a trainman employed by the C.N.R.

"Mrs. Peter Budnyk recalls that several years ago, she and her husband found themselves riding on car No. 42 on Mr. Budnyk's birthday.

"A friend of ours asked the conductor if Peter shouldn't have a free ride," she said. "The conductor told us he should have the whole car to ride in all day" (Bob Shields, *Edmonton Journal*).

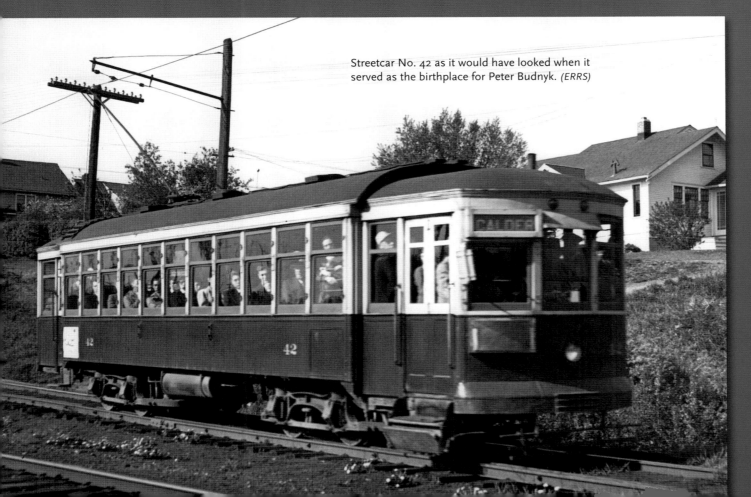

Streetcar No. 42 as it would have looked when it served as the birthplace for Peter Budnyk. *(ERRS)*

Today, Streetcar No. 42 carries much of the passenger load at Fort Edmonton Park. *(ETS)*

The 49th Battalion on a route march in Edmonton in 1915.
(City of Edmonton Archives, unaccessioned fonds)

49TH BATTALLION.
ROUTE MARCH
6/4/15.

In August 1914, Edmonton men, many of whom had served in South Africa at the turn of the century, again rushed to serve King and Empire when war was declared in Europe. Most of the city's influential residents were recent British immigrants or the inheritors of strong patriotic traditions, and this was reflected in the immediate turn-out of hundreds at the recruiting stations. In February 1915, the 19th Alberta Dragoons became the first Edmonton unit to see active service in France.

The ranks of other battalions also quickly swelled as patriotic fervour swept the city. The 9th Battalion of the Canadian Expeditionary Force was formed largely from the 101st Regiment (Edmonton Fusiliers) under Lt. Col. E.B. Edwards. The 51st, 63rd and 66th battalions saw recruits flocking to the colours as well. The need for more recruits grew as the war dragged on, and the 138th, 194th, 202nd and 218th battalions also were raised in the city. Among the new battalions was the 49th, which retained its connection to its city of origin throughout the war. (The 49th later marched into the Second World War as The Edmonton Regiment, earning the right to add "Loyal" to the name at pivotal victory at Ortona.) ERR men would serve in many of these units before the First World War ended.

The First World War took a heavy toll. Of the 4,050 Edmonton men who served in the 49th Battalion in France and Belgium, 977 were killed or were reported missing and presumed dead. Another 2,282 sustained wounds. ERR men were numbered among the casualties in this and other battalions. On 15 June 1915, Sergeant William McCann of the 9th Battalion was killed in action in Flanders. McCann, a conductor on the Edmonton Radial Railway for over three years before enlisting, left a widow and three children living in East Edmonton Gardens. McCann was the first of a number of ERR men who would make the ultimate sacrifice during the Great War (*Edmonton Journal*).

With its labour force reduced by wartime enlistment, the city struggled to carry on as floods—both human and natural—swept the city within a year of the outbreak of conflict. In mid-June 1915, Edmontonians turned out to assist displaced Europeans. "Scores of prominent citizens were on hand early to make things comfortable for the refugees," the *Edmonton Journal* reported, adding that within a few weeks, natural disaster challenged the city with refugees from among its own ranks when the North Saskatchewan River overflowed its banks, striking hardest in the low-lying river valley flats that were the city's industrial heartland. Given wartime financial constraints, economic recovery was lethargic, and people were slow to move back into the valley community (Tingley and Bunner).

Women filled a larger role in industrial and civic life, becoming the first in Canada to be eligible to vote in civic and municipal elections. The women of Edmonton joined others in the province and country to work toward female suffrage and other more dubious goals such as prohibition. Many served as jitney drivers. Jitney service, a form of shared taxi operating on a regular or semi-regular route, is said to have unintentionally appeared in Los Angeles in 1914 when L.P. Draper accepted a jitney (slang for a nickel) from a stranger for a brief ride in his Model T. Without realizing it, Draper had launched a phenomenon that rapidly swept across North America and that threatened the financial welfare of public transit systems. In the United States, the powerful political allies of the electric interurban railway systems soon implemented regulations that made it difficult for jitneys to operate. The *Electric Railway Journal* called the jitneys "a malignant growth," and "this Frankenstein of transportation." When the United States entered the war in 1917, the American Electric Railway Association contended that jitney drivers should be drafted into military service, arguing that "men engaged in nonessential automobile service of this nature should be forced to obtain some useful occupations or compelled to enter the service" (*Journal of Law and Economics*).

The jitney craze hit the Canadian West by mid-November 1914 when the first jitneys appeared in Vancouver. By April 1915, 325 were in service, and by June, 664 jitney drivers were licensed. The City substantially reduced the number by requiring drivers to post hefty bonds.

Jitneys also appeared in Edmonton in early 1915. That July ERR Superintendent J.H. Larmouth expressed his concern in a letter to the City's commissioners. Edmonton already had made an effort to control the jitney invasion by passing a restrictive bylaw, but provincial courts ruled against it. Larmouth estimated that the City was losing at least $5,000 monthly to the rival service, a small sum today but at the time roughly equal to the cost of four to six working-class homes. Larmouth reported that "jitneys are still operating in Edmonton and are not subject to any regulations." The City Solicitor was given the task of drafting another bylaw that required licensing fees of $6 annually for jitneys and their chauffeurs (*Edmonton Journal*).

Public concerns over Edmonton Radial Railway service began to be voiced with more determination and persistence as the war neared the end of its first year. Women were especially critical of streetcars that required them to step up over half a metre to gain entry, hardly in keeping with the decorum of the day. On 29 September 1916, streetcar No. 77 began a test run along Jasper Avenue with new steps lowered to half the original height. The innovation was met with immediate satisfaction by women riders (*Edmonton Journal*).

While the usual dissatisfaction with the perceived lack of service to some districts remained constant, the mounting street railway deficit became the central issue. The Edmonton Property Owners' Association endorsed a resolution to amend the City Charter to establish an independent directorate to operate the ERR. Unlike the City commissioners, the independent board would have to go before the citizens and be elected. The *Edmonton Journal*, one of the principal critics of the ERR at the outbreak of the war, mounted a disparaging editorial campaign aimed at transit financial practices.

Jitney buses at Sarcee Army Camp, Calgary, Alberta, in the early years of the First World War. *(Glenbow Archives PD-351-123)*

The 51st Battalion, Canadian Expeditionary Force, marches
down Jasper Avenue on its way overseas in 1915.
(Glenbow Archives NC-6-1392)

The Watershed Year of 1915

One of the most devastating natural disasters in Edmonton's history occurred at the end of June 1915. The first warning that a potentially destructive flood was approaching reached the city on the Saturday night, 26 June 1915, when people first noticed that water was rising rapidly on the banks toward the river flats. News from Rocky Mountain House told of the North Saskatchewan River rising six metres very rapidly, and warned those downstream to take precautions. By Monday morning reports of the spectacular nature of the flood had spread throughout the city, and "a small army of men arrived in the flooded areas to help in the relief work" (*Edmonton Journal*).

The disaster was so overwhelming that few could grasp its enormity at first. Thousands of men, women and children were drawn to the river escarpment to watch the spectacle. Several thousand more gathered at the top of the stairs at McDougall Hill to watch efforts to save the Low Level Bridge, where excited rubberneckers attempted to get onto the endangered structure despite the best efforts of the Edmonton police. The High Level Bridge, too, was clogged with spectators, while the Mill Creek Bridge, with its streetcar rails, was completely submerged under over four metres of raging water and suffered extensive damage (*Edmonton Bulletin*).

Power, water and light services were soon lost in the river's rampage. The street railway shut down at ten o'clock in the morning, and the thousands of people who had flocked downtown to view the unfolding drama in the river valley were forced to walk home.

The Low Level Bridge was withstanding the terrific pounding from the river, but tons of debris jamming against the upstream side were putting the structure under enormous pressure. The *Edmonton Bulletin*, powering its presses with gasoline engines while pressmen set type by gas lamp, reported daily on the danger: "Now and again barns, shacks, and even large houses were swept down on the bosom of the torrent and crashed with mighty force against the girders of the bridge, until it was finally decided that something would have to be done to protect the structure from entire demolition, so grave was the danger" (*Edmonton Bulletin*).

Overnight two Canadian Northern Railway locomotives with loaded ballast cars were driven onto the bridge to help it withstand the pressure of strong currents wearing away the piers. In the event the bridge might collapse, the engines kept up a head of steam, and the engineers were in readiness to pull the ballast cars off the bridge if possible.

Measurements made at the Low Level Bridge indicated that the river peaked at 11.25 metres above its low-water mark and rose eight metres between Saturday night and Tuesday morning. This was almost as high as the flood of August 1899, but the devastation was much greater, almost all of it confined to the valley flats, where much of the city's industrial wealth was concentrated. The river valley had grown up considerably in the first 15 years of the new century, and the destruction was a personal tragedy for those who lived on the flats and a trauma for the city as a whole. Estimates of property damage approached the million-dollar mark in a time when a modest home could be purchased for about $1,000.

Residents canoe down the street during the 1915 flood. Notice the flooded streetcar tracks in the foreground of the picture. (*City of Edmonton Archives EA-10-877*)

By mid-afternoon of 29 June, the water had receded one and half metres, and later that day workmen were able to free much of the debris piled up against the bridge. Following a loud "crunching and crackling of timber," the many observers watched as "the erstwhile chicken coops, barns, woodshed and shacks which have been cluttered under the bridge sailed down the Saskatchewan at a rate of speed seldom attained before today" (*Edmonton Journal*).

By 4 July crews were hard at work repairing the downed telephone wires and other services. Other crews were putting the Low Level Bridge back into operation (*Edmonton Bulletin*).

Sickness remained a concern for some time following the flood. On 30 June, T.H. Whitelaw, the Medical Officer of Health, published a public notice warning of the dangers of polluted water (*Edmonton Journal*).

Two Canadian Northern Railway locomotives and several freight cars were stationed on the Low Level Bridge to try to hold it down under the pressure of the 1915 flood. The engines kept steam up and were prepared to drive off the bridge if it gave way. (*City of Edmonton Archives EA-25-30 and EA-25-10*)

Reporting on a July meeting of citizens, the paper argued that an independent board "would remove the street railway department, the biggest deficit producing utility the City has, out of the realm of municipal politics, and give it an opportunity to live a clean life and a chance to make good without the interference of unclean meddlers." Although the resolution failed, it was the canary in the mine warning of deep dissatisfaction even during the overwhelming concerns of wartime.

Meanwhile, on 20 July 1915, Alderman R.N. Frith gave notice of motion on a resolution calling upon City Council to demand the resignation of ERR Superintendent Larmouth. Although Larmouth was not forced out, plans were quickly developed to deal with costs, deficits and other public complaints. Among the changes was the appointing of J.H. Moir to the new position of traffic manager in August 1915. Moir was typical of early management, having worked his way up through the system after his first appointment as Chief Inspector. The veteran Moir proposed a more efficient schedule, general fare reductions of six for a quarter and workingmen's rates of eight for a quarter when he assumed his new job. It was also hoped that Moir's background would ensure better relations with the emerging

union. This hope was not, however, borne out in the events of the 1917 strike (*Edmonton Journal*).

New routes and schedules went into effect a month later. The Low Level and High Level bridges were linked by a "15-minute belt," with alternate cars running over the High Level to Bonnie Doon and McKernan Lake. A streetcar now passed over the High Level Bridge every seven and a half minutes. The Highlands was served by streetcars running north on 101 Street, west on Nelson (107 Avenue) and around 124 Street, east on Jasper Avenue and then to the end of the line. Additionally, the practice of reducing service by half after 10:00 PM was ended. Smokers were allowed to indulge their habit in the rear vestibule of the streetcars. "If smoking becomes a nuisance, then it will be stopped," the *Edmonton Journal* reported, "but if the smokers will recognize their limitations and not blow clouds of smoke in the faces of passengers getting on and off the cars, they may have their weed while travelling."

In spite of efforts to shore up crumbling pubic relations and enhance revenue, the ERR was under serious financial pressure by September 1915, forcing the City Solicitor to propose a bylaw for the consideration of the commissioners. "A Bylaw for the Relief of the Street Railway System"

Tracks built along Portage Avenue (now Kingsway) were never used because the district was not serviced until buses were in use. This kind of overly enthusiastic building could have been the source of charges of mismanagement against the ERR.
(Glenbow Archives NA-1652-15)

The challenge of the high step for women in long dresses is evident in this view of Streetcar No. 64, stopped near the CPR station on Jasper Avenue to allow a female passenger to disembark and a male passenger to board. *(Glenbow Archives NA-1328-64862)*

provided for $131,992 to be charged to the general municipal debt for paving between the tracks of the expanding system (*Edmonton Journal*). That same month, a specially commissioned investigative report on the ERR under the chairmanship of H. Milton Martin, assisted by J.A. Bullman and William M. Sheppard, brought in damning conclusions, adding to the rising voice of dissatisfaction. After what was essentially an audit of ERR capitalization, depreciation and resource management, the Martin report concluded that "if the street railway department of Edmonton had in the past been conducted on sound business principles, it would have earned sufficient to meet all proper charges and that there would not have been a deficit such as the City now faces.

"It cannot be denied that this department has been severely mismanaged in almost every direction, and that this is primarily responsible for the serious condition of affairs. It is only too apparent that there has been lacking the acumen necessary to grasp the situation, and that matters have been permitted to drift along without earnest endeavour being made to place the affairs of the department on a business basis" (*Edmonton Journal*).

Recommendations of the Martin report—"a sorry report . . . that the committee has to make" opined the *Edmonton Journal*—included the reduction of capital, adjustment of interest on overcharges, adjustment of depreciated charges, reduction of stores on hand and operating expenses, and the placing of the ERR under an independent commission. The *Journal*

trumpeted that its previous censure had been vindicated and that mismanagement, not simple overextension of the line, as the ERR had argued, had resulted in operating deficits.

The Martin report led to several reforms in financial procedures and reporting practices at the Edmonton Radial Railway, although many of the other problems identified continued in some form and were even further exacerbated by wartime equipment and parts shortages, and growing ridership placing stress on existing resources.

Public concern over service standards and deficits was only deepened by several spectacular accidents caused by brutal winter weather. On 16 January 1916, Car No. 23 was "breaking the rail" (the first car over the track without the benefit of a sweeper) when it could not supply enough sand to control its speed as it dropped down toward the Low Level Bridge. As the speed picked up, Motorman William Johnson, an 18-year veteran, did his best. Conductor Warmington warned the three passengers to lie on the floor and hold onto the seat legs. No. 23 ploughed into the sharpest turn on the Low Level Belt, rushing down 97 Avenue (Saskatchewan) and hitting 100 Street (Currie), one of the sharpest turns in the city. The car jumped the track, snapped off a telephone pole and rolled six metres into a garden, where it came to rest on its side. Motorman Johnson was pinned under the heater, where spilled coals set his uniform afire. Passengers put out the fire with snow. This was Car No. 23's second accident. It had been seriously damaged at the Grand

Streetcar No. 23 after the 1913 accident at the Alberta Avenue Grand Trunk Pacific Railway crossing.
(Glenbow Archives NA-1328-1956)

Trunk Pacific Railway crossing on 118 (Alberta) Avenue when a train switching cars struck it on 12 September 1913 (*Edmonton Journal*; Hatcher and Schwarzkopf).

The following year, a highly publicized accident occurred when a high-profile businessman, W.W. Prevey, manager of the Edmonton City Dairy, was struck by a streetcar on 99 Street. Prevey received serious head injuries and suffered from temporary paralysis, though he recovered and continued to play a leading role in business and politics, serving as a City councillor in 1918–19 and a Liberal MLA from 1926–30. Another spectacular accident occurred in June when a broken trolley wire at 109 Street and 99 Avenue dropped onto the roof of Car No. 22, burning the new trolley to its trucks and providing an exciting diversion for passengers and pedestrians for an hour or so (*Edmonton Journal*).

Only two weeks after the January 1916 runaway accident, the system was virtually immobilized by blizzard conditions, the situation worsened by previous austerity measures that came back to haunt the ERR. A roadmaster had previously inspected tracks and switches in the early morning to ensure that all were clear before the heavy traffic commenced, but road crews were giving less attention to these details by early 1916. One of the two sweepers went out of operation, and the second wore out its bristles valiantly trying to keep the tracks clear. Around noon all cars were ordered back to the barns, and riders were left to their own resources, frequently trudging through bitter cold and drifting snow. The following Monday "half of the south side [had] to walk to their places of business." Everyone agreed this was the greatest winter crisis of the ERR to this point (*Edmonton Journal*). In July another scandal blackened the ERR's reputation when a number of five-for-a-quarter tickets were stolen. The ERR had no option but to quickly suspend use of these tickets (*Edmonton Journal*).

The rising demand for privatization of the ERR reached a crescendo in business circles by late 1916. "If the city cannot make the street railway pay, it should give other agencies a chance to provide as good and as cheap a service without loss to the municipal treasury," the *Edmonton Journal* editorialized. Mayor Henry stood firm on the principle of public ownership, while pointing out that the resulting revenue from costly ERR extensions had more than paid for the expenditures (*Edmonton Journal*).

Supporters of privatization within City Council took up the cause with the support of the Edmonton Board of Trade that had adopted the recommendation of H. Milton Martin in September. The Milton motion stated that ". . . as a report from the committee on civic interest dealing with the street railway situation was considered by the council, this report recommended that tenders be received for the leasing of the street railway for a period of twenty years at an annual rental equal to at least the fixed charges including sinking fund and in addition thereto, a sum sufficient to wipe out the present existing deficit against that utility and that the tenders be called for to this connection on specification or details prepared beforehand by an expert railway solicitor after a thorough investigation and report by an experienced railway traffic man, and that no variations of the conditions of the lease, once prepared, be considered" (*Edmonton Journal*).

Facing mounting citizen, business and City Council protest, the long-awaited extensions of the radial railway into the northwest, including Elm Park, Calder and West Edmonton, were shelved. Mayor Henry met community delegates in an effort to blunt criticism by pointing out that the Board of Railway Commissioners would have to give their permission for the ERR to cross the Grand Trunk Pacific Railway line before service could be extended to new districts. Negotiations with the federal government for permission to install crossings could be lengthy, he advised. The right-of-way was central to the operation of rail companies, and anything that could affect their unfettered use of this privilege, such as cross traffic, always was carefully scrutinized at length. Wartime constraints also undoubtedly were a significant factor as well (*Edmonton Journal*).

In November 1916, streetcars sporting new colours of brown and yellow made their first appearance on the line. It was concluded that the original red and green faded too easily, requiring frequent repainting and creating an attendant cost that could not be supported in budget-sensitive times. In February 1916, it was decided to paint all City vehicles the same brown and yellow as the streetcars. This was the first case of a uniform colour for municipal vehicles in Edmonton; previously the other vehicles had remained the colours in which they had been purchased (*Edmonton Journal*).

The horrific cost of the global conflict was, however, hitting the home front by the end of 1916. In September word reached Edmonton that Lance Corporal Nield of the 51st Battalion, a conductor with the ERR before enlistment, had been wounded in France. Only days later, on 23 September, Conductor Thomas Burke was reported killed in action in France after only three weeks in the trenches. Burke had left with the first company of the 101st Fusiliers in August 1914. Conductor T.E. Greenaway of the 63rd Battalion, who had worked as an ERR conductor for three years, was reported killed in action the same day (*Edmonton Journal*).

In 1917 the Edmonton Radial Railway began to make its appeal directly to Edmontonians through advertising. "It takes sixty passengers per car per hour to make the utility pay," the first advertisement stated. "It is only when all the citizens use the street railway exclusively that the system will pay and result in a better service" (*Edmonton Journal*). A second advertisement attempted more directly to evoke sympathy for the beleaguered service by noting that "[some-times] the people forget the daring of the earlier undertaking, the amount of capital invested, the [employees] dependent upon its continuance, the part it has played in development and helping to develop the city of Edmonton" (*Edmonton Journal*). Edmontonians were reminded that the "cost of living may soar and the prices of food stuffs may reach the danger point, but the car fare remains the same" (*Edmonton Journal*). Businesses assisted by advertising their locations on streetcar lines. When the Hotel Selkirk promoted dancing in its ballroom during February 1917, most of its advertisement consisted of directions and schedules for the ERR service (*Edmonton Journal*).

The ERR's public relations campaign extended to the jitney threat with one advertisement directly pleading for Edmontonians' patronage. "Ride the streetcars daily," it implored. "Ignore their competitor. It is your own street car system and you suffer if the street railway suffers" (*Edmonton Journal*). But it was probably another bylaw inspired by Calgary's jitney regulations that finally countered the jitney invasion. The new 1917 bylaw tightened regulations for the licensing of jitneys and their chauffeurs, requiring that routes and tariffs of fares be filed with the City. Breaches of the bylaw were provided for through a series of fines (*Edmonton Journal*). The *Edmonton Journal* reported that the city was "perhaps the only city on the continent which has had an attack of 'jitneyitis' and rallied." In April the newspaper reported that not one jitney was in operation in Edmonton. "Now the street railway is the sole conveyor of nickel riders in Edmonton and hopes to pick up the prestige it lost through the jitneys, increase the revenue, and so give a better service." Such jitneys as remained converted to taxi service, an example being Dale, Farney and Murray, which expanded Farney Auto Livery to provide taxi and touring car service from the Big 4 Garage on Jasper Avenue (*Edmonton Journal*).

Besides beating back the jitney invasion, the ERR also attempted to shrink deficits in 1917 by increasing the use of one-man cars on the Spruce Avenue and Calder lines, with the possibility of expanding their use to the Highlands route and inner city belts. Superintendent Moir endorsed their success, and it was hoped they would be introduced throughout the system soon. Of course, such a service would reduce the labour requirements of the ERR at a time of wartime shortages as well (*Edmonton Journal*).

Soon after the introduction of the one-man car, Motorman A.R. Mason led a delegation to protest the new system (*Edmonton Journal*), the opening salvo in contract negotiations with the City. At a meeting of the utilities committee on 21 August, a labour delegation requested amendments

The Death of William Woodroofe

Edmonton was shocked to learn in October 1916 that former Superintendent William Turton Woodroofe, a corporal in the 66th Battalion, had been either killed or wounded. He was later reported killed in action. Woodroofe had replaced R.H. Knight as Superintendent of the ERR in 1912. Before this he had worked for the British Columbia Electric Railway Company in Vancouver. Woodroofe oversaw the extensive pre-war extension of trackage and services before being replaced by J.H. Larmouth in 1914. After leaving the ERR, Woodroofe worked as a consulting engineer for the Edmonton Interurban Company, which was planning lines beyond those existing to St. Albert. He then worked for the Alberta government in its rural telephone line extension program to the northwest of the city (*Edmonton Journal*).

A Record of Sacrifice

A proud moment for the ERR occurred when a concert was held in April 1916 at Albion Hall to benefit the Red Cross and the many men of the Edmonton Radial Railway who had enlisted in the armed forces. In reading out a list of 71 enlistees, Magistrate P.C.H. Primrose reminded the crowded hall that few organizations in Alberta had answered the call to arms to the same degree as the ERR.

In the 101st Regiment (and later the 9th Battalion): Privates Tuck, Parrock, Ramsey, Burke, Hollands and McPherson; Corporal Hutton; Sergeants Mortingley, McCann and Mattingly.

In the 49th Battalion CEF: Privates Dowdell and Green.

In the 51st Battalion: Sergeants Murphy and Johnson; Corporal Baxter, Privates Whitehead, McGowan, Nield, Osborne, H. McPherson, Fox, W. Whitehead and Eames.

In the 66th Battalion: Corporal Woodroofe; Privates McEwan, Dryden and Greenaway.

In the 63rd Battalion: Sergeant-Major Walker; Privates J. Walker, Collier, Mowat and Flemming.

In the 138th Battalion: Corporal Hiel; Privates Berry, Blake, Palmer, Watt, Cody, McMasters, Knight, Davies, A. Albery and H. Albery.

In the 143rd Battalion: Privates Wilkie and Bampton.

In the 45th Battalion: Private Saunders.

In the Transport Battalion: Privates Tetrault and Massie.

In the Engineers Battalion: W.V. Kennedy.

In the 19th Alberta Dragoons: Private J. Finlay.

In the Royal Rifles: J. Wintringham.

In the 194th Highlanders: Privates Thompson, Greig, Rennie, Ferguson, Smith, Hodgson, Yell, Houston, Le Bouthilier, Patterson, Houghton, Whirter, Moir and Lammie.

In the 202nd (Sportsman's) Battalion CEF: Sergeant Bebbington; Privates McDonald, Dwyer, Pitts, Ostrander and McCowan (*Edmonton Journal*).

The ERR placed advertisements in the *Journal* in 1917 urging the public to choose streetcars over other forms of transportation (*Edmonton Journal*).

Edmonton Municipal Railway

Your Patronage

Better service should be the aim of all endeavor. With consistent patronage and co-operation we can give a steadily improving service. Wherever conditions have warranted the street railway has been extended and is giving service to-day.

Sometimes the people forget the daring of the earlier undertaking, the amount of capital invested, the employes dependent upon its continuance, the part it has played in development and helping to develop the city of Edmonton.

Ride the street carefully. Ignore their competitor. It is your own street car system and you suffer if the street railway suffers.

---

to their agreement to provide for an increase of 20 percent in wages and a rate of 55 cents hourly for operators of the contentious one-man cars. The workers' primary argument centred on the rapidly increasing cost of living (*Edmonton Journal*).

ERR employees watched with interest the labour unrest stirring throughout the country as a result of wartime inflation. On 11 July, the Toronto Street Railway conductors and motormen walked out for a day to back their demands for wage increases (*Edmonton Journal*). On the night of 31 August, the ERR men met to discuss their demands for increased wages. City Council had offered some minor concessions the previous afternoon, but these were rejected and the members passed a strike vote. Mayor Henry called an emergency City Council meeting the next morning to secure aldermen's unanimous support for holding firm on City's position. All 172 ERR workers walked out immediately.

Management took punitive approach with Superintendent Moir giving notice that he would hire back experienced men "who would be given such standing as the traffic manager may decide upon. The agreement is at an end, the union will not be recognized," he went on, "and the [employees] of the civic transit system will in some cases receive less money than they had been offered, but because they refused that offer, and went out

McNeill's taxi fleet lined up in 1914.
(City of Edmonton Archives EA-423-51)

on strike, the members of the council are firmly determined they must suffer the consequences." Special constables were sworn in and posted at the car barns, while all employees were ordered to turn in their uniforms (*Edmonton Journal*).

For a while it looked like a revival of the jitney was in the works as private cars once again took to the streets. John McNeill, with Twin City Transfer, provided motorbus service to the Highlands, while other private cars served Jasper Avenue.

With the Labour Day weekend past, Manager Moir was busy hiring strike-breakers, and within a few days he had 45 men ready to work. Returned servicemen were not permitted to work for the ERR because they were still employed by the Department of Militia and Defence, but their wives and sweethearts were eager to work at the City's rates, and the Next-of-Kin Association was reported to have up to 30 women prepared to take strikers' jobs. Meanwhile A.R. Mason, president of Local 569, was arguing the strikers' case, accusing the City administration of forcing the strike (*Edmonton Journal*).

By 5 September, three cars were running, and the strikers requested an emergency meeting at which they would agree to return if all members were taken back by the ERR without discrimination and an overall raise of 10 percent were granted. City Council rejected the offer and threatened the strikers who had not yet returned their badges and uniforms with action through their bonding agency. The strikers held firm, and public opinion was swinging in favour of the workers, with Alderman W.H. Clark in particular speaking for their case in City Council (*Edmonton Journal*).

By 8 September, five cars were running on both sides of the river and half-hour service was offered on 124 Street and to the packing plant. The following day the number was six. The Monday morning deadline imposed by City Council for men to return to work was looming, with both sides apparently intransigent. The federal Department of Labour attempted to break the impasse in a telegram encouraging the strikers to return to work and suggesting that arbitration would be forthcoming. The international union, in turn, sent communication in support of the strikers, while locally the machinists in the Grand Trunk Pacific and Edmonton, Dunvegan and

British Columbia shops voiced their support. Strikers were reported to be grounding power wires to interrupt service. The labour situation grew more precarious by the day (*Edmonton Journal*).

The strike ended abruptly on the morning of 11 September when 125 men reported for work at the barns. They returned on the City's terms, starting at 30 cents per hour and rising to 40 cents in increments. The City still refused to recognize the union. There would be no agreement. The 10-day strike was "a quiet kind of an affair, as strikes go," the *Edmonton Journal* concluded.

At this point the Industrial Disputes Act kicked in, and the union executive served Mayor Henry with an application for the appointment of a Board of Conciliation and Investigation. The union chose Henry A. Mackie as their representative on the three-man board. Union local president A.R. Mason insisted that by returning to work the strikers had only been following advice of the Fair Wage Commission and were not giving up their cause. He also insisted that the ERR's refusal to reinstitute workers according to seniority was discrimination. The demand for an agreement with a further wage increase remained on the strikers' agenda (*Edmonton Journal*).

When the Department of Labour requested that Edmonton name its representative to the Board of Conciliation and Investigation, City Solicitor Bown replied that the City had rejected any case sufficient to name such a board. Bown then asked the Minister of Labour to reconsider calling the board. At this point, it was clear to the union that they would receive no satisfaction from this process. Another mass meeting held in St. Faith's Church on 28 November to review labour grievances was followed by another strike vote at the car barns (*Edmonton Journal*). Labour relations between the City and the ERR had reached their lowest ebb to date.

Meanwhile, the City pressed on with the implementation of the one-man car system and soon had 17 in operation. The popular belt line between Jasper and 107 avenues, which had been discontinued for several years, was restored as the Figure 8 Route, with its cars marked in green and white with a superimposed numeral 8. Four cars ran each way. A new belt line also was planned for construction on the south side (*Edmonton Journal*).

Labour strife grew more significantly across Canada as the war entered its final year in 1918. Toronto street railway employees loudly protested the training and employment of women as conductors to meet wartime labour shortages. A civic workers' strike in Winnipeg led to a sympathy strike at the street railway, with one union man warning that "[not] a wheel will be turned until the strike is settled." The strike shut down streetcar service for three and a half days. Striking electricians and street railway workers in British Columbia brought the streetcars to a halt in Vancouver, North Vancouver, South Vancouver and New Westminster in mid-July. Workers succeeded in obtaining an eight-hour week, time-and-a-half for overtime and a starting wage of 40 cents per hour. Such a settlement made a strike look attractive to the Edmonton operators (*Edmonton Journal*).

A mass meeting of civic employees was held in Albion Hall on 7 June 1918, at which representatives of the separate unions discussed the need for a municipal workers' union to give their concerns more political influence. It was decided to seek a charter from the Dominion Trades Council modelled on a similar Calgary union, thus creating the Edmonton Trades and Labour Council. Alf Farmilo, the fiery labour organizer who would rise to prominence through the Edmonton Trades and Labour Council during the 1919 general strike, was present at the meeting to advise on the best way to organize (*Edmonton Journal*).

On 30 July 1918, Local 569 approached City Council to request a wage increase starting at 35 cents hourly and rising to 40 cents the second year. The City's Utilities Committee had been attempting without success to work out an arrangement with the car men for months. The Utilities Committee was chaired by Alderman Orlando Bush with Alderman H. Milton Martin and Mayor Harry Evans as the other members. Evans, with his greater experience in dealing with labour issues, took a more conciliatory position in negotiations, and an agreement was reached on 14 August that gave operators of the one-man cars a 45-cent starting hourly rate to be increased to 50 cents by New Year. Operators of the two-man cars received the 35-cent hourly rate demanded. However, subsequent talks broke down over the issue of taking back strikers. Superintendent Moir declared that he "had taken as many of the old men back as he intended to take back as long as he had anything to do with the department." Alderman Bush countered that the Utilities Committee had "promised protection to these new men. For my part as

long as I am a member of the city council I will stand to protect them." Furthermore, the City Solicitor offered the opinion that the agreement requested by the union would be illegal, although Mayor Evans suggested that a bylaw might prove a way to address the demand. Both sides again were temporarily in deadlock, but soon would resolve their issues until the next confrontation following the end of the war (*Edmonton Journal*).

A new streetcar schedule went into effect on Sunday morning, 21 July 1918, with the hope that it would prove a more efficient and profitable response to the unrelenting customer demand for improved service. North Edmonton cars, designated by their blue signs, operated south on 101 Street, east on Jasper and north on Namayo. Fifteen-minute service was promised, leaving Jasper and 101 Street at three minutes past the hour. The Figure 8 cars, designated by their green and white signs, ran south on 101 Street and then south on Namayo from 111 Avenue, and then west on Jasper Avenue. The 124 Street and 118 Avenue cars, with their green signs, turned back from 106 Avenue on Namayo and also adopted the existing schedule. The blue and white cars continued to run between 80 Street and 118 Avenue and 124 Street and 118 Avenue by way of Namayo (97 Street). Sunday service had the 142 Street trolleys leaving 142 Street at 10:00 AM and providing half-hour service until 11:30 PM to accommodate church services and other social functions (*Edmonton Journal*).

Superintendent Moir also routed more cars past department stores, which greatly increased revenues. Still mindful of the jitney threat, Moir also suggested extending the spur line at the Exhibition Grounds east to a point near the midway, "to combat the jitney inroads on the receipts for the fair period" (*Edmonton Journal*).

In the further pursuit of profit, the ERR increased fares to seven cents by mid-1918, though conductors still sold five tickets for a quarter before 8:30 AM. The "Town Bellman," a local opinion column in the *Edmonton Journal*, observed that fare increases were in line with those across the continent. "It must be admitted, of course," the Bellman nevertheless snipped, "that Detroit people are able to get cars when they want them."

By mid-1918 the ERR was finally showing signs of turning the corner of deficits. "That the street railway is gradually receding from being the wobbly member of Edmonton's utilities and assuming the pedestal of profit earning

The 49th Battalion Victory Parade on Jasper Avenue on 22 March 1919. Of the 45,136 Albertans who served overseas, 6,140 were killed and thousands more were wounded. (*City of Edmonton Archives EA-255-15*)

services is shown by Supt. Moir's report for July," the *Edmonton Journal* declared. The ERR had benefited from the decision to hold the summer fair again, despite the fact that the war had not officially drawn to a close, but nevertheless, important strides had been made.

As the war entered its final months, the deadly impact on ERR men in uniform continued. Private Eugene McDonald, who had enlisted with the 202nd Battalion before transferring to a Calgary battalion, was seriously injured in action in September. Acting Sergeant-Major M.J. Murphy, an ERR motorman and a Military Medal award-winner, died of wounds that same month while serving with the 51st Battalion. Lieutenant H.C. Saunders, Royal Air Force, a former engineer with the ERR, was reported missing in September as well. Saunders had joined the 47th Battalion, was wounded at the Somme and had received the Military Medal before transferring to the RAF. At the request of the Great War Veterans' Association, J.H. Moir recommended free rides for returning veterans dependent upon crutches (*Edmonton Journal*).

When the war finally ended, spontaneous peace celebrations were held throughout the city. An impromptu parade was organized around 4:00 PM near Namayo and 104 Avenue. A motor truck pulling a wagon loaded with children was struck by a streetcar driven by Motorman–Conductor Finley, throwing many of them to the street and slightly injuring two. The event seemed an ironically fitting conclusion to the war years for the ERR when every silver lining had its cloud. The transit service had struggled through the four years of labour strife, manpower shortages, budgetary restraint, citizen protest, and City Council and media criticism. Still the system had managed to muddle through and in the end receive the ultimate local accolade. The *Edmonton Journal* declared that it was no longer, at least for the present, the city's "white elephant." The Edmonton Radial Railway was still a public utility and finally operating in the black.

Works Cited

Edmonton Bulletin. 29 June 1915; 30 June 1915; 4 July 1915.

Edmonton Journal. 28 June 1915; 29 June 1915; 30 June 1915; 15 July 1915; 21 July 1915; 26 July 1915; 27 August 1915; 3 September 1915; 10 September 1915; 28 September 1915; 29 September 1915; 24 November 1915; 17 January 1916; 31 January 1916; 2 February 1916; 20 April 1916; 31 May 1916; 10 July 1916; 19 September 1916; 20 September 1916; 23 September 1916; 3 October 1916; 13 October 1916; 30 October 1916; 6 December 1916; 13 January 1917; 10 February 1917; 22 February 1917; 19 April 1917; 24 May 1917; 11 June 1917; 14 June 1917; 11–13 July 1917; 21 August 1917; 1 September 1917; 4 September 1917; 5–6 September 1917; 7–8 September 1917; 11 September 1917; 13 September 1917; 20 September 1917; 29 September 1917; 17 October 1917; 21 November 1917; 13 May 1918; 24–25 May 1918; 7 June 1918; 6 July 1918; 11 July 1918; 20 July 1918; 25 July 1918; 30 July 1918; 8 August 1918; 9 August 1918; 10 August 1918; 15 August 1918; 24 August 1918; 31 August 1918; 14 September 1918; 17 September 1918; 26 September 1918; 27 September 1918; 30 September 1918; 12 November 1918.

Electric Railway Journal, cited in *Journal of Law and Economics*. October 1972.

Hatcher, Colin K., and Tom Schwarzkopf, *Edmonton's Electric Transit: The Story of Edmonton's Streetcars and Trolley Buses*. West Hill, Ontario: Railfare Enterprises Limited, 1983, p. 184.

Shields, Bob. "Edmonton Man Recalls Birthday In Street Car," *Edmonton Journal*, 7 September 1952.

Tingley, Ken, with Paul Bunner, *Heart of the City: A History of Cloverdale from Gallagher Flats to Village in the Park*. Edmonton, Alberta: Cloverdale Community League, 2005, pp. 72–81.

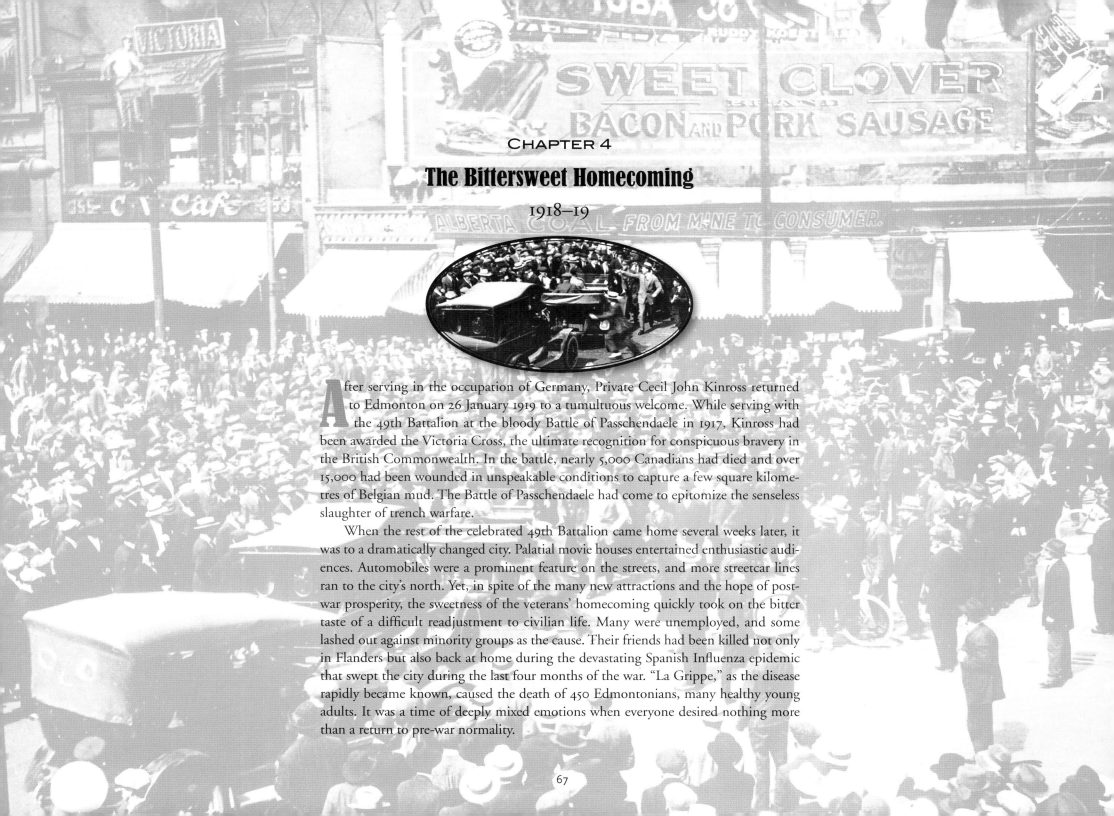

CHAPTER 4
The Bittersweet Homecoming
1918–19

After serving in the occupation of Germany, Private Cecil John Kinross returned to Edmonton on 26 January 1919 to a tumultuous welcome. While serving with the 49th Battalion at the bloody Battle of Passchendaele in 1917, Kinross had been awarded the Victoria Cross, the ultimate recognition for conspicuous bravery in the British Commonwealth. In the battle, nearly 5,000 Canadians had died and over 15,000 had been wounded in unspeakable conditions to capture a few square kilometres of Belgian mud. The Battle of Passchendaele had come to epitomize the senseless slaughter of trench warfare.

When the rest of the celebrated 49th Battalion came home several weeks later, it was to a dramatically changed city. Palatial movie houses entertained enthusiastic audiences. Automobiles were a prominent feature on the streets, and more streetcar lines ran to the city's north. Yet, in spite of the many new attractions and the hope of post-war prosperity, the sweetness of the veterans' homecoming quickly took on the bitter taste of a difficult readjustment to civilian life. Many were unemployed, and some lashed out against minority groups as the cause. Their friends had been killed not only in Flanders but also back at home during the devastating Spanish Influenza epidemic that swept the city during the last four months of the war. "La Grippe," as the disease rapidly became known, caused the death of 450 Edmontonians, many healthy young adults. It was a time of deeply mixed emotions when everyone desired nothing more than a return to pre-war normality.

Presentation of Cecil Kinross (VC Recipient) to the King and Queen during their Royal Tour visit to the Alberta Legislature in 1939. (*City of Edmonton Archives EA-29-89*)

The quarantines, school closures and general restrictions placed on public gatherings by the City's Health Officer had led to a very lean period for the ERR in late 1918. Superintendent Moir reported that passenger numbers had been very low in the autumn but were showing signs of improvement as reports of the dreaded disease declined. It took a lot to keep Edmontonians off the ice, and Moir reported that skaters were riding the ERR to various rinks, boosting revenues once again.

The arrival of the Spanish Influenza in the fall of 1918 prevented labour action in Edmonton, though long-standing grievances continued among the men. Likewise, public protest over service had gone underground briefly, only to fester and re-emerge as vocal as ever (*Edmonton Journal*). Wartime material shortages had prevented the expansion of ERR's fleet, and crowded streetcars were the predictable result. The South Side Community League took the lead in protesting rush hour crowding on ERR cars in January 1919. The league, publicly supported by recently elected Mayor Joe Clarke, demanded, among other improvements, two doors at the front of all one-man cars and better waiting facilities. In a letter published in the *Edmonton Journal*, Clarke lashed out at the ERR in his famously undiplomatic manner: "I have received more complaints against the street railway service since taking office than all the other departments of the activities of the municipality put together. I find in making the most elementary suggestions of

City residents wore surgical masks for safety during the 1918–19 flu epidemic.
(*City of Edmonton Archives 2003-25-126, EA-10-2767*)

improvements or regulations that for some reason the traffic manager [John H. Moir, referred to as Superintendent by this time elsewhere] now in charge is of the opinion that he doesn't have to pay any attention to the mayor's office. . . . However, the street railway can and must be improved and I am prepared to tackle that job single-handed or with the support of the South Side Community League or any body that will prevent work being stopped once it is started" (*Edmonton Journal*).

A few days later, debate in City Council chambers turned acrimonious when military veterans returning to work on the ERR challenged the manner in which their seniority was applied. The veterans held the view that foreign workers and wartime enemy aliens were not only taking their former jobs, but also undermining core British values of Canadian society. Such unfortunate nativism was sometimes given voice in the post-war years by the Great War Veterans' Association (GWVA), and at the organization's insistence, a survey was conducted into the numbers of recent immigrants working at the ERR. The GWVA's case was seriously undercut when the results showed that only 8 percent of ERR employees were recent arrivals to the city. At the same time, it was reported that the ERR boasted the largest

People attending a peace parade in 1919 wearing masks that were part of the response to the 1918–19 flu epidemic.
(Glenbow Archives NC-6-4200)

City payroll in the city, so the results were probably a good indicator of the larger situation. Clearly, recent immigrants were not overrepresented in civic departments after the war. The truth was far from it (*Edmonton Journal*).

Other lingering issues made their way into the debate when some aldermen expressed concern that disaffected ERR operators eager for another strike were deliberately undercutting the service and that communication had broken down between Moir and the commissioners on one side and City Council on the other. These concerns were highlighted in a public meeting that followed (*Edmonton Journal*).

A month later, a large number of dissatisfied citizens assembled in the City Council chambers to voice concerns over transit service. Topping the list were overcrowded and untidy streetcars, general inefficiencies, and late-owl cars not stopping for riders. The return of the two-man car, seen by many as providing superior service, was demanded. "Having a live subject on the boards, the citizens turned out in good force," the *Edmonton Journal* reported, "despite the wintry blasts during the evening." Superintendent Moir defended his department, explaining that replacement parts had been difficult to obtain during the war and that slow service was partly the result of the frequent railway crossings over which the ERR had to pass on its daily runs. Moir went on to remind the citizens' group that the additional operating costs of two-man service would drive the ERR deeper into debt (*Edmonton Journal*). Alderman J.A. Kinney, chair of the Utilities Committee, countered that people were more concerned with adequate service than the ERR's debt (*Edmonton Journal*).

Attempting to address the issue of war veteran's seniority, Alderman Kinney moved that the question be settled as though there had been no war,

but his committee was deadlocked on the vote. A war veterans' group in attendance demanded that they be excused from taking their turn on the spare list, and Secretary A.H. Dugdale of the Great War Veterans' Association demanded that repatriated veterans be moved to the top of the seniority list immediately. Another delegation demanded that seniority not be influenced by the earlier strike. "The meeting was the warmest of its kind for some time," a local newspaper reported ironically, "and evoked several warm passages between the different parties." For all the debate, nothing was settled. There would be no concerted movement on the grievances of either the ERR

Putting a Name to a Face

Many long-term employees of the ERR like Frederick Wood were returned veterans. A number went on to become long-term employees of the ETS, as it was later named.

During ETS Centennial Celebrations, a photo of Frederick William Wood (1898–1972) was used in a display to show a typical inspector, though his identity was not known until his daughter came forward to attach a name to this outstanding historic image. Wood served in the armed forces in World War One, rose from motorman to inspector, and also drove a bus. He was president of the ATU Local 569 in the 1930s and '40s. He retired in 1962.
(*Provincial Archives of Alberta BL616.6*)

Crowds filling the streets on 10 June 1919 during riots that
broke out during the Winnipeg General Strike, a labour action
lasting from 15 May to 25 June. (Glenbow Archives NA-1775-2)

men or the public at this time. This changed in a couple of months when events in Winnipeg fanned the flames of discontent throughout the West, including Edmonton to a much less violent extent (*Edmonton Journal*).

Public discontent was further exacerbated in the spring of 1919 when the five-for-a-quarter ticket strips were replaced by four-for-a-quarter tickets after 8:30 AM, whether sold on or off the streetcars. After 12:30 PM, cash fares for rides after 12:30 PM were raised to ten cents. An *Edmonton Journal* headline complained that street railway tickets were "rapidly reaching the luxury class." Strathcona residents raised the cry of unjust treatment, claiming that the new fares contravened the Amalgamation Agreement of 1912, which many felt guaranteed a five-cent fare. Legal action was threatened, although never carried out. The City claimed, correctly, that the amended charter (Section 39, 1918) gave the City full power to charge such tolls and fares on any of its tramway lines "provided that the passenger fares are uniform throughout the city" (*Edmonton Journal*).

In early 1919, the labour strife that had gone underground during the war and the influenza epidemic resurfaced (*Edmonton Journal*). Fred Ackland, the federal Deputy Minister of Labour, concluded that a joint request from the City and the labour union local for a conciliation board to resolve issues could not be granted unless non-union ERR employees also agreed to the process. Ackland reminded Clarke that while a conciliation board had been offered during the 1917 strike, the City had questioned the Labour Minister's jurisdiction and had even obtained an injunction restricting the inquiry. The Department of Justice had subsequently rendered the opinion that if an employer was a municipality or controlled by municipal authorities, the Minister of Labour could establish a board of conciliation only if both parties agreed to the measure. Although F.C. Harrison, the Labour Department representative in Calgary who had dealt with the 1917 case, travelled to Edmonton to discuss the matter, no conciliation board seems to have been established (*Edmonton Journal*).

J.F. Lymburn, representing non-union street railway workers before City Council, argued that they had not had an opportunity to voice their grievances regarding seniority, which they felt was unfairly administered by the ERR in favour of union members and military veterans. He cited the case of one non-union worker whose seniority would be reduced from number 36 to number 122. Mayor Clarke postponed any decision on the matter, which would "be considered at a future meeting according to the ruling of the mayor." Like the conciliation board, this issue also seems to have faded away in the broader turmoil arising in the wake of the Winnipeg General Strike (*Edmonton Journal*).

The Winnipeg General Strike began on 15 May 1919 when almost 30,000 workers walked off the job to protest poor wages and working conditions amidst the turmoil of post-war unemployment and rising inflation. It ended more than a month later after the arrest of strike leaders and the infamous charge of the Royal North-West Mounted Police into a crowd of strikers that left 30 injured and one dead.

The Winnipeg General Strike galvanized labour discontent across the Canadian West and deepened the divide between management and labour, as well as between radical and moderate factions within the trade union movement. On the more conservative side were the traditional craft unionists represented by organizations such as the Edmonton Trades and Labour Council (TLC), while more revolutionary elements were represented by the new but growing One Big Union movement. The OBU was a largely western Canadian phenomenon influenced by the French syndicalist workers' movement of the early twentieth century. The OBU, dominated by members of the Socialist Party of Canada, publicly expressed solidarity with the Russian Bolsheviks and organized sympathy strikes in Calgary, Vancouver and Edmonton in support of the Winnipeg General Strike. The organization's radical agenda, however, never took root among largely conservative western trade unions, and its membership waned throughout the 1920s. But during its brief heyday, as a voice for alienated trade unionists, the One Big Union raised the fear that the recent example of the Russian Revolution would tip the majority of workers towards more confrontational labour activity.

On 28 April 1919, the Edmonton Trades and Labour Council (TLC) was deeply divided over whether to allow sympathizers of the highly controversial One Big Union among its ranks. Council Secretary Alfred Farmilo moved to expel all OBU delegates and to deprive them of their voting rights. Over half

the members walked out of this stormy meeting. The TLC later denounced the radicals as Bolsheviks in its *Edmonton Free Press*, as did other newspapers.

Joseph White, the street railwaymen's local secretary of the Amalgamated Transit Union (ATU) took the side of the One Big Union, protesting the expulsion of OBU sympathizers in a letter to the Edmonton Trades and Labour Council in May and giving notice that the ATU would withdraw from the Council until OBU supporters had been reinstated. Farmilo called the bluff, recognized the ATU's withdrawal, and stated that when they decided to return to the fold, all back dues would have to be paid in full. He further claimed that since the previous strike, when the streetcar men had returned without a settlement, the union had settled its account with the Trades and Labour Council (*Edmonton Journal*). The ATU withdrew from the TLC.

Although the ERR members of ATU Local 569, who had been without a settlement for two years, believed their concerns were downplayed or ignored by the Council, few seem to have been willing to openly support the One Big Union initiative. They were reluctant to support the Winnipeg strike with gusto because of the widespread view that the strikers were more ideologically committed to extreme political action. Few Edmonton labour unionists could be counted among the extreme radicals at this time. This probably accounts for the fact that the local sympathy strike commencing on 26 May 1919 never became general or unduly disruptive in Edmonton. On 23 May, City Council unanimously passed a vote of confidence in the ability of the Edmonton Trades and Labour Council to avert a strike in the city, despite the deteriorating labour situation throughout the West. Nevertheless, a general strike hit Edmonton on Monday morning, 26 May,

Workers marched on 10 June 1919 in the streets of Winnipeg, during the General Strike.
(Glenbow Archives NA-1775-4)

Strikers from the One Big Union at Drumheller, Alberta, in 1919. Many southern Alberta miners supported radical union action, but the One Big Union did not make inroads in Edmonton, where more conservative craft unionism held sway. *(Glenbow Archives NA-2513-1)*

following an Edmonton Trades and Labour Council vote that favoured a walk out by a factor of over three to one. Member locals voted 34–4 in favour of the strike. The streetcars were slated to stop running at eleven o'clock that morning (*Edmonton Journal*).

ERR employees withheld transit service only briefly. "Hopes of an early morning and late afternoon street car service were held out at general strike headquarters at noon today" (*Edmonton Journal*), came the news on 28 May 1919, although a proposal to cut off power to all services except hospitals and other essential services was threatened. William Marshall, chairman of the general strike publicity committee, announced that curtailed streetcar service would be provided for an hour or two in the mornings and afternoons. "The executive committee is recommending this in order that school children who have long distances to go to school will be able to take the cars as before," Marshall declared. "It is not the intention, however, to limit passengers to school children." By this time, the taxi drivers also had gone

on strike. The *Edmonton Journal* reported that "Apart from the lack of street cars, the city is not being seriously inconvenienced by the general strike. Stores are open as usual, most of the restaurants are open with the master barbers working alone and the railways are still carrying passengers" (*Edmonton Journal*).

The work stoppage in Edmonton was virtually at an end by the following day when the central strike committee made further concessions that allowed streetcar personnel to return to work if the other civic employees also returned. "Members of the street railway men's union favor a complete resumption of work if the civic block [employees] return," a front-page newspaper story stated. To the activist members of the union, it seemed that little had been gained by the sympathy strike. The prevailing public attitude seems to have been summed up by an editorial in the *Edmonton Journal*: "The issue between those employers in Winnipeg whose dispute with their employees was the original cause of the trouble is one over which Edmonton can have no control," it argued. "To punish those in Edmonton whose attitude towards organized labour has been satisfactory in the eyes of organized labour itself, because of the actions of those people in Winnipeg with whom they have had nothing to do, is the limit of absurdity and unfairness." The streetcar men voted to return to work, and on 30 May full service was restored (*Edmonton Journal*).

Though the streetcars were soon on the rails again, the sympathy strike spread by early June to the Cardiff and Morinville coalmines, where the OBU was more influential. The ERR warned that if coal could not be brought in from the Tofield mines or Canadian Northern Railway stocks, service might have to be curtailed again. Fortunately, this never proved necessary. The *Edmonton Journal* proclaimed that the city was "back to normal" on 31 May. "From now on," an editorial concluded, "we may expect this city to resist more strongly than ever the program of the O.B.U." ERR Superintendent Moir's salary was increased by over 15 percent from $2,556 to $3,000, presumably for successfully weathering the labour storm. By 18 June, the streetcars were running again in Winnipeg, with the Edmonton strike officially ending six days later—some time after it was an accepted fact, although some disruption in streetcar service lingered until the very end (*Edmonton Journal*).

No sooner had the labour situation essentially returned to normal than demands for service improvements erupted again among the perpetually insistent ridership. In early July, in an effort to promote attendance at south-side public events, T.P. Malone, a south-side businessman, encouraged the South Side Community League to demand the extension of ERR service down 109 Street to the Athletic Grounds with return via 104 Street. Nothing came of the proposal at the time, and the "stub line" running south down 104 Street, then west on 76 Avenue toward McKernan Lake remaining the principal southern service (*Edmonton Journal*).

The best the ERR could offer was a new service schedule that went into effect on 3 November 1919 to provide 15-minute service at rush hours on the Low Level Bridge and Bonnie Doon lines, and a streetcar every seven and a half minutes over the High Level Bridge. Upgraded service was expected soon on the Alberta Avenue line as well. As the second post-war winter began, Edmontonians hoped the worst of the service crunch might be over (*Edmonton Journal*). Shortage of rolling stock, weather disruptions and ever-present power problems all conspired to make the final months of the year difficult. A "Warning to Citizens" from the City Commissioners on 10 December notified Edmontonians that additional cars could not be provided for the busy Christmas season. "We respectfully ask your hearty co-operation," the communiqué requested, "by shopping well in advance of Christmas, and as early in the afternoons as possible to avoid overcrowding of cars during evening rush hours" (*Edmonton Journal*).

On 15 December 1919, the collapse of power plant machinery under the demands of the heavy seasonal load forced the commissioners to order a further reduction in that afternoon's service. "Thousands of people were obliged to shiver in doorways and many, loaded down with Christmas purchases, slipped and ploughed homewards," the *Edmonton Journal* complained the next day. Two days later, the power plant experienced more

The original officers of the Amalgamated Transit Union Local 569 in 1911. Top row, left to right: W.H. Clark; A.J. Campbell; A.H. Elliott (President); A. McCulloch (Treasurer); A. McCann (Fin. Secy.). Bottom row, left to right: H.D. Hughes; T. Ferrier; H. Montgomery; J.M. McCready; R.F. Murphy; A. MacDonald. *(ATU 569)*

problems, and the commissioners were forced to curtail streetcar service even more drastically, taking 31 of 56 cars out of service. Even street lighting was reduced to a dim glow by the shortages. Nevertheless, by Christmas Eve, the ERR provided additional streetcars for holiday church services with "extras" running on the main lines after midnight to take the faithful to mass or late-night services (*Edmonton Journal*).

Simmering labour unrest, material shortages and service reductions all took their toll on the ERR's reputation during 1919, but nothing damaged public confidence as much as a series of notable accidents beginning on 12 August when a streetcar collided with a Canadian Northern Railway train on the Low Level Bridge they had shared since 1908 without mishap (*Edmonton Journal*). Then, in the early morning of 22 October, Car No. 21, eastbound from 142 Street along 102 Avenue, jumped the tracks while crossing the bridge between 130 and 132 streets and crashed into Groat Ravine 12 metres below. Miraculously, none of the six passengers was very seriously injured, although the streetcar was shattered to splinters by the impact. A later investigation revealed that No. 21 was speeding when a snow-filled dip in the tracks at the west end of the bridge caused it to jump the tracks. When the motorman and his passengers arrived at the General Hospital, they realized one passenger, A.J. Adams, was missing. As it turned out, he had crawled out of the wreck, helped rescue other victims and then set out for work afoot, simply saying, "Goodbye, I have to get to work."

Fearing litigation, Mayor Clarke forbade any non-municipal witnesses to testify at the subsequent inquiry. The 142 Street Community League accused Clarke of blocking the investigation, and a second inquiry was called. Eventually, an inspection of all bridges carrying streetcar traffic resulted from the uproar (*Edmonton Journal;* City of Edmonton Archives).

Edmonton's dream of post-war modernization and civil reestablishment was not to be realized in 1919, though a hollow victory of sorts was eked out when the Edmonton Radial Railway announced its first surplus since 1912 at the height of the pre-war economic boom. This news, despite influenza, economic stagnation and the sheer magnitude of a decade of physical demands on the system left the ERR looking forward to the 1920s, hoping for a brighter day for the urban transit system and the city it served (*Edmonton Journal*).

The Certificate of Establishment for ATU Local 569 in 1911. Left column, top to bottom: A. Elliott; W. Magirl; Geo. Turgeon; Hugh Montgomery; E.G. Ramsey. Right column: E. Turnbull; N. Turgeon; E. Pascoe; A. McDonald; A. McCulloch. The certificate is signed "8th Day August 1911, W.D. Mahon, International President."
(ATU 569)

Works Cited

Bercuson, David J., "Syndicalism Sidetracked: Canada's One Big Union," in *Revolutionary Syndicalism: An International Perspective*, edited by Marcel van der Linden and Wayne Thorpe. Aldershot, England: Scholar Press, 1990, pp. 221–36.

City of Edmonton Archives. Accident File.

Edmonton Journal. 19 October 1918; 27 November 1918; 25 January 1919; 28 January 1919; 6 February 1919; 12 February 1919; 17 February 1919; 18 February 1919; 14 April 1919; 15 April 1919; 22 April 1919; 29 April 1919; 20 May 1919; 24 May 1919; 26 May 1919; 27 May 1919; 28 May 1919; 29 May 1919; 30 May 1919; 31 May 1919; 7 June 1919; 12 June 1919; 3 July 1919; 14 August 1919; 22 August 1919; 22 October 1919; 1 November 1919; 12 December 1919; 17 December 1919; 19 December 1919; 24 December 1919.

No. 21 streetcar after it crashed into Groat Ravine in October 1919.
(Glenbow Archives NC-6-4795)

CHAPTER 5

The Edmonton Radial Railway in the Doldrums

1920–29

Whatever made the 1920s roar in Paris and New York was missing in Edmonton. No Lost Generation artists haunted the Left Bank of the North Saskatchewan River, and only a few local architects were influenced by the flamboyance and modernism of the Art Deco style, which reacted against years of wartime austerity. There were some flappers, of course, but of a more subdued type befitting life in a provincial capital still under the powerful influence of socially conservative forces.

Edmonton's population grew by only 22 percent during the post-war decade, from 61,045 in 1920 to 74,298 in 1929, barely a ripple compared with the dramatic expansion of the pre-war years. Only the fleeting outburst of oil speculation following the discovery of oil at Fort Norman in the Northwest Territories in 1920 gave a foretaste of the city's future. For the time being, Edmonton remained an agricultural supply centre rather than the bustling industrial metropolis many had predicted during the early surge of development. Growing farm production remained one of the few bright spots in the regional economy during the decade.

Many Edmontonians responded to the post-war malaise of high unemployment and sluggish growth by banding together to boost their community. On 24 January 1921, the Edmonton Federation of Community Leagues (EFCL), an umbrella community organization, was established. The EFCL rapidly grew to the largest organization of its kind in Canada, exerting its influence through both social activities and

COMMUNITY LEAGUES

FOSTER CLEAN SPORT

MOTHER EDMONTON

INDUSTRY · ENERGY · ENTERPRISE

The Edmonton Federation of Community Leagues' float participating in its first Dominion Day parade. *(City of Edmonton Archives EA-496-6)*

Announcer R.W. Drake at the CJCA microphone in about 1922. *(City of Edmonton Archives EA-244-6)*

political advocacy. Transit service remained among the more important concerns motivating the various community leagues as they became established throughout the city.

Community leagues across the city took enormous pride in the international fame brought to their city by the McDougall Commercial High School girls' basketball team coached by the legendary principal J. Percy Page. Before the Grads were disbanded in 1940, they had won an astonishing 96 percent of their 522 games, including four Olympic tournaments and every Canadian championship from 1922 to 1940. Edmontonians loved their hockey then as now, and they thrilled at the exploits of the Edmonton Eskimos Hockey Club as they defeated the Regina Capitals to win the 1923 Western Canada Hockey League prize before losing to the Ottawa Senators in their challenge for the Stanley Cup.

Edmontonians began to keep abreast of their city's accomplishments through the new medium of radio when the first local radio station, CJCA, signed on air on 1 May 1922 from a corner of the *Edmonton Journal* building. Communications pioneer G.R.A. Rice would begin his career as

The Edmonton Commercial Grads at the height of their glory days in about 1926. *(City of Edmonton Archives EA-10-2060)*

manager at CJCA before launching Sunwapta Broadcasting with partner Hans Neilson. The University of Alberta launched the city's second radio station, CKUA, in 1927. The Edmonton Newsboys Band, organized in 1914 through the *Edmonton Journal* when John Michaels of Mike's News fame and Alderman Joseph Driscoll started a subscription list among city businessmen, really came into its own during the 1920s as it was acclaimed as one of the finest bands in the world (*Edmonton Journal*).

The community spirit generated by the city's civic-minded organizations' growing list of events and accomplishments did not, however, transfer to the glue that held many of these threads together—the transit system. Throughout the 1920s, the Edmonton Radial Railway grew slowly, struggling to consolidate and upgrade the infrastructure and rolling stock that had been thrown together pell-mell during its hectic first decade and then left to deteriorate during wartime shortages of money and material. The ERR's principal preoccupation during the period was simply to catch up to demand, but trials assailed it on every front.

The decade began with rumours that Superintendent John H. Moir would be forced to resign by the City Commissioners. The irascible, outspoken Mayor Clarke was the chief proponent of the move, having crossed swords with Moir on more than one occasion. Clarke's main concern was the slow completion of the ERR line extension to the horse show pavilion located at the Exhibition Grounds, which at the time also doubled as the main ice arena. Hockey fans were transit riders, and their numbers in 1919 contributed to the first increase in ridership numbers the ERR had seen since 1912. Mayor Clarke laid the blame for the loss of additional revenue occasioned by the slowness of track completion squarely at the feet of Moir.

Superintendent Moir, at what became the end of his tenure, responded by undertaking an ill-fated ERR extension along 127 Avenue and a double-track line along 78 Street to the Exhibition Grounds to capitalize on the increased demand for transit service. The Exhibition Grounds loop consisted of about 1,200 metres of track, while the 127 Avenue extension provided the 800 metres of track needed to upgrade service to Calder residents and workers at the Grand Trunk Pacific Railway roundhouse. Construction began in October 1919, but severe weather in November slowed the work,

which was not completed until the following spring. Moir's fate was sealed by the weather-related delay (Buck).

Mayor Clarke invoked his authority under the City Charter in early 1920 to suspend Moir immediately, "which will be as early after 10 o'clock Wednesday January 7 as it is possible to find you," he notified the hapless object of his outrage. Clarke planned to replace Moir with William James Brumlees, who was selected on the basis of his seniority in the department, a demand made by the street railway union. Inspector Andrew Robertson was to become Brumlees' chief assistant

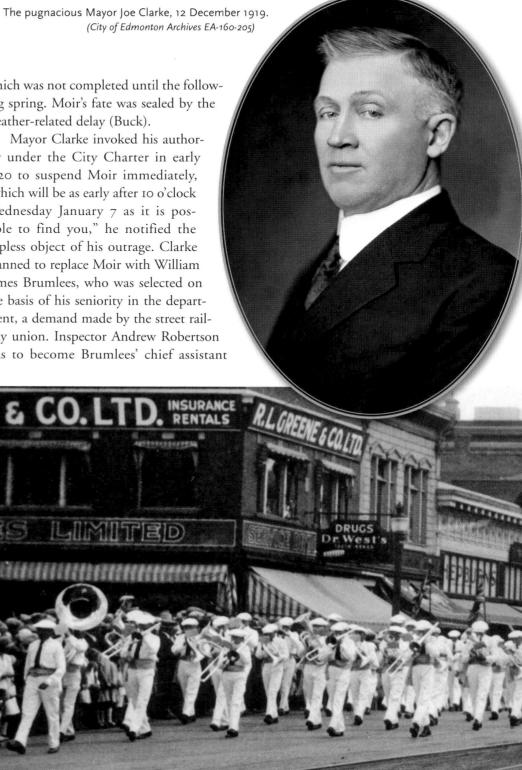

The pugnacious Mayor Joe Clarke, 12 December 1919.
(City of Edmonton Archives EA-160-205)

with special responsibility for administration and operation of the car barns. Inspector Thomas Ferrier was to become senior traffic inspector responsible particularly for the provision of service during the power shortages and outages that still routinely occurred, especially during winter (*Edmonton Journal*).

Not all civic officials endorsed Mayor Clarke's heavy-handed decision. "Mr. Moir gave the city better service last year than ever before," Alderman Andrew McLennan protested. "This is not a fair way of treating a man who has given good service to the city." Alderman Henri Martin argued that Moir was the most efficient superintendent in the ERR's history, that he had advanced the system under adverse conditions and that he had been constantly hampered by interference from the mayor. Moir himself argued against his suspension, insisting that he had followed all orders and that construction delays were the result of adverse weather conditions, not management bungling. Rumours circulated that Moir would soon be appointed superintendent of the Calgary transit system, a position that ultimately went to Edmonton City Electrical Engineer R.A. Brown.

A compromise of sorts was struck at a meeting of the Utilities Committee on 10 January 1920. Mayor Clarke agreed to withdraw his suspension of Superintendent Moir, and Moir agreed to resign at the end of 30 days, until which time he would be on leave with pay. Perhaps feeling embarrassed, the commissioners granted two months severance pay to Moir (about $500) before turning him loose, a victim of "Fightin' Joe" Clarke's displeasure (*Edmonton Journal*).

Only days later, Albert Walker Haddow, previously appointed a City Commissioner, was sworn in as the new Public Works Commissioner of a reorganized three-man Public Works Commission board. One of the first demands of the new board was that they would henceforth make all decisions regarding the dismissal of senior City employees. The unfortunate case of Superintendent Moir thus played an important role in provoking civic reform to limit the arbitrary authority of the mayor's office, although Moir would not benefit from this reform.

The Edmonton Newsboys Band marches along the ERR tracks during the Dominion Day parade in 1927.
(City of Edmonton Archives EA-502-14)

John. H. Moir's 12-year career with the ERR started as a track-layer in 1908. He quickly worked his way up to construction foreman and motorman during 1908, then inspector, becoming chief inspector in 1910. In 1915 he was appointed traffic manager. During the mayoralty of W.T. Henry in 1917, he became the general superintendent of the department. He left in early 1920 after disputes with Mayor Clarke (*Edmonton Bulletin*).

CANADA,

Province of Alberta

To Wit:

I, *John Moir*

do solemnly promise and declare that I will truly, faithfully and impartially, to the best of my knowledge and ability execute the office of *Traffic Manager Street Railway*

to which I have been elected or appointed in this city, and that I have not received and will not receive any payment or reward or promise thereof for the exercise of any partiality, malversation, or undue execution of the said office, and that I have not by myself or partner, directly or indirectly, any interest in any contract with, or on behalf of the said city save and except that arising out of my office as

Traffic Manager, St Railway

Sworn before me at Edmonton,   So help me God

Province of Alberta, this 17

day of *Sep* 19 15

The official oath of office, sworn by John H. Moir when he accepted the post of Traffic Manager with the ERR in 1915.
(*City of Edmonton Archives MS-209-162Moir*)

W.J. Cunningham, Superintendent of City Power, took the additional role of Manager of the Street Railway Department on 1 January 1925, succeeding R. Colwell, who started in the position in 1921 and resigned in 1924 to move to Winnipeg. Cunningham would play a dominant role in rationalizing and expanding transit services during his tenure, although the cauldron of lingering troubles brewing on his watch was nothing if not daunting. A decade of almost unbridled growth followed by economic downturn and war had left a legacy of aging, inadequate and poorly maintained trackage, rolling stock and electrical generation. Keeping the brew simmering was pent-up demand for costly improvement and expansion of services, and ready to stir the pot was City Hall with its ubiquitous demands for austerity.

Though Cunningham must have cast a wary glance over his shoulder at the fate of Moir, he nevertheless moved quickly to address the changing role of the public transit system in the post-war era.

One of Cunningham's first orders of business was the completion of the 101 Street underpass, which had begun construction the year before. The tunnel between 104 and 105A avenues, constructed in cooperation with the Canadian National Railway, was conceived as part of an effort to deal with growing congestion in the busy downtown. Months of disruption to downtown traffic and ERR service followed before the project was completed in the summer of 1925. This project was the first of several that would see the ERR update its routes, equipment and service under the new superintendent.

Summer construction on 97 Street near Frank Ropert's Grocery just north of 107 Avenue. The dome of the original St. Josaphat's Ukrainian Catholic Church is visible above the buildings.
(*Provincial Archives of Alberta A2377*)

Albert Walker "Bert" Haddow, 1887–1958, Edmonton Public Works Commissioner, 1920

Bert Haddow was appointed City Engineer in 1910 and returned to that role in 1921 after only a year on the commission board, but he maintained an active and influential involvement in transit issues throughout his long career.

Haddow was born in Simcoe, Ontario, and graduated from Queen's University with a degree in Civil Engineering in 1909 before moving to Edmonton the following year. He joined the Engineering Department, serving the City well until retiring in 1950 *(Edmonton Journal)*.

A young Bert Haddow with A. Latournell.
(City of Edmonton Archives EA-10-1601)

William John Cunningham, Edmonton Radial Railway Superintendent

William John Cunningham was born in Altringham, Cheshire, England, where he was raised, educated and first worked for the Altringham Electrical Company. He later graduated from the College of Technology affiliated with Manchester University. After immigrating to the United States in 1907, he moved to Montreal, where he worked for a time at Ellis, Chambers & Bullock, Limited. By 1913 he was in Calgary, where he worked his way up to the position of assistant superintendent of the municipal power plant by 1915.

During the First World War, Cunningham briefly served overseas with the Munitions Department, with Vickers Limited and for four months aboard HMS *Valiant*. For the rest of the war, he was assigned to the Royal Arsenal at Woolich. After the war, he returned to his former position in Calgary until appointed to replace C.E. Cope as Superintendent of the Civic Power Plant in Edmonton in 1919. He became Superintendent of the ERR in 1925.

William Cunningham died on 13 May 1934 following a stroke. Still serving as superintendent of the Street Railway and Power Plant at the time of his death, he was replaced by Thomas Ferrier *(Edmonton Bulletin; Edmonton Journal)*.

> December 30th 1919
>
> BYLAW No. 45 , 1919.
>
> A Bylaw to appoint W. J. Cunningham Superintendent of the Civic Power Plant, including Pumping Station and Sub-stations.
>
> The Municipal Council of the City of Edmonton, duly assembled, enacts as follows:
>
> 1. W. J. Cunningham, now of the City of Calgary, in the Province of Alberta, is hereby appointed Superintendent of the Power Plant of the City of Edmonton, including the Pumping Station and all substations, for the term of one year from the first day of January, 1920, at the yearly salary of Three Thousand and Six Hundred Dollars in the usual course of Civic salary payments.
>
> DONE and PASSED in Council this Thirtieth day of December 1919.
>
> MAYOR.
>
> CITY CLERK.

The City of Edmonton, Bylaw 45, 30 December 1919 appointing W.J. Cunningham as Superintendent of the Civic Power Plant for a one-year term, which was subsequently adjusted to a permanent position.
(City of Edmonton Archives)

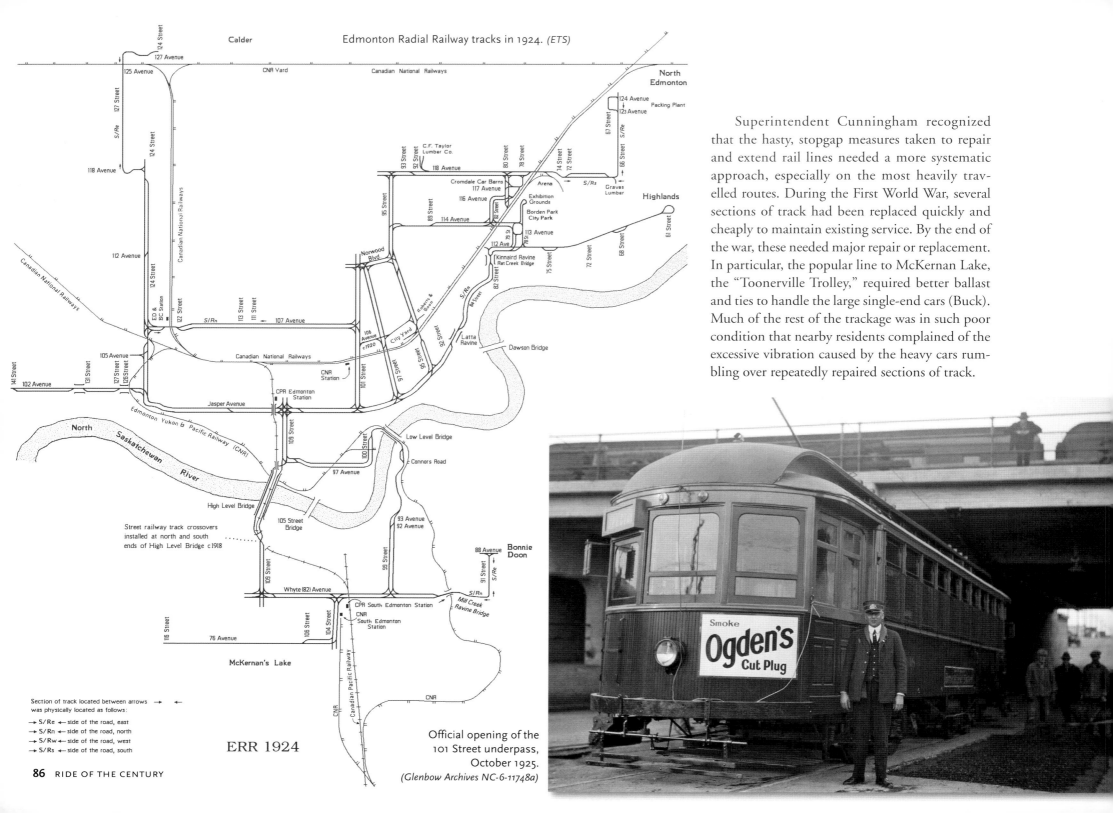

Edmonton Radial Railway tracks in 1924. (ETS)

Superintendent Cunningham recognized that the hasty, stopgap measures taken to repair and extend rail lines needed a more systematic approach, especially on the most heavily travelled routes. During the First World War, several sections of track had been replaced quickly and cheaply to maintain existing service. By the end of the war, these needed major repair or replacement. In particular, the popular line to McKernan Lake, the "Toonerville Trolley," required better ballast and ties to handle the large single-end cars (Buck). Much of the rest of the trackage was in such poor condition that nearby residents complained of the excessive vibration caused by the heavy cars rumbling over repeatedly repaired sections of track.

Street railway track crossovers installed at north and south ends of High Level Bridge c 1918

Section of track located between arrows → ← was physically located as follows:

→ S/Re ← side of the road, east
→ S/Rn ← side of the road, north
→ S/Rw ← side of the road, west
→ S/Rs ← side of the road, south

ERR 1924

Official opening of the 101 Street underpass, October 1925.
(Glenbow Archives NC-6-11748a)

Cunningham returned to the proven concrete-slab construction methods introduced in 1913 for a comprehensive rail replacement program that would finally be completed in 1936. Requiring the complete replacement of both the tracks and concrete roadbeds, the program was very labour-intensive and expensive. The screw spikes used to anchor rails to the ties were more costly than the wartime hammer-driven spikes, but they were much more durable, and the new grooved girder rails also were a major improvement over the old T-section rails. Finally, the old hard-drawn copper electrical wires, which deteriorated quickly under Edmonton's harsh operating conditions, were replaced with a more durable copper and cadmium alloy wire, the so-called bronze trolley wire (Buck).

Ridership increased on the ERR to the point that, by 1924, it was exceeding the capacity of the direct current plant by 25 percent. Despite warnings from the powerhouse superintendent, the ERR continued to place excessive demands on power generation. The system had little choice. On 20 February 1927, the inevitable happened when the old 1912 power plant steam engine broke its connecting rod while operating at full capacity. Within a week, the ERR was forced to reduce service by half. Makeshift measures could no longer do, and a study undertaken by Superintendent Cunningham reported in 1928 that the City power equipment was obsolete and could no longer meet the demands of the ERR. A new power plant was installed by December 1929, alleviating the perennial problem of power supply—at least for a while (Buck).

The 101 Street underpass just prior to completion.
(Glenbow Archives NC-6-11749b)

The little streetcar information kiosk that resided in downtown Edmonton for years, November 1923.
(Glenbow Archives NC-6-10830)

A work crew outside the Alberta Hotel replacing ERR tracks near 97 Street in May 1929.
(Glenbow Archives ND-3-4670a)

STREET CAR INFORMATION BUREAU
CARS TO ALL PARTS OF THE CITY LEAVE THIS CORNER

WEST BOUND	EAST BOUND	
BONNIE DOON VIA High Level	HIGHLANDS	All White
SOUTH SIDE	101 ST. & SPRUCE	Red & White
SOUTH SIDE VIA Low Level	95TH STREET	All Red
WEST END	NORTH EDMONTON	All Blue
WEST END	80 ST. & 118 AVE.	Blue & White
CALDER & 124 ST. VIA 101 St.	95 ST. & 105 AVE.	Green & White
TO ARENA & EXHIBITION GROUNDS		Green & Red

The busy intersection at Jasper Avenue and 101 Street in the early 1920s, shortly after the new wye track was installed.
(City of Edmonton Archives EA-10-354)

Weather continued to bedevil the transit system during the winter, the worst being 1928–29, one of the coldest on record, when temperatures frequently plunged to –40°C. The new girder rails began to sheer where the new system of joints had been used. The susceptibility of even the improved tracks to cold-weather damage thus continued to plague the system for years to come.

Cunningham also faced a system undergoing inevitable change resulting from technological innovations. Laundry, meat and especially large industrial and construction deliveries from the warehouse district had been a valued source of supplementary revenue for ERR during the early years, but by the 1920s, the decline in construction and the rise of truck transport had rendered the service less essential. In any event, the ERR needed to focus all its resources on catching up to passenger demand. The downtown tracks were a web of spur lines serving warehouses and department stores, but by mid-decade, the ERR began to pull up these lines, including the previously busy spurs from 95 Street into the City yards and the former Roberts and Boon Wholesale warehouse, and from 118 Avenue into the Graves Lumber Yard (Buck).

To shift more revenue to line extension and repair, the ERR began another round of cost-cutting measures. The south-side barns were closed in May 1921, and the temporary track on Whyte Avenue west of 109 Street was removed. At the same time, plans were in the works to introduce more permanent routes targeting areas of heavier passenger demand. In order to have more routes originate and end at the busy Jasper Avenue and 101 Street intersection, a combination wye and crossover was installed. Such installations allowed the single-end cars to turn without backing out into busy vehicular traffic.

The information kiosk on 101 Street in 1929, looking north from the *Edmonton Journal* building. *(Glenbow Archives ND-3-4840)*

Other cost-cutting measures included the phasing out of horse-drawn maintenance equipment in keeping with the general trend toward more efficient mechanized transport. Although horses remained on the city scene delivering ice, bread and milk for some years after, the general character of the main streets was transformed by motor traffic during the 1920s. The Preston sprinkler car, S-1, used for cleaning horse droppings, was retired at the end of the "sprinkling season" in 1921, while the McGuire-Cummings sprinkler, S-2, continued in service until October 1922. The old horse-drawn tower wagon purchased in 1910 also was obsolete by 1923. The wagon was sold, though the tower assembly was kept and later mounted on a truck. Near the end of the decade, the ERR built a weed-control car to apply weed killer to the unpaved tracks. A warning light on the car advised anyone in the vicinity to stay well back from the toxic spray (Buck).

ERR street-cleaner S-1 at the Jasper Avenue and 101 Street wye exchange, 1913.
(Glenbow Archives NA-1328-64341)

The downtown wye in July 1929.
(Glenbow Archives ND-3-4830)

The ERR weed-sprayer car at work, June 1934.
(City of Edmonton Archives EA-160-636)

The S-1 near the intersection of Jasper Avenue and 99 Street during the early years of the First World War.
(Provincial Archives of Alberta B4852)

A crew stringing streetcar wire using the horse-drawn tower wagon.
(Provincial Archives of Alberta A4709)

The Observation Car shortly after it began
regular service in the summer of 1920.
(Provincial Archives of Alberta A4848)

Throughout the decade, the ERR introduced new safety technology to cope with the increasing volume of vehicle and pedestrian traffic on city streets. An electrically operated wig-wag signal, which warned of approaching trains, was installed at the crossing at 107 Avenue and 121 Street in 1925, the only such safety device to be installed since one appeared on Strathcona Road in 1912. As traffic noise increased, it became harder for pedestrians and motorists to hear the foot-operated gongs that warned of streetcars operators' intent, so Westinghouse air whistles operating off the air brake valve replaced the earlier gongs. The first experimental pneumatic automatic-door treadle system for passenger unloading was installed on Preston Car No. 74 in 1926. The innovation, though designed to improve passenger safety and system efficiency, was not successful because the public was reluctant to use the new-fangled contraption and insisted on exiting by the wrong door. Widespread installation of treadles would have to wait until a later date (Buck).

In 1926, in keeping with its new passenger focus, the ERR adopted a new red, cream and black colour scheme for the fleet and phased out the venerable old name *Edmonton Radial Railway*, which gradually disappeared from the cars. Cars now were identified by the car number in yellow, as well as black numbers on a letter board affixed above the vehicle vestibule. Edmontonians expressed their preference for the new modern look over the old brown and yellow livery.

Even though the budget remained a constant concern, the ERR nevertheless recognized the value of public relations and civic boosterism during a time much in need of something to celebrate. One such popular effort involved constructing a special events Observation Car. The ERR had planned for a sight-seeing car, modelled on similar car operating in Calgary, as early as 1914, but the war had postponed the plan. Using the frame and trucks of Car No. 22, which had been destroyed by fire in 1917, the ERR began construction of the long-awaited sightseeing car in 1919. Brought into service on Dominion Day 1920, the new streetcar sported a canvas roof, white livery with gold and red trim, and "ERR" emblazoned on the dash. The Observation Car remained in service until 1935 (*Edmonton Bulletin*; *Edmonton Journal*).

By the end of the 1920s, the ERR appeared to be narrowing the gap between passenger demands and the service that could be effectively delivered throughout the city. Or had passenger demands simply declined in response to the financial realities now apparent to most?

No new rolling stock or motive power was added to the fleet between 1914, when Preston streetcars Numbers 75 through 81 were purchased with a service flat car, and 1930, when five new Ottawa cars (Numbers 80 through 84 with No. 80 and 81 taking over previous fleet numbers). A ballast spreader was added in 1922, a wrecker in 1925 and a weed killer car in 1928. *(See Fleet List in Appendix.)*

As early as February 1920, in response to the continuing demand for expanded service, City Commissioner Arthur W. Ormsby (former Superintendent of the Power and Light Department) had proposed a municipal motorbus service for outlying districts, in particular 142 Street, McKernan Lake and Bonnie Doon. He argued that Edmonton should follow the lead of Winnipeg, which had augmented its streetcar service with motorbus routes to good effect. Though the idea failed to gain traction and streetcars remained the mainstay of public transit in Edmonton for many years, Ormsby's proposal contained the seed of the future development of the transit system that would begin to germinate in the following decades (*Edmonton Journal*).

A Preston streetcar lavishly decorated to commemorate the Diamond Jubilee of Canadian Confederation at the Dominion Day parade in 1927. The civic motto is proudly emblazoned on the bumper.
(City of Edmonton Archives EA-10-2295)

Early advertising was a precursor to the later "vinyl-wrap" buses in its full-scale presentation. The "Big Fun Festival" ran at the Rialto Theatre in 1921. Notice the lanterns fore and aft, and the rear-view mirror.
(Glenbow Archives ND-3-1070)

Works Cited

Buck, George H. *A Technological History of Municipally Owned Public Transportation In Edmonton: 1893–1981.* Edmonton, Alberta: University of Alberta Thesis, 1985, pp. 121–23, 132, 134, 135–46, 205–08, 373, 376, 386.

Edmonton Bulletin. 8 January 1920; 14 May 1934.

Edmonton Journal. 4 March 1914; 20 December 1919; 5 January 1920; 7 January 1920; 10 January 1920; 12 January 1920; 20 January 1920; 23 January 1920; 17 February 1920; 14 May 1934; 23 July 1958.

CHAPTER 6

The Great Depression

1930–39

The first neon signs to light Jasper Avenue in 1929 ironically heralded not a return to prosperity, but the Great Depression. Triggered by the Wall Street crash of Black Thursday, 24 October 1929, a chain of events sank North America into a long period of economic distress, political unrest and social upheaval. At its peak in Canada in 1933, unemployment reached 27 percent, export markets for agricultural commodities shrank by half, and a fifth of the Canadian population was dependent on government assistance. Worst hit were regions that relied on primary industries such as farming, where the economic malaise of plummeting cereal grain prices was compounded by prolonged drought. Across the prairies, businesses closed their doors as soup kitchens opened theirs. Farmers abandoned the land, and some small towns simply disappeared.

Luckily, Edmonton was cushioned from the worst lows of the 1930s because dust-bowl conditions never reached the parkland. Though the city was dependent on the health of the parkland agriculture industry, which suffered from low agricultural prices, Edmonton did not fare as badly as many prairie cities to the south. In fact, the city grew modestly but steadily during the Great Depression, reaching just over 90,000 in 1939, as those driven off the land migrated north in search of employment and a new life.

Population growth in the 1930s continued to be as mixed a blessing for the Edmonton Radial Railway as it had been in the 1920s. On the one hand, it meant increased revenues as the Great Depression forced greater use of the transit system among more ranks of society. On the other hand, it also meant relentless pressure on the system for expansion at a time when it could be least afforded, especially after the economically listless post-war decade when needed repair, replacement and extension had already been hindered by years of wartime shortages of equipment and material.

Superintendent W.T. Cunningham had cautioned the City of the imminent need for more passenger rolling stock as early as 1928. By 1929 this shortage had led to the reinstatement of old Car No. 3, a stopgap measure until five new cars could be purchased from the Ottawa Car Manufacturing Company in June 1930. The new Ottawa cars were characterized by many new technical improvements and were the only all-metal cars ever operated by the ERR. The cars retained the use of wood only for the roofs and interiors, and featured the now-popular, elegant double-wide cherry-wood folding doors, operated by air cylinders, in the front vestibule as well as treadle-operated exit doors in the middle right side. Front centre windows came equipped with a hand-operated windshield-wiper, the first to be used in the system. Ten electrical heaters were located under the seats in addition to the tried-and-true coal-fired Peter Smith heaters. Push-button switches located along the sides of the interior allowed passengers to signal through a buzzer that they wished to get off at the next stop. The Ottawa cars could accommodate 51 passengers on their leather-upholstered seats and on a distinctive little semicircular seat located in the rear vestibule (Buck).

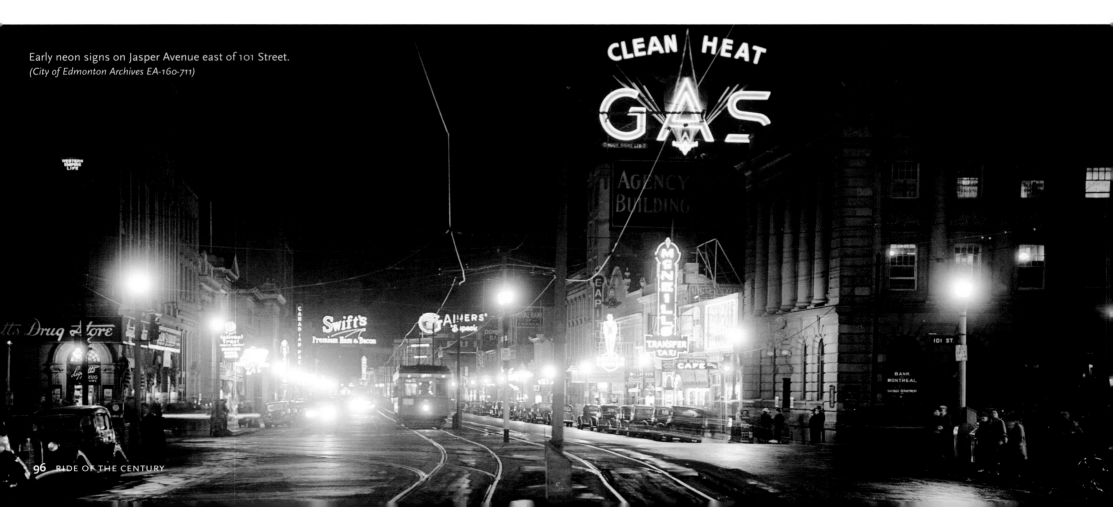

Early neon signs on Jasper Avenue east of 101 Street.
(City of Edmonton Archives EA-160-711)

An interior view of streetcar No. 74 in 1928. Note the mesh windows. These earlier cars did not have the leather-upholstered seats of later models. *(Provincial Archives of Alberta A6019)*

Most of the streetcars introduced in the 1930s, including the Ottawa models, continued the trend away from double-end cars that began in the 1920s. The single-end cars required wyes to turn, and in 1930, a wye that had been removed at 95 Street and 106 Avenue in 1921 was restored *(Buck)*.

Two of the Ottawa streetcars purchased in 1930 on the blue-and-white route on Jasper Avenue during 1938. *(Provincial Archives of Alberta BL243.2)*

It was fortuitous that Superintendent W.J. Cunningham oversaw both the ERR and the power utility at this time and was able to take some initial steps toward alleviating the persistent power shortages that had plagued the system from the outset. In his reports on rolling stock shortages, Cunningham also had pointed to the need for more direct-current electrical substations to feed the energy needs of the ERR. The Depression brought an end to the plan, and some outlying sections of the ERR continued to suffer from low voltage, especially north of 118 Avenue to Calder, which required the installation of a voltage booster in 1934. As a cost-saving measure, Cunningham recommended that mercury-arc rectifiers be installed throughout the system because they did not require onsite operators at all times (Buck; City of Edmonton Archives).

When citizens complained that heavy static interference from trolley wires hampered radio reception along streetcar routes, Cunningham had radio interference suppressors installed on all streetcars by the end of the 1930s. The suppressors, consisting of a large choke coil and a capacitor connected in parallel and housed in metal boxes, were installed in series with the trolley poles. The resulting high-series impedance suppressed the static being broadcast by the streetcars to the relief of Edmonton's many Jack Benny devotees, who during the Depression demanded their distractions more than ever (Buck).

Depression or not, some additional track was required urgently. Under pressure from the University of Alberta, whose students relied even more heavily on the streetcars during the Depression, the ERR finally agreed in 1930 to inaugurate service to the campus, but with the anticipation of a heavy financial loss. In return the University deeded to the City the west half of 112 Street as well as a 30-metre-wide strip to extend Saskatchewan Drive through the campus (*Edmonton Bulletin*).

Superintendent W.J. Cunningham died suddenly on 13 May 1934 and was replaced by Thomas Ferrier. In June 1936, Acting Superintendent Ferrier warned the City that it would be unwise to postpone track upgrading indefinitely. As a result, heavily used sections on 97 Street between 108 and 111 avenues and between 111 Avenue and 95 Street were replaced. Little track replacement work would occur after 1937 (Buck).

Although the need for track repair and replacement was repeatedly made obvious by the City Engineer's reports, the financial demands of the Depression meant that little upgrading could actually occur. By 1937, to respond to the long-standing degradation of trackage that had overtaken substantial sections of the lines, the ERR modified a number of routes to divert traffic away from the most eroded sections. As a stopgap measure to repair the most severe rail corrugation, the ERR also purchased a rail grinding device pioneered by the Toronto Transportation Commission. The grinder consisted of abrasive blocks situated above each rail that were held in a steel yoke installed beneath a streetcar. A lever and spring activated the device so that it pressed against the railheads, abrading them as the car travelled along its route. In 1938 the grinder replaced the herbicide dispensing apparatus on the weed-killer car, which, after being fitted with two motors, performed much of the rail grinding operation (Buck).

Rail grinder used for track maintenance. *(Colin Hatcher)*

Streetcars, including No. 39, trundle down Jasper Avenue at night in 1930. *(Provincial Archives of Alberta BL2135)*

A.W. Haddow.
(City of Edmonton Archives EA-10-1597)

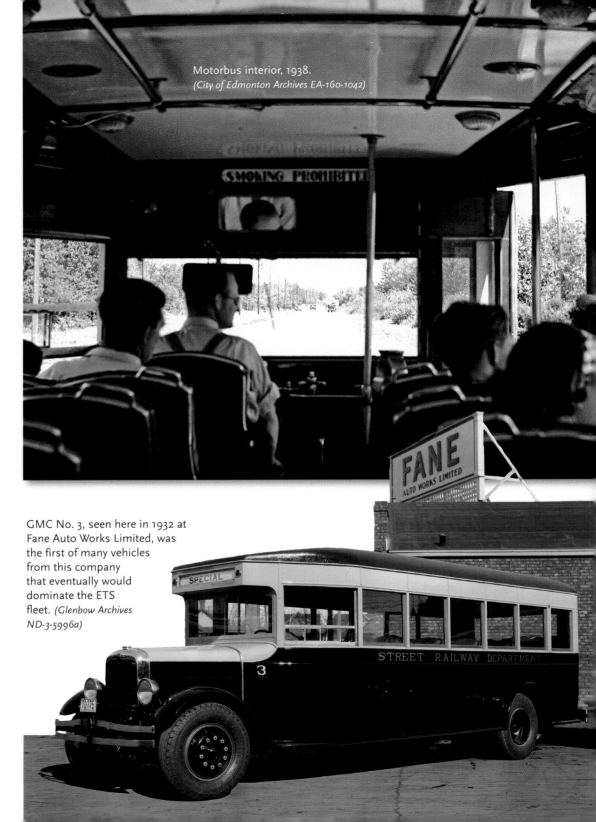

Motorbus interior, 1938.
(City of Edmonton Archives EA-160-1042)

SMOKING PROHIBITED

FANE
AUTO WORKS LIMITED

SPECIAL

STREET RAILWAY DEPARTMENT

3

GMC No. 3, seen here in 1932 at Fane Auto Works Limited, was the first of many vehicles from this company that eventually would dominate the ETS fleet. *(Glenbow Archives ND-3-5996a)*

In 1931 City Engineer A.W. Haddow reported that the trestle bridge over Penitentiary Ravine (later named Latta Ravine) was unsafe for streetcars. Depression budgets did not allow for replacement, so Haddow devised a temporary solution in the form of a diversion that started near both ends of the existing bridge and ran around the head of the ravine. This strange little diversion went into service in 1932 and remained until 1945 even after a new bridge was built in 1936.

While the streetcar remained king of the Edmonton transit system during the 1930s, the Edmonton Radial Railway made its first tentative experiments with motorbuses in 1932 when the two bridges on 102 Avenue were deemed inadequate for use by the ERR, particularly the one at 131 Street, which the City Engineer reported was near collapse and requiring extensive repair. A motorbus replaced the heavier streetcars on this route on 25 January 1932, the same day the bridge was closed. The service proved so successful that the tracks west of 124 Street along 102 Avenue were pulled up later that year, ending streetcar service for Groat Estate and Glenora. "If the motorbus proves satisfactory, it will be used more freely in the outlying parts of the city, where good roads permit," a newspaper report observed, "and so conserve the street cars for the more central areas" (Buck; *Edmonton Bulletin*).

Three gasoline buses were purchased in 1932, one from Leyland Motors, a Cub (No. 1), converted to diesel five years later, a second from the White Truck Company (No. 2) and a third from General Motors (No. 3), also converted to diesel in 1937. Another GMC motorbus was leased from Bus Universal Supply Ltd. in 1938, followed by the purchase of another Leyland Cub motorbus (No. 5). Rubber-tired electrically powered trolleys, the so-called "trackless trolleys," followed in 1939 with the purchase of three trolley coaches from Associated Equipment Company and the English Electric Company (Numbers 101–03), and three coaches from Leyland Motors and the Park Royal Coach (Numbers 104–06). The transition to trackless systems

reduced the ongoing costs associated with track maintenance and the need to lay track along new routes. Routes No. 10 and No. 14 appear to have been the first to fully implement the permanent transition in August 1938.

On 22 December 1937, the City Commissioners delivered a sobering report to City Council on what years of financial restraint had wrought on the ERR. The report emphasized once again the extensive and costly repair, replacement and expansion the streetcar system required after years of neglect. The report also identified this work as the prime culprit in the large capital deficit under which the City was suffering. A year later, a report written by Norman F. Wilson, a consultant with Wilson and Bunnell, recommended that consideration be given to ending streetcar service entirely in favour of the less costly alternatives of motorbuses and trackless trolleys.

Later the same year, adoption of the recommendations of Wilson's report led to the introduction of the trolley coach system to replace the decaying street railway that now was considered too expensive to repair. Motor coaches had been introduced as early as 1931 simply as economical feeder vehicles to serve low-volume routes, but they would become the hallmark of the transit system in the near future (City of Edmonton Archives).

In his 1938 annual report to City Council, Superintendent Ferrier confirmed that "the Department intends to convert certain routes from street car

Motorbus No. 1, a Leyland Cub, one of three buses purchased in 1932.
(Glenbow Archives ND-3-6431)

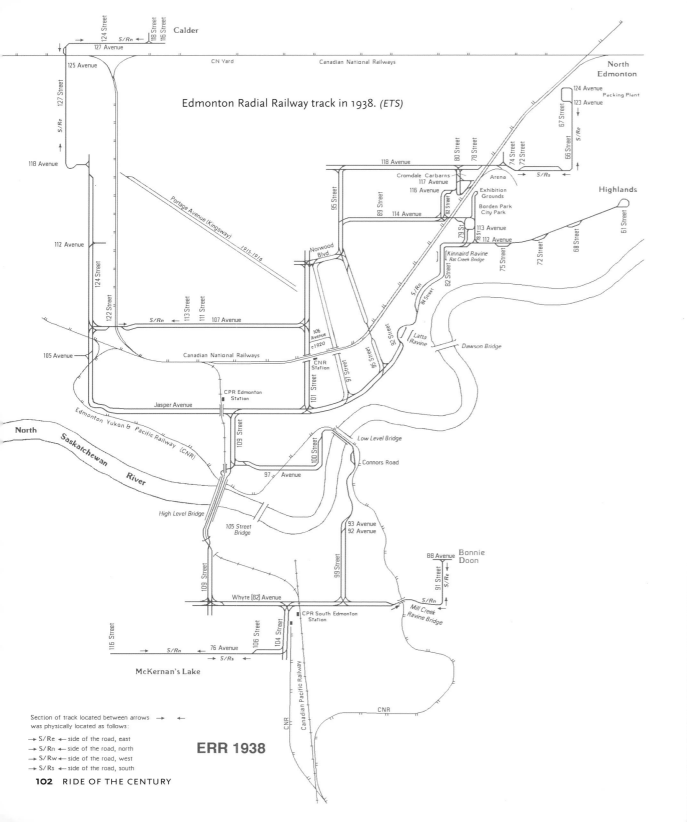

Edmonton Radial Railway track in 1938. *(ETS)*

Calder

North Edmonton

Highlands

CN Yard   Canadian National Railways

124 Avenue   Packing Plant
123 Avenue

127 Avenue
125 Avenue

Portage Avenue (Kingsway) *1915-1916*

118 Avenue
Cromdale Carbarns
117 Avenue   Arena
116 Avenue   Exhibition Grounds
114 Avenue   Borden Park City Park
113 Avenue
112 Avenue

Norwood Blvd.

Kinnaird Ravine
Rat Creek Bridge

112 Avenue

106 Avenue c1920

107 Avenue

Canadian National Railways

CNR Station

Latta Ravine

Dawson Bridge

CPR Edmonton Station

Jasper Avenue

Edmonton Yukon & Pacific Railway (CNR)

North Saskatchewan River

Low Level Bridge

Connors Road

97 Avenue

High Level Bridge

105 Street Bridge

93 Avenue
92 Avenue

Bonnie Doon
88 Avenue

Whyte (82) Avenue

Mill Creek Ravine Bridge

CPR South Edmonton Station

76 Avenue

McKernan's Lake

Canadian Pacific Railway

CNR

Section of track located between arrows → ← was physically located as follows:

→ S/Re ← side of the road, east
→ S/Rn ← side of the road, north
→ S/Rw ← side of the road, west
→ S/Rs ← side of the road, south

ERR 1938

Utility Substation No. 600
10643–124 Street
Built in 1938

Substation No. 600 was designed by the prominent Edmonton architect John Martland, who emigrated from England in 1910 and worked with Roland W. Lines before joining the City's Building Inspection Department. In 1912 Martland returned to private practice with David Hardie, later rejoining the City as a Telephone Department drafts-man to work on a new telephone building. In 1919 he was transferred to the Engineer's Department, which was in charge of all City architectural work, and by 1926 he was appointed head of the City's building department. Martland retired from the City in 1944 but continued in private practice with T.G. Aberdeen until 1953 when he retired to Victoria, British Columbia. He died in December 1957. Substation No. 600, an elegant little landmark, is a reminder of his work for the City *(Edmonton Journal)*.

Interior of Substation No. 600 in 1939.
(City of Edmonton Archives EB-28-462)

to electric trolley bus operation." The ERR and city administration agreed to introduce the first route on the Low Level Bridge crossing. Since the bridge deck needed considerable repair, as did Scona Road, the ERR built a loop on 99 Avenue just east of 100 Street to enable the trolleys to double back before having to cross. This ended streetcars crossing the Low Level Bridge. Since trolley buses required even more power than streetcars, an automatic substation with a mercury-arc rectifier was finally constructed near the southeast corner of 124 Street and 107 Avenue in 1938. Substation No. 600 finally made possible dependable service in the west end of the city.

As the Depression deepened, voices of dissent grew across the prairies. On 20 December 1932, crowds of distressed Edmontonians converged on Market Square in the city centre to protest their plight only to be dispersed with violence by mounted police. The unionized workers of the ERR grew bolder and pushed for more day-to-day involvement in decision-making. In January 1935, the wives of 60 Edmonton motormen signed a petition that argued for shift rotations that would free their husbands from being permanently assigned to the night shift. Until this time, seniority determined shifts, and those with longer service naturally chose the preferred day runs. The wives urged "in the name of justice and fair play" that "their husbands be given an opportunity to have some time in their families' company." A local newspaper concluded that it "isn't right that men should be forced to work 15 or 16 years on night runs with never a chance at a day run. A more humane system must be adopted. If the men [of the ERR] can't reach a decision, then the Council will have to." In 1936, after much agitation within the local unions, junior motormen were assigned day shifts with senior motormen under a pairing system. This new shift rotation

plan was the first time the old-boy system had been breached in a Canadian street railway. Prior to this time, the men with seniority formed an entrenched clique that controlled the shifts (*Edmonton Bulletin*).

The union also pressed for needed safety improvements. One necessary, minor change involved the addition of more windshield wipers on cars. The first manually operated ones proved unsatisfactory because they required a motorman to keep one hand on the controller and the other on the brake valve control while the streetcar was in motion. By 1936 several automatic pneumatic wipers made by the National Pneumatic Company were being installed on some cars, but the cost prevented their rapid spread throughout the fleet.

AEC trolley bus No. 101, the first trackless trolley, on Jasper Avenue and 101 Street, October 1939.
(*Provincial Archives of Alberta BL260.1*)

It was not until March 1940, in response to the union local, that Trico Wiper Company wipers were installed in most of the cars as a safety measure to deal with the heavy snows of the Edmonton winters.

Despite the deep economic malaise of the Great Depression, the Edmonton Radial Railway could boast that it ranked second in ridership among Canadian transit systems in 1932. Good fortune continued to fall on the ERR in 1933 when it posted a profit of $8,029, its second year in the black since inception. The following year brought more good news as profits rose to $21,748 even as a large amount of indebtedness was retired, reducing the appropriation necessary for interest and redemption from $177,697 to

$111,152. In 1934 Acting Superintendent Thomas Ferrier reported an increase of more than one million passengers, and the number of riders continued to grow throughout the decade. Besides increasing its profit, the street railway put $37,000 into the fund for renewals and reserve, compared with $26,000 in 1933. Obviously, many Edmontonians were relying upon their transit system as they commuted to work, or rode to sports or cultural events. Paradoxically, in a time of great restraint, the ERR, the "white elephant" of the City, became profitable in more sustained manner than in the past.

By the late 1930s, just as the country was beginning to drag itself out of the Depression, newspapers began carrying ominous stories of the rising

AEC trolley without wipers in about 1939.
(City of Edmonton Archives EA-75-856)

tide of violence in Europe and Asia. Imperial Japan was driving its military and economic agenda into Manchuria and Indochina. Italy was crushing Abyssinia (Ethiopia), while Adolf Hitler's Third Reich annexed Austria and Czechoslovakia in the face of an ineffective League of Nations.

Considerable public sentiment in Canada ran against involvement in the second European war in a single generation. To shore up support within the British Commonwealth, Great Britain dispatched King George VI and Queen Elizabeth on a Royal visit to Commonwealth countries, including scores of stops across Canada and official events such as the unveiling of the new National War Memorial in Ottawa. When they arrived in Edmonton on

2 June 1939, thousands of men, women and schoolchildren crowded bleachers along Kingsway Avenue, renamed in honour of the Royal visit. Ironically, the Royal party rode in cars, even though streetcar rails laid on this route in 1912 had never been used. The Royals' Canadian tour was seen as an omen of the impending war that would call on many of the young people waving the sea of Union Jacks to make the greatest sacrifice for their country.

Veterans of the Edmonton Radial Railway, like other Edmontonians and Albertans, could remember well the privations wrought by the First World War, and they braced themselves for what was to come (*Edmonton Bulletin*).

Pullman trolley with wipers in about 1944.
(*City of Edmonton Archives EA-75-857*)

The No. 11 streetcar was extravagantly decorated with lights in commemoration of the Coronation of King George VI in May 1937. The Radial Railway, as in the past, was an integral part of Edmonton's response to such special, patriotic events. *(City of Edmonton Archives EA-10-903)*

The Coronation car illuminated for night display in May 1937. *(City of Edmonton Archives EA-160-396)*

Works Cited

Buck, George H. *A Technological History of Municipally Owned Public Transportation In Edmonton: 1893–1981*. Edmonton, Alberta: University of Alberta Thesis, 1985, p. 148; p. 153; pp. 151–52; 212–16; 390–405; 405; 407; 408–416.

City of Edmonton Archives. "Memo to the City Commissioners from the Superintendent of Electric Light and Power Department," RG11 Class 3 File 4, 20 October 1938.

City of Edmonton Archives. MS420, Llew Lawrence.

Edmonton Bulletin. 15 December 1930; 17 December 1930; 19 December 1930; 19 February 1934; 23 February 1934; 19 November 1934; 23 January 1935; 19 August 1936.

Edmonton Journal. 11 December 1957.

CHAPTER 7

Here Come the Trolleys

1938–40

During 1938 the City adopted the recommendations of a very influential report presented to City Council in December 1937 by Commissioner R.J. Gibb. The Gibb Report presented a prioritized inventory of those sections of track likely to require reconstruction over the next 10 years and compared the estimated costs of street-car track repair and replacement with the elimination of tracks and the introduction of electric trolleys augmented by diesel motorbuses for some feeder lines. The report would result in the most far-reaching changes to ERR since its inception 30 years before.

The Gibb Report reminded City Council that with "regard to financing rehabilita-tion . . . our street railway system has not been on a paying basis since its inception, and . . . has gone behind to a total of $1,407,655." Commissioner Gibb recommended that fares be raised 20 percent, which he calculated would generate at least $60,000 additional revenue annually. This amount would fund the cost of the transition from streetcars to trolleys, he estimated. Ever the cautious manager, Gibb advised that a rec-ognized transportation expert review his recommendations before City Council made a long-term commitment to trolley buses and fare increases. Engineering consultant Norman F. Wilson of Wilson and Bunnell, a Toronto firm, was engaged later that year to review Gibb's recommendations and investigate further.

Wilson supported Gibb's pronouncements on the financial health of the ERR and the compelling necessity of increasing the fare. The street railway "has since its

The upper deck of the High Level
Bridge on 18 October 1948.
(Provincial Archives of Alberta BL1527.2)

commencement in 1908 failed to meet its full costs by $50,000 per year," he confirmed. Wilson recommended the fare increase "from 5 for 25¢ to 4 for 25¢ . . . such change in fare being calculated to yield 17 1/2% additional revenue, adequate with the surplus from operations to meet all capital costs of extensions if made at a uniform rate." The Wilson Report went on to make several important recommendations based on the prediction that the proliferation of private automobiles would limit public transit growth over the next decade. "Streetcars everywhere are a declining industry," Wilson warned. "On this account, an average increase of traffic on the street railway in Edmonton of 125,000 passengers per year is all that is estimated upon, with 15,800,000 [rides projected] in 1950 when a population of 100,000 is anticipated" (City of Edmonton Archives).

The coin box in the passenger entry in a trolley in 1946. *(City of Edmonton Archives EA-75-852)*

The driver's compartment in the new trolley as it appeared in 1940 at the AEC plant in Montreal. *(Provincial Archives of Alberta A13838)*

Ignoring the clouds of war gathering over Europe, the report failed to recall the substantial increase in ridership occasioned by the First World War. But in defence of Wilson, his population estimate could not have anticipated the post-war oil boom that would propel Edmonton's population in 1950 to 50 percent higher than his forecast, perhaps proving once again that prophecy should be left to prophets (City of Edmonton Archives).

Responding to Wilson's analysis, Gibb sagely reminded City Hall that the plan was dependent on increased revenue from the new fare structure. He cautioned City Council to "eliminate certain remaining [streetcar] sections, but . . . leave the final decision as to the balance of the system for future determination." Gibb doubtless reasoned that the nickel fare remained too dear to Edmontonians and that the political will to introduce publicly unpopular fare increases was yet to develop, even if the action improved the financial health of the transit system (City of Edmonton Archives).

For the first stage in the transition to trolleys, the Wilson Report proposed the purchase of six buses to serve a route from Whyte Avenue via McDougall Hill to a downtown loop running from Jasper Avenue and 104 Street to 115 Avenue and 85 Street. The report also recommended the redevelopment of the upper deck of the High Level Bridge for trolley use. City Engineer A.W. Haddow was dispatched to Montreal and Toronto to assess the feasibility with the CPR and Canadian Bridge Company engineers, but this would become yet another recommendation that was never implemented in spite of readily apparent benefits. Streetcars would continue to make use of the upper deck of the High Level Bridge until the last streetcar in the fleet passed over in 1951.

Commissioner Gibb and Superintendent Ferrier's report also described other continuing challenges facing the crumbling ERR streetcar network, including system safety. Along with recommendations for street paving, power pole and electrical line replacement, and track lifting in preparation for the new trolley service, they pressed for repair of the deck of Mill Creek Bridge that "has become quite dangerous and must be replaced this year." The report further proposed implementation of diesel bus service for the Bonnie Doon stub line (99 Street and Whyte Avenue) to the existing terminus by 1940 and for Rossdale via McDougall Hill, Jasper Avenue and 109 Street the following year. It also recommended that by 1941 trolley bus

service be extended through the centre of the Norwood District from 111 Avenue and 95 Street, via 111 Avenue east to 91 Street and north on 91 Street to 115 Avenue, then east to the intersection of 85 Street and the Fort Trail. Finally, the report urged that a trolley bus beltline for the south side via the High Level Bridge be completed in 1942, "or later as war and financial conditions will permit" (City of Edmonton Archives).

Construction on the first phase of trolley service moved smoothly and fairly rapidly except for the extension of the service from 111 Avenue and 95 Street to the car barns, necessary for the elimination of streetcar service on 114 Avenue, as contemplated in the Gibb Report. "However," Gibb reported in 1940, "as the cutting of an existing service is always a contentious matter, it was felt that this extension had better be left until people in the Norwood District had seen trolley buses in operation" (City of Edmonton Archives).

While the new trolley coaches did not require tracks, they did need adequate streets, preferably paved, and new power lines in order to operate. Roadwork commenced just after the Royal visit of 1939. Track was taken up and roads paved for the first sections of the trackless trolley system on 99 Street from Whyte Avenue to 93 Avenue, and on 95 Street from Jasper Avenue to 111 Avenue (*Edmonton Journal*). Other significant road improvement projects involved rebuilding the Low Level Bridge deck and Scona Road.

Further preparatory work involved a new electrical delivery system. While the streetcars had used a straight ground-return of electrical current through the tracks, the new trolleys required the addition of a return wire, usually placed next to the curb and running a standard two feet away from the positive wire. The installation of overhead switches also was necessary at points where two sets of overhead wires met or crossed. These switches needed heavy-duty steel and Bakelite insulators rather than the previously adequate hickory insulators used on the old streetcar lines. Trolleys also needed to navigate around obstacles in the street such as parked wagons or trucks, so steel or carbon shoes with grooved wheels were required to keep the trolley poles connected to the overhead wire.

Even as the ERR turned to implementing the most significant improvement in service in many years, the international rearmament race that presaged the outbreak of hostilities in Europe caused a shortage of construction materials for trolleys that were expected to be in service by July 1939 (*Edmonton Journal*). Trolley service thus was launched with just two coaches on Sunday, 24 September 1939, following several trial runs downtown. The first route started on 111 Avenue, ran south on 95 Street, west on Jasper Avenue to 100 Street, then north to 102 Avenue, west to 102 Street and finally south to Jasper where it turned east for its return to 95 Street. The *Edmonton Journal* reassured that the new coaches, while unfamiliar to most of its readers, were equipped with auxiliary batteries in case of a power failure, an eventuality that Edmontonians knew was probable after decades of power shortages on the streetcar lines (*Edmonton Journal*).

As with virtually every significant change to the public transit system, the plan to replace streetcars with trolleys was not without public controversy. Ride comfort, speed of service and the opinion of experts from other cities were all challenged by those seeking to preserve the original street railway system. David Duncan, president of the Edmonton Public Ownership League, led the fight to keep the streetcars with Lawrence L. Alexander

addressing the Street Railway Committee in 1940 to give voice to the popular resistance. In a lengthy denunciation, Alexander offered objections that still resonate today. In colourful and at times inflammatory prose, he contended that the changes meant less comfortable travel due to road surface and trolley design; that the public did not, in fact, want the changes, but were being led by consultants; and that improvements, such as greater speed, were created by reducing service—in this instance, by reducing stops on the routes rather than introducing faster rolling stock.

Gibb and Ferrier's cautious approach to replacing streetcars with trolleys may have been influenced by such outspoken criticism. "We should examine conditions since the introduction of trolley bus service," they cautioned. "Particularly we should determine whether the operation of this service is shaping up successfully or not. . . . We believe it is generally conceded that the trolley buses themselves are more pleasant to ride in, and are quieter than diesel equipment. The real test of popularity, however, is in the increase in patronage reflected in increased cash receipts."

One of the first trolleys emerging from the Low Level Bridge in 1939.
(City of Edmonton Archives EA-75-876)

The old ERR tower apparatus on 118 Avenue and 95 Street in 1939. Originally pulled to work sites by a horse team, it was eventually mounted on a truck to install the post-war trolley lines. *(City of Edmonton Archives EA-160-1107)*

An early south-side AEC trolley on 99 Street near 83 Avenue in 1939. *(City of Edmonton Archives EA-75-870)*

DEANS GROCERY & MEAT MARKET

"An Alberta Product"

Blue Willow

An AEC trolley on 95 Street near 107A Avenue in 1939. *(City of Edmonton Archives EA-75-875)*

Mr. Alexander Addresses City Council

Lawrence L. Alexander was the streetcar's most vociferous champion. His address to Edmonton City Council was dripping with irony and wit.

A trolley interior in 1940.
(Provincial Archives of Alberta A13839)

At the risk of appearing to be nothing more than a miserable knocker, I would like to ask . . . [what] is the reason for the tremendous enthusiasm which the City Council, the Commissioners, and in general most of the people connected with the operation of the City utilities, seem to have worked up for the replacing the street-railway system with buses? I can assure you it is not by any means unanimously shared by either the residents of the city in general or by users of the street-railway system. Yet this enthusiasm . . . seems to amount almost to a mania. Not only is the bus regarded as a superior form of transportation, but it seems to be regarded as the only form of transportation. After reading some of the eulogies of trolley-bus service which have been quoted in our papers, I have been positively amazed to go out into the street and see that such a thing as a street car even exists, and have been even more amazed on getting on board one of these archaic forms of transportation, to find them rather comfortable.

I would like to go on record now as saying that I have travelled on the new buses and have found them about as uncomfortable a form of transportation as I have ever had the misfortune to come across. Maybe I am built the wrong way, but I have not yet been in one of these buses in which I have not had to nearly double up like a jack-knife in order to sandwich myself into one of the seats. In addition, I feel sure that the seats on these buses . . . must either have been designed by one-legged men and cripples, or by a professional contortionist. I hate to contemplate the dilemma of those who live in districts where they must use the buses constantly and cannot decide whether to have the right leg cut off, in which case they can sit only on the right side of the bus, or of losing the left leg, in which case the amputation will do them good only when sitting on the left side of the vehicle.

In the Wilson report, that great work of literature which I had the pleasure of reading in full last year . . . Mr. Wilson waxes eloquent on the "desire of people to-day to ride on rubber" and he continues with poetic fervour to picture the way in which these buses will float noiselessly along the street without presumably a jar or a bump. Maybe Mr. Wilson got his ideas in some other city where the pavement is smoother. . . .

I have rather a feeling that there is being an attempt made to compare the buses with our street cars in an attempt to discredit the latter. There is no question that the buses are faster. . . . I would like to point out that one way in which the extra speed has been gained is by cutting out of half the stops. I don't doubt the street car service could be greatly accelerated if the cars had to stop only every two blocks (City of Edmonton Archives).

An AEC trolley interior in 1939. *(City of Edmonton Archives EA-75-911)*

They need not have worried. Edmontonians took to the new service in large numbers, and it was not long before a sizeable petition was received requesting improved trolley service from 99 Street and Whyte Avenue to Connors Road and 99 Street via 91 Street, then uptown via McDougall Hill. "We recommend delay in this project to find out more about operating conditions over gravel roads," wrote Gibb and Ferrier. "It may prove necessary to pave the bus route, as was done on 102nd Ave. west to Jasper Place. Such a length of pavement would involve us in about $35,000.00 even for three inch bituminous surface." Popular opinion won the day and Connors Road was soon paved to allow expansion.

Ironically, the success of the conversion from streetcars to trolleys generated more challenges for the system to grow even more rapidly. "In buying equipment we had estimated on a 50% increase at peak hours," Gibb conceded. "Fortunately, or unfortunately, the peak load has turned out to be over 100% increase on the Low Level route. This increase has taxed capacity of our equipment to the utmost, indeed we have not sufficient buses and three additional ones have been ordered. For the same reason, we have not been able

to go to 104th St. and 82nd Avenue as first anticipated, and we feel that an extension of the service to that point now would only accentuate the peak load trouble."

The Edmonton Radial Railway celebrated its thirtieth anniversary in 1938. Superintendent Thomas Ferrier had started with the ERR in 1908 as a motorman. W.J. Brumlees, line and track foreman, Inspector Peter Fleming and Motorman George A. Berry also had started that year. The times were changing, and many other long-term employees were retiring. In 1940 Robert Chalmers and Robert Lindsay retired after over 30 years of service. Both had come to the ERR from Glasgow, where they had been conductors on the horse-tram system (*Edmonton Bulletin*).

The first trolleys arrived amid the uncertainty and confusion attending the outbreak of the Second World War. On 1 September 1939, the newsboys were called in early in anticipation of the news that conflict had erupted in Europe. As dawn broke, they ran through the streets crying, "War Extra! Polish Cities Bombed!" Residents of the Arlington Apartment threw open their windows to investigate the ruckus to find a guard with fixed bayonet posted at the armoury entrance across the street (*Edmonton Journal*). The British passenger

Rolling west on Whyte Avenue near 98 Street during the first year of the Second World War when horses and carts were still in evidence on city streets. *(City of Edmonton Archives EA-75-868)*

Trolley No. 106 stops at Connors Road to let a
passenger exit in Cloverdale on 4 May 1940.
(Provincial Archives of Alberta BL287.3)

One of the Leyland trolley buses shipped on 1 September 1939, still in original British colours, arrives on the train in Edmonton just ahead of the export ban on metals from England, as confirmed by C. Hatcher. *(ETS)*

ship *Athenia* had already been torpedoed by a German submarine with loss of several Edmonton lives, and at first it was also feared that the new British trolleys had gone down with the ship. Mayor Fry denied the rumour and reported on 5 September that the first two trolleys had been shipped from England on 1 September, and were thought to be already in Canadian waters. The next two had been shipped the following day, the day before London declared war. It was felt, however, that the final two, although ready to ship, might be delayed until a convoy system could be organized for transatlantic shipping. On 7 September, a ban on all shipments of "war-useful metals from England" was announced (*Edmonton Journal*).

Crews worked hard to pour six inches of concrete on 95 Street north of Jasper Avenue to 111 Street, part of the six-mile route planned for the first trolleys. A two-inch layer of asphalt was rapidly laid atop the concrete as the trolleys arrived. Work was then to commence on 99 Street between Whyte Avenue and 93 Avenue.

The first two cream-and-red trolleys were unloaded at the Canadian National Railway yards on 12 September. The $17,000 trolley buses could seat 38 passengers with room for thirty more standees during rush hours. Maximum speed was estimated at 40 miles per hour, and the operating cost was estimated at 18 cents per mile (*Edmonton Journal*).

As the roadway and electrical network were prepared, a company representative from the Associated Equipment Company of Canada (AEC) of Montreal trained the first drivers, who included James Billingsley, Thomas McWhirter, Lionel Fouracre, Edward Hillary, Harry Humpish and Gordon Murray. Billingsley and McWhirter had been driving streetcars previously, while the others were enthusiastic new trolley drivers (*Edmonton Journal*).

Edmontonians were able to take their first trackless trolley ride over a 3.25 kilometre downtown loop on Sunday, 24 September 1939. Installation of the overhead wires was complete on the north side and was progressing across the river as well by that time.

The second delivery of trolleys on 20 September contained two unexpected passengers who were the first, albeit unofficial, riders of the trolleys. Their names were Hughie and Walter, although nothing else is known about them. They had ridden the 3,200 kilometres from Toronto to Edmonton on the same flatcar as the buses. They kindly left a note of thanks to the Edmonton Radial Railway. "Dear Sirs," it began. "We wish to thank you for the use of your new trackless trollies [sic]. Due to the fact that it was very cold outside we were forced to ride [inside] of No. 103 from Toronto to Edmonton. We wish to tender our apologies for not first seeking your permission, but due to the fact that we were so far away and did not possess any stamps we took the liberty of entering and riding in your cars."

Hughie and Walter had only one concern. "There is one more item we would like to mention and that is due to a very speedy and forced evacuation we found it necessary to leave half a loaf of bread and a pound of bologna." The two hoboes, veterans of riding the rails during the Depression, added, "If it would not be too much bother to you we would appreciate it very much if you would send same by return mail to the above address. We would not bother you with such a small matter, but many of the boys have obtained abnormal appetites due to the prolonged diet they have been on." Every courteous, the wandering correspondents concluded, "Trusting you will give this your immediate attention. We remain, Yours truly, Hughie and Walter." The return address was given as "Jungles, Ltd.," the transient settlement located near the Calder freight yards. Superintendent Thomas Ferrier reportedly gave the bread and bologna to some small boys playing around the Calder yards (*Edmonton Journal*).

Edmontonians took to the unfamiliar three-axle, six-wheel vehicles in such numbers that three of the new trolleys had to be put into operation on the first day of service. The *Edmonton Journal* opined that the arrival of the trolleys marked a "long-awaited, revolutionary change in the municipal transit system of Alberta's capital." They also were "free of gear-shift jolts, vibration, noise and smell" the newspaper enthused. The acceleration was another feature praised by one and all. The *Edmonton Journal* went on to recall the recommendation of Norman D. Wilson that the High Level Bridge be converted to a four-lane, double-deck bridge by 1947, and envisioned the new trolley system as fitting into that plan in a way that the old streetcars could not. Only a war remained to be won before these dreams could be realized.

The trolleys were introduced at the end of two decades of financial restraint and on the cusp of another global conflict. The number of passengers riding the ERR would soar during the Second World War, continuing the trend of relentless stress on a system reacting as best it could to global forces shaping the local scene. But one thing was certain: In the next 70 years, the trolleys would become as integral a part of the Edmonton scene as the original streetcars that represented to many the heart and soul of public transit during the Edmonton Radial Railway's first stage of evolution.

Works Cited

City of Edmonton Archives. Commissioner R.J. Gibb and Superintendent T. Ferrier. *Report on the Edmonton Street Railway, Edmonton, Alberta*, 1 May 1940. RG 8.10 file 188.

City of Edmonton Archives, Lawrence L. Alexander addressing the Street Railway Committee in 1940. RG 8.10 file 188.

Edmonton Bulletin. 10 November 1938; 6 January 1939; 6 January 1940.

Edmonton Journal. 19 May 1939; 1 September 1939; 5 September 1939; 8 September 1939; 12 September 1939; 20 September 1939; 21 September 1939; 25 September 1939.

A streetcar rolls by a sign exhorting the public to be patriotic supporters of England and Churchill in the war effort. The advent of the Second World War extended the life of streetcars on many lines because trolley replacements were not available. *(Pattison Hook Signs)*

CHAPTER 8

The Friendly Invasion

1940–45

Life in Edmonton rapidly took shape around the war effort after the call to arms in September 1939. The Prince of Wales Armouries once again became the heart of Edmonton amidst a makeshift community of military tents and barracks springing up outside its brick walls. Another generation of young men—and this time women as well—prepared to serve their country. Edmontonians would serve in every theatre of war and in every branch of the armed services.

Edmonton, although far from the major theatres of war, played a significant role in the global air war and continental defence plan. The British Commonwealth Air Training Plan (BCATP) established an Air Observer School and Elementary Flying Training School at Edmonton's airport, Blatchford Field. The airport was rapidly expanded under federal government control to ferry thousands of American Lend-Lease fighters and bombers over the hastily organized Northwest Staging Route to reinforce the Union of Soviet Socialist Republics after the German invasion in June 1941. On one memorable day, 860 aircraft passed through, making Edmonton the busiest airport on the continent.

Air traffic volume soon pushed Blatchford Field beyond its capacity, and in September 1944, the Namao Airport, the largest airfield in North America at the time, opened. Aircraft Repair Ltd. (later known as Northwest Industries), owned by local aviation pioneer Leigh Brintnell, employed approximately 3,000 Edmonton men

Royal Canadian Air Force cadets march along the Whyte Avenue streetcar tracks in May 1942.
(Glenbow Archives ND-3-9054a)

Roll Of Honor
STREET
RAILWAY DEPARTMENT
Enlistments

NAME	DATE	UNIT	
J.F.Wallace	Sep 6th, 1939.	1st Batt. Edm Reg.	
T.M.W.Gunn	Sep 25th, 1939.	61st Batt. R.C.A	
J.L.Hussey	Sep 27th, 1939.	9th Ar.Typ.R.C.E.	Discharged Feb 25th
C.J.Pugh	Sep 28th, 1939.	R.C.N.	
S.Barbam	Oct 15th, 1939.	R.C.A.F.	
D.C.Deane	Oct 7th, 1939.	R.C.Cps.of Sig.	
J.Cherrington	Oct 12th, 1939.	R.C.Cps.of Sig.	Discharged Apr 28th
J.E.McKay	Jan.21st, 1940.	C.A.S.F.	
G.T.Wiles	June 5th, 1940.	Vet.G.of Canada.	
H.Huttspich	June 8th, 1940.	R.C.A.F.	
W.Newley	Aug 11th, 1940.	R.C.A.F.	
J.Thompson	Sep 8th, 1940.	M.T.C.Camrose.	
B.M.Stein	Oct 7th, 1940.	C.F.Cps.	
J.Cherrington	Oct 11th, 1940.	Edm F.(M.G.)	Discharged Oct 27th
H.Hillary	Oct 21st, 1940.	R.C.A.F.	
M.M.McLaughlin	Dec 19th, 1940.	R.C.A.F.	
J.C.Ross	Jan 23rd, 1941.	R.C.A.S.Cps.	
E.N.Eggen	Jan 31st, 1941.	1st A B Co.	
A.F.Dyer	Feb 8th, 1941.	R.C.A.F.	
R.E.Rushton	Mar 17th, 1941.	R.C.N.	
R.M.Laurie	Apl 25th, 1941.	R.C.O Cps.	
W.Ness	May 1st, 1941.	R.C.A M Cps.	
R.E.Driscoll	May 2nd, 1941.	R.C.A.S.Cps.	
H.S.H.Hayden	June 17th, 1941.	R.C.A.F.	
E.A.McCray	July 7th, 1941.	R.C.A.F.	
A.A.Clarke	July 25th, 1941.	R.C.N.	Discharged Sep 2nd
J.Alison	Aug 8th, 1941.	R.C.A.F.	
F.Billingham	Aug 9th, 1941.	R.C.A.F.	
R.E.Rushton	Aug 9th, 1941.	R.C.A.F.	
H.Hannah	Dec 28th, 1941.	R.C.A.	
A.M.Kinsman	Dec 8th, 1941.	R.C.A.F.	
L.S.P.Dalton	Jan 5th, 1942.	R.C.A.F.	
W.Greig	Mar 7th, 1942.	Cps.of M.S.C.	

The Roll of Honour for the Street Railway Department attests to the service of employees, who came forward to enlist during the Second World War as they had in the First. *(ATU 569)*

A wartime conductor and "conductorette" on the job in October 1944. *(Provincial Archives of Alberta BL805.3)*

and women to repair damaged Allied aircraft (Ivany). The ranks of workers swelled yet again after the Japanese attack on Pearl Harbor on 7 December 1941 when Edmonton became the supply, communications and transportation centre for the massive North American defence projects of the Alaska Highway and the Canol Pipeline. The "friendly invasion" of a large number of American construction and service personnel had an enormous impact on the city (Boddington).

Most new military recruits and members of the wartime workforce used the Edmonton Radial Railway for transportation, and their ranks increased ridership beyond limits that had become unacceptable even before the war. As early as November 1938, with no financing available for additions to the transit fleet, the ERR had been obliged to lease two General Motors coaches from the Bus Universal Supply Company of Alberta to serve Forest Heights in partial fulfilment of its commitment to address growth in new districts.

As the war effort grew between 1940 and 1942, public transit ridership increased by approximately 40 percent—ironically, an unwelcome windfall for the ERR. The federal government requested more extensions to provide transit service to the Aircraft Repair Ltd. facility and Blatchford Field even as the wartime federal Transit Controller was limiting the availability of trolleys and motorbuses. As an interim measure, the ERR leased two more coaches from the Checker Taxi Cab Company to serve the needs of shift workers, and plans to abandon streetcar service were temporarily postponed. The ERR trolley fleet grew in any way it could with an assortment of disparate models as rolling stock of any description was made available. Three Macks, 16 Pullman-Standards and two ACF-Brills were purchased between 1943 and 1945 (Buck).

In July 1942, several routes were proposed for the new streetcar line to Aircraft Repair Ltd. The most popular proposal called for a single-line of open track construction along 124 Street between 118 Avenue and 125 Avenue with a switch at 125 Street to allow streetcars to turn east or west. The eastern leg of track was to be built near the aircraft repair depot, where it would terminate in a loop. The western leg was to connect with the existing single-track line on 127 Street (the Calder Line). The proposal also called for the removal of the existing track on 127 Street between 118 and 125 avenues, previously part of the old Edmonton Interurban Railway. The Dominion Transit Controller approved the plan in the interest of the war effort, and construction was completed by March 1943 (*Edmonton Bulletin*).

In the past, most track construction had ended when winter hit the city, but the demands of war required pressing forward. The construction of the new line to the aircraft repair centre proved that open track construction could continue during the winter months if absolutely necessary (*Edmonton Bulletin*).

The Street Railway Department (SRD) urgently needed more motorbuses for feeder routes to the new line, but the diesel fleet had been fraught with difficulties since the tentative beginning of motorbus service in 1932. The new diesels were unpopular with the public, and many complained about the sooty smoke they belched from exhaust pipes venting near the rear wheels. For a brief period, some annoyed Edmontonians sent their cleaning bills to the City in protest. Personnel at the City garage tried adding volatile fluids to the fuel in an attempt to achieve better combustion, and the

Car No. 114, a new Pullman-Standard trolley purchased in 1944.
(City of Edmonton Archives EA-75-857)

manufacturer, Leyland, supplied new stacks that vented the exhaust above the roofline between the rear windows. The vertical pipes only made matters worse by allowing soot to accumulate in the stacks when the Leylands were idling. When they left the curb, heavy clouds of soot settled on nearby pedestrians. New pipes were installed to route the exhaust towards the centre of the street into the path of oncoming traffic (Buck).

The City found rolling stock where it could, and in August 1939 purchased a surplus British-built Leyland diesel motorbus (Number 558) from the Toronto Transportation Commission and had it shipped by rail to Edmonton the following month (City of Edmonton Archives). The bus became No. 4 in the Edmonton fleet, and would later become a travelling library car to supplement the streetcar first used for this innovative service.

In addition to the fleet colours of red and cream, the paint scheme on the Leyland bus included an orange band bordered by thin black lines that ran around the body below the windows. Between 1939 and 1941, six new diesel-powered Leyland buses were ordered, bringing the total number of motorized buses in the fleet to 10 (Buck).

In 1942 the City Commissioners petitioned the Dominion Transit Controller for the allocation of three to four motorbuses to replace the Leylands that were already beginning to fail. Their small engines had proved inadequate for the steep hills on the river valley routes, and heavy use coupled with the difficulty in obtaining parts from Europe during wartime left Leyland Nos. 1 and 3 in bad condition by 1944. They were sold to a local mining company.

The desperate search for rolling stock led the Street Railway Department to the American factory of the Ford Motor Company, where three Ford 27 buses, not produced in Canada during the war, were purchased. The American War Production Board allowed Ford to manufacture and export specific models such as the Ford 27, named for its 27-passenger capacity. These export buses, equipped with heaters for the more robust northern climate, were known in Canada as the Ford 29-B Victory model. In keeping with wartime austerity, the new Fords dispensed with the orange band with black borders found on the Leylands. Three more virtually identical Fords arrived in December 1944 and January 1945.

Trolleys purchased in 1939 lined up at the south end of the Cromdale Garage in 1946. (City of Edmonton Archives EA-75-860)

Trolleys parked inside the Westwood Garage, likely with the buses posed to promote the facility when it was new. Westwood garage was the 2009 location of the last trolley run in Edmonton. *(City of Edmonton Archives EA-75-865; ETS personnel assisted in identification of the image)*

No. 11, a Ford 29-B Victory model
purchased in 1943 on the Highlands run.
(City of Edmonton Archives EA-75-907)

With the demands of war production restricting the availability of new rolling stock, every mishap to a car presented a potential crisis. In March 1943, streetcar No. 28 was badly damaged by fire and could not be returned to service without extensive rebuilding, especially to the interior and the roof. The SRD undertook the reconstruction of the damaged streetcar even though the process, given the shortage of materials, would take three years. The roof and sides were replaced, new sashes and an arched roof were constructed to resemble the big Preston streetcars, and the front vestibule was widened. Replacement seats were scavenged from the now unused Observation Car. The roller sign was mounted in the letter board located above the central window. The rebuilt car finally went into service in April 1946.

Rebuilt streetcar No. 28. *(Les Corness)*

Early Motorbuses

By 1943 the SRD fleet included 13 motorbuses:

1932 Purchases
No. 1 Leyland (gasoline)
No. 2 White Truck Company (gasoline)
No. 3 GMC (gasoline)

1939 Purchases
No. 4 Leyland (gasoline)
No. 5 Leyland (diesel)

1940 Purchases
No. 6 Leyland (diesel)
No. 7 Leyland (diesel)

1941 Purchases
No. 8 Leyland (diesel)
No. 9 Leyland (diesel)
No. 10 Leyland (diesel)

1943 Purchases
No. 11 Ford (gasoline)
No. 12 Ford (gasoline)
No. 13 Ford (gasoline)

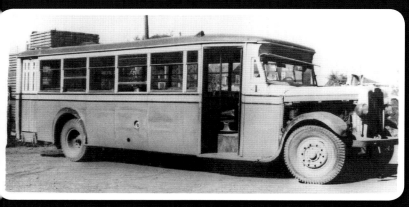

Leyland No. 4. *(ETS)*

The Leyland No. 5 sporting the 1946 ETS oval decal. *(ETS)*

While struggling to keep a miscellany of rolling stock on the streets to meet the growing demand, the Radial Railway fought its own battle against the bitter winter weather of the war years. The entire fleet of 72 vehicles—including 59 streetcars, six trolley buses and seven motorbuses—had to be turned out when a cold snap hit Edmonton on 10 December 1940, and the old nemesis of power outages struck again:

"Trams Stalled, Lights Out When Snow Breaks Circuit

"Soft, wet snow fell on cracked insulators and caused a short-circuit on high voltage city power lines shortly after 6:00 PM; darkened the plant for 10 hours; turned out lights in most of Edmonton for about 30 minutes; stalled 25 street cars and one trolley bus and made lights flicker or go out in remote parts of the city. It caused a spectacular bluish glare, which could be seen over a wide area. The break had nothing to do with the City power plant; it was a 'localized' condition caused by the weather. All trams in North Edmonton were stalled for about 25 minutes, said Mr. Ferrier. City electric crews toiled until 4:00 AM to restore power at the Canada Packers plant" *(Edmonton Journal)*.

A derailed streetcar on the High Level, 14 February 1948. *(Provincial Archives of Alberta Gs193.2)*

The combination of war and weather would add to the collection of stories that Edmontonians would tell for years to come. When a terrible blizzard hit the city in November 1942, the friendly invasion of American soldiers turned out in large numbers to help civilian workers clear the streets to keep the streetcars running. Another storied moment of streetcar history occurred during a severe summer storm in 1940 when a tram stalled on the High Level Bridge in a windstorm:

A Critical Moment When Tram Stalls on Bridge

"At the peak of an 80-mile-an-hour gale, motorman L. Gamble displayed unequalled heroism. The trolley was blown from the overhead feed wire on the [High Level] bridge, stalling the tram. The motorman forced his way outside to return the trolley to the wire, while the passengers had to be forcibly held in the car; two women forced their way outside but were pushed back inside before the wind blew them over the bridge. The passengers held the door shut, while Motorman Gamble went to the rear of the car. He found that he could control the trolley by handling the rope attached to it.

"Despite the terrific gale he climbed to the top of the car, grasped the trolley itself, and after several attempts, attached it to the wire. Then he clambered down, and the passenger guarding the door let him in to the vestibule. He continued the trip across the bridge while everyone breathed heavy sighs of relief. Mr. Gamble has been a motorman for only a year, but his act was described as very heroic, courageous, and altogether "very fine." There were about 20 or 25 people riding the white sign car at the time it was stalled on the bridge. Mr. Gamble deserves a gold medal for downright bravery" (*Edmonton Journal*).

The Olive Marjorie Ainslie Story

Edmonton Street Railway conductorettes in 1945. Front row: L. Bly, A. Koselski, M. Brownoff, M. Sifert. Second row: J. Berg, M. Oliver, L. Warburton, P. Maines, L. Michetti, S. Anderson, B. Broadhead, A. Halowchak. Third row: J. Bateman, E. MacDonald, M. Haire, E. Cameron, D. Scott, L. Coutts, N. Lundeby, E. Anderson, L. Pinder, C. Place, N. Felming. Back row: R. Gibeault, V. Page, W. Whitford, O. Ainslie, A. Bard, E. Wells, L. Tyler, L. Lindley. *(Mrs. O. Ainslie)*

Olive Marjorie Ainslie is at the centre of the back row of this McDermid Studios group photograph of ERR conductorettes at the end of their wartime service in 1945. Olive Ainslie was born in Edmonton in 1920, the daughter of Frederick and Ruby Mason. Her father Fred was a supervisor with the ERR, so she was personally aware of Edmonton's transit system as she grew up. Young Olive was tall and athletic, played basketball in school and was invited to try out for the famous Edmonton Grads basketball team.

Olive worked on the Edmonton Radial Railway cars as a conductorette during the Second World War, having married Angus (Gus) Ainslie in 1942. Olive recalls one episode when they were crossing the open upper deck of the High Level Bridge and one of the trolley lines broke, leaving the streetcar stalled half way across. Olive was worried that she might be called on to climb to the top of the streetcar to reset the trolley back on the line because the wartime operator had an injured leg and would be unable to make the ascent safely. Fortunately, a supervisor was on board to make the repair. Olive made many good friends among ERR personnel and passengers, who would occasionally slip her a present like cheese or coffee, which were in short supply during wartime. She also remained very close to her fellow conductorettes after the war (ETS Centennial Interviews).

To sustain civilian morale through the difficult war years, the ERR redoubled its efforts to provide social benefits to the community in cooperation with other public service agencies. The advent of specialty cars, and in particular a travelling library car, was an innovation on this front. City Librarian H.C. Gourlay approached the Street Railway Department in May 1941 with a proposal to have retired streetcar No. 14 refurbished as a mobile branch of the Edmonton Public Library to serve residents of outlying neighbourhoods in greater Edmonton. The SRD agreed, and the new library car was completed in early October 1941. All but four windows were covered over, seats were removed and the interior was fitted with bookcases secured to the walls. Interior lighting was provided by the original lamps, which ran along the length of the body, while additional lamps were placed over the front and rear doors. The exterior was painted blue between the base and the belt rail, and ivory above the belt rail. "Edmonton Public Library" signage was painted in black letters at the centre of each side above the belt rail, which also was painted black (Buck; *Edmonton Journal*).

Streetcar No. 14 and the old Leyland Library Bus No. 4, both of which did yeoman service for the Edmonton Public Library in the rapidly expanding districts of the city for many years. Later versions operated by the Edmonton Public Library were known as bookmobiles.
(Provincial Archives of Alberta PA454.1)

The travelling library car visits an Edmonton
school a week before Christmas in 1947.
Jack Fearon often drove these cars.
(City of Edmonton Archives EA-600-643a)

The Library Car required special rail sidings on which it could be parked in neighbourhoods served. The first of these, installed in Calder, was a short open-track extension built on the northern end of the open track wye on 127 Street. In North Edmonton a short stub line was constructed from the loop on 124 Street.

Victory in Europe Day on 8 May 1945 and Victory over Japan Day on 15 August 1945 marked the formal end of hostilities in the European and Pacific wars. During that spring and summer, the growing realization that the world had been fundamentally changed swept through the global community. Shock at the atomic bomb attacks on Hiroshima and Nagasaki, revelations of the genocide that occurred in the death camps of Eastern Europe, the horrendous casualty lists and the massive dispersal of populations all brought home the brutal nature of modern mechanized warfare. At the same time, a sense of euphoria and optimism found expression among the returning veterans as they turned their energy toward post-war reconstruction and civil reestablishment.

Edmonton grew almost 25 percent during the war years from a population of 90,419 in 1939 to 111,745 in 1945. The city had been drawn further into the continental and international political and economic world during those critical years. The wartime search for strategic reserves of oil, while secondary to the building of transportation routes and provision of a security zone on the continental northern perimeter, soon would pay off, and Edmonton would almost immediately enter a new era of prosperity with its related challenges.

Works Cited

Ainsley, Olive. ETS Centennial Interviews, 2007–08. Edmonton, Alberta: ETA Archives.

Boddington, Steve. *Canadian Social Studies,* Volume 26, Number 1, Fall 2001.

Buck, George H. *A Technological History of Municipally Owned Public Transportation In Edmonton:* 1893–1981. Edmonton, Alberta: University of Alberta Thesis, 1985, p. 416; 440; 443; 437–39; 449–50; 451–55; 551; 553; 566.

City of Edmonton Archives. Letter to the City Commissioners from the Toronto Transportation Committee, 1 September 1939.

Edmonton Bulletin. 7 November 1942; 22 February 1943; 23 March 1943.

Edmonton Journal. 6 December 1940; 15 December 1940; 13 August 1940; 14 October 1941.

Ivany, Kathryn. *Heritage Fair Resource Package.* Edmonton, Alberta: 2002.

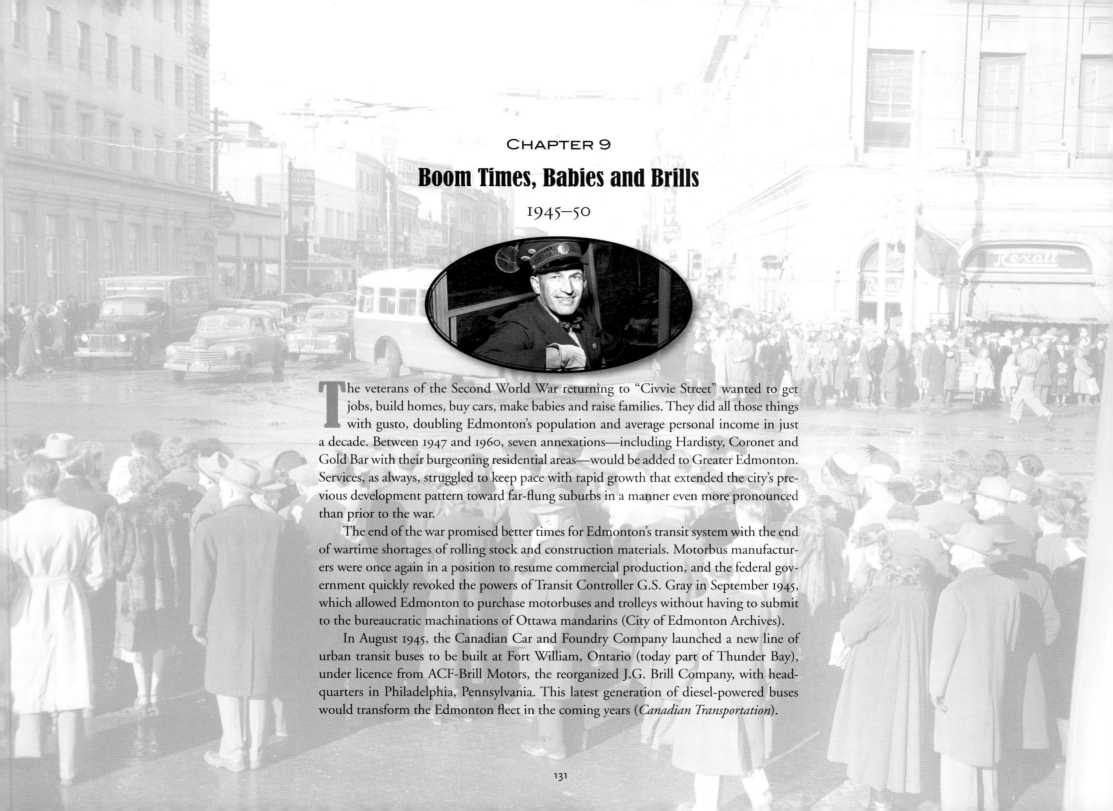

CHAPTER 9

Boom Times, Babies and Brills

1945–50

The veterans of the Second World War returning to "Civvie Street" wanted to get jobs, build homes, buy cars, make babies and raise families. They did all those things with gusto, doubling Edmonton's population and average personal income in just a decade. Between 1947 and 1960, seven annexations—including Hardisty, Coronet and Gold Bar with their burgeoning residential areas—would be added to Greater Edmonton. Services, as always, struggled to keep pace with rapid growth that extended the city's previous development pattern toward far-flung suburbs in a manner even more pronounced than prior to the war.

The end of the war promised better times for Edmonton's transit system with the end of wartime shortages of rolling stock and construction materials. Motorbus manufacturers were once again in a position to resume commercial production, and the federal government quickly revoked the powers of Transit Controller G.S. Gray in September 1945, which allowed Edmonton to purchase motorbuses and trolleys without having to submit to the bureaucratic machinations of Ottawa mandarins (City of Edmonton Archives).

In August 1945, the Canadian Car and Foundry Company launched a new line of urban transit buses to be built at Fort William, Ontario (today part of Thunder Bay), under licence from ACF-Brill Motors, the reorganized J.G. Brill Company, with headquarters in Philadelphia, Pennsylvania. This latest generation of diesel-powered buses would transform the Edmonton fleet in the coming years (*Canadian Transportation*).

Jasper Place in 1948 showing ETS motorbus service to outlying communities. Jasper Place was a separate community at the time, and bus service only ran from the terminal stop to the 149 Street boundary.
(City of Edmonton Archives EA-10-166)

The Gordon Oleschuk Story

Although many ERR veterans returned to their positions with the transit system after the war, some found it difficult to obtain work. Gordon Oleschuk, who retired in 1984, today spends many happy hours driving streetcars for the Edmonton Radial Railway Society at Fort Edmonton Park. He also drove the ceremonial Streetcar No. 1, restored for the ETS Centennial in 2008. Gordon went to work for the ETS 60 years before the centennial celebration. Harvey Clark, an ETS driver he knew, suggested the ETS for Gordon, who was driving a delivery truck in 1948. Gordon recalls the difficulty faced by men with Ukrainian or Polish names at the time. "It took me months to get onto Transit," he remembers.

"There is quite a history behind this," he recalls. "Every time I went in (Don MacDonald was the Supervisor then), they were hiring. You know, I could stop in every Monday, and they would ask me a few questions, but when it came down to what was my name, 'Well, not right now. Maybe in a week. Call in a week.'

"I would get the same story over and over again. The only way I got on was [that when] I left the office that day Walter [Hill] . . . was putting people on streetcars, and somebody hadn't shown up. He asked me if I was looking for a job.

"I said, 'Well, yes!'

"He said, 'Just a minute.'

"So he went back into Don MacDonald's office, came back and said, 'You fill those [forms] out and get your medical.' And that's how I got on with Transit."

Later, in the Inspectors' office at the Scona Garage, Gordon met Jim Moir and Jim Allan. "They asked me what my name was," he recalls. You know the word I got? They asked me if I would change my name. My brother was the same way," he adds. "He came out of the [Royal Canadian] Air Force and tried to get onto the police force. He got the same thing. He changed his name, and they hired him right away" (ETS Centennial Interviews).

Streetcars, photographed here by R. Harrington, still ran on Jasper Avenue in 1949.
(Provincial Archives of Alberta A8412)

Brill Motors' new C-36, available in either gasoline-powered or electric trolley models, featured a new lightweight aluminium alloy unitized chassis developed from wartime aircraft design and construction techniques. With its motor mounted midway in the chassis to allow more usable passenger space, the C-36's streamlined, modern look may not have driven off the pages of Buck Rogers, but it represented a leap forward as revolutionary as the replacement of the horse-drawn stage coach with the electric streetcar. An extruded aluminium "rub rail" running along the exterior panels just below the windows protected the panels from daily scrapes and bumps and added to the sleek look. The public appreciated the Brill's contemporary design. Inside, in keeping with the use of modern materials, linoleum-covered plywood replaced the hardwood flooring previously used in Edmonton buses, and tubular seating, including four longitudinal seats, was covered with green faux-leather.

Bernie Budney, who worked on the Brills' bodywork very late in their lifespan, found it quite a challenge. "All the parts were obsolete. You had to find a part and make it work," he recalled (ETS Centennial Interviews).

Streetcar No. 20 at the end of its service. *(City of Edmonton Archives EA-600-312d)*

No. 26 Brill C-36 on the road in 1946. *(City of Edmonton Archives EA-75-854)*

Edmonton ordered a dozen 36-passenger models in December 1945 and seven more in February 1946. Delivery was delayed due to the backlog of orders that had accumulated at the Canadian Car and Foundry during wartime. In the meantime, the City leased more Ford buses from McMullen and Noullett, an arrangement that lasted until the first Brills arrived in December 1946 (Buck).

The new Brills, painted in the same colours as the wartime Fords, with three ETS decals affixed around the front, were numbered 17 through 35 and arrived just in time to remind Edmontonians of an old problem of public transit coaches in Edmonton. In the depths of the Edmonton winter, heaters proved inadequate, and cold fingers, toes and ears caused a litany of complaints from riders. Modifications, including wood-frame window sashes to restrict heat loss, were made in 1946 to rectify the problem. The Brill's Hall-Scott engines also caused problems as their pistons collapsed in little over a year due to the use of low-octane fuel. The engines had to be replaced over an extended period. But for all its initial failings, the C-36 began to settle into a long and venerable service (*Canadian Transportation*; Buck).

The ETS ordered an additional 18 C-36s (Nos. 36 through 53) between December 1947 and January 1950. These were identical to the first Brills with the exception of minor modifications that improved the technical performance, such as exterior plugs to allow batteries to be charged without removing them from the bus, and dust shields for the brakes. ETS also ordered five Twin Coach 44-S gasoline buses in early 1950 (Nos. 54 to 58). Manufactured by Twin Coach of Kent, Ohio, they featured a steel frame and seated 44 passengers. These were followed by a propane-powered 44-S (No. 59) (Buck).

No. 27, a Brill C-36, with the new decal introduced in 1946 displayed prominently on the front.
(Provincial Archives of Alberta, Missionary Oblates, Grandin Collection, OB6162)

No. 21, one of the new Brill C-36s, at
Jasper Avenue and 101 Street in 1952.
(Provincial Archives of Alberta PA57.4)

The Speedy Brills

The Brills were favourites with drivers. ETS operators "T.H." and "D.M." related stories about both their speed and agility.

Said T.H., "They were a great bus, those Brills. You could have that bus up to 30 miles an hour in a half a block. Just responsive—just touch the door and it was open. You could get people in and out of there. Unbelievable! Nice bus to drive. [Because they were a] little shorter, you could zip through traffic pretty good. They were fast!"

"We took a Brill out in Northlands," remembered D.M. "At that time it was all open except for the racetrack, and it had that mound of dirt up there. Howie Crities was driving, and he says, 'We'll go for a spin around.' He sees a black dog chasing one of those big rabbits out there. 'I'll cut him off, I'll cut him off!'

"Jeez, the first thing I know he's goin' up on the side of this racetrack. Bus falls over.

"I says, 'Howie, what're we going to do now?'

"He says, 'I don't know. Let's walk back and don't say anything. We'll go get it tonight.'

"We had to go get it that night."

Don MacDonald, Tom Ferrier and S.B. Derbyshire inspecting No. 55, one of the new Twin Coach 44-S gas buses on 16 June 1950.
(City of Edmonton Archives EA-600-4549)

Transit Name-Changes, 1946–1993

As the streetcar era drew to a close with the replacement of the original fleet by motor- and trolley buses, a new name was needed to reflect the new reality of transit in Edmonton.

On 16 July 1946, the names *Edmonton Radial Railway* and *Street Railway Department* were replaced by *Edmonton Transportation System* (ETS), which was abbreviated to *Edmonton Transit System* on 29 April 1947. A new oval decal, red with "ETS" written in yellow and outlined in black, was designed and first used in 1946.

The new logo adopted in 1947.

In 1977 the name was changed to Edmonton Transit, which lasted until 1993, after which it reverted to the name Edmonton Transit System (ETS).

Other logos used by Edmonton Transit through the years.

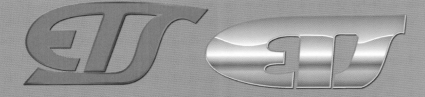

Operator Bill Seaton, who retired in April 1949, logs his two-millionth mile at the wheel.
(City of Edmonton Archives EA-600-2287a)

While expanding the fleet, the ETS finally responded to continuing public pressure by beginning to convert the smelly old Leyland buses from diesel to gasoline engines in 1948. The diesel experiment, which began in 1936 with engines converted from gasoline, was at an end, although a new generation of diesels would return in force to Edmonton streets in the mid-1960s. Interest now shifted to propane, a cheap and plentiful by-product of the petroleum refining process that was established in Edmonton with the discovery of oil at Leduc in 1947. In December 1949, a propane system was installed on No. 14, one of the wartime Victory Fords, and the experiment proved successful enough to choose propane power for one Twin Coach 44-S bus and 10 more 45-S models ordered in 1950. Superintendent Donald MacDonald noted in 1958 that the early Victory Ford conversion to propane was the first such use of the fuel by a Canadian transit system (Buck; *Edmonton Journal*).

New coaches became more readily available after many years of shortages, allowing some obsolete vehicles to be finally retired. Among these was old No. 4, which was sold to the Edmonton Public Library in 1948 and converted to a bookmobile to serve the rapidly expanding suburbs. Many baby boomers still recall making their weekly trips to this little travelling library as it stopped in their neighbourhood.

To service the growing fleet, a new bus garage and shop were constructed on the west side of the Cromdale car barns to replace the main Civic Garage (Buck).

As more motor coaches came into service, Edmonton's beloved streetcars disappeared, though the increase in ridership following the war and the initial difficulty in finding buses to replace them resulted in a delay in the total elimination of the streetcar for six years. In fact, to maintain service, some construction of open streetcar lines was undertaken following the war, despite the frequently stated intent to replace the streetcars. One busy streetcar line that could not easily be replaced by buses was the single-track line to Calder. ETS constructed a second open track line in 1946 along 124 Street parallel to the one built in 1942–43, eliminating the need for passing sidings and accommodating the demand for improved service. This line, the last constructed for streetcars, began at 118 Avenue and proceeded north to a point just south of the switch at 125 Avenue, where it connected with the other track (Buck).

The Leyland No. 4 interior during its use as a bookmobile. *(Provincial Archives of Alberta PA454.5)*

The Leyland No. 4 "Lioness" purchased in 1939 was converted to a bookmobile in 1951 after being taken out of the fleet. It also was designated as a mobile command post for emergency services. *(Provincial Archives of Alberta PA454.2)*

The Edmonton Transit System's conversion from streetcars to electric trolleys and gasoline buses, and the resultant abandonment of the street railway track system, transformed the character of the city's streets. The process began in 1939 with the first trolley route and advanced more rapidly after the end of the Second World War. Wherever the new routes ran, paved streets either preceded them or followed shortly thereafter, and open-construction streetcar tracks disappeared, though the process was not without complication. In 1948 plans were made to remove existing streetcar tracks on 124 Street from 107 Avenue to 118 Avenue, then to pave 124 Street in preparation for trolley service. The removal of the 124 Street tracks south of 118 Avenue isolated the heavily used track north to Calder from the remaining street railway system. The Calder section required construction of temporary storage and service tracks since the nine streetcars remaining on that section were unable to return to the streetcar barns. Four spur tracks, one of which

doubled as a wye, were installed on the east side of 124 Street immediately north of 118 Avenue.

The discovery of oil on 13 February 1947 ushered in Edmonton's long-awaited second boom. When Imperial Oil Leduc #1 blew amid much fanfare, it set in motion developments that would shape Edmonton's destiny. The following year, the first oil refinery was established in Clover Bar. Though it was only the old Norman Wells refinery that had first been shipped north during the wartime Canol Pipeline project, it was a start. The British–American and McColl–Frontenac companies soon followed with major refineries. Within three years of Leduc #1, the first inter-provincial oil pipeline connected Edmonton with Ontario markets.

With the advent of oil-based prosperity, Edmonton realized that civic growth would require more long-term planning. No longer could civic services always be rushing to catch up to demand. The City launched an

Preparing 107 Avenue for paving as trolleys began to replace streetcars in May 1947. *(City of Edmonton Archives EA-600-120b)*

Bus Etiquette

Public sentiment following the Second World War favoured stability and conservative family values. Politeness and decorum were stressed, and youthful exuberance was suspected as a disturbing sign of social unrest or disintegration. Juvenile delinquency became a virtual obsession during the post-war baby boom years, and behaviour on the bus was no exception. In 1948 City Council passed a sweeping resolution to remind the city's youth of proper conduct aboard the transit system:

WHEREAS for the purpose of ensuring as far as possible the safety, comfort and convenience of passengers on said System [ETS] and to protect the vehicles and equipment of said System from damage, it is desirable to pass a bylaw regulating the conduct of persons using the vehicles of the said System.

NOW THEREFORE the Municipal Council of The City of Edmonton, duly assembled, enacts as follows:

1. No person shall use any profane, abusive or foul language in or upon any vehicle owned, used or operated in connection with the said System.

2. No person shall conduct himself in a disorderly manner in or upon any vehicle owned, used or operated by or on behalf of said System.

3. No person shall annoy, incommode or inconvenience any other person in or upon any vehicle owned, used or operated by or on behalf of said System.

4. No person shall smoke any tobacco or any other substance in or upon any vehicle of the said System.

5. Except the duly authorized employees of the said System or except in emergent circumstances requiring quick exit for safety reasons, no person shall (a) open any entrance or exit door of any vehicle of said System; (b) interfere with any bolt or fastening of any door, nor in any way interfere with the door closing mechanism, nor prevent the door closing mechanism from operating, so as to permit any person to enter any of said vehicles.

6. No person shall interfere with the windows, apparatus or equipment of any of the windows of any of the vehicles of the said System, except to open or close the same for the reasonable need of ventilation in cases where said windows are provided with manual operation thereof for passenger use.

(City of Edmonton Archives)

aggressive, far-reaching planning program in 1947 when Noel Dant became the City's first post-war town planner. Dant would radically change the character of future development, leaving his mark in the traffic circles, curbs, crescents, cul-de-sacs and service roads that broke up the old rectilinear grid pattern that had exemplified Edmonton's earlier development. Though each neighbourhood in the spreading suburbs would be reached by public transit service, the planning philosophy would ultimately come to favour the transit system's immediate rival—the private automobile.

The number of private automobiles in Edmonton increased sharply after the Second World War, not just reflecting but surpassing the continental trend. The Wilson Report of 1949 bowed to the inevitable by recommending that the busy three-part wye used to turn streetcars at 104 Street and 82 Avenue be relocated as an open-track loop to the east side of 109 Street north of 82 Avenue to better accommodate the increasing use of cars. The ETS ultimately built the loop on the east side of 109 Street immediately south of 84 Avenue. The Wilson Report also recommended terminating one streetcar route at the north end of the High Level Bridge. An open track loop at 98 Avenue just to the north of the bridge between 109 Street and the CPR tracks was built to allow streetcars to run back to the south side of the city and turn around near 109 Street and 84 Avenue. These two open-track loops were the last sections of street railway track to be constructed for ETS.

The streetcar era officially ended in the early morning of 2 September 1951 when the 98 Avenue to 109 Street loop finally closed. A month later, when Princess Elizabeth and Prince Philip visited the city, they encountered a bustling resource-driven city bursting with wealth, energy and confidence. Though the Hotel Macdonald still dominated the river valley skyline during the 1950s, an annex would be built just east of the hotel, its International style described by local wits as "the box the hotel came in." Beneath the annex, Edmonton's first underground parking lot opened to accommodate the downtown traffic of the bustling post-war economy. From this point onward, the personal car would come to dominate the shape, growth and cultural fabric of Edmonton, a seemingly irresistible trend that also would define the progress of ETS in the coming decades.

The Ken Strachan Story

The operators during the post-war period were generally a gracious and public-oriented group of men. Ken Strachan, back from service overseas with the Royal Canadian Air Force, joined the ETS in 1947, the last man to be hired under compulsory military service rules. He was No. 374 when he was turned in, reflecting the number of drivers in ETS that year. The ETS allowed him to buy back his service time toward his pension, and he began a long career with the City. He recalls that the streetcars were hard to train on, cold and hard to start in the winter and uncomfortably hot in the summer.

Although many drivers left for high-paying work in the oil fields in the 1950s, Ken stuck with the ETS. In 1968 he became Chief Inspector. He recalls how the ETS "was one big happy family" that bowled, danced and played hockey together. Ken compared transit workers' community spirit to other public services. "I would compare driving a public bus to going out to dinner," he concluded. "When you go into a café, if there is someone to meet you and they're quite jovial, then your meal is better. And it's just the same thing when you get on the bus. It makes the day go better" (Strachan).

The Cromdale body shop Christmas party of 1952 shows the ETS "happy family" celebrating together. Back row: J. Iwaskow, Charlie Ness, Dan Snatynchuk, Bill Marriott, Sig Hope, Jack Gaitts, Ernie Landridges, Jim Peden and Sid Boultan. Front row: Art Howark, Ernie Cliff, Greg Craigie, George Norrie and Charlie Lisson. *(ATU #569)*

The 1944–45 Street Railway Hockey Club, Independent Hockey League champions for the year with the Gas Co. Trophy. Sports teams played a part in building camaraderie among ETS employees and hockey had a long tradition within the system. Back row: H. Rattenbury (equipment manager), N. Guild (secretary-treasurer), A. Curfman (president), R. Magee (manager) and J. Gaitts (trainer). Centre row: D. Smart (forward), J. Maday (forward), J. (Phats) Faulder (defence), C. Newsome (defence), A. McSporran (defence and coach), M. Darling (forward) and W. Weeks (defence). Front row: G. McPherson (forward), R. Graham (captain and forward), R. Campbell (goal), R. Walker (forward) and R. Crossland (forward). *(ATU 569)*

Works Cited

Budney, Bernie. ETS Centennial Interviews, 2007–08. Edmonton, Alberta: ETS Archives.

Buck, George H. *A Technological History of Municipally Owned Public Transportation In Edmonton:* 1893–1981. Edmonton, Alberta: University of Alberta Thesis, 1985, p. 160; 452; 457; 461; 464; 465–67; 468–70.

Canadian Transportation, 1945, p. 453–54.

City of Edmonton Archives. G.S. Gray, Transit Controller, to Commissioner R.J. Gibb, 13 September 1945.

City of Edmonton Archives. 9 August 1948, RG8/A97-82.BL1172.

Edmonton Journal. 14 March 1952.

Oleschuk, Gordon P. ETS Centennial Interviews, 2007–08. Edmonton, Alberta: ETS Archives.

Strachan, Ken. ETS Centennial Interviews, 2007–08. Edmonton, Alberta: ETS Archives.

No. 107, one of the Leyland "Park Royal" trolleys, purchased in 1942 and in service until 1951, running down McDougall Hill with the Hotel Macdonald in the background, prior to the construction of the Annex. This model was painted ivory and orange, with an orange band and black stripes.

CHAPTER 10

When the Car Became King

1950–59

The last streetcar made its official farewell journey on Saturday, 1 September 1951, 43 years after entering service. Car No. 1 left 97 Street and Jasper Avenue at 8:00 pm, rumbled west on Jasper to 109 Street and wheeled south across the High Level Bridge to the turnaround on 84 Avenue. The venerable No. 1 had travelled an estimated 2.4 million kilometres during its long service, a distance equal to 60 trips around the planet.

Radio station CJCA, in a program sponsored by Gainers to commemorate the end of the service, presented reminiscences about Streetcar No. 1. Recalling incidents from its exciting dash across the country with CNR and CPR competing to deliver the first car and thus secure the contract to ship others for the fledgling ERR, to its role in the unique and eccentric run to McKernan Lake on the "Toonerville Trolley" line, the program highlighted aspects of ETS history that were retiring with the car. "There never was a streetcar like the one that ran to McKernan's Lake," said the broadcaster. "The Toonerville Trolley started at South Edmonton's busiest intersection, lurched south on the Calgary Trail to get up speed, and then bounced wildly to a solitary terminus among the trees and creatures of the forest at 118 Street. No thrill ride on the Exhibition ever offered the exhilaration of that desperate, careening journey on the uncertain two-mile track" (CJCA).

Old No. 1 was fittingly decked with flowers before trundling down Whyte Avenue to the official opening of the new South Side Garage, where its replacement motorbuses

"Old Faithful," Streetcar No. 1, retired in 1951.
(City of Edmonton Archives EA-10-1391)

1908 OLD·FAITHFULL 1951
RETIRED 1,500,000 MILES OF
AFTER SERVICE

Trolley buff Norm Corness poses for his brother's camera on 118 Avenue at 124 Street about 1942. Car 51 in the background is the blue-and-white. The sign reads "Noon Hour Extra." This car travelled six blocks beyond the regular terminal to turn, then lay over briefly before returning to the downtown area. Considerable revenue was generated over the noon hour as many people working in the downtown area went home for lunch. On February 21, 1943, Calder cars began to operate on new trackage extended north behind Car 51 from this point. *(Photo courtesy Norm Corness. Text courtesy Colin Hatcher)*

would be serviced. Among the approximately 50 guests who packed the last ride were Mayor Sid Parsons; Superintendent Thomas Ferrier and "Dad" Miller, the motorman on the first streetcar in 1908; and J.C. McDougall, son of former Mayor John A. McDougall, who had presided over the inauguration of the Edmonton Radial Railway a half century before. McDougall carried with him the first strip of streetcar tickets he had purchased many years before. Tom Ferrier moved about the car recording for posterity the names of No. 1's last riders. "The sound of street cars pounding over the rails was missing from the Edmonton scene Tuesday for the first business day since 1908," the *Edmonton Journal* observed wistfully. A chapter in the city's transit story had been closed.

In the early hours of the next morning, Streetcar No. 1 left the barns again to convey many of the same party on a sentimental, unofficial last ride. Tom Ferrier again took down their names. Among the riders was Norm Corness, a lifelong streetcar enthusiast, who disembarked early at 101 Street and Jasper and so regretted not having his name on the second list. As a youth living near 124 Street and 118 Avenue, Norm had assisted in turning the trolleys around at the end of the line. Years later he fondly

reminisced about the youthful pranks he and his friends had played on ERR passengers and staff. When the streetcar crossed the upper deck of the High Level Bridge, "We used to try and rock the streetcar to scare some people," he recalled. At other times, "[if] we didn't like the conductor, we would take the poles off, and he would have to go back to put them on." Virtually every significant memory of his youth included the streetcars that carried him and his pals around the city to sports contests and other events. "They were all lined up at the end of the game. Every route went to First and Jasper" (*Edmonton Journal*). Norm Corness's last ride signed *finis* to a generation of fond memories.

Crowds view the first numbered streetcar, visible to the left of Twin Coach No. 74, as it takes the last ceremonial run in 1951. The event was an early example of ETS providing service to special events. In this case, it was a "Park and Ride" for the final run of the streetcars in the city.
(*City of Edmonton Archives EA-1-1374*)

The official last ride on an Edmonton streetcar.
(City of Edmonton Archives EA-10-1376)

The Arlene Meldrum Story

Streetcars played a role in the daily lives of Edmontonians, and not everyone loved the thrill of the High Level Bridge trip. During the Centennial celebrations, Arlene Meldrum recalled her experiences. Born Arlene Jones, she was raised in Edmonton, graduated from the University of Alberta in 1951 and married in 1952. She worked at Rutherford Library to the spring of 1953 and took many streetcar rides in her life.

"I hated the streetcar going across the top of the High Level Bridge because if you did dare to sit on the outside seat you looked straight down. It was pretty scary," Arlene remembers. "We lived on 115 Street just north of Jasper. . . . I should have been able to go to Vic, but they had [too many] students . . . there was just this overflow of students. One year they put one room of us from that . . . area into McDougall High; then the next year, they opened [Garneau] and the top floor was for high school. They took us over and stuck us there, which

meant I had to go over the High Level Bridge for three years during high school, three years during university and then I chose to get a job at the Rutherford Library. . . . So there I had to go every day of my life on . . . 'my favourite little route'. It was like [the streetcars] rattled across, and then you had to go up this hill to get to the [south] side. It was quite a production.

"Nobody drove their kids anywhere in those days. The boys would just keep their gear in their duffle bags and hop on the streetcar and go out to their game at the Gardens. . . . The city was smaller. You lived in your community, but when you took the streetcar, it was kind of a regular form of transportation. It wasn't like you were being hard done by. My father had a car, and he took it to work," Arlene observed, but the family still used the ERR regularly.

"I don't remember myself sitting down and crying" when the streetcars ended in 1951, she noted. "So the streetcar and I probably ended our careers together" (ETS Centennial Interviews).

Arlene Meldrum passed away in 2010.

Arlene Meldrum during the ETS Centennial celebrations in the summer of 2008. Arlene thoroughly enjoyed the experience. "I had my own bus driver, I had my own photographer, I had my own script man," she fondly recalls. "That was kind of a fun day because any place I wanted to go, I had my own bus." *(ETS)*

Arlene Meldrum (nee Jones) poses on Streetcar 37 when she was a university student just after the war. "My mother was involved with the IODE (Independent Order of the Daughters of the Empire) at that time," she recalled, "and it was the thing to do in those days to have fashion shows . . . as a money-raising thing . . . and I think that must have been how I got into it because I remember a bunch of us did other fashion shows. My skirt was so tight around the bottom and the steps were so high [that] it was kind of tricky to get on and off with any elegance or dignity at all. It was a struggle to be graceful all the time." *(Provincial Archives of Alberta PA927.5)*

It also was a sign of the times that three days before the last ride, Ferrier announced that work had already begun on tearing up the streetcar tracks on 109 Street. The hope was that this could be completed before an anticipated Royal visit, ensuring a smoother limo ride for their Majesties. The tracks on Whyte and Jasper avenues soon followed, and the federal Steel Controller seized most of the tracks to alleviate post-war metal shortages.

Even before streetcars were retired in 1951, the look of ETS had changed. Span wires replaced the centre poles on Jasper Avenue in 1948. Overhead wire replaced ground wires, onto which the trolleys clamped rather than hooked. Improved insulators and aerial switching assemblies also were installed. The ETS then handed over all the duties relating to power supply to the Electric Light and Power Department in 1951.

This new chapter of Edmonton transportation history had been partly presaged in 1949 by two events. The first was the twinning of the Low Level Bridge to speed rapidly increasing auto traffic across the North Saskatchewan River between the sprawling new suburbs to the north and south. Suburbs also required their own services. Westmount Shopping Centre became the first of many when it opened in August 1955, following the completion of the Groat Bridge, which, in turn, opened up the west end for further suburban sprawl that would soon be crowded with more shopping centres, diners, groceterias, drive-in restaurants and parking lots.

The second local event of 1949 to auger the immediate future was the opening of the Starlite Drive-In on Country Club Road. Few doubted that the car would become king of Edmonton streets when over 600 of them

Tracks being removed from the upper deck of the High Level Bridge on 28 March 1967.
(Provincial Archives of Alberta J74)

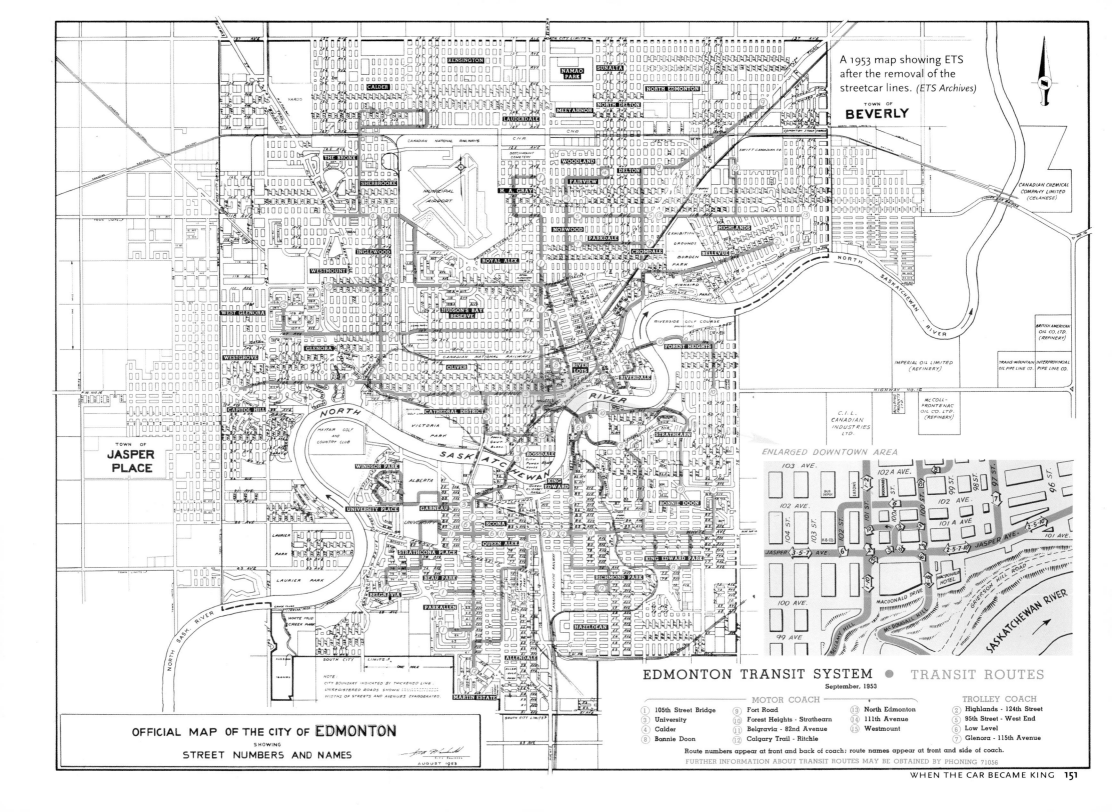

A 1953 map showing ETS after the removal of the streetcar lines. *(ETS Archives)*

OFFICIAL MAP OF THE CITY OF **EDMONTON**
SHOWING
STREET NUMBERS AND NAMES

AUGUST 1953

EDMONTON TRANSIT SYSTEM • TRANSIT ROUTES

September, 1953

ENLARGED DOWNTOWN AREA

NOTE:
CITY BOUNDARY INDICATED BY THICKENED LINE.
UNREGISTERED ROADS SHOWN
WIDTHS OF STREETS AND AVENUES EXAGGERATED.

MOTOR COACH			TROLLEY COACH
① 105th Street Bridge	⑨ Fort Road	⑬ North Edmonton	② Highlands - 124th Street
③ University	⑩ Forest Heights - Strathearn	⑭ 111th Avenue	⑤ 95th Street - West End
④ Calder	⑪ Belgravia - 82nd Avenue	⑮ Westmount	⑥ Low Level
⑧ Bonnie Doon	⑫ Calgary Trail - Ritchie		⑦ Glenora - 115th Avenue

Route numbers appear at front and back of coach; route names appear at front and side of coach.

FURTHER INFORMATION ABOUT TRANSIT ROUTES MAY BE OBTAINED BY PHONING 71056

arrived for the opening. Hundreds more were turned away. Alf J. Hooke, Minister of Economic Development, officially opened the Starlite, proclaiming it proof positive that Edmonton was "one of the most progressive cities in Canada." Other drive-ins soon followed, making the city what some local boosters proclaimed as the drive-in theatre capital of the world. By 1956 Waterloo Motors led all North American dealers in sales, and it was not long before automobile ownership rates in Canada ranked among the top five in the world. When successive waves of local sporting excellence were celebrated, it would be automobiles that provided parade transport for the homecoming heroes of hockey, curling and football before the throngs that crowded Jasper Avenue (*Edmonton Journal*).

As the trolley era drew to a close, Superintendent Thomas Ferrier took his leave. Not long after his last streetcar ride, he retired, having shepherded the transit system through the crucial transition from streetcars to trolleys. Though he remained committed to the electric trolley as the workhorse of

the fleet, his last recommendations included ordering more motorbuses to serve the new routes into the distant suburbs. Ferrier had experienced the effects of two world wars on public transit, and with an eye on the growing Korean conflict and Cold War hostilities, he reasoned that more "independent vehicles" should be brought into the fleet "so that possible new industrial or military areas may be served." On Ferrier's recommendation, 10 propane-powered Twin Coach 45-S buses (Nos. 60 through 69) were ordered to take advantage of the fuel's lower costs. As a cost-saving measure, ETS drivers

Waterloo Motors in 1951. The *Edmonton Bulletin* reported on 19 May 1950 that Alberta had the greatest demand for cars, both new and used, of all Canadian provinces, helping support large and elegant dealerships, such as Waterloo Motors. *(City of Edmonton Archives EA-88-139)*

Early Twin Coach 45-S No.77 sporting the 1960s logo.
(Doug Cowan)

ferried them from the Fort Erie, Ontario, manufacturer in December 1950. Five minor accidents on the trek home more than offset the savings. When 13 additional 45-S models (Nos. 70 through 82) were ordered from Twin Coach that same month, they were delivered by a private firm (Buck).

The proliferation of suburbs brought familiar pressure on the Edmonton Transit System to service low-density developments, where routes characteristically had to be operated at a loss. By the time ETS ordered a further 12 Twin City 52-seat propane-powered FLP-40 buses in 1951 to service outlying districts, Canada had been swept into the Korean War, and the federal government had once again assumed wartime production management powers of the Fort Erie bus plant. For the ETS, it was "déjà vu all over again." When the buses could not be built in Canada, the City turned to Twin City's Kent, Ohio, plant only to learn that the demands of the war had also reduced production output south of the border. When the new buses had not arrived by 1952, the contract was renegotiated, and the first eight, Nos. 401 through 408, finally arrived in Edmonton in May 1952.

While the City waited, ETS shifted into a familiar emergency management mode by ordering six C-37DT Mack diesel-powered buses to fill the gap (Nos. 94 through No. 99). Fortunately, these Macks had better transmissions and heating systems than their predecessors, and they served the system well. Even with reliable new rolling stock, as winter drew close, the *Edmonton Journal* reported that the City might request local firms to stagger their hours of business to avoid possible overcrowding of ETS vehicles (*Edmonton Journal*; Buck).

Ritchie residents Mrs. V.R. Speare, Mrs. F.R. Hamm and Mrs. A.E. Tyldesley protesting new bus routes on 21 November 1950 that left the area with half hour service, except in rush hour, when buses ran every 15 minutes *(Edmonton Bulletin)*. *(City of Edmonton Archives EA-600-6164)*

A new bus is inspected on 24 September 1947 by Superintendent Tom Ferrier, on the left, with Mr. Kerr and Mayor Harry Ainlay. *(City of Edmonton Archives EA-600-420a)*

The inspection party of Ferrier, Kerr and Mayor Harry Ainlay boarding the bus. *(City of Edmonton Archives EA-600-420b)*

ETS buses are serving the 101 Street retail area. The T.Eaton store addition is under construction, and the Greyhound Bus Depot and warehouse district are in the background.
(Provincial Archives of Alberta BL1753.1)

In the fall of 1950, the reconstruction of Connors Road from the south end of the Low Level Bridge was beginning to take shape. Graded east of the EYP rail line, the new road was designed to accommodate trolley bus service to Bonnie Doon. In the background, the construction of the Hotel MacDonald annex can be seen. *(City of Edmonton Archives, EA-600-5027a)*

possible historical preservation, was stored outdoors, where it became a victim of the elements and vandals. Only through the long and meticulous efforts of the Edmonton Radial Railway Society was it restored in time for the ETS Centennial celebrations. (*Edmonton Journal*; ETS Centennial Interviews).

The streetcar was gone, but the trolley had not seen its last days in Edmonton just yet, despite the increased reliance upon motorbuses. With motorbuses in short supply, four new Brill T-48A trolleys were purchased from Canadian Car and Foundry Company in December 1951 (Nos. 193 through No. 197). Six more were ordered in August 1954 (Nos. 197 through No. 202). All would provide long service before being retired between 1975 and 1978 (*Edmonton Journal*; Buck).

As diesel fuel became lower in price, it began to replace propane power for motorbuses, ending a long and successful experiment in alternative fuels. In 1955 the ETS ordered 10 new diesel-powered General Motors Corporation TDH-5105s (No. 409 through No. 418) similar to the Macks ordered four years earlier. Like the first Brills that became a fleet staple, the move to GMCs heralded a significant change that would leave its mark for decades to come. The GMC buses were judged to be superior to all other models in the fleet at the time, and five more were ordered in 1956 (Nos. 419 through No. 423), followed by 10 more in 1958 (Nos. 424 through No. 433). All were produced in Pontiac, Michigan. Citizen complaints about the diesel fumes, however, continued, and the ETS tried a chemical additive called Allmask, which partly reduced the distinctive, unpleasant odour (*Edmonton Journal*; Buck).

ETS also was forced into more extreme stopgap measures such as purchasing used rolling stock from other transit systems and acquiring new versions of technology on its way out. The aging Ford and Leyland motorbuses, purchased between 1932 and 1946, desperately needed replacement, so ETS acquired 11 used 1946-model Brill C-36 gasoline motor buses from the former power company in St. John, New Brunswick, in April 1951 (Nos. 83 through No. 93). Red Deer equipment broker G.L. Sorenson ferried the C-36s to Edmonton. Even with these additions to the fleet, only two of the most decrepit Leylands could be retired. Leyland No. 6 was sent to the Edmonton Public Library to serve as another bookmobile. The last Leylands and Fords would not disappear from the fleet until they were sold in the summer of 1954.

Several old streetcars remained in fairly good operating order, and it was hoped that buyers could be found for them. When no buyers came forward, the streetcars were stripped and sold like the others. Some streetcar bodies continued to serve the ETS as storage sheds near the Cromdale car barns for several years. Others found novel second lives in St. Paul, Ponoka, Bremner, Wabamun and other locations. One became an office for a Vegreville auctioneer. Another served for several years as an Edmonton diner under dispensation of a special permit from the building department. Several more found useful life as granaries and lakeside summer cottages. Streetcar No. 1, retained for

No. 185, one of the new Brill T-44 trolleys purchased in 1948, on Jasper Avenue in May 1950.
(Provincial Archives of Alberta Rs96.4)

No. 189, a Brill T-44 trolley, in 1953 near the Hudson's Bay Company department store. Five T-44 models purchased in May of 1949 were operating by the end of that year. *(Provincial Archives of Alberta B5038)*

A diesel Ford served Edmonton Public Library users in the 1950s as a bookmobile. *(Provincial Archives of Alberta PA454.4)*

Library Car interior. *(Edmonton Radial Railway Society)*

Model T48A trolley No. 194, purchased in 1952, operating along Jasper Avenue in the 1960s with the new logo. *(Doug Cowan)*

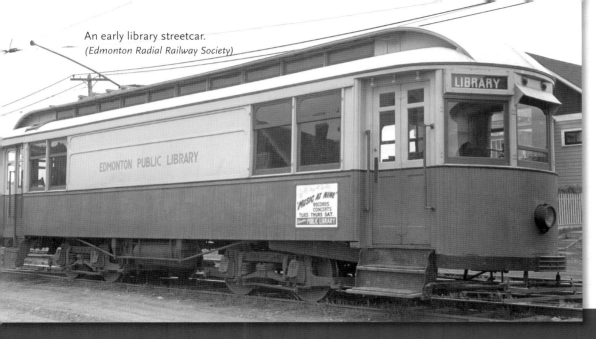

An early library streetcar.
(Edmonton Radial Railway Society)

The ETS was also becoming an innovator in areas other than fuels. In 1952 new buses arrived with two-way radios to add to security and to deploy the fleet more efficiently. The *Edmonton Journal* reported in January of that year that this was the first such application of the technology by a Canadian municipal transit system. The experiment was not continued, however, and radios would not become standard on buses for another two decades.

Bodywork represented another area where the ETS was a leader. Fibreglass reinforced resin panels were installed on buses starting in 1954 to reduce the cost of repair. This use apparently inspired the manufacture of fibreglass sports car bodies.

Superintendent Thomas Ferrier

Thomas Ferrier spent 43 years with the Edmonton Transit System. He immigrated to Canada from Scotland in 1906 and came to Edmonton two years later. He recalled how, on his arrival, he was "driven from the south side CPR station in a stage coach down Scona Hill towards the north side. The ruts on Scona were about two feet deep and the floor of the coach was scraping the ground." Ferrier's first impression was hardly promising for the man who would play such a prominent role in bringing public transit to the city.

Ferrier's first role with the new Edmonton Radial Railway was as a conductor on the Low Level Bridge line to Strathcona, one of a two-man team that operated each streetcar at the time. "The power was so low at times," he recalled, "I remember occasions when we had to leave the car on the street overnight because there wasn't enough to drive them to the barns."

Ferrier rose to Inspector in 1911, then Chief Inspector and Traffic Supervisor, and finally Superintendent from 1934 until his retirement. Assistant Superintendent Donald L. MacDonald replaced Ferrier in 1952.

Ferrier oversaw the ETS's transition from streetcars to trolleys and buses, and the implementation of the modern post-war system before his retirement.

The Ferrier Garage, an important garage in the ETS system, named in his honour, commemorates the contribution of Thomas Ferrier today (*Edmonton Journal*).

Portrait of Thomas Ferrier at his desk. (*ETS Ferrier Garage*)

Artist's concept painting of Ferrier Garage before it was built. (*ETS Ferrier Garage*)

The interior of a GMC in 1957.
(City of Edmonton Archives EA-301-11)

Twin Coach No. 59, purchased in 1950, was one of the units outfitted with two-way radios in 1952. *(ETS)*

The South Side Garage

As the ETS fleet grew to over 160 buses in 1950, the need for more garage space resulted in the construction of the South Side Garage at 10310 – 83 Avenue, where up to 90 buses and trolleys could be stored. Assistant Superintendent Donald L. MacDonald supervised the planning of the project that was completed in August 1951.

The *Edmonton Journal* enthusiastically reported that the new South Side Garage was a marvel of automation. "From the moment one enters the building there is the impression that everything is operated by pushing buttons." When buses entered the garage, they were automatically washed as they passed through a series of sprayers. (Interestingly,

it was found that the automatic washers often abraded the ETS decals, necessitating replacement by cast aluminium crests.) The buses then passed into storage or into a shop for repairs. Though the ETS initially described the South Side Garage as an experiment in improving system efficiency, the state-of-the-art structure proved its worth over the years.

The South Side Garage's (later known as Scona Garage) brick façade, three storeys high at one corner, remains a landmark in Old Strathcona to this day. The popular Old Strathcona Farmers' Market began outside the garage in 1983 and later moved inside the immense interior to be joined in 1989 by Chinook Theatre and Fringe Theatre Adventures, which became a vital part of the Edmonton arts scene (*Edmonton Journal*; Buck).

South Side Garage is known today as the Strathcona Farmers' Market. *(ETS Archives)*

Representatives of the ETS fleet lined up on 19 February 1958 at the south end of Scona Garage on 83 Avenue. From left to right: No. 33 Brill C-36 motorbus; No. 82, Twin Coach, propane; No. 415, GMC TDH-5105, diesel; and No. 116, Pullman Standard Trolley. Route numbers are posted on placards on each bus. *(Provincial Archives of Alberta Ws165)*

Even as changes were made, some things remained as reminders of less automated days. Ticket collecting, which would be transformed in years to come with automatic machines, still involved paper tokens.

By 1956 both Edmonton and Calgary had ridden the wave of the Alberta oil boom to the distinction of being the fastest growing cities in Canada. During the decade, Edmonton grew by 75 percent, from 148,861 residents in 1950 to 260,733 in 1959, much of the growth channelled into sprawling new subdivisions designed for access by private automobiles. As the first generation of ETS management passed the torch to their post-war inheritors, the new rules for future growth recognized that Edmontonians loved their cars.

Cromdale Memories

In the old Cromdale Garage much of the mechanical work was performed with what amounted to antique tools. Glen Benson was one of the first licensed mechanics to apprentice there after gaining his credentials at SAIT. Most of the mechanics there at the time were grandfathered in and had been trained on the job, while others had recently arrived from wartime experience in the RCAF. After apprenticing at the Scona Garage, Benson became a permanent employee at the Cromdale in August 1955.

Benson recalled the conditions: "I walked into the old Cromdale Shops on my first day. I walked into where they parked the trolleys. I walked in that small door, and it was dark with just a few incandescent bulbs glowing, and I thought, *God, what have I got myself into? This dark old hole of a place?* The guys that worked there over the years didn't have the right equipment and didn't have the training, so over a period of years we did change a lot and we got the . . . tooling and equipment we needed—like, for example, tow trucks. We used to tow these darn buses with little 4x4s with a steel tow bar, and you had to have a driver in the bus and hopefully he had enough air to operate the brakes. If you come down McDougall Hill and it's slippery, and you try to brake, and you jack-knife. . . . Things like that were just hairy to operate.

"Many of the streetcar tools still were produced in the blacksmith shop at the Cromdale Garage, especially the larger tools.

Mechanics bought their own tools until about the 1970s. Some mechanics came in from Finning and other companies with their own fancy kits, like the pre-electronic socket sets, etc. As is so often the case even now, it was the employees who made the difference. In the 1950s, the ETS still had a Machine Shop, Welding Shop and Blacksmith Shop." Benson recalls two English and Scottish blacksmiths and their two helpers who made many tools such as jigs. These were pre-computer days, and "We had a couple of fantastic machinists back then. It was marvellous to watch them [work]."

Benson also recalled the characters he had worked with through the years. "We had one old mechanic when I started at Cromdale, and we would put the bus up on the hoist, one of the small gas Brills. He would get his ball peen hammer and bang all around the bus, the skirts, and the bumper, to knock dirt out, because when you were working underneath you would bang your head and the dust would go down your neck. You could see the shape of the bus on the floor in dirt." Benson recalled another mechanic working on one of the old Mack diesels. "He had the manifold off with flames pouring out of the exhaust ports as he worked—roaring away. . . . He was a strange old bird" (ETS Centennial Interviews).

FAIRBANKS

Superintendent Donald L. MacDonald

Don MacDonald in 1951. *(City of Edmonton Archives EA-43-3)*

Expansion and change were the hallmarks of the administration of D.L. MacDonald, the Superintendent who moved ETS into the modern era of transit. D.L. (Don) MacDonald was born and raised in Edmonton, where he attended McCauley Public School and Victoria High School and earned the Gyro Scholarship for the highest scholastic standing in Edmonton.

MacDonald graduated from the University of Alberta in 1944 with a B.Sc. in Electrical Engineering. During his university days, he took the University Naval Training Course, and in 1943 served on convoy duty in the dangerous North Atlantic as an engineering officer aboard HMCS *Huron*. After being demobilized in 1946, he joined ETS, where he took an active part in the post-war conversion from streetcars to trolleys and buses.

MacDonald later worked as a design engineer, technical assistant and assistant superintendent until replacing his mentor, Tom Ferrier, as Superintendent in 1952, a position he held until the late 1970s when he moved to Portland, Oregon.

MacDonald demonstrated his commitment to public transit and the city through serving as president of the Canadian Transit Association and first president of the Alberta Productivity Council, organized by the Canadian Manufacturers Association and the Alberta Research Council, which was dedicated to developing more productive industrial methods in Alberta *(Edmonton Journal)*.

Works Cited

Benson, Glen. ETS Centennial Interviews, 2007–08. Edmonton, Alberta: ETS Archives.

Buck, George H. *A Technological History of Municipally Owned Public Transportation In Edmonton: 1893–1981.* Edmonton, Alberta: University of Alberta Thesis, 1985, pp. 472–73; 474-77; 479; 486; 494.

CJCA, *Sentimental Journey*, script, courtesy of Norm Corness, 1951.

Corness, Norm. ETS Centennial Interviews, 2007–08. Edmonton, Alberta: ETS Archives.

Edmonton Bulletin. 21 November 1950.

Edmonton Journal. 17 June 1949; 23 April 1951; 25 May 1951; 15 August 1951; 16 August 1951; 17 August 1951; 29 August 1951; 30 August 1951; 31 August 1951; 4 September 1951; 28 September 1951; 29 October 1951; 29 December 1951; 19 January 1952; 29 March 1952; 27 May 1958; 13 September 1958; 25 February 1961.

Meldrum, Arlene. ETS Centennial Interviews, 2007–08. Edmonton, Alberta: ETS Archives.

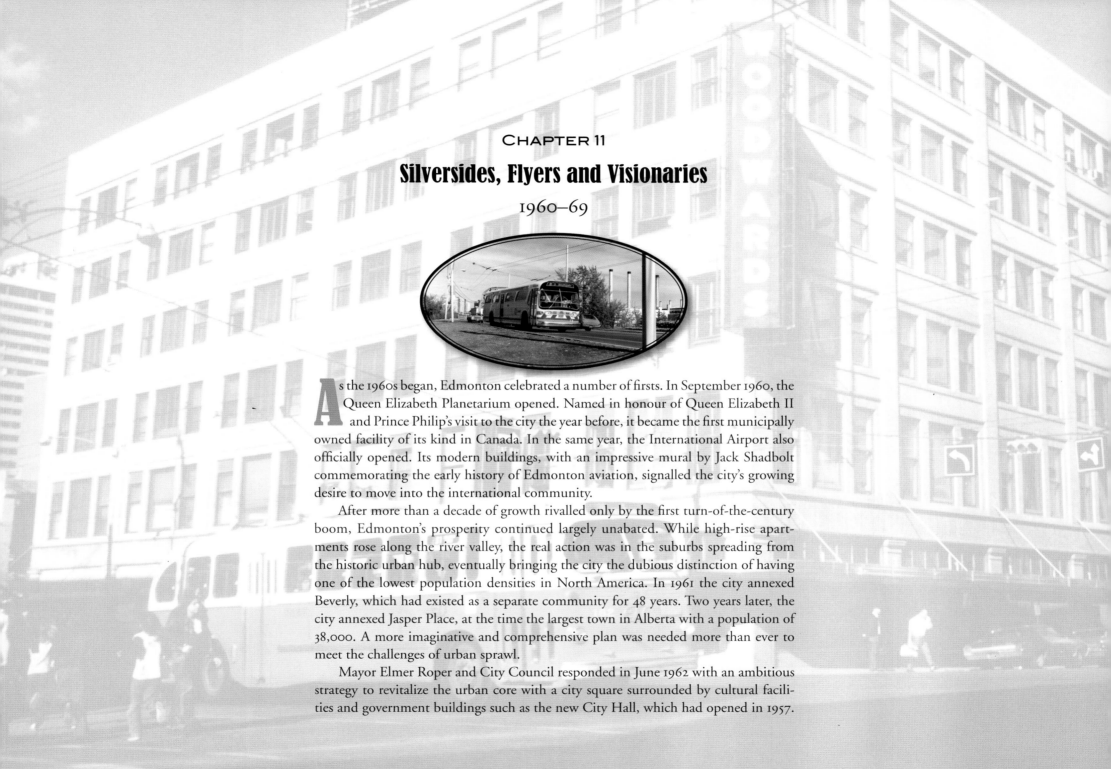

CHAPTER 11

Silversides, Flyers and Visionaries

1960–69

A s the 1960s began, Edmonton celebrated a number of firsts. In September 1960, the Queen Elizabeth Planetarium opened. Named in honour of Queen Elizabeth II and Prince Philip's visit to the city the year before, it became the first municipally owned facility of its kind in Canada. In the same year, the International Airport also officially opened. Its modern buildings, with an impressive mural by Jack Shadbolt commemorating the early history of Edmonton aviation, signalled the city's growing desire to move into the international community.

After more than a decade of growth rivalled only by the first turn-of-the-century boom, Edmonton's prosperity continued largely unabated. While high-rise apartments rose along the river valley, the real action was in the suburbs spreading from the historic urban hub, eventually bringing the city the dubious distinction of having one of the lowest population densities in North America. In 1961 the city annexed Beverly, which had existed as a separate community for 48 years. Two years later, the city annexed Jasper Place, at the time the largest town in Alberta with a population of 38,000. A more imaginative and comprehensive plan was needed more than ever to meet the challenges of urban sprawl.

Mayor Elmer Roper and City Council responded in June 1962 with an ambitious strategy to revitalize the urban core with a city square surrounded by cultural facilities and government buildings such as the new City Hall, which had opened in 1957.

In March 1965, Sir Winston Churchill Square was named to commemorate the great British wartime leader who died that year. The Edmonton Art Gallery opened that year, and by 1966 the CN Tower opened to anchor the downtown at its northern boundary. A modern downtown library was planned to mark the Canadian Centennial the following year. The square began to coalesce around the City Hall with innovative architectural forms that transformed downtown core. New cultural facilities drew more Edmontonians back to the downtown, and while many drove private cars, others wished to take public transit—if such connections were available from the suburbs.

A farsighted plan was sorely needed by ETS, which faced sizeable difficulties resulting from a familiar problem. Decades of patching together the public transit network in response to the shifting tides of boom and bust, war and peace, had left the system perpetually attempting to respond to growth after it had already reached the crisis point rather than anticipating the future and planning for it. The network struggled to provide adequate service to the burgeoning, distant suburbs, where the array of transfer points was scattered and frustrating. Peak commuting hours resulted in a crush of riders. Transit planning, like urban planning, had to take a long view that could respond to challenges before they became pressing and immediate.

Superintendent Don MacDonald would prove to be the right person at the right place at the right time to bring a new vision to the Edmonton Transit System. In the preface to his 1961 *Report on the Present Operation of the Edmonton Transit System with a View to Determining a Policy for the Future Operation of the System*, he pointed to the need for a systematic, thorough approach that would integrate urban and transit planning, launch the city into the computer age and put the ETS back on the rails, both literally and figuratively. "With the recognition that Edmonton's phenomenal growth of

No. 423, a GMC TDH-5105, passing the new City Hall on 20 August 1957.
(Provincial Archives of Alberta BL2395.1)

the past decade will continue," MacDonald wrote, "It is of primary importance that principles be determined for the development of the Edmonton Transit System and for its role in the evolving general plans for the Greater Edmonton area.

"There are as yet no tried nor proven solutions to the urban transportation problems developing in the major cities of North America, but the severity of the problems facing many other cities in more advanced stages of their traffic and transit difficulties has produced much new awareness, thinking, discussion, theories and plans for study by civic authorities, the general public, planners and designers and transportation authorities. . . .

"The planning of transit 'networks' and 'service standards' must be closely coordinated with traffic, parking, and city development plans. It might be suggested that a study of the organization to best do this be made, bearing in mind certain trends to approaching the transportation problem as a whole such as in the present *Transportation Study of the Edmonton Metropolitan District*. The *District Transportation Study* is establishing methods through the use of computers for the prediction of transportation needs and their related problems dealing with the many aspects of the Edmonton and District transportation picture (it should be noted that the city's new computer and others that will be available will be capable of operating on these new transportation study methods)" (MacDonald).

What would emerge during the decade was a series of short-term measures to address existing problems while studies setting a new direction for the future were conducted and evaluated. Every new suburb required new bus routes to serve its mostly young working families, but the ETS remained short of buses. To fill the gap in the fleet, 15 Blue Bird school buses were purchased to service annexed

areas until the necessary buses could be acquired. Nos. 855–874 arrived between September and December 1964, and also served as school buses.

As the suburban baby boomers flooded the public schools, university and new Northern Alberta Institute of Technology, the city responded with new schools and temporary portables. ETS responded to the demand by striking a deal in 1961 with the Edmonton Public School Board to provide school bus service. The first three bright yellow school buses (Nos. 801–803) were purchased from the Oneida Company. Two more buses—Nos. 804 and 805, fitted with bodies from Carpenter Body Works of Milton, Ontario, and similarly painted—were mounted on International Harvester chassis and engine assemblies. Fifteen more school buses (Nos. 830–844) were ordered

the following year from the Carpenter, Superior and Bluebird companies. Each bus seated 72 children. Ten more Carpenter and Blue Bird school buses were added in 1963 (Nos. 845–854). By 1967 the ETS school bus fleet would grow to 80 units (Buck; ETS *Annual Report*).

Suburban sprawl fuelled by major annexations placed the bus at the forefront of ETS's efforts to meet the immediate demand for new routes. In January 1960, the General Motors Company sent a demonstration model of the company's latest municipal bus, the TDH-5301, to Edmonton. The model met with approval with its up-market features, superior hot-water heating and fluorescent lighting. In February 1960, ETS ordered the first five TDH-5301s (Nos. 434–438) to be driven immediately to Edmonton from the Pontiac, Michigan, plant. The model's distinctive slanted windows and fluted aluminum side panels gave it a streamlined look, and ETS drivers soon were referring to it as the "Silverside." Standee windows running above the main passenger windows contained green glass to reduce heating and glare.

ETS operator Brian Ernest directs the driver of a yellow school bus. (ETS Archives)

ETS Goodwill Ambassadors

The Pipes and Drums of Edmonton Transit were established in 1964 to represent the transit system at public events. After making their first public march during the Canadian Centennial Year, the Pipes and Drums travelled widely in Alberta and abroad, becoming one of the foremost goodwill ambassadors for the city. In 1968 they visited Helena, Montana, to honour the Special Service, also known as the Devil's Brigade, a joint Canadian-American force that distinguished itself during the Second World War. In later years, they also participated at the Commonwealth Games, Universiade and other major events.

ETS Pipes and Drums at the Capital Ex Parade in 2008. (ETS)

The ETS Pipes and Drums performing at the opening ceremony for the Clareview LRT station in 1981. (ETS)

The design of the TDH-5301, known at ETS as the "Silverside" when it was first introduced in 1960. This illustration from promotional material focused on the merits of the hot water heating the bus featured. *(ETS)*

With its seating capacity of 51, the Silverside soon became the staple of the bus fleet. Five more, assembled at the London, Ontario plant, were ordered in June 1962 (Nos. 439–443), and a further 30 (Nos. 444–473) were ordered for delivery the following year. Twenty upgraded TDH-5303 models (Nos. 474–493) joined the fleet in 1964 and another 17 were ordered in 1966, primarily to serve the needs of suburban districts. Smaller buses were kept in the fleet to serve routes crossing the narrow High Level Bridge. ETS ordered 10 GMC models in 1968 and 15 more the following year (Buck; *Edmonton Journal*; *Canadian Transportation*).

Despite the sizeable purchase of new GMC buses, the demands of population growth kept many older buses in service in spite of rising maintenance costs. In 1962 ETS purchased 20 used 38-S and 41-S Twin Coach buses (Nos. 501–520)

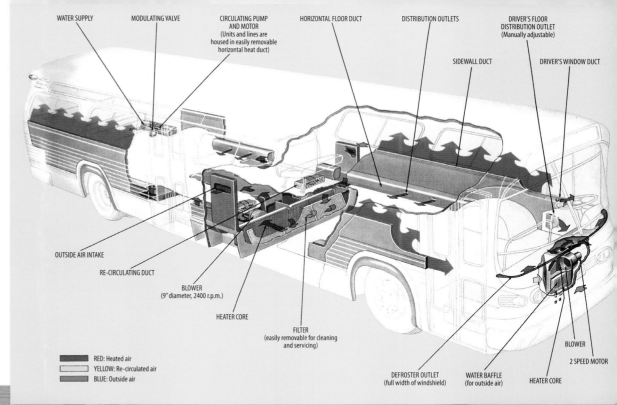

WATER SUPPLY — MODULATING VALVE — CIRCULATING PUMP AND MOTOR (Units and lines are housed in easily removable horizontal heat duct) — HORIZONTAL FLOOR DUCT — DISTRIBUTION OUTLETS — DRIVER'S FLOOR DISTRIBUTION OUTLET (Manually adjustable) — SIDEWALL DUCT — DRIVER'S WINDOW DUCT — OUTSIDE AIR INTAKE — RE-CIRCULATING DUCT — BLOWER (9" diameter, 2400 r.p.m.) — HEATER CORE — FILTER (easily removable for cleaning and servicing) — BLOWER — 2 SPEED MOTOR — DEFROSTER OUTLET (full width of windshield) — WATER BAFFLE (for outside air) — HEATER CORE

RED: Heated air
YELLOW: Re-circulated air
BLUE: Outside air

No. 438, one of the first five GMC TDH-5301 buses, was driven from Michigan to Edmonton in February 1960. *(ETS)*

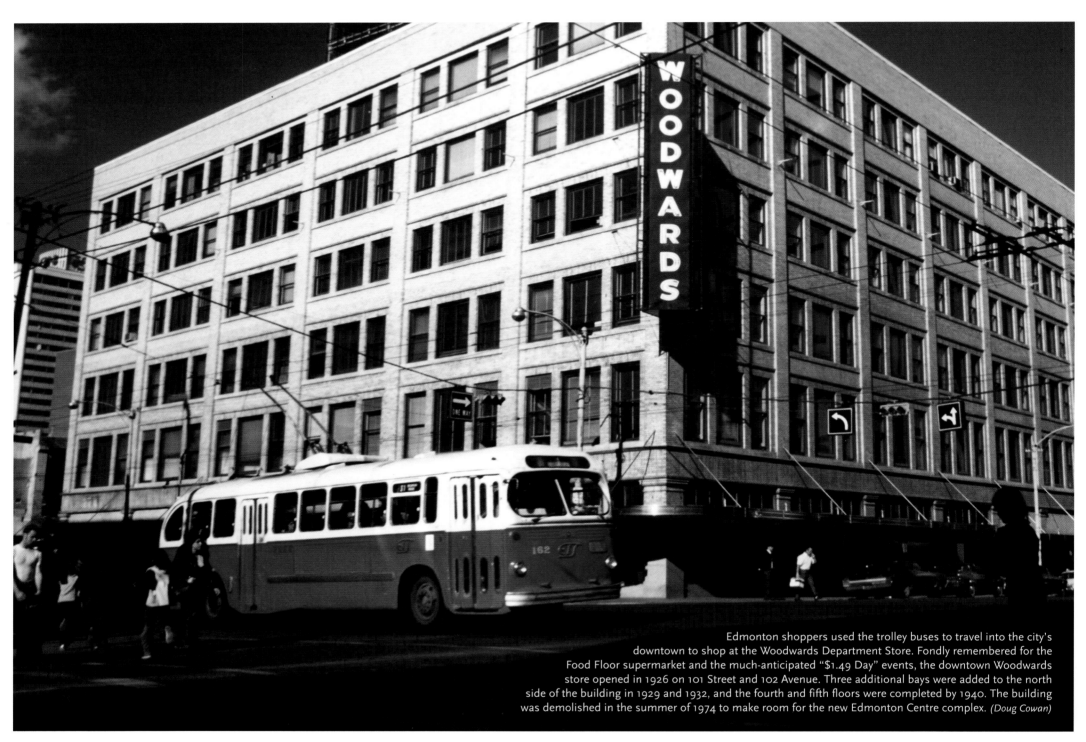

Edmonton shoppers used the trolley buses to travel into the city's downtown to shop at the Woodwards Department Store. Fondly remembered for the Food Floor supermarket and the much-anticipated "$1.49 Day" events, the downtown Woodwards store opened in 1926 on 101 Street and 102 Avenue. Three additional bays were added to the north side of the building in 1929 and 1932, and the fourth and fifth floors were completed by 1940. The building was demolished in the summer of 1974 to make room for the new Edmonton Centre complex. *(Doug Cowan)*

JUST ARRIVED!

Edmontonians will experience the ultimate in modern bus transportation this week when three Japanese custom-built buses will be placed in service on city routes.

The proto-type buses were purchased by the Edmonton Transit System in a recent transaction with Mitsui & Co. Ltd., of Japan. The acquisition is the first of its kind made by ETS for transportation vehicles. Current and past vehicles have been of Canadian design and manufacture.

Nissan Motors Ltd., Japan, designed and manufactured the new buses specifically for Edmonton's transportation needs and it is hoped that they will prove superior to models now in use. If they do, taxpayers will not only enjoy more efficient, comfortable bus transportation but also reap the benefits of more economical operational costs for such vehicles. The price tag for one of the new Japanese manufactured buses is $29,800.00 — which, compared to current prices on Canadian manufactured vehicles, is considered a bargain.

from the Winnipeg Transit System to alleviate rush-hour congestion. Older Twin Coach 44-S and 45-S models were kept in the fleet by converting them to air suspension to improve ride and reduce maintenance costs. Only gradually throughout the decade could ETS phase out the old C-36 gasoline buses, Mack C-37DT diesels, Twin Coach FLP-40 propane buses, and several Twin Coach 38-S and 41-S models (Buck; *Edmonton Journal*).

While having made a significant commitment to expensive GMC rolling stock, mostly imported from the United States, Superintendent MacDonald recommended that other better-priced foreign models not be overlooked in fleet expansion planning. Among coaches tried in small numbers was a Mitsubishi-Fuso model purchased in 1964. Powered by a rear-mounted four-stroke V-8 engine with an improved heater suitable for western Canada, it was painted in a special ETS colour scheme and designated No. 10. While powerful, the engine was prone to breakdown, and with parts difficult to obtain, the Mitsubishi-Fuso proved unsatisfactory. Nissan Motor Company also provided a prototype, model 6RLA110-K2, to ETS specifications, and three (Nos. 601–603) were ordered in April 1964 with a further 10 modified versions delivered in 1965. In May 1964, the British Daimler and Duple companies produced another prototype (SRC6), and after trying three prototypes (Nos. 701 to 703), ETS purchased 25 for delivery in 1966. Finally, a Western Flyer bus, model D700A (No. 700), manufactured in Winnipeg, was ordered in June 1969. While the only purchase from the company at this time, the Flyer proved reliable and would play a larger future role with ETS, especially as trolleys were replaced in the 1970s. (Buck).

One of the ten Nissan 6RLA110-K2 diesel buses in the second order that remained in service with ETS from 1966 to 1974. *(Doug Cowan)*

Teaching General Motors a Lesson

Rick Paul described the situation with the experiment designed to cut costs by cutting out GM: "Daimler and Nissan buses were here when I started in 1965. Due to training and parts issues, each type of bus was kept in one garage. The Daimlers operated out of Scona and the Nissans out of Westwood.

"The powers that be at the time were annoyed with GM for charging too much. GM wouldn't negotiate the prices. So Edmonton Transit said, "Fine, we'll teach you a lesson," [and they purchased the Daimler and Nissan busses instead.] I don't know how naïve they were because no one teaches GM a lesson. The Daimler and Nissan buses were a piece of junk and were gone within ten years.

"The purchase dates and retirement dates of these units tells the final story—what was saved and what was lost in short life for the import buses:

"1964 – 3 Nissans
       (retired 1973);

"1966 – 10 Nissans
       (retired 1974);

"1966 – 3 Daimlers
       (retired 1973);

"1967 – 25 Daimlers
       (retired 1973–74)
(Paul)."

In 1967 the experiment with Japanese and British buses was abandoned. Superintendent MacDonald lamented that all had experienced technical problems and that a "great deal of development must be accomplished to provide suitable equipment to meet the stringent requirements of bus operation here" (Buck). As a result, the ETS turned again to GMC and ordered another 25 TDH-5303 models in November 1966 (Nos. 511–535), which were delivered in 1967 (Buck).

Daimler No. 701, a diesel prototype, on display at the Northwest Trade Fair in May 1966. *(Provincial Archives of Alberta PA744.22)*

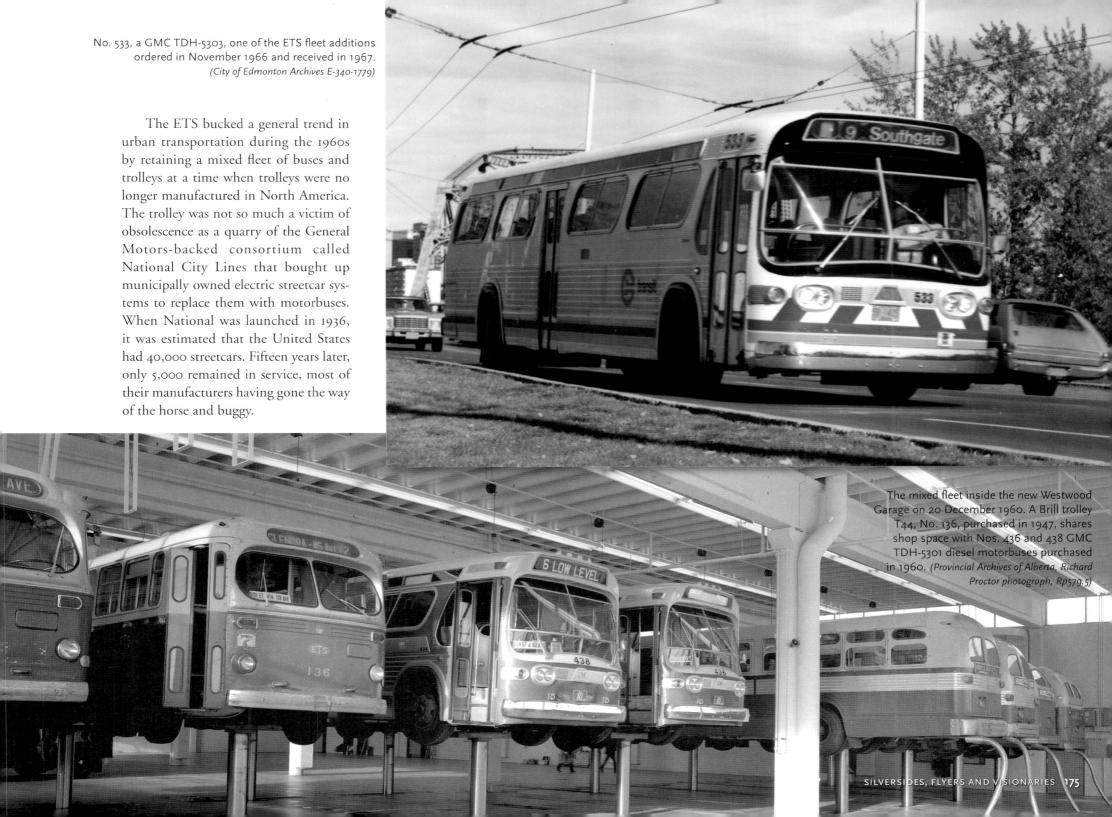

No. 533, a GMC TDH-5303, one of the ETS fleet additions ordered in November 1966 and received in 1967.
(City of Edmonton Archives E-340-1779)

The ETS bucked a general trend in urban transportation during the 1960s by retaining a mixed fleet of buses and trolleys at a time when trolleys were no longer manufactured in North America. The trolley was not so much a victim of obsolescence as a quarry of the General Motors-backed consortium called National City Lines that bought up municipally owned electric streetcar systems to replace them with motorbuses. When National was launched in 1936, it was estimated that the United States had 40,000 streetcars. Fifteen years later, only 5,000 remained in service, most of their manufacturers having gone the way of the horse and buggy.

The mixed fleet inside the new Westwood Garage on 20 December 1960. A Brill trolley T44, No. 136, purchased in 1947, shares shop space with Nos. 436 and 438 GMC TDH-5301 diesel motorbuses purchased in 1960. *(Provincial Archives of Alberta, Richard Proctor photograph, Rp579.5)*

As a result, the ETS was obliged to purchase used surplus rolling stock as other cities divested themselves of their trolley fleets. Ten used T-44 trolleys were purchased in 1962 from the British Columbia Electric Company. The T-44s, built in 1947, were similar to trolleys Nos. 131–177 with a few modifications. Four years later, 10 more surplus 1949-model T-44s were purchased from the Regina Transit System, while another 15 came from Winnipeg in 1969 to provide parts for the trolleys remaining in the ETS fleet. The fleet list numbers suggest that some of the Regina trolleys were in good enough shape to be used in the system as rolling stock, not just as parts. Keeping the trolleys on the streets allowed the ETS to finally retire the last Macks, Pullman-Standards and two ACF-Brills by 1966. The Canadian Car and Foundry trolleys were upgraded with air suspension systems between 1960 and 1964 (*Edmonton Journal*; Buck; *Edmonton Transit News*).

As the bus fleet grew substantially in the 1960s, the need for garages in more outlying areas became critical. The Westwood Garage, completed in 1960, was expanded to accommodate 200 buses in the spring of 1968. (That September it would also serve as a garage and repair facility for the Can-Am racecars when they came to town.) The Westwood extension allowed more vehicles to be housed at the Cromdale Garage, and with the completion of the Davies Shop in 1967, the ETS began catching up on the backlog of fleet maintenance (ETS *Annual Report* 1968).

Labour relations reached a low point when ETS members of the Amalgamated Transit Union went on strike in mid-August 1969. W.L. "Bill" Mack, president of Local 569, stated that the City had triggered the strike by shortening their agreement by four months, and insisted that wages and benefits were not an issue. Other union officials, however, pointed to wage parity with the Edmonton Police Department as a concern. Transit workers, they claimed, had been losing parity since 1940. The strikers, wearing distinctive arm- and hatbands, attempted to prevent non-union members from crossing picket lines at four ETS offices and garages.

Amalgamated Transit Union picketers at the Westwood Garage on 15 August 1969. *(Provincial Archives of Alberta J364.1)*

Westwood Garage

Westwood Garage in 1960.
(City of Edmonton Archives EA-97-461)

Construction on Westwood Garage on 107 Street and 120 Avenue commenced in October 1959, but workers immediately encountered problems with the excavation that delayed its completion until 1 December 1960. The building was designed under the supervision of William Telfer, Assistant City Architect, with Bennett and White Alberta Ltd. as the general contractor. The Westwood Garage was an impressive structure with a vast storage area covered with distinctive 58-foot clear spans designed to allow the parking and turning of the large buses dominating the fleet during the 1960s. It also included an isolated fuelling station and administrative offices.

Robert (Bob) Lane shouldered the responsibility of managing the new Westwood Garage. Lane had started with the ERR in 1926, spending two decades as a streetcar operator and another six years as a trolley driver. After some time as a relief inspector and

instructor, he was named ETS Director of Personnel. Maintenance was under the direction of John Elock, an RCAF aero-engine mechanic who began work for the transit system in 1945. Another RCAF veteran, F.J. (Jack) Dorsey, the engineering assistant to Superintendent MacDonald, was responsible for the smooth operation of all the mechanical equipment within the transit system, and during the construction of the garage, he supervised equipment installation. Jack Dorsey was born in Iroquois Falls and later moved to Innisfail, where he was educated. After five years in the RCAF as an airframe mechanic, Dorsey studied aeronautical engineering at the Calgary Technical School. After working for several years with Northwest Industries and A.V. Roe, he arrived in Edmonton in 1952 to work again for Northwest Industries. In 1953 he joined ETS as engineering assistant to the Superintendent *(Edmonton Journal)*.

Assistant City Architect William Telfer supervised the design of the Westwood Garage and established a cutting-edge modern look for ETS. *(Provincial Archives of Alberta, Richard Proctor photograph, Rp579.1)*

ETS Advertising Takes a New Twist

ETS advertising during the 1960s became more sophisticated than the self-serving appeals of early eras. The new pitch appealed not so much to supporting survival of a city utility as to touting the personal benefits of public transit to citizens. Advertising focused on themes of safety, economy, accessibility and convenience, and the transit user was now depicted as the modern urban sophisticate. The new ad campaigns also linked public transit to cultural and recreational activities Edmontonians loved.

The economy of public transit over the private automobile was featured in another ad in *The Edmontonian*.
(*City of Edmonton Archives*)

The stress of commuting in private automobiles was contrasted with the relaxation of the transit experience in another ad in *The Edmontonian*.
(*City of Edmonton Archives*)

The ETS could provide easy access to special events, including cultural exhibitions such as art displays like this one held at Meadowlark Shopping Centre.
(*City of Edmonton Archives*)

During the 1960s, *The Edmontonian* ran a series of ETS advertisements stressing the personal benefits to transit riders. This advertisement is explicit in citing the rise in traffic fatalities as a reason to take the bus.
(*City of Edmonton Archives*)

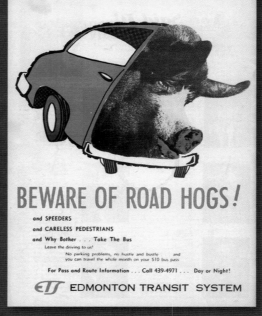

The dreaded "Road Hog" in one issue of *The Edmontonian* was contrasted with the safe, courteous ETS driver in another. (*City of Edmonton Archives*)

GOOD LUCK ESKIMOS

Take the easy, enjoyable way . . . Go ETS to the Eskimo Football Games.

No parking problems, no heavy traffic to fight. Convenient, quick, economical service.

Call 439-4971 for information, 24 hours a day.

EDMONTON TRANSIT SYSTEM *ETS*

Regular routes also serviced events such as Eskimos games, with the ETS depicted as a strong supporter of Edmonton's sports teams.
(City of Edmonton Archives)

Public transit depicted as the perfect, safe transport for couples.
(City of Edmonton Archives)

COMPLETE COMFORT IN 65

MEN'S FASHIONS BY EATON'S

WITH *ETS*

You don't ride on a bus . . .
You ride In it!
And when you ride in an E.T.S. bus . . .
You ride in relaxed, Complete, Comfort!

INCIDENTALLY . . .
Your courteous E.T.S. chauffeur . . .
Gets you there SAFER!

EDMONTON TRANSIT SYSTEM
For information 24 hours a day—phone 439-4971

He's Gone To The Game . . . I Told Him To Take The Bus

This gal knows — there's no worry about parking problems and heavy traffic when you take the bus to the stadium — Courteous ETS drivers take over all these annoyances — chauffeur you comfortably and safely to and from the game

PARKING'S A PROBLEM?

For convenience, safety and economy — she's wise to recommend the bus.

For route and pass information telephone 439-4971

It's Safe, Convenient and Economical to **TAKE THE BUS**

ETS EDMONTON TRANSIT SYSTEM

Taking your wife's advice— always a wise choice.
(City of Edmonton Archives)

YOUR OWN BUS

Here's the easy enjoyable way to go to all the Eskimo Football Games.—CHARTER A BUS—No traffic worries—no parking problems—just convenient, quick, economical service in the company of your friends.

Why not get a group together now—arrange for a Charter Bus from your neighborhood—or from a pre-game supper at your favorite restaurant.

Call **439-4971**—for information and charter service, 24 hours a day.

EDMONTON TRANSIT SYSTEM *ETS*

Charter service was offered as a solution for large parties wanting easy access to public events.
(City of Edmonton Archives)

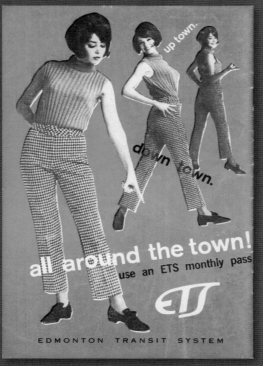

all around the town!
use an ETS monthly pass!
up town. down town.

ETS

EDMONTON TRANSIT SYSTEM

SPECIAL GAL

Who is the special gal?

If she's a housewife, she knows a food special from a bad buy. If she's a career girl, she's well informed on budget-priced clothing. And whoever she is, she knows the best time to go shopping.

She avoids the "lunch bucket" crowd. (The rush to work crowd. The rush to home people). Why not try it yourself. Try the "off peak" bus hours. And you'll find out who the next special gal will be.

She'll be you.

EDMONTON TRANSIT SYSTEM *ETS*

Some ads of the 1960s appealed to the style of public transit users, while others appealed to their intelligence.
(City of Edmonton Archives)

Suddenly, over 50,000 transit commuters had to find other means of getting to work. Staff Inspector George Mitchell arranged to have traffic directed by policemen at major downtown intersections, while Superintendent Don MacDonald, who used the buses, was depicted in the press riding his bicycle to the office in the morning. Service resumed 31 August, just over two weeks after the walkout. Many strikers felt then, as now, that the settlement was an unsatisfactory conclusion after the time and effort expended and the financial loss suffered (*Edmonton Journal*).

While working hard to meet the immediate challenges of growth and labour relations, ETS launched a series of transportation studies early in the decade in an effort to forecast the demand for public transit and respond with a long-term plan. The *Metropolitan Edmonton Transportation Study* (*METS*) was the first of several influential plans that opened the political debate on transit that still occupies the city today.

The *METS* plan, tabled in 1962, predicted that ridership to the downtown would grow from 27 to 35 percent of the Edmonton population by 1980, a tripling of the transit load carried in 1961. The plan proposed to meet the challenge of continuing urban sprawl through a network of new roadways that, in a sense, returned to the familiar structure of the original radial railway. A major freeway would ring the downtown with five freeways radiating out to suburban neighbourhoods. The radial freeways would open up the suburbs in the southeast part of the city via a major arterial thoroughfare through Mill Creek Ravine; in the south, along 110 Street; in the west, via MacKinnon Ravine; in the northwest, via Kingsway and the western perimeter of the airport; and in the northeast, near the CNR tracks. Express buses would travel radial freeways on dedicated bus lanes, while in the downtown, the ETS would literally rise above peak-hour traffic congestion on a series of elevated high-speed roadways dedicated exclusively to public transit. While visionary, the report failed to provide cost estimates for the expressway network and did not address growing traffic problems around the University of Alberta. Nor did it anticipate increasing environmental concerns and the importance of preserving the river valley ravines as unspoiled parkland.

The *Canadian Bechtel Study*, a decidedly different vision for transit in the future, was also was delivered in 1962. The first conceptual exploration of the feasibility of contemporary rapid transit technology, the Bechtel Study proposed a tunnel in the congested downtown core connected to feeder lines to the southeast, the northeast using the CNR right-of-way, the north running along or near 97 Street, the southwest over the High Level Bridge, the west to Jasper Place, and the northwest using the CNR right-of-way. Most importantly, the Bechtel Plan provided specifications for equipment and construction to achieve the highest standard possible.

J.J. Bakker, a transportation engineer and consultant, reviewed both the *METS* and Bechtel proposals in his report *Public Transportation in Edmonton* for City Commissioner S.J. Hampton in January 1968. While Bakker noted that the *METS* was a visionary document, he expressed concern about its lack of cost estimates, solutions for traffic problems around the University of Alberta, and unrealistic ridership expectations. Pointing out that freeway construction in Edmonton was already falling behind schedule, Bakker rejected the freeway proposals at the heart of the *METS* plan, especially the elevated roadways dedicated exclusively to public transit. The "feasibility of the *METS* proposed elevated busways would appear to be open to serious question," he concluded. "It appears that notwithstanding Provincial aid, the finances are not available to implement the freeway proposals as proposed in METS by the year 2000, even though METS suggested 1980." The *METS* was received with some serious scepticism by ETS too, although the ring route and freeway elements of the study would leave a lasting legacy. Bakker also noted that the *METS* ignored the reality that express buses in Edmonton, as in other cities, had not proved profitable and had not attracted park-and-ride users.

Bakker was more supportive of the Bechtel plan. "The proposed Bechtel Rapid Transit Tunnel (or some modification thereof) through downtown would appear to be a practical and relatively inexpensive structure," Bakker concluded, somewhat optimistically. "The City Engineer's Department has a wealth of experience available on tunnelling . . . that should be utilized in the planning, design and construction of any subway tunnel." Though the tunnel sparked continuing civic debate, City Hall decided fairly quickly to approve construction (Bakker).

EXHIBIT 8

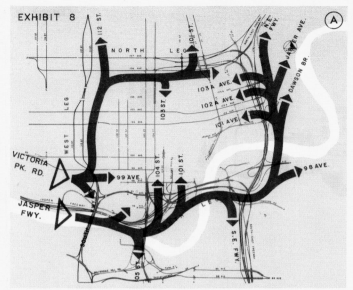

JASPER FREEWAY & VICTORIA PARK RD. TO STUDY AREA

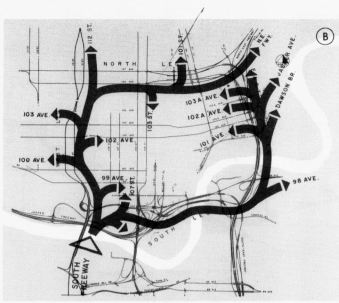

SOUTH FREEWAY TO STUDY AREA

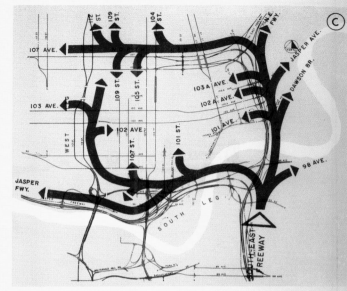

SOUTH-EAST FREEWAY TO STUDY AREA

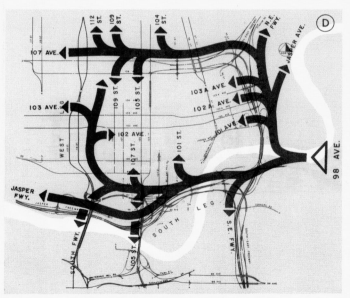

98 AVE. TO STUDY AREA

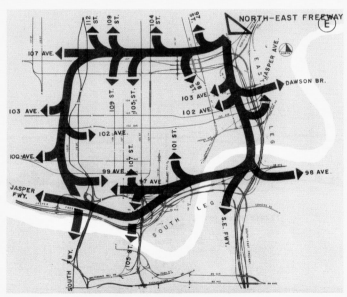

NORTH-EAST FREEWAY TO STUDY AREA

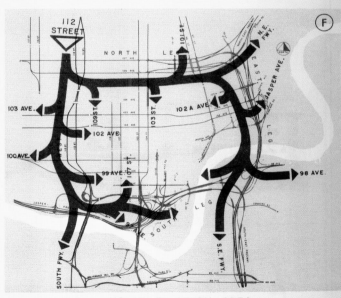

112 ST. TO STUDY AREA

CITY OF EDMONTON
DOWNTOWN FREEWAY LOOP
PRELIMINARY PLANS
PHASE I DEVELOPMENT
TRAFFIC DISTRIBUTION

One plan to relieve downtown traffic congestion envisioned a freeway circling the city centre. *(ETS)*

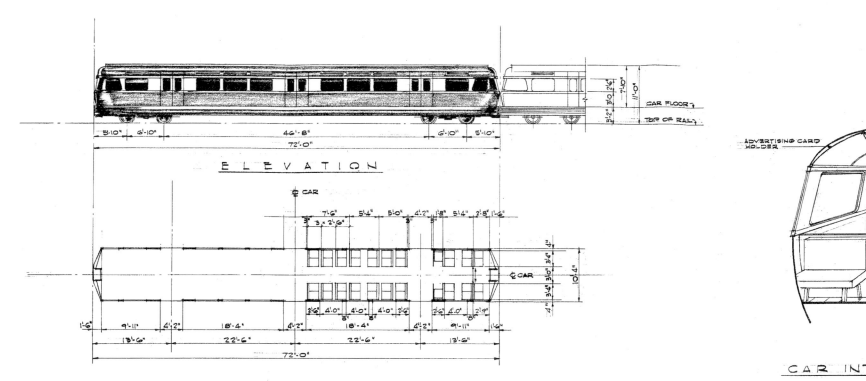

E L E V A T I O N

P L A N

NOTE: SHOWN SEAT LAYOUT TO BE SYMMETRICAL ABOUT SHORT AXIS OF CAR.

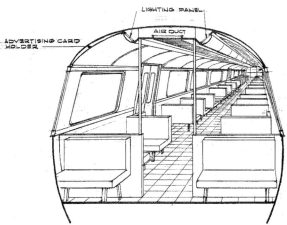

C A R   I N T E R I O R   V I E W

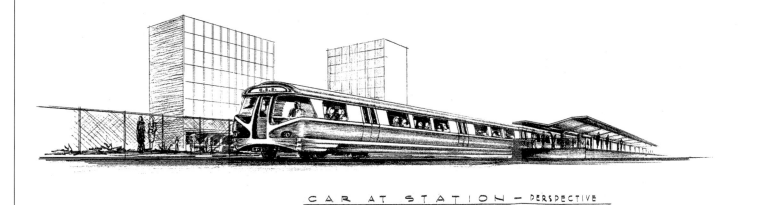

C A R   A T   S T A T I O N — PERSPECTIVE

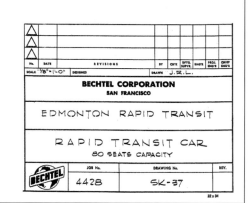

BECHTEL CORPORATION
SAN FRANCISCO

EDMONTON RAPID TRANSIT

RAPID TRANSIT CAR
80 SEATS CAPACITY

JOB No.	DRAWING No.	REV.
4428	SK-37	

Bechtel's plan for rapid transit rolling stock. *(ETS)*

The *Bakker Report* warned that ETS was facing a crisis. "In order to retain its downtown patronage it will have to operate more miles, since the population has moved to the outskirts. . . ." It also stressed that "vehicular interference," especially downtown, was slowing the transit system's service delivery. "New and unproductive areas have to be served by transit as a matter of policy. However, the patronage does not satisfy the present criteria that the transit riders should be paying for their service through fares (or that 'the transit system should not have a large deficit')." Bakker urged that a larger portion of the cost be borne by the casual rider rather than the regular transit user (Bakker).

The *Bakker Report* hit a responsive chord in its conclusion that "The early establishment of a rapid transit line would provide the opportunity at this stage of Edmonton's development of encouraging concentrations of development along [the] southwest–northeast corridor line. This line would also give the opportunity to provide the system with feeder buses and private cars." The provision of large park and ride lots along the route, Bakker concluded, would allow public transit to finally "cater to the automobile age" (Bakker).

In an effort to integrate elements of both the *METS* and Bechtel proposals into high-density development for the city centre, the *Downtown Plan* of 1963 recommended exclusive transit lanes on Jasper Avenue, 101 Street and 102 Avenue; one-way streets and a bus pedestrian mall on 102 Street between Jasper Avenue and 102 Avenue; and additional exclusive pedestrian ways.

Some of these plans were implemented. The one-way system, introduced on 2 July 1967 in the downtown core, brought some alleviation of congestion. Bakker cautioned, however, "[It] should be realized that high density development is continuing faster than expected. . . . The traffic congestion will therefore continue to increase and in turn will increase the frustration of the motorist and also of the transit system in providing a reasonable and regular service" (Bakker).

In addition to the *Downtown Plan*, the city's *General Plan* for 1967 projected that by 1974 Edmonton would reach the minimum requirements for rapid transit as defined by the American Transit Association. These criteria included a metropolitan population of 500,000 with an urban core

of 80,000 and an estimated travel time from home to work of 30 minutes or more. The *General Plan* advocated that existing rail facilities be used for mass transit, including the Calder Yards and the CPR southeast branch. Bakker's response warned that "employment centres that have adequate free parking facilities like in the South-East are not attractive for rapid transit. . . . Rapid transit can only compete to areas of high density employment surrounded with [sic] an area of traffic congestion, and with a parking shortage." A southeast line could be successful only if high-density residential areas were developed in the area, he noted. Finally, Bakker observed that while the *General Plan* and the *METS* presumed traffic distribution to the city centre of 73 percent by private car and 27 percent by transit during peak rush hours, the City had, in fact, pegged public transit's portion at closer to 50 percent (*The General Plan*).

A signal moment in ETS history occurred in 1967 when City Council approved a high-capacity rail rapid transit link along the Canadian National Railway's right-of-way from Edmonton's northeast to the downtown. Superintendent MacDonald reported in 1968 that the route would not serve areas covered in the *METS* freeway construction proposal "until much later than the 1980–85 target dates when it had been indicated that these facilities would be required." MacDonald felt this represented "a reasonable and simple approach toward the goal of providing 'balanced transportation' for the citizens of Edmonton . . . at least cost for the system." It was hoped this project could be coordinated with the CNR Redevelopment Scheme, expected to commence in about two years time.

Secrecy was maintained while property around the planned stations required for park and ride lots could be assembled. At the same time, the City tried to acquire heavy transit vehicles used for the Canadian Centennial World's Fair, but when Montreal retained the vehicles, Edmonton was obliged to move definitively toward light rail transit. Plans called for the first rapid transit line to be operational by 1973 (*Annual Report*).

A rapid increase in funding was required to sustain service, overcome inflation and maintain an adequate fleet during the 1960s. Between 1961 and 1968, Edmonton City Council passed 10 bylaws authorizing over $8 million for ETS extensions, a new garage, extensive electrical and mechanical installation and equipment, and architectural and engineering costs (City of Edmonton Archives). City Council passed several bylaws throughout this decade for ETS service extensions: $900,000 was authorized in March 1961; in November 1961, an additional $200,000; another $500,000 in March 1962; a further $1 million in May 1963; in May 1964, $200,000 was approved; in November 1964, $500,000; and $1.5 million was authorized in May 1965. In November 1965, Edmonton City Council passed a bylaw to authorize $1.35 million in transit funding for a new ETS garage, extensive electrical and mechanical installation and equipment, and architectural and engineering costs. In February 1967, another bylaw authorized a further $1.2 million for ETS extensions. And in 1968, $515,000 was authorized for further extensions.

As the 1960s drew to a close, the City and ETS could look back with some satisfaction on a decade that had transformed urban and transit planning. After half a century of remaining perpetually reactive in the face of progress and growth, city planners and politicians had finally taken the initiative. By all appearances, the ETS was finally catching up and was prepared for the future. But as the 1970s approached, an international oil crisis would propel Edmonton and Alberta into another unforeseen feverish boom when the best laid plans of transit would be sorely tested once again.

Works Cited

Bakker, J.J. *Public Transportation in Edmonton*, for City Commissioner S.J. Hampton, January 1968.

Buck, George H. *A Technological History of Municipally Owned Public Transportation In Edmonton: 1893–1981*. Edmonton, Alberta: University of Alberta Thesis, 1985, pp. 490–92; 495; 498–502; 506–07; 508; 509–10; 582–85; 586.

Canadian Transportation. February 1960.

City of Edmonton Archives. Bylaws, Boxes 8–9, RG8/A96/203.

City of Edmonton. *The General Plan*, August 1967.

Edmonton Journal. 25 January 1960; 25 February 1961; 3 November 1962; 15 August 1969.

Edmonton Transit News. Vol. 3, No. 11, November 1975.

Edmonton Transit System. *Annual Report*, 1968.

MacDonald, Edmonton Transit System, *Report on the Present Operation of the Edmonton Transit System with a View to Determining a Policy for the Future Operation of the System*. August 1961, p.4, 24–29.

Paul, Rick. Communication to Ken Tingley, 2008. Edmonton, Alberta: ETS Archives.

The Edmontonian. Vol. 1, No. 49 1964; Vol. 2, No. 4, 1964; Vol. 2, No. 11, 1964, p. 29; Vol. 2, No. 17, 1965; Vol. 2, No. 21, 1965; Vol. 2, No. 35, 1965; Vol. 3, No. 3, 1965; Vol. 3, No. 4, 1965; Vol. 3, No. 25, 1966; Vol. 3, No. 44, 1966; Vol. 4, No. 27, 1967; Vol. 5, No. 21, 1968.

CHAPTER 12

Here Come the Seventies

1970–79

ere Come the Seventies, a popular Canadian documentary television series, set the tone of the new decade with confident predictions that technological marvels would transform the future. The baby-boomer generation was entering the work-force in record numbers, and their youth and exuberance provoked change at every turn.

Early in the decade, the Progressive Conservative Party, under the charismatic leadership of the 43-year-old Peter Lougheed, swept to power, ending 36 years of unin-terrupted Social Credit government. In a prescient move, the new governing dynasty was quick to further the development of oil and natural gas resources. Two years later, when the Organization of Oil Producing and Exporting Countries (OPEC) embargo sent crude oil prices into the stratosphere in Europe and North America, Edmonton was thrust onto the national stage to a degree not seen since the Second World War.

The city rode the crest of a superheated economy throughout the 1970s, attract-ing thousands of new workers and striving to meet the demands of a rapidly increas-ing population. Seventy-six thousand new citizens, an increase of 18 percent, swelled the city's population in the decade. Downtown growth accelerated swiftly with the construction of 26 high-rise towers. The initial phase of Edmonton Centre opened in May 1974, while other buildings in the heart of the city sprang up to the west of Churchill Square. The new Law Courts opened on the square in 1972, and the striking Citadel Theatre opened four years later.

Edmonton's downtown skyline, looking north from the river valley, in the 1970s.
(City of Edmonton Archives EA-340-496)

A bustling Jasper Avenue in 1970, as passengers disembark from buses lined up on the Klondike Days Parade Day. *(Provincial Archives of Alberta J510.2)*

The James Macdonald Bridge opened in October 1971 as the culmination of a series of new bridges to handle the rising influx of suburban commuters into the downtown, and shopping centres became a feature of their drives home. In 1970 the new Southgate Shopping Centre was advertised as the largest west of Toronto; in August 1972, the Londonderry Mall did it one better—or at least one bigger.

The new Edmonton Coliseum (now called Rexall Place) opened in November 1974. With the opening of Commonwealth Stadium in 1978, Edmonton became the centre of wave after wave of sporting achievement that soon had the city billed as the City of Champions. Following in the winning tradition of the Edmonton Flyers and the Edmonton Oil Kings, the Alberta Oilers came to town in 1972 as one of the founding franchises of the new World Hockey Association. The renamed Edmonton Oilers soon would become one of the proudest standard bearers for the city. The Edmonton Eskimos, after languishing for some time, burst back onto the scene, winning five consecutive Canadian Football League Grey Cups starting in 1978.

Trolleys parked at Jasper Avenue and 110 Street on Parade Day for the annual Klondike Days Festival. *(Provincial Archives of Alberta J510.1)*

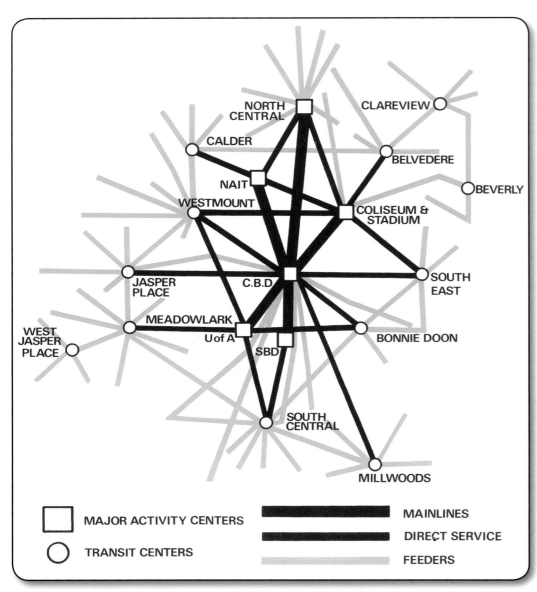

NORTH
CENTRAL

CLAREVIEW

CALDER

BELVEDERE

NAIT

BEVERLY

WESTMOUNT

COLISEUM &
STADIUM

JASPER
PLACE

C.B.D

SOUTH
EAST

MEADOWLARK

U of A

BONNIE DOON

WEST
JASPER
PLACE

SBD

SOUTH
CENTRAL

MILLWOODS

☐ MAJOR ACTIVITY CENTERS   ████ MAINLINES

○ TRANSIT CENTERS   ████ DIRECT SERVICE

                                  ▬▬▬ FEEDERS

The Transit Plan Concept depicting transit centres and connectors linking
major activities (contained in the Transportation Plan Part I adopted by
City Council on 15 July 1974); service plan utilized feeder service and timed
transfers to mainline and direct routes. *(ETS)*

truly comprehensive transportation study synthesized the various reports
prepared for the City between 1963 and 1970 and led to a new chapter in
The City of Edmonton General Plan when the revised Transportation Chapter
was approved in 1973.

The *City of Edmonton Transportation Plan Part I* rejected the costly five
radial roadways and downtown loop recommended by the *Metropolitan
Edmonton Transportation Study* (*METS*) plan. Terry Cavanagh, a City
Alderman at the time, recalled that Council did not consider *METS* as a
serious contender in the development plan. *METS* presupposed "a tremendous amount [of development] in the downtown area. We were going to
have [the roadways] up above, like they do in Chicago, for example. . . .
It never came to anything. More talk than commitment."

The new planning guidelines required consideration of public transportation in the preparation of all new subdivision plans, emphasis on rapid
transit in all future plans, consideration of environmental concerns in all
public transportation planning, and provision for bicycle and pedestrian
routes. Among the specific measures called for were the introduction of
transit centres throughout city, the provision of mainline service between the
transit centres and major trip generators such as the University of Alberta
and the downtown core, provision of Light Rail Transit service to key metropolitan population nodes, and provision of mainline service radiating from
the downtown distribution system. The idea was to provide arterial roadways into and around new developments that were "to meet the objectives of
decreasing the percentage of the daily work trips by private auto to the area."
Corridors were to be protected for future transportation needs, and a city
ring road concept more in tune with emerging conditions than the METS
plan was to be established (City of Edmonton).

The choice of the automobile as Edmontonians' favourite transportation was beginning to be challenged with new priorities for operating
standards. Meeting basic operating standards would be the ETS goal for all
users, no matter where they lived. Standards were to be a function of walking
distances from the passenger's residence or place of work, frequency of service, hours of service, loading conditions, trip times, transfer convenience,
safety and reliability (City of Edmonton).

City planning initiatives of the 1960s began to be implemented in the
1970s. More comprehensive plans followed after the Province passed *The
City Transportation Act* requiring every city to "prepare a comprehensive
transportation study report for the development of an integrated transportation system designed to service the needs of the entire city." Edmonton
City Council then passed *The City of Edmonton Transportation Bylaw* (Bylaw
3655, 23 December 1971, amended by Bylaw 3853, 27 March 1972). This first

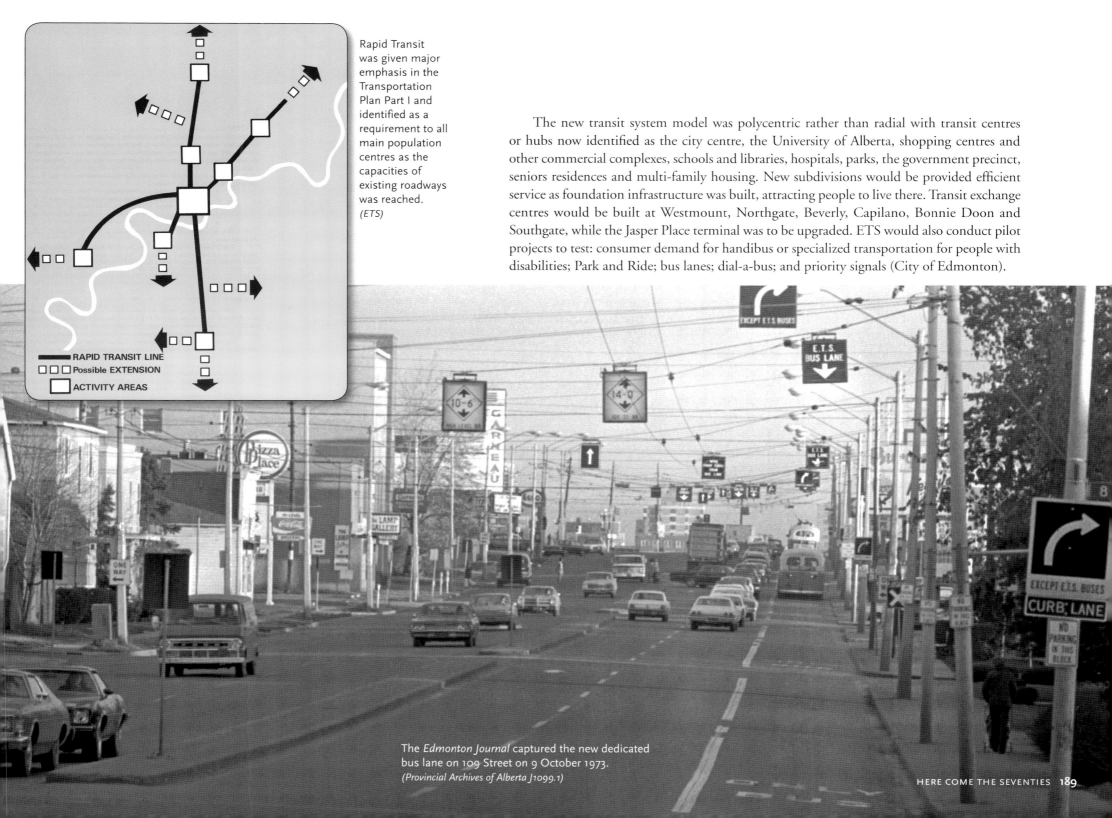

Rapid Transit was given major emphasis in the Transportation Plan Part I and identified as a requirement to all main population centres as the capacities of existing roadways was reached. *(ETS)*

— RAPID TRANSIT LINE
□□□ Possible EXTENSION
□ ACTIVITY AREAS

The new transit system model was polycentric rather than radial with transit centres or hubs now identified as the city centre, the University of Alberta, shopping centres and other commercial complexes, schools and libraries, hospitals, parks, the government precinct, seniors residences and multi-family housing. New subdivisions would be provided efficient service as foundation infrastructure was built, attracting people to live there. Transit exchange centres would be built at Westmount, Northgate, Beverly, Capilano, Bonnie Doon and Southgate, while the Jasper Place terminal was to be upgraded. ETS would also conduct pilot projects to test: consumer demand for handibus or specialized transportation for people with disabilities; Park and Ride; bus lanes; dial-a-bus; and priority signals (City of Edmonton).

The *Edmonton Journal* captured the new dedicated bus lane on 109 Street on 9 October 1973.
(Provincial Archives of Alberta J1099.1)

That's Roadeo—Not Rodeo

Bus Roadeos were an example of how drivers were encouraged to improve their skills to meet the goals set by service standards. The Bus Roadeo was a skill-and situation-based obstacle challenge in which drivers demonstrated and improved their skills through friendly competition.

Bus Roadeo event held with the Commonwealth Stadium in the background. *(ETS Archives)*

The ETS held its first annual Bus Roadeo in the Clarke Stadium parking lot on 13 September 1975, with competition in six categories:

Event 1: competitors with 20-years-service and over. Winners: W. MacLean, H. George, C. Wilson.

Event 2: competitors with 15–19 years service. Winners: B. Todd, F. Stelter, B. Prokopiw, M. Huber, P. Klein, H. Wilkerson.

Event 3: competitors with 10–14 years service. Winners: J. Doucette, E. Burke, G. Nadema, R. Fester.

Event 4: competitors with 5–9 years service. Winners: L. Dettman, G. W. McKee, G. F. McNee, A. Wuschenny, M. Hanson, K. Ruth, A. B. Wildeboer.

Event 5: competitors with under 5 years service. Winners: G. Kennedy, G. Beattie, J. Wishman, R. Aslin, D. L. George, D. Tiedmann, G. Kjar, J. Dunbar.

Event 6: Grand Championship. Winners: W. MacLean, B. Prokopiw, E. Burke, L. Dettman, D.L. George *(Edmonton Transit News)*.

Mayor Bill Smith driving a bus in the 2001 Edmonton Bus Roadeo. *(ETS Archives)*

Bus Roadeo events in 2001 with the Coliseum (now Rexall Place) in the background. *(ETS Archives)*

Edmonton Transit operators compete in the 1978 National Bus Roadeo in Toronto, Ontario. *(ETS Archives)*

DATS Comes to Edmonton

Specialized transportation for people with disabilities followed a roundabout journey before it was fully integrated into Edmonton Transit operations. The Edmonton Handi-Buses Association applied for and received a Local Initiatives Program grant to operate two special vehicles to transport physically disabled adults to work, medical clinics and schools. This service operated between 1 January and 30 June 1974. Greg Latham, who worked at Edmonton Transit from 1973 until leaving as Transit Manager in 1994, worked on special projects and helped launch the DATS service. He praised the experiment as "the first of its type in North America" (ETS Centennial Interviews).

Ken Thomas was a leader in the local movement that galvanized the public and political determination necessary to establish the Disabled Adult Transportation System (DATS) in Edmonton. "I remember the day I took part in my first protest outside City Hall in July 1974," he recalled.

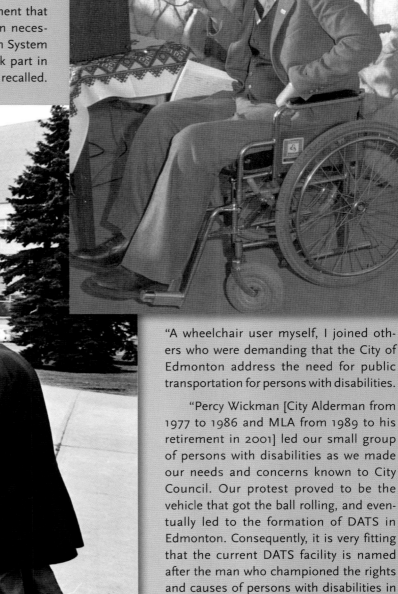

Percy Wickman. *(City of Edmonton Archives EA-289-85)*

"A wheelchair user myself, I joined others who were demanding that the City of Edmonton address the need for public transportation for persons with disabilities.

"Percy Wickman [City Alderman from 1977 to 1986 and MLA from 1989 to his retirement in 2001] led our small group of persons with disabilities as we made our needs and concerns known to City Council. Our protest proved to be the vehicle that got the ball rolling, and eventually led to the formation of DATS in Edmonton. Consequently, it is very fitting that the current DATS facility is named after the man who championed the rights and causes of persons with disabilities in Edmonton" (ETS Centennial Interviews).

Mayor William Hawrelak wheels a passenger into a DATS van at City Hall on 29 April 1975. *(Provincial Archives of Alberta J1847)*

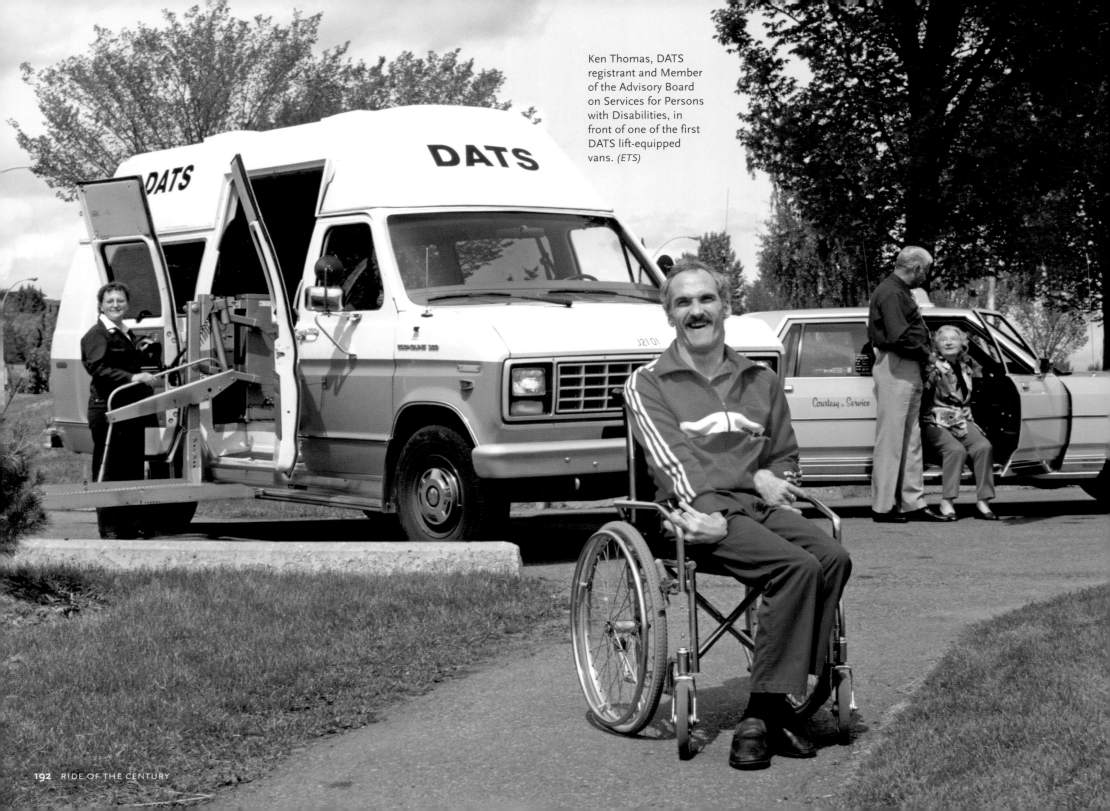

Ken Thomas, DATS registrant and Member of the Advisory Board on Services for Persons with Disabilities, in front of one of the first DATS lift-equipped vans. *(ETS)*

Following this early experiment in service for disabled riders, City Council passed a motion authorizing a feasibility study to examine the possibility of developing a "public transportation system specifically designed for the physically handicapped." Aldermen approved the Disabled Adult Transportation System in November 1974, and a two-year pilot project, jointly funded by municipal, provincial and federal governments, was launched in 1975. City Council approved the pilot project and provided interim funding enabling two city operators, the Edmonton Handi-Buses Association and Edmonton Handy Limousine Service, to provide service until the pilot project was initiated. The pilot operated from April 1975 until March 1977 (Stewart; Nowicki).

The mandate of DATS was to provide affordable transportation within the City of Edmonton to physically disabled people, either ambulatory or in wheelchairs, over the age of 16, who could not use regular transit services. Diamond Cab was awarded the first DATS contract in 1974, but the Edmonton Handi-Buses Association took over in June 1975. In 1975 approximately 36,000 trips were provided at a cost of $5.66 per trip. Customers were charged fifty cents per trip.

The arrangement with Edmonton Handi-Buses lasted until 1977. At that time, City Council voted to continue DATS service but moved its management to Edmonton Transit, which received its DATS operational budget from the Social Services Department.

Based on the results of the pilot project (1975–77), City Council and Administration concluded that the proposed service "provides a social service for individuals eligible for this form of transportation," and that "costs and benefits of providing DATS clearly outweigh the costs and benefits of not providing DATS and having handicapped individuals dependent on public assistance." It also was noted that while current capital and operating costs of DATS were carried by the municipal tax base, the province was directly benefiting by cost reductions in social assistance to the physically disabled. The DATS budget was transferred from the Social Services Department to the Transportation Department in 1980.

The first DATS fleet. (ETS)

Edmonton Transportation contracted DATS services to Baxter, Hicks and Stevenson, and Briggs Brothers Student Transportation Ltd. in 1981. By January 1985, three separate DATS services were operating under the two independent contractors, an awkward system that produced some administrative problems. That year DATS implemented a computerized Brokerage Demonstration Project to match individual or group transportation needs with the most appropriate and cost-effective vehicle service available. Under the brokerage system, the City provided the scheduling and dispatching services to improve reliability and cost effectiveness.

The City owned 30 lift-equipped small buses that were operated by contracted drivers; all sedans and some lift-equipped buses were owned, maintained and operated by contractors. DATS driving services were initially awarded to two independent contractors with payment based on hours of service rather than on a flat per-trip basis.

In September 1987, the Edmonton Brokerage Demonstration Project was declared a success on the basis of increased flexibility and improved service response time provided without any increase in the operational budget.

Starting in 1988, payment to contractors reverted to a per-trip basis when analysis showed it would be less costly than the hourly contract option. About the same time, the City awarded contracts on a one-contractor-per-route basis, which was seen as providing a higher quality of service. By mid-1997, delivery of service had been fully converted to a contracted environment with contractors once again owning all vehicles.

The eligibility criteria remained unchanged until September 1987 when the policy was updated to include youth 13 to 15 years of age for travel during off-peak for non-educational purposes. The impact of this change on total ridership was minor, but a significant expansion of the program occurred in May 1989 when City Council approved a change to DATS eligibility to include cognitive or mentally disabled persons.

In 1993 City Council directed the Office of the Auditor General (OAG) to audit the DATS operation.

On 28 September 1993, the OAG tabled its report *Special Investigation Custom Transportation Services (DATS) Transportation Department*. The OAG concluded that DATS provided a higher level of paratransit service at a lower cost of service than most Canadian municipalities. However, the OAG expressed concern about the organization's lack of responsiveness to emerging issues that could rapidly erode the current level of service. In OAG's opinion, the current level of service provided by DATS was not sustainable given the increased demand in service that was forecast in the near future, stagnant levels of provincial funding and municipal budget constraints.

The OAG report contained 25 recommendations to improve the efficiency, effectiveness and economy of DATS, encouraged the creation of a strategic plan, and acted as the catalyst for a future travel-training program. A strategic plan was prepared for the DATS program and approved by City Council in September 1994. The plan identified five major strategic goals, including development of demand management strategies to address short- and long-term funding shortfalls. Foremost were establishing a family-of-accessible-services concept that would see DATS services complemented by the new low-floor buses and other accessibility improvements to the LRT system, and the introduction of community bus service. Funding was granted by Council to pursue development of a travel training program.

In the fall of 1994, public meetings and focus groups were conducted to review future service options for DATS. The public consultation participants agreed on the essential nature of DATS services and supported the family of services and travel training initiatives.

Both the DATS Strategic Plan (1994) and the ETS Horizon 2000 plan (1996) banked on the introduction of low-floor and community buses as key elements of the ETS family of accessible transit service.

In September 1998, the Alberta Labour Relations Board determined that independent DATS owner-operators and their back-up drivers were employees of the City, resulting in DATS drivers, excluding commercial transportation companies, becoming City employees. In October 1998, the Amalgamated Transit Union Local 569 was certified to represent the DATS drivers, and the first collective agreement was executed on 26 April 2000 after going through mediation. The agreement provided employees with benefits and an adjustment to their per-trip remuneration, but maintained other characteristics of the operation such as the vehicles being owned and operated by the employees. This working relationship with the new work group was very unique not only for Edmonton but the paratransit industry.

In 2002 the Office of the City Manager conducted a review of the DATS program. While recognizing that the status quo delivered the most cost-effective service, the review identified two principal reasons for change in the DATS service model: first, the previous model of an employee and contractor owner-operator fleet was characterized by reliability issues with vehicle and driver back-up coverage; and second, the model was unsustainable because of the different remuneration of the ATU Local 569 DATS drivers versus the ATU Local 569 main bus operators.

Several operational models were presented to City Council in the DATS Review, and in early October 2002, Councillors approved the Hybrid Business Model, a blend of public and private enterprise. The lift-equipped vans would be owned and maintained by the City, and operated by City employees paid hourly wages. The sedan and passenger van service would be contracted to private operators.

The second component of the DATS Review—policy considerations—was approved by City Council on 2 July 2002. Thirty recommendations were approved in the areas of patrons' eligibility and certification; operations; governance roles and responsibilities (equitable relationship with the province); the auditor's benchmarking study and a review of the 1994 DATS Strategic Plan implementation. The administration reported back to the Transportation and Public Works Committee on a semi-annual basis on the status of implementation of the recommendations, including the new business model.

The second collective agreement for the DATS drivers, executed on 18 April 2004, provided for transitioning to the new business model, including hourly wages and modified working conditions with an implementation no later than the end of July 2005.

City Council approved capital budget adjustments at the end of April 2004 for the acquisition of a City-owned lift-van fleet and construction of a new DATS facility. The funding for 81 additional lift-equipped vans would complement the existing fleet of 10 City-owned DATS vehicles. The new DATS facility was located at the former Telus maintenance yard at 86 Street and 58 Avenue, where renovations and building additions would convert the facility to a fully operational garage.

The new business model was implemented in July 2005. Coinciding with the new service model was installation of new on-board computer and automated vehicle location/global positioning technology (AVL/GPS) in the City-owned and contracted fleets, and DATS dispatch centre.

Over several years, DATS evolved from a lean operation using independent owner-operators and contracted companies to a high-tech operation with a municipal fleet of lift vans housed in a City-owned garage with service supplemented by contracted sedan and minivan service.

Bill Smith, former Mayor of Edmonton, recalled how DATS service commenced with "a mixed bag of City employees, contract drivers, some people who loaned their vehicles, some [who] didn't. It really was a mess. You didn't have direct communication and responsibility for how [the contractors] operated." He credits the role of the union in integrating DATS with ETS and concludes, "I'm very proud to say that we have the best operation in Canada because it's all part of Edmonton Transit."

DATS now operates out of the Percy Wickman Garage, completed in 2006 and named in honour of the long-serving alderman and MLA who was an advocate for the rights of the cognitive and physically challenged citizens of Edmonton. This innovative service provides convenient, affordable transportation within Edmonton to physically disabled adults, both wheelchair-dependent and ambulatory, over the age of 16, who are unable to use regular transit service. Today, it provides full door-to-door subscription, reservation and charter service to registrants. In 2008 the fare for a DATS trip, which numbered 870,000 per year, was $2.50 one-way.

Technology continues to improve DATS service. The Interactive Voice Response, implemented in May of 2008 (an automated system that calls ahead to clients to alert them that their ride is 10 minutes away), and Trapeze, launched in November 2008 (an automated scheduling package), make the system highly responsive to riders' needs. The addition of the Customer Care Centre, launched in March 2008, pushed customer service satisfaction levels to about 90 percent (Stewart; Nowicki).

Community input has helped shape DATS since its inception. In 1975 the DATS Advisory Committee was created to advise City administration on policy formulation, service planning and operation. The group was comprised of 11 disabled Edmontonians and included representatives from the United Way. The next phase of evolution was the Custom Transportation Services Advisory Board, formed in 1986 with 13 members, including users of the services and citizens at large who provided consumer advocacy and advice on eligibility and service concerns. The Council-appointed board grew to 15 members, before being consolidated in 1994 with the LRT Advisory Board into the Edmonton Transit System Advisory Board. A consumer advocacy group, the DATS Advisory Group, with 12 members, now provides advice to the Manager of Edmonton Transit and Director of DATS.

Percy Wickman Garage. *(ETS)*

The Edmonton Transit System's efforts to enhance service standards benefited from a broad reorganization of City departments that consolidated all urban transportation in the new and enlarged Engineering and Transportation Department. City Engineer George Hodge became the first supervisor, and former planning staff at the ETS formed the core of the new Transportation Planning Branch; D.L. MacDonald, ETS General Manager, became the first director. The main tasks facing the Transportation Planning Branch were another review of the scattered transportation plans commissioned before 1971 and an assessment of the expanding transportation needs of the city. "It is abundantly clear," reported Acting General Manager S.R. Daviss in his 1971 *Annual Report*, "that the public transit system is entering an era where it must play a much greater role in the journeys of citizens within this city if the overall transportation network and its facilities are to effectively cope with Edmonton's continued rapid growth."

As a part of the transit system's efforts to work more closely with all stakeholders, Llew Lawrence, Director of Marketing and Development, launched *Edmonton Transit News,* the monthly newsletter distributed to all ETS employees, in November 1973. "Its purpose," wrote Lawrence, "is to

Local 569 picket line, 29 November 1973.
(Provincial Archives of Alberta J1130.1)

provide a means by which a two-way flow of information between ETS management and ETS employees can take place on a regular basis." Lawrence identified two concerns repeatedly voiced by employees: the need to hear from management about recent developments "instead of having to wait and hear it from the local news media. And, why can't there be a means by which employees' ideas for improvements can be heard, given the consideration they deserve, and put into practice if warranted?" Lawrence credits the newsletter with helping to improve communication within ETS (*Edmonton Transit News*).

While the newsletter was a step in the right direction in improving internal communication, continuing labour discord resulted in the third major strike in ETS history in 1973. The members of Amalgamated Transit Union Local 569 went on strike on 26 November backed by a membership vote of over 92 percent. Workers demanded a 28 percent increase in their average hourly wage to $5.68,

Members of ATU Local 569 on the picket line on 7 December 1973.
(Provincial Archives of Alberta J1135.1)

The ETS strike meeting chaired by Mayor Ivor Dent with Commissioners George Hughes and Phil Walker, and Harold Hill, Director of the Labour Relations Branch, 29 November 1973.
(Provincial Archives of Alberta J1149)

A cartoon in the *Edmonton Journal* expressed public opinion about the inconvenience caused by the strike.
(Edmonton Journal, *ETS Clipping Files*)

"Stop griping — the transit strike can't last forever!"

NORTHWEST EDMONTON

A Christmas shopper hitchhikes home from downtown on 15 December 1973 as the strike drags on.
(*Provincial Archives of Alberta J1140.2*)

while the City was offering just over $5.00. The strike, lasting over 50 days, did not end until January 1974, and it left a legacy of resentment and distrust. Particular vitriol was directed at Chief Commissioner George Hughes, who frequently released City offers through the media, contrary to the stated desire to maintain more direct contact with employees. At the end of the strike, a 31-month contract saw wages increase for drivers to $6.12 by June 1975 and to $7.15 for tradesmen. ATU 569 members were guardedly optimistic about the settlement. The real victory, as noted by one driver in the *Edmonton Journal* on 18 January 1974, was that drivers were worth the money, and were "not puppets to be pushed pulled and pushed around by the Mayor or anyone else."

Fallout from the strike resulted in the formation of the Edmonton Transit Union Management Consultation Committee, a joint employee–management group, in late 1976. Its terms of reference included the promotion of better communications, "mutual respect and understanding throughout the system," the promotion of "harmonious relations" between the union and management, a dialogue concerning ways to improve work conditions and staff development, and the discussion of collective agreements. The first members were R.J. Matthews, W.L. "Bill" Mack, R.H. Garside, B. McLean, L.F. Wiebe, E. Paterson and C.T. Smyth. G. Hodge and G. Harris were co-chairmen. This committee provided further evidence of planning designed to increase employee satisfaction (*Edmonton Transit News*).

The critical importance of long-range planning became ever more evident as ETS ridership surged during the early and mid-1970s. By 1974 the system carried 40 million passengers annually, ranking twentieth in overall North American passenger trips, eighth in total number of annual rides per capita, and first among cities of similar population. That year every man, woman and child in Edmonton made 90 trips yearly on the bus. (The figure was subsequently adjusted upward to 102 rides per capita, far higher than the 77 rides in Calgary.) The ETS fleet included over 380 buses, 525 drivers and a further 170 maintenance workers. There were 470 miles of bus routes on which ETS vehicles accumulated 9 million miles annually. "The overall number of miles driven by ETS buses daily is more than enough to go once around the equator," the *Edmonton Transit News* proudly proclaimed that year. Desmond Liggett, an ETS transit analyst, reported that "more and more people are taking a bus and leaving the gas guzzling, traffic congesting, polluting cars at home, so the sooner the new buses and trolleys arrive, the better." Liggett warned that soon "there won't be any room for the extra people who want to ride the bus" (*Edmonton Transit News*).

More transit vehicles would require more maintenance garages. The ETS assigned Jack Dorsey, Engineering Assistant in the Equipment Section, to initiate planning and supervise construction of the Coronet Garage at 58 Avenue and 87 Street in 1975. (The Coronet facility opened in 1976 and has been renamed for Thomas Ferrier.) Almost every decade had seen construction of a new garage, and the Coronet Garage would exemplify the ideas

Trolley No. 191, a Brill T-44, leaves the garage on 4 January 1974 following the strike. (*Provincial Archives of Alberta J1153.6*)

of the 1970s. After 18 designs were submitted to transit employees for review, the final concept was forwarded to the City Architect. "We asked for lots of windows and they gave us lots of windows," Dorsey reported, "but they used a variety of shapes and sizes, and a variety of outside finishes, so that the outside appearance is extremely pleasing. It isn't a big, flat concrete box." Don Collins was hired by the Architectural Branch to oversee the project on site. "Having been in the business himself," Dorsey observed, "he knows all the dodges and shortcuts that contractors try to get away with to save a nickel." Mark Byrne took over as facility supervisor when Coronet opened (*Edmonton Transit News*).

During the 1970s, ETS planned and implemented important route revisions as part of a coordinated scheme to integrate a light rail transit component in the general strategy, especially in the northeast corridor. Five new routes and six route revisions were implemented on 1 September 1974, providing peak industrial service, especially to the more outlying areas of the city (*Edmonton Transit News*).

Traffic congestion along transit routes led to the first traffic light designated exclusively for ETS use on 111 Street at 57 Avenue. These lights began operating on 24 June 1974. Bus drivers needing to cross 111 Street could now use a remote control to operate the signal. The light would stop traffic on 111 Street for ten seconds, just enough time to make the turn onto 57 Avenue unimpeded by cars. This experiment proved successful, and more such lights would be introduced by ETS (*Edmonton Transit News*).

The environmental benefits of public transit were beginning to be celebrated by the general public during the decade, as this little poem by a satisfied rider suggests.

While many Canadian cities scrapped their trolleys during the 1970s, some major metropolitan centres such as Toronto, Hamilton and Vancouver set another example by rebuilding their lines. Edmonton followed a path between the two extremes. "This return to favour of the electric vehicle has been due in large part to the growing concern for the reduction of air pollution and the conservation of natural resources,"

Don't Cuss the Bus

There's much to be said for, and nothing to dread
    In riding a transit bus.
With no disrespect to the family car,
    It seemingly saves much fuss.
No need to keep your eyes on the road,
    They are free to wander at will.
In the wink of an eye, after heaving a sigh,
    Your thoughts go all willy-nill.
In the rambling, shambling, quaking, shaking,
    Shuffling to and fro'
The tensions which have been building up
    Quite suddenly seem to go.
You are now free to think, or catch forty winks,
    As the driver propels you up hill.
And now if you crash, you can holler "whiplash"
    And not have to pick up the bill.
And then if your goal is pollution control,
    You're sure to chalk up a plus.
Yes, there's much to be said for, and nothing to dread
    In riding a transit bus (*Edmonton Transit News*).

                –Zelta W. Whitfield

Advertising in the 1970s stressed the safety and reliability of the ETS service. Note that one advertisement features a female driver, another change in the 1970s. *(ETS)*

The ETS Flyers hockey team in 1977–78.
(ETS Archives #2.1.5 H1)

Robert "Bob" Clark, Edmonton Transit Development Supervisor, reported in 1973. While the disadvantages of trolleys were acknowledged—vehicle unavailability, high installation costs, routing inflexibility, route shutdown during trolley breakdowns, and aesthetic concerns about trolley wires—several advantages of trolley buses over gas or diesel were identified. These included higher operating speed, lower operating cost, more economical use of fuel, lower noise levels and much lower air pollution (Clark).

Llew Lawrence, Director of Operations and an ardent trolley advocate, weighed in on the issue in a speech presented in the early 1970s. He touched on the difficulties associated with the trolleys, notably the loss of skills in construction and maintenance of overhead lines, the increase in traffic congestion, the length of the trolley buses, and the failure to move switches and curves from outdated locations. But Lawrence also noted an important change that had received little public press but had been most appreciated by operating personnel—the switch to K&M elastic suspension for the trolley overhead lines. This was such an improvement that, with the addition of induction control switches, it was nicknamed "speedwire" by enthusiastic operators (Lawrence).

Edmonton remained committed to the trolley fleet as the workhorse for daily service, but after over 25 years in service, many of the old CCF Brill T-44s had developed structural and other problems associated with age. Facing similar problems in 1970, the Toronto Transit Commission decided to rebuild its trolley fleet rather than convert to diesel buses. The TTC rebuilt the electrical systems and installed them in new bodies supplied by the Western Flyer Company of Winnipeg. Several Canadian cities followed suit, among them Edmonton, which had consulted Toronto since the earliest days of the Edmonton Radial Railway. In 1972 the City received a TTC E10240 demonstration model and purchased 37 of the same model the following year. (These looked virtually identical to the 51 D10240 buses purchased in 1969.) Assembly plant relocation and labour problems at Western Flyer delayed delivery until October 1974 with the final buses arriving in August 1975. ETS then installed the electrical systems at the Davies Shop. When the Calgary Transit System ended its trolley service in 1974, ETS was provided with an additional source of trolley replacement components.

ETS employees expressed their affection for the venerable trolleys, dubbed the Flyers, by changing the name of their hockey team to the ETS Flyers in the spring of 1976 and sporting new sweaters with a crest displaying a new Flyer bus with wings and Local 569 emblazoned on its side (*Canadian Coach*; *Edmonton Transit News*; *Edmonton Journal*).

The ATU 569 Flyers hockey team badge.
(ETS Archives #2.1.5 A1)

The new Flyers, though of tried and tested design, were not without their problems. A three-sided housing on the rear of the roof designed to hold optional air conditioners scraped against trolley ropes, fraying them or actually disconnecting the pole from the wire. Flyer had to design a more streamlined housing to fix the problem. Another irritant was remedied when the old familiar treadle to open central exit doors was replaced by a paddle-shaped gate in 1979 in response to their tendency to stick during cold winter (*Transit Canada*; Buck).

The ETS began to systematically install two-way radios in every vehicle during the mid-1970s in a return, finally, to the experimental use of radios during the Korean War. The ETS, which dropped the *S* and was renamed Edmonton Transit or ET for the period of 1977–97, established its own radio network to assist bus, trolley and LRT operations and security. Each bus now sported a small antenna encased within a plastic dome on the roof.

ET changed its colour scheme and logo in early 1976 in keeping with name change. The design firm of Daly, Gervais, Matthewman recommended a comprehensive integrated visual identity program, including the LRT. The familiar bullet-shaped logo was replaced by a design featuring a directional arrow-tail enclosed in a circle. Edmonton Transit buses were now painted white above their fluted aluminum panels, as well as in areas below the panels. Borders around the windshield were painted black to reduce reflection and glare. The lower parts of the body featured a yellow-and-blue-stripe design. The blue Scotchlight stripes, impregnated with reflective beads to enhance night visibility, were positioned 60 centimetres above the ground to be at the level of auto headlights. Bus numbers were placed directly above front doors and the operator windows, as well as centred above the rear window. The former ETS crest was replaced by a distinctive blue Flying *E* decal, followed by the word *Transit* in black (*Edmonton Transit News*).

A Flyer E10240 trolley near the landmark Irving Kline clock on Jasper Avenue, 7 December 1974, with the optional air conditioner housing.
(Provincial Archives of Alberta J1633)

When the *S* was dropped from the transit system name, a stylized *E* became the new symbol. The Flying *E* was reversed on the street side of each bus, giving the impression that it formed the fletching on an arrow being fired in the direction of travel. The new logo earned the nickname of Pacman for its resemblance to the popular game symbol. *(ETS)*

Edmonton Transit System
Owned and operated by the City of Edmonton

A Flyer on Route 3 featuring the new colour scheme with the bus number painted above the door. It is followed by the 1949 Brill 153, one of the units kept running to support the system during the Commonwealth Games. *(Doug Cowan)*

Trolley No. 202, the T-48A retained as an example of the units that were once a staple of the ET fleet. The trolley is seen here outside the Edmonton Exhibition Grounds with the Northlands racetrack building in the background. *(Doug Cowan)*

The influx of Flyers allowed ET to retire some of its dilapidated Canadian Car and Foundry trolleys, though the process was delayed when some of the old fleet was retained for emergency use during the 1978 Commonwealth Games. The last run was a special charter on 19 November 1978. By the end of the 1970s, ET had the smallest trolley fleet since the end of the Second World War, despite its continuing commitment to trolleys. ET kept two original T-44 trolleys, Nos. 148 and 191, and one T-48A trolley, No. 202. The role of trolleys in the ET fleet would be debated persistently in the next decades and not finally decided until 2008 (Buck).

In July 1976 a joint proposal to investigate the operational and economic feasibilities of using large-capacity articulated buses in Alberta was submitted to the provincial government by Edmonton and Calgary. Funding for the project was approved under the Alberta Urban Transportation Research and Demonstration Program, and a steering committee comprised of representatives from Alberta Transportation, Edmonton Transit and Calgary Transit was established to coordinate the project.

The Steering Committee resolved to evaluate two articulated diesel bus models taken under lease from Sweden's Volvo and West Germany's MAN for a period of 24 months, commencing in September 1977. The study concluded that the buses were suitable for local operating conditions and that significant cost savings could be achieved through system-wide integration of articulated buses. The province, however, felt it was desirable to gain further experience with other articulated vehicles. More tests were conducted in the early 1980s, but it was not until 2001 that articulated buses finally came into service (Keshwani).

The Volvo articulated bus on display at its unveiling in front of City Hall on 19 July 1977. Rick Paul confirmed that the articulated buses did not go into regular service until 2001. (Provincial Archives of Alberta J3491)

The MAN articulated bus, one of the models on trial in the 1970s. *(ETS)*

ET disposed of most of its foreign and prototype vehicles when all the Nissan and Daimler-Duple buses, used only for charters and standby, were withdrawn from service in 1973–74, most having lasted only about a decade. No. 707, a Daimler, was retained as the Infobus. Billed as "a mobile showcase for public transit in Edmonton, past, present and future," the Infobus made its debut in the 1975 Exhibition Parade with a display of Edmonton Transit artefacts and information on current routes and services. It also sported audiovisual displays and stood out through its sparkling white and orange body "with coloured super graphics." All the remaining gasoline and propane-powered Twin Coach buses were retired by the end of 1975, many having served the ETS for over 25 years. More importantly, in 1978 ET sold the entire fleet of General Motors TDH-5105 buses purchased between 1955 and 1958. Only No. 432 was retained as a reminder of that model's contribution to the fleet (*Edmonton Journal*; *Edmonton Transit News*; Buck).

Daimler No. 707 serving as the Infobus. *(ETS Archives)*

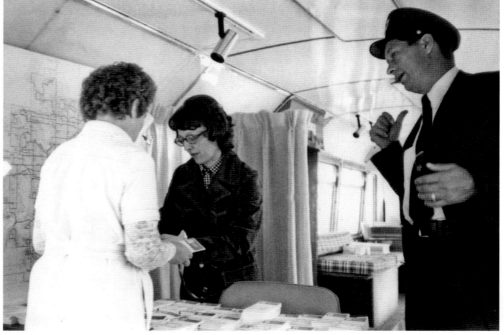

The interior of the Infobus. *(ETS Archives)*

GMC No. 434, a TDH-5301, and GMC No. 583, a TDH-5307N, being prepared for a school field trip at the Westwood Garage, 25 November 1976. *(Provincial Archives of Alberta J2888)*

"Beware the Ides of March." The *Edmonton Journal* recorded GMC No. 317 following a mishap on McDougall Hill after a spring snow on 15 March 1978. No. 317 shows the new logo. *(Provincial Archives of Alberta J3917)*

No. 324 passing the Alberta Legislature around 1974. This bus sports the old ETS logo rather than the new Edmonton Transit symbol. *(Provincial Archives of Alberta Ws350)*

the 1970s led City Council to approve the purchase of 373 more GMC T6H-5307N buses in five years to meet increased demands placed on the transit system. Those ordered in 1975 were equipped with automatic transmissions with three forward speeds. Forty of the 1979 delivery featured digital destination signs instead of the old roller signs so familiar to transit riders over the years. These signs could send messages as well, like the tried and true "Go Oilers Go." Eighteen D10240 Flyers also were added in 1977 (Buck).

Digital signage on buses continued the process of improving vehicle identification that began with the colour coded routes in the early years of the Edmonton Radial Railway. In September 1962, in an earlier effort to improve signage, ETS had designated exclusively north-side routes with the prefix *N* and south-side routes with *S*. Many complaints resulted from

A GMC T6H-5307N with the old roller signage picking up students at the university terminal for the Mill Woods run in 1977. *(City of Edmonton Archives EA-340-1778)*

Superintendent D.L. MacDonald had made the case for standardizing the ETS fleet in 1964, and by 1980, virtually the entire fleet consisted of GMC models, achieving the goal for better or worse. "The motorbus, which had once been intended as a feeder vehicle for streetcar lines and (later) trolley bus lines was now the unquestionable mainstay of Edmonton Transit's passenger fleet," concludes George H. Buck, educator and transit historian.

In 1972, 34 new GMC buses were ordered (Nos. 536–69). The new T6H-5307N buses were similar in appearance to the 5303 model already in service. Catalytic mufflers directed exhaust away from the bus above street level through a vertical stack that worked much better than the early experiments with vertical stacks during the Second World War. The ETS ordered 31 more GMC buses and 10 from Flyer Industries Ltd. (the former Western Flyer Company) in 1974. Extremely rapid urban growth during

No. 936, a GMC T6H-5307N, with the first digital signage.
(City of Edmonton Archives EA-340-1776)

signage that was "too difficult to read—there is confusion between 5, S5, N5 and U5—displays are different between buses on the same route and so on." In August 1975, Bob Clark, Transit Development Supervisor, introduced "the first signs of a radical change which will help our passengers know where we are going without having to check so often with the operator or telephone information service." On N-Day (New Number Day) in 1976, the old "Silversides" and Flyers all got standard sign boxes. Bus routes were renumbered 1 through 99, eliminating the letter prefixes. To avoid the previous confusion, front signs indicated only the terminal on a large curtain. The old white capitals on a black background were replaced by "clear modern lettering in black on a white background." The bus stop signs were redesigned to incorporate the new logo accepted as part of the new ET visual identity program. (Hatcher and Schwarzkopf; *Edmonton Transit News*).

Route Destination Signs to Change to a Total Numerical System.

Why the Change is Being Made:

1. The alphabetical prefix system no longer accurately represents our routes. The combined numbers and letters system was adequate for a small system where N-meant north, S-south, etc., however, with services now operating through two or more sectors of the city, the alphabetical prefixes have led to confusion. A total number route will eliminate this problem.

2. To remove confusion arising from similar numbers, eg. S5 — J5; not knowing what the prefix meant, some patrons assumed that these buses operated in the same vicinity.

How the Change is Being Made:

The changeover is being phased in slowly. All new routes and those routes that have had service improvements made will now carry a straight number designation. The completion of this program is scheduled for early December, 1976.

Initially, the changeover may cause a bit of confusion but once worked out, Edmonton Transit is positive your public transportation system will be easier to use.

We ask for your patience and assistance in this program.

NOTE: Individual Route Brochures for these new services will be available from your bus driver for several days before and after the September 5th service changes. Or you may call Transit Information at 439-6363 and we will drop the brochure(s) in the mail to you.

transit zone

New Transit Zone Sign

The new Transit Zone sign illustrated on the left will replace the existing bus stop sign presently used by Edmonton Transit.

The new Transit Zone sign is another component of the system's visual identity program.

These new Transit Zone signs will begin appearing in downtown Edmonton effective September 5, 1976. The remaining Transit Zone signs will be phased in over the next two years.

Motorist Take Notice:

— under **Bylaw 3100** it is an offence to park, stop or lay over in a transit zone. Disobedience of this law will lead to a stiff penalty.

 Edmonton transit

Public information about the new numbering and logo used on ET signs. *(ETS)*

A bus with roller signage passes through a bus gate at Clareview on 13 February 1979. *(Provincial Archives of Alberta J4450)*

Uniforms Through the Years

Uniforms were updated in 1978 as a part of the ET new look, though the trousers still sported a fob pocket dating to the early days when operators carried pocket watches. ET remained one of the few transit operations to retain this traditional feature.

Murdock McIntyre, who started with the system in 1947, reminisced about the changes: "The blue serge uniform remained almost unchanged from the very first days of the Edmonton Radial Railway. The present uniform was preceded by two other basic designs." The early dark-blue serge uniform featured a military stripe on the trouser leg that was later eliminated and then reappeared. McIntyre recalled that the stripe was not popular when it was reintroduced in the 1950s on light-blue serge uniforms that were worn by operators between the early 1950s and 1978. Transit men usually wore their uniforms socially as well as at work, but this proved difficult with the stripe. "When you think of the wages in those days," he recalled, "the uniform, which used to wear like it was made of steel, was just one of the side benefits that went along with the job." The bulky long overcoat of the early years eventually gave way to more comfortable pea jackets, and still later, nylon parkas. Army khaki was popular in shirts. McIntyre also recalled that streetcar operators after the Second World War often wore US army surplus sheepskin-lined boots in winter *(Transit News)*.

The new ET uniform that appeared in 1978.
Left to right: Dennis Cardall, LRT Inspector;
Vern MacKenzie, LRT Inspector; Don MacDougall,
Surface Inspector. *(Provincial Archives of Alberta J3966)*

Get Me to the Church on Time

ETS driver Daryl Stubbington chartered a bus for his wedding to Janet Highstead in 1976. After first delivering Janet to the church for the ceremony, the bus took the wedding party on a festive jaunt around the city, bedecked for the occasion by the bridegroom *(Edmonton Transit News)*.

ETS driver Daryl Stubbington and Janet Highstead board the decorated bus for their wedding ceremony in April 1976. *(Provincial Archives of Alberta J2386.2)*

ETS bus decked out for the nuptials of Daryl Stubbington and Janet Highstead. *(Provincial Archives of Alberta J2386.3)*

The Kathleen Andrews Story

Kathy Andrews was "turned-in" as the first fully qualified female ETS operator on 8 May 1975. There were a few uncomfortable moments, but she recalls those days mostly with good humour. "At one union meeting, the first one, at the Masonic Lodge, I remember so well all these men around me. And the speaker said, 'Fellow Brothers, and . . . Sister." And everyone turned around to look at me. Well, I laughed."

Although now retired, she recalls, "I still feel like I work for Transit. I'm on the payroll. I still have my payroll number to cash my pension cheque, so as far as I'm concerned I'm still part of the team. I was trained well. I got excellent training at Edmonton Transit. I still drive one school bus part-time. I still wake up at 5:30 in the morning" (ETS Centennial Interviews).

Operator Kathy Andrews takes the wheel in May 1975. She was the first female driver in a system that had resisted the move for some time. *(Kathy Andrews)*

Kathy Andrews at her job in the information office. *(ETS Archives)*

Kathy Andrews was the first woman to become an operator with the ETS. Her son and daughter also drive, bearing out the axiom that the Edmonton Transit System remains a family in many ways to this day. Kathy was born in 1940, in Rochdale, England, just outside Manchester, where her father, a transit driver, taught her to drive. Joseph Smith, her father, was in the National Fire Service during war, while her paternal grandmother and mother owned a little shop on Yorkshire Street. Kathy was born in the family residence above the shop. During her infancy, she took almost nightly trips to the bomb shelters during the Blitz, often in a basket with the dog and cat.

The family immigrated to Edmonton in March 1954 after Kathy's uncle attended a lecture about Alberta and asked, "Why don't we move to Canada? It looks like it's going to blow wide open." The Smiths first lived in Oliver, where Kathy attended Oliver Jr. High School and swam competitively under coach Dave Sissons at Oliver Swimming Pool. Later in life, as a single mother of two, she went to City Personnel to seek a job opening. She was directed to Transit, where the restrictive employment bans had just been lifted. When she contacted Llew Lawrence, he encouraged her to apply as a driver, and she was transferred over from the City Information Department, where, at her request, she was trained and worked briefly.

Edmonton became more integrated within its expanding metropolitan area during the 1970s. The City of St. Albert launched bus service to Edmonton, painted in its own distinctive colours, but with the system operated, stored and maintained by ET personnel. In the interest of uniformity, St. Albert chose the same GMC T6Hl-5307N buses by now quite familiar to Edmontonians. The County of Strathcona began operating 10 of the same model GMC buses under a similar arrangement in 1977. These new routes to outlying regions fulfilled in some measure the early interurban railway dreams of the Edmonton Radial Railway (Buck).

The decade would end on an upbeat note. Edmonton's Light Rapid Transit system, the first of its kind in Canada, began operation in April 1978, ready to carry the throngs of sports fans to the official opening of Commonwealth Stadium and the XI Commonwealth Games held 3–12 August 1978. The city basked in the international limelight. Local champions such as Graham Smith, Cheryl Gibson, Diane Jones-Konihowski and John Primrose proved that Edmontonians had the right stuff.

Edmonton prizes its magnificent river valley and ravines, and in July 1978, in time for the Commonwealth Games, Capital City Recreation Park opened. This ambitious project brought more people into the valley to walk, run, cycle, picnic and play team sports. Mayfair Park, later renamed Hawrelak Park, had opened in 1967 to form the cornerstone of the project that, among other things, forestalled the use of the river valley and its tributary ravines as rapid traffic throughways, although not until after some very heated debates.

The 1970s was a decade of rapid change for the ETS during which the LRT was finally launched and special services such as DATS began to meet the special needs of transit passengers. Amidst all the change, a concerted effort was made to coordinate the planning, design and maintenance of the public transit system into the larger scheme urban planning. Through a series of studies and departmental reorganizations, the ETS emerged as a full partner with other City departments in shaping the future. The momentum achieved in the previous decade gained force in the 1970s and would achieve its fullest expression in the decades to come.

The Light Rail Transit train with Commonwealth Stadium in the background. *(City of Edmonton Archives EB-28-1612)*

Works Cited

Andrews, Kathleen. ETS Centennial Interviews, 2007–08. Edmonton, Alberta: ETS Archives.

Buck, George H. *A Technological History of Municipally Owned Public Transportation In Edmonton: 1893–1981.* Edmonton, Alberta: University of Alberta Thesis, 1985, pp. 513–14; 515; 518–28; 529; 591; 592–93.

Canadian Coach. June 1971; February 1972; May/June 1973.

Cavanagh, Terry. ETS Centennial Interviews, 2007–08. Edmonton, Alberta: ETS Archives.

City of Edmonton, Engineering and Transportation Department, Transportation Planning Branch. *The City of Edmonton Transportation Plan Part I,* June 1974, pp.1–40; 41–62.

Clark, Robert R., Transit Development Supervisor, Edmonton Transit System, Transit Development Section. "Comparison of Trolley and Diesel Buses," *Report No. 1,* November 1973.

Dorey, Margaret. Communication to Ken Tingley, 2008. Edmonton, Alberta: ETS Archives.

Daviss, S.R. *Edmonton Transit System Annual Report,* 1971, pp. 2–3.

Edmonton Journal. 6 January 1973; 18 January 1974; 1 August 1975.

Edmonton Transit News. November 1973; February 1974; May 1974; June 1974; November 1974; June 1975; July 1975; August 1975; October 1975; January 1976; March 1976; April 1976; May 1976; September 1976; October/ November 1976; November 1978;

Hatcher, Colin K., and Tom Schwarzkopf. *Edmonton's Electric Transit: The Story of Edmonton's Streetcars and Trolley Buses.* West Hill, Ontario: Railfare Enterprises Limited, 1983, p. 167.

Keshwani, Salim. "Articulated Bus Demonstration Project," *Transit News,* Vol. 10, No. 1, Spring 1983, pp. 14–16.

Latham, Greg. ETS Centennial Interviews, 2007–08. Edmonton, Alberta: ETS Archives.

Lawrence, Llew. "Why Have Trolley Buses?" *Transit News,* Vol. 9, No. 4, November/December 1983, p. 1.

Nowicki, Dennis. ETS Centennial Interviews, 2007–08. Edmonton, Alberta: ETS Archives.

Stewart, Jim. Communication to Ken Tingley, 2008. Edmonton, Alberta: ETS Archives.

Stewart, Lorna. Communication to Ken Tingley, 2008. Edmonton, Alberta: ETS Archives.

Thomas, Ken. ETS Centennial Interviews, 2007–08. Edmonton, Alberta: ETS Archives

Transit Canada. November/December 1977.

Even with the new LRT playing a vital role in moving crowds to Commonwealth Stadium during the 1978 Commonwealth Games, additional buses were needed. Here, a bus on loan from Calgary Transit helps out. *(ETS Archives)*

CHAPTER 13

Light Rail Transit—From Vision to Reality

1960–79

Edmonton experienced rapid transformation and growth during the 1970s, especially after the Organization of Petroleum Exporting Countries (OPEC) drove oil prices to new highs. Created in September 1960, OPEC rose to international prominence during the 1970s after its members had taken control of their domestic oil industries in the effort to influence international oil pricing. Within the larger cartel, the Organization of Arab Petroleum Exporting Countries was established following the Six-Day War of 1967 to exert pressure on the larger body for an oil embargo against pro-Israeli western nations following the Yom Kippur War in 1973.

The price of oil had risen a modest 15 percent between 1948 and 1960, but by the end of 1974, it had quadrupled to US$12. The Iranian Revolution and subsequent Iran–Iraq War then sent the price rocketing from USD$14 in 1978 to USD$35 two years later. The surging price of crude led to greater prosperity throughout Alberta, which was archly referred to as the land of "blue-eyed sheiks" in the rest of Canada. Yet, ironically, it was oil prosperity that encouraged Edmontonians—individually and collectively—to re-examine their attitudes toward "King Car" and to seek alternatives in cheaper and more environmentally friendly forms of pubic transit, especially Light Rail Transit, which represented a return to the steel rails and wheels that had been abandoned two decades before.

In truth, the visionary planning that laid the foundation for the LRT dated back to the decommissioning of the streetcars in 1951, but it took until the early 1960s for the rapid transit dream to take coherent shape in D.L. MacDonald's *Report on the Present Operating Conditions of the Edmonton Transit System With a View to Determining a Policy for The Future Operation of the System* in 1961. An attached article by Gilbert Burck described the problems of a city dependent on the private automobile: "Crowding is not necessarily the result of too many citizens; a small city can be more congested than a large one. "Crowding" means that the citizens have arranged something—usually their traffic—stupidly. . . . Today what complicates and multiplies the age-old problem of urban congestion, of course, is the motorcar . . . [which] uses nine times as much space as a human being takes on up in a public conveyance, and while parked takes up as much space as an office" (Burck).

Burck went on to sagely point out how the effort to escape commercial core congestion through decentralization simply duplicated the problem in the suburbs and resulted in "progressive disintegration, with . . . central business district(s) declining . . . blighted areas expanding, and . . . mass transportation going bankrupt or being abandoned" (Burck).

Burck's observations described faraway Chicago, but they resonated in Edmonton. By the early 1960s, Edmonton was already beginning to experience noticeable traffic congestion and increasingly limited and expensive parking in the downtown commercial core. The rush to house the influx of new energy workers in the suburbs during the 1970s exacerbated a worsening situation. The more far-sighted argued that freeways feeding into downtown would not be enough to meet Edmonton's future needs. After all, the experience of European cities with light rail transit systems had demonstrated that freeways carried far fewer commuters per hour during peak demand hours than light rail lines. A better balance between the increasingly dominant car culture and public transit could only be achieved through transportation planning integrated into larger development plans.

Neither was decentralization the answer to congestion because keeping the downtown central to the city's life was deemed essential to the future. The May–June 1978 issue of *Rail and Transit* noted that no North American city dependent on freeways had a strong, vibrant downtown core. The publication also lauded Edmonton's achievement in operating the first LRT in North America, despite the city having the lowest gasoline prices (69.9 cents per gallon, or 15.4 cents per litre) and the highest per capita number of cars (1.3 for every man, woman and child) on the continent.

Llew Lawrence, Director of Marketing and Development at Edmonton Transit until 1978, recalled that Edmonton's system planning at the time remained "freeway-oriented despite reports that pointed out freeway faults." In fact, "METS [Metropolitan Edmonton Transportation Study] made no mention of a public transportation component." Nevertheless, Lawrence felt that City Council and the general public were experiencing an "awakening which said freeways destroy the physical and social fabric of urban centres. . . . Predictions of the high cost and low productivity of an all-bus system forced a look at the rail mode."

Edmonton, like most North American urban centres, bowed to the necessity of examining alternate visions of public transit. Internationally, urban planners were debating how historical districts could be preserved, how transit systems could be environmentally sustainable through innovative technologies, and how both preservation and growth could be accommodated within a single far-reaching public transit policy. City Council, Lawrence recalled, instructed planners "to include a public transportation component with heavy emphasis on the use of exclusive rights of ways to make public transportation more cost efficient."

Lawrence also pointed out that changes in attitude "did not happen accidentally. People worked from inside and outside the transit system to inform the public about forces for change and alternate solutions.

"Rail transportation was quite radical. In the early '60s, the mention of rapid transit in Edmonton brought immediate comparisons to the London subway, Tokyo people-pushers or the very expensive BART system in the San Francisco Bay area. By 1972 this had changed. Through travel many Edmontonians had come in contact with European systems, where LRT was successfully serving urban centres with fewer than 1 million inhabitants. These systems were modern tramways and quite within the means of small cities" (Lawrence).

Light rail transit had been a long-time dream for Edmonton Transit Superintendent D.L. MacDonald. Former mayor Cec Purves recalled how MacDonald presented this vision clearly and consistently. "Don kept

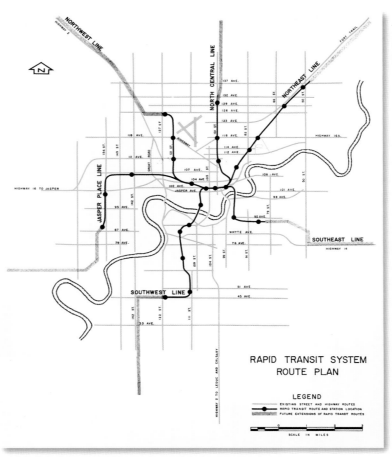

The map of the Bechtel Plan showing streets and highways existing at the time and proposed routes for rapid transit. *(ETS)*

RAPID TRANSIT SYSTEM
ROUTE PLAN

LEGEND

EXISTING STREET AND HIGHWAY ROUTES
RAPID TRANSIT ROUTE AND STATION LOCATION
FUTURE EXTENSIONS OF RAPID TRANSIT ROUTES

SCALE IN MILES

bringing in [how] Light Rail Transit is better planning. . . . All of us in Council were aware . . . that if the city kept growing . . . we would have to do some things in those areas. As far as I'm concerned, he was right to . . . get Council to start thinking about LRT." To mark Don MacDonald's contribution to light rail transit development, the new LRT operations garage would be named in his honour in 1983.

Don MacDonald's ambition from the beginning was to develop an underground metro system. "It is inconceivable that the city should reinvest in vehicles geared only to surface traffic conditions for the central area of the city far into the future," he concluded. Instead, he argued how "a new system must be developed for the transportation of people within approximately a four-mile core of the central area of Edmonton, involving people travelling at different levels for safe, efficient movement." MacDonald's *Edmonton Transportation Plan for the Future* fleshed out his vision in 1961. The scale of the plan would evolve over the coming decades, but the development of LRT would adhere to MacDonald's original subway concept forming an integral part of the rapid transit system (*Canadian Transportation*).

Canadian LRT models were found in the much larger metropolitan centres of Toronto, which began operating its subway in 1954, and Montreal, which completed its Metro in 1966, just in time for the World's Fair the following year. An underground LRT system, however, was an impressive project for a city the size of Edmonton, which in 1960 had a population of just under 270,000. In particular, it was financially ambitious even when, in 1973, the city was beginning to benefit from the increased oil prosperity and had a population of over 400,000. Edmontonians had seen the boom and

bust cycles of resource prosperity before. It was not until the Alberta government committed significant funding to support the project in 1974 that fully comprehensive planning for design and implementation of a metro system commenced with *The Edmonton Transportation Master Plan*.

The eventual master strategy for LRT development was rooted in earlier plans beginning with the Canadian Bechtel plan, commissioned in 1962. It envisioned a rapid rail system that could shuttle passengers along the north–south axis of the downtown and the university campus, using existing railway right-of-ways to the northeast, an underground line along 102 Avenue through city centre to Jasper Place, then along the north escarpment of the North Saskatchewan River to cross the river near the High Level Bridge. A further report produced by J.J. Bakker in 1968 also included a rapid rail transit system in its overall public transportation strategy. A *Rapid Transit Executive Report* emerged from the general debate in 1968, and City Council unanimously endorsed the concept of a rapid rail transit system for Edmonton. This in turn led to a more ambitious round of studies.

The De Leuw Cather study, *Rapid Transit Feasibility Study Northwest–Northeast Line, November 1970*, continued to favour using the existing CNR right-of-way connecting 118 Avenue and Kingsway, running southeast to the CN Tower, then northeast to return to 118 Avenue and the Edmonton Exhibition Grounds in an 8.3-kilometre route. A follow-up study, the *Rapid Transit Feasibility Study University Line, January 1971*, recommended adding a 6.6-kilometre route south of the University of Alberta, beginning at 72 Avenue and 114 Street, tunnelling beneath 114 Street and surfacing to the east between 111 and 110 streets to cross the upper deck of the High Level Bridge.

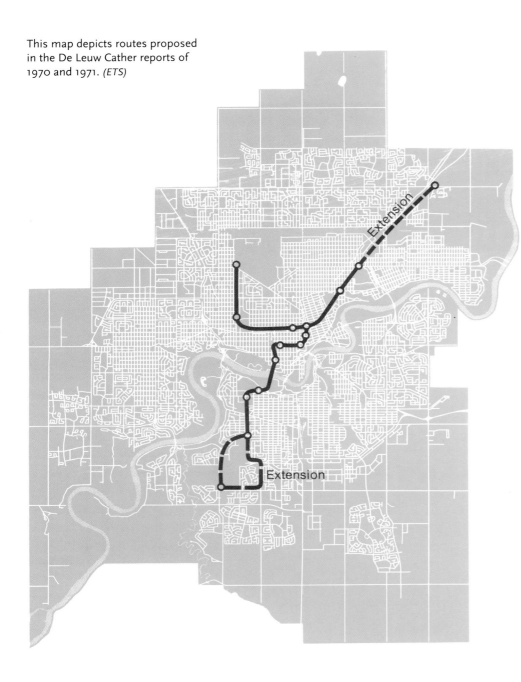

The line would then follow the CPR right-of-way north to 100 Avenue, where it would move underground to turn east along Jasper Avenue as far as 99 Street, then above ground to 97 Street to connect with the Northwest–Northeast Line. The De Leuw Cather proposal bears a close resemblance to the LRT routes that would eventually cover 12.59 kilometres, with 4.7 kilometres underground.

Dr. Gerry Wright, an associate professor at the University of Alberta, became another vocal proponent of the benefits of rapid rail transit. His 1972 report, aptly subtitled *The Immediate Answer for Edmonton*, embraced light rail transit as the responsible answer to the many problems wrought by unrestrained car culture on Edmonton. As an advocate for the preservation of historic districts and a founding member of the Old Strathcona Foundation, which successfully protested a planned freeway through the valuable heritage district of Old Strathcona, Wright gave passionate expression to the progressive aspects of light rail transit and rallied others to the cause.

As with most innovations, Light Rail Transit was not universally applauded. John Reid, who was the first Chief Instructor for the new LRT operators, later was transferred to Operations to oversee LRT development. Reid recalls a particular meeting with a group of city councillors from several cities in the United States. One councillor "didn't approve of the LRT. . . . He stood up, and he was quite fierce in his manner. He addressed the people and said it was too expensive and it wouldn't work.

"He said, 'I would like to ask Mr. D.L MacDonald why you chose such a strange rail gauge as 4 foot 8 1/2 inches?'

"And D.L. MacDonald stood up and calmly said, 'Because, Sir, it's the gauge of the Roman chariots.'

"Then he sat back, and there was a silence of total confusion. . . . [The councillor] was afraid to follow it up. . . . The only snickering going on at the back was Dave Geake and myself. We were busting a gut because that was the truth. When the Romans built the roads in Britain, they made the groove smooth so you could ride your chariots without getting bumped out.

"Then, when Britons began mining coal, they would haul the coal with coal wagons, and when they decided to put them on rails they just put the

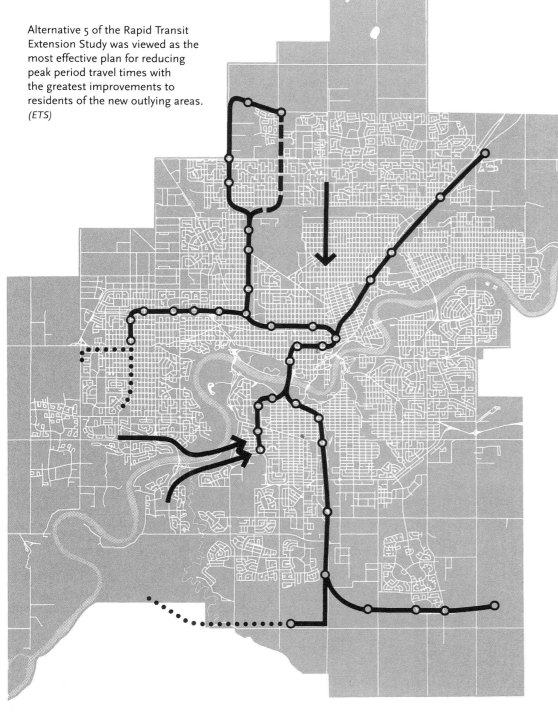

Alternative 5 of the Rapid Transit Extension Study was viewed as the most effective plan for reducing peak period travel times with the greatest improvements to residents of the new outlying areas. *(ETS)*

Figure 9.1   Alternative 5

━━━━ Rapid Transit Routes
╍╍╍╍ Alternative RT Alignment
●●●●● Possible Future Extensions
➤ Main Bus Service

flanged wheels on and laid down the rails. D.L. MacDonald handled it so beautifully" (Reid).

To implement Edmonton's commitment to light rail transit, the City appointed D.L MacDonald as the first Manager of Transportation Planning in 1972. His first *Report of the Transportation Planning Branch* was presented on 13 August 1973, and City Council quickly made an application to the provincial government for the funds necessary to implement the renewed emphasis on rail transportation expressed in the report.

The Rapid Transit Extension Study was initiated in December 1974 by the Transportation Planning Branch of the Engineering and Transportation Department, and carried out in accord with the direction of the Transportation Plan Part I. The Study was completed in 1977 and consisted of detailed analyses and evaluations of a range of alternative light rapid transit plans using population and employment projections to the year 2001. Service characteristics of the alternative rapid transit plans were reviewed and it was found that a better level of service could be provided than with expanded bus service. While the Study did not determine the next stage and timing of rapid transit development, it did identify that based on development and population projections, the southern fringes of the City would experience the greatest growth and on this basis the south corridor should receive the highest priority for the next rapid transit line.

City Council launched the *South Corridor LRT Functional Design Study* on 11 October 1977, just as construction of the first phase neared completion and after recommendations from the *Rapid Transit Extension Study* were approved. Council approved the South Corridor LRT as the next major extension of the system and charged the Planning Department with initiating a functional planning study and exploring necessary funding arrangements. Edmonton Transit already was making both short-term and long-term plans to build on its first successes (City of Edmonton).

Construction of the 95 Street Portal started in 1974. *(ETS)*

Following years of planning, strategizing, lobbying and designing, provincial funding was finally provided in the wake of the new oil boom. B.W. Booker Engineering Ltd. conducted the first engineering studies, beginning with the projected tunnel section from Jasper Avenue to the 95 Street level-crossing at the Canadian National Railway tracks just north of 105 Avenue. City Council accepted the Booker proposal for the 6.9 kilometre Northwest–Northeast Line, estimated at a cost $50 million (it would eventually cost $64.9 million), and construction began in March 1974.

A sod-turning ceremony on 30 September 1974 took place at the 95 Street portal, where boring operations commenced almost immediately. That same month, the City instructed a local construction firm to begin the 2.6-kilometre tunnel using an open cut-and-cover method in which a trench was dug, a concrete tunnel installed and the soil returned to cover the trench. Circular underground boring techniques were used where the line passed beneath existing structures. The tunnel would run from near 101 Street under Jasper Avenue to the 95 Street portal. The original plan was to have the LRT line pass under the tracks, but budgetary constraints later necessitated the retention of the level crossing and the modification of the portal to improve sight lines for the LRT operator (Buck).

Selecting underground rather than surface construction for the downtown section of the line was contentious for both financial and public relations reasons. Dave Geake recalls how Edmonton Transit was "roundly criticized for the expense of going underground in [the] downtown area." The decision was, however, carefully considered after discussions with transit officials in the densely populated centres of Frankfurt, Hanover and Rotterdam, who advised that underground routes in the heart of the city would avoid surface traffic congestion that would only increase in the future (Geake).

New Construction, New Challenges

The 95 Street portal produced some unexpected challenges. The roof of the portal originally extended to the edge of the sidewalk, creating problems for trains entering the tunnel. Dave Geake recalled how it came to be "reconfigured."

"On the Friday of the September long weekend," he said, "about four o'clock [Motorman] Rudy announced, 'I gotta go.' This despite the discussions of how the pantograph [the assembly providing the electrical connection to the overhead electrical lines], could not react within the necessary four or eight feet to allow the train to enter the tunnel smoothly. Came back on Tuesday morning and it was just a pile of rubble and the debris was being cleaned up. The top was pushed back to where it should be in the first place" (Hatcher).

The portal at 95 Street caused problems with the sightlines for equipment entering the tunnel. When an impromptu demolition occurred, the portal was reconfigured to allow enough distance for the electrical apparatus on the top of the train to enter the tunnel. *(ERRS)*

Churchill Station tunnel under construction with the Post Office in the background. This view shows the scene from the rail bed.
(ETS Archives)

ETS personnel worked with Jasper Avenue merchants to offset the impact of LRT construction. *(ETS)*

LRT construction inevitably resulted in closed streets and snarled traffic. Jasper Avenue merchants voiced their concerns very publicly over the loss of pedestrian and vehicle traffic when the 1975 construction of the Central Station ultimately closed access to Jasper Avenue along its busiest section. That year Jasper Avenue businesses formed the Downtown Area Rapid Transit Committee (DART) to attract pedestrian traffic to their isolated locations. The City of Edmonton and ETS did what they could to support the local merchant group by trying to minimize construction disruption.

The City was forced to adopt the disruptive cut-and-cover excavation method for the massive two-level underground structures of the Central and Churchill stations because they were beyond the capacity of existing boring technology in the 1970s. Meanwhile, the Lovat Tunnel Equipment Company

Community Concerns

What a lot of people remember about LRT construction is the mass disruption and confusion that ruled on downtown streets for what seemed an eternity. ...particularly if you were an owner of an affected business.

DART - (Downtown Area Rapid Transit Committee)

DART - (Downtown Area Rapid Transit Committee) a joint City Business Committee issued a sidewalk superintendent certificate and sponsored promotions to help counteract the disruption of construction at ground level on Jasper Avenue in the summer of 1975.

Edmonton Journal promotional page August 8, 1975.

of Toronto fabricated a mole to bore tunnel sections passing under existing buildings. The Edmonton Water and Sanitation Department held the contract to oversee this task because of their experience with similar tunnelling operations for the municipal water system. The Lovat excavator consisted of a circular steel tunnelling shield enclosing a six-blade cutting wheel equipped with carbaloid teeth suitable for chewing up the subsoil. A laser beam coupled to computer technology kept the direction of the mole straight and true, and a conveyor belt system carried away the spoil. The tunnelling phase was completed in mid-1977. Tunnelling firsts included the first use of a hydroshield tunnel boring machine in North America and the first time the sequential excavation method was used for soft ground in North America (*Edmonton Journal*; Buck; www.edmonton.ca).

The cut-and-cover tunnel construction method in front of the Post Office. *(ETS)*

The cutting head of the Lovat excavator, also called the "mole," that was used to bore the tunnels on the original LRT line. (ETS)

Using a crane to move the excavating mole from Churchill Station to Central Station at 99 Street and 101A Avenue. (Doug Cowan)

Construction of the street level entrance to Central Station on the southeast corner of Jasper Avenue and 100 Street. (ETS)

Construction of the interior of Central Station. *(ETS Archives)*

Cut-and-cover construction along 97 Street. *(Doug Cowan)*

Construction commencing on Churchill Station (99 Street), with care taken to avoid damaging a tree planted by Queen Elizabeth on a visit to the city. *(Doug Cowan)*

Construction of the double-track surface lines along the CNR right-of-way was undertaken during 1977. Several overpasses and an underpass near 66 Street also were built in conjunction with the concrete and steel stations terminating at the Belvedere Station adjacent to 129 Avenue.

Light Rail Transit rolling stock needed to be electrically powered light-weight vehicles travelling on steel rails over a grade isolated from residential areas, commercial buildings and traffic routes. Only two light rail manufacturers existed in North America during the early 1970s, so Llew Lawrence used his personal vacation to evaluate European rapid transit rolling stock at the request of D.L. MacDonald. He travelled to Frankfurt, literally on a busman's holiday, to examine the UT model LRT car manufactured by the West German Waggonfabrik Uerdingen, better known as Duewag. John Reid reported that he came back saying, "That's the car for us." This decision gave Edmonton the distinction of being the first Canadian city to adopt Light Rail rather than Heavy Rail Transit that used heavier and noisier vehicles that caused more vibration (Reid). Edmonton approved a bid from Duewag for 14 cars (Nos. 1001–14) with U2 engines designed for double-end operation, harkening back to the very first Edmonton Radial Railway streetcars.

LRT construction on Jasper Avenue west of 103 Street. (ETS)

LRT construction on Jasper Avenue east of 101 Street. (ETS)

Interestingly, in some fundamental ways Light Rail Transit represented a return to the past and the original streetcars that had served the city for over four decades. Track construction methods and rolling stock had antecedents dating from the earliest subway systems of Europe. In fact, Buck describes the LRT as "modified versions of underground and street railway construction methods first developed during the nineteenth century." The cut-and-cover technique, for example, was pioneered by the London underground in 1860, while James H. Greathead invented circular boring machinery for tubular subterranean rail lines completed in London in 1870. Buck also observes that even the rails were similar in cross-section to the T-rails used by the early Edmonton Radial Railway, although much heavier (Buck).

John Reid, Chief Instructor at Edmonton Transit in 1977, found value in this return to the past. "We were very fortunate right off the bat that there were a number of [senior drivers] who had streetcar experience," he recalled. "They had started on streetcars and they were going to quit on streetcars. And they did" (Reid).

The U2 could pull up to six cars and was equipped with either two direct-current or four alternating-current motors. Three more cars were added in 1979 (Nos. 1015–17) and four more in 1982 (Nos. 1018–21).

Though designed and built in Germany, 35 percent of the first U2's components were manufactured in Edmonton. The 24.3-metre-long cars were the first off the line with triple trucks and articulation to allow for tighter cornering. Each car carried 161 riders standing, 64 seated. The Edmonton prototypes, designated RTE1, were powered by two Siemens 150kW direct-current motors mounted longitudinally on the front trucks. The cars thus offered the flexibility of operating as single units or in trains of up to four cars. Most U2 cars (Nos. 1001–14) were in operation by the end of 1977 and were used to train operators in 1978.

Workers lay track for the LRT along the CNR right-of-way. (ETS Archives)

The international publication *Rail Travel News* commented on the success of Edmonton's LRT project. Writer Robert W. Ryerson took a test trip on 20 December 1977 with Murdock MacIntyre, who started his career on the last of the streetcars, Dennis Twarog, who drove the car, and Dave Geake. Ryerson described them as "interested and knowledgeable employees." He praised the DuWag car as "the Mercedes Benz of the traction world." Ryerson explained that DuWag cars were chosen because "There is no Federal funding ready to pick up the tab for mistakes in Edmonton, therefore there is no room for Buck Rogers technology. The DuWag cars, the Siemens overhead, and the Siemens signal systems are all evolutionary rather than revolutionary." Ryerson noted that Edmonton Transit "will accomplish the trick of building and operating a rapid transit line by next spring, in less time than if has taken to shake the bugs out of some other systems' rolling stock. The reason, he concluded, was the expertise of the employees: "'experts' of all stripe will beat a path to Cromdale's door. It won't matter what they say, one way or another. Clark [Rail Operations Supervisor], Geake and Twarog and all the others will make it work" (*Rail Travel News*).

Edmonton Transit embarked on an extensive public relations campaign to inform the public about the new Northeast LRT line. A series of community meetings were held in Northeast Edmonton, brochures and other publicity on the new service were widely distributed in the community, and a steady stream of stories were circulated to media providing news of construction progress and the forthcoming launch of service. Edmonton Transit was careful to inform Edmontonians about how to use the new service as well as how bus routes in the northeast were to be integrated into the new LRT service.

The first five of 10 eventual LRT stations were officially named in June 1975, well in advance of completion: Central (101 Street and Jasper Avenue), Churchill (99 Street and 102 Avenue), Stadium (84 Street and 112 Avenue), Coliseum (118 Avenue and 75 Street) and Belvedere (129 Avenue at Fort Road). Edmonton Transit felt that the early naming of LRT stations was important so the public could "refer to these stations with clarity and consistency from the early construction stage through to public use in 1978." Work commenced on the underground Central Station and Churchill Station at about the same time tunnelling began (*Edmonton Transit News*).

The first light rail transit vehicles had to be lifted off the train in two parts and pushed by hand into the Cromdale Garage. A lot of coordinated manpower was required. (*ERRS*)

The Cromdale Garage on 18 April 1977 with the first, as yet unpainted, LRT vehicle on site. (*Doug Cowan*)

The first light rail transit vehicles arrived by rail in Edmonton in the early morning hours of 11 April 1977. (*Doug Cowan*)

The soon-to-be familiar yellow-and-blue-striped LRT vehicle was showcased at Klondike Days in 1977, giving Edmontonians firsthand experience of the new LRT cars. *(Doug Cowan)*

The first group of LRT inspectors. Back row from left: John Reid, LRT Instructor; Gerry Michael, George Glazerman, Murdoch McIntyre, Dave Johnman, Bob Podmoroff, John Couy, Al Biggelaar, Verne MacKenzie, John Elniski and Larry Barber. Seated from left: Jack McLachlan, Earl Solomon and Brent Kiernan. *(ETS)*

On 23 July 1977, Mayor Terry Cavanagh officially received the keys to the first LRT vehicle when its assembly at the Cromdale Garage was completed. *(ERRS)*

The public got a first real taste of light rail service on 18–20 April 1978 when Edmonton Transit invited citizens to take a free ride on the new LRT. Teeming crowds, excited to see more evidence of their city's entrance onto the stage of world firsts, took the opportunity to be on the historic ride. After this shakedown of the new system, the official opening was held on 22 April, with Mayor Cec Purvis and the Hon. Hugh Horner, Minister of Transportation, presiding at the ribbon cutting at Central Station. The line opened for service the following day. Edmonton Transit reported with some pride that "The smooth entry into service of Edmonton's LRT has created a tremendous impression all over North America and in other parts of the world."

After one more day of free rides on 23 April, regular service on the first 6.9 kilometres of the line opened on 24 April with the very first train departing Cromdale Garage at 5:22 AM as it headed north to Belvedere Station. The trip took 12 minutes, less than half the time needed by car, Edmonton Transit estimated. Service was provided by 14 Light Rail Vehicles (LRVs) operating between Belvedere Station and Stadium Station by way of a stop at Coliseum Station near the Northlands Coliseum and continuing via a tunnel beneath 99 Street to the Central Station at Jasper Avenue and 100 Street, stopping on the way at Churchill Station. Each train consisted of two coupled cars with three-car configurations added as needed during peak hours. Trains ran at five-minute intervals in peak hours, a 10-minute schedule in off-peak times, and every 15 minutes on evenings and Sundays. However, low volumes at first led to weekend closure of alternate entrances to the system for a while.

An early test of public confidence in the Edmonton Radial Railway had been providing service to the Edmonton Exhibition in 1909, and the first major trial for the LRT also came within months with the staging of the XI Commonwealth Games, 4–12 August 1978. With private automobile parking nonexistent at most sports venues, Edmonton Transit spent over two years intensively planning for the transportation of athletes, dignitaries, coaches, media and spectators. Event preparation encompassed coordination with Police, Engineering, Planning, and the Parks and Recreation departments, the City '78 Committee and the Commonwealth Games Foundation.

To meet the transportation demand, a fleet of 724 buses was assembled using Edmonton, Calgary and Red Deer rolling stock. Edmonton Transit conveyed almost two million spectators to events over the nine days of the Games, and on August 8, the LRT system set a ridership record of over 69,000 people. The City's Disabled Adult Transportation System (DATS) recorded more than 2,000 trips for disabled visitors attending the Games' events. When the last bus left Commonwealth Stadium after the closing ceremonies, the department's job was done. Employees had forgone vacations and had worked long and hard hours throughout, but everyone took pride in the accomplishment. The Games were a shining moment for the city, and Edmonton Transit had played its part well passing the gargantuan test with flying colours (Edmonton Transit System).

J. Reid, Supervisor of LRT Operations; M. McIntyre, Senior Training Instructor; and R. Craig, Supervisor of Safety and Training, in front of one of the LRT vehicles in 1977. *(ERRS)*

Introducing the Public to New LRT Lines

ETS publications helped citizens appreciate the benefits of the new Northeast LRT line.

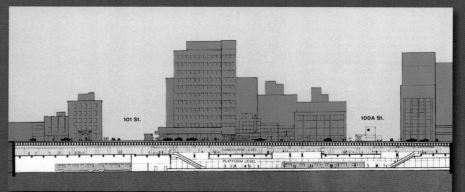

101 St. 100A St.

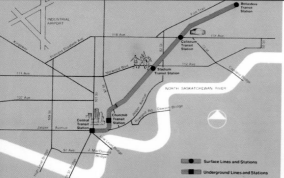

Public transit for Edmontonians will be complimented by a new comfortable and quiet L.R.T. line in early 1978. Edmonton will be the first city in Canada with a population base of under 1 million to have such a system. As well, Edmonton will be only the third city in our country to have a Light Rail Transit line.

Edmontonians have been strong supporters of public transit. In recent years, our city has firmly established itself as a dynamic centre of business and industry. As the population grows, residential areas have sprung up outside of the centre core. Edmonton's northeast area is presently experiencing some growing pains. While this growth is a "plus" for Edmonton, it has also caused unpleasant traffic congestion and overcrowded buses — two things we'd all be happier without. Various solutions to this bumper-to-bumper problem have been examined.

Freeways, for example, have been examined; however any advantage will be lost in a few short years as growing populations will again cause the same problems we have now. As well, the residents of the northeast area have stated strongly their opposition to disruption of their community environment by additional automobile traffic. The solution, then? Light Rail Transit.

It's quite an undertaking — designing a system that will comfortably carry between 5,000 to 6,000 people per hour in each direction during peak periods. Work has already started on this $64.9 million project. Like the building of Edmonton's impressive Coliseum, the construction of the 4½-mile northeast Light Rail Transit line represents a real challenge to design and engineering skills. One mile of the line will be under the bustling commercial core of downtown Edmonton; the remaining 3½ miles will use the existing Canadian National Railway Line.

Transit Ridership Growth from 1969 to 1976

TOTAL RIDERSHIP

Year	Ridership
1969	36,553,010*
1970	38,465,710
1971	39,909,983
1972	40,722,137
1973	42,745,877*
1974	45,668,346*
1975	51,223,597
1976	56,476,582

*Adjusted figures on daily average.

Edmonton's L.R.T. line will initially have five stations. The Central Transit Station (Jasper Avenue and 101 Street) will be located in the heart of the business and shopping district. The Churchill Transit Station (102 Avenue and 99 Street) will give easy access to the Library, Art Gallery, new Citadel Theatre, and Churchill Square. Both of these stations will be underground.

Two of the remaining surface light rail stations are planned for major public complexes. The Stadium Station will be a real convenience for sport enthusiasts, who have in the past, experienced annoying traffic tie-ups. The Coliseum Transit Station (Coliseum, Exhibition Grounds, Northlands Park) will receive the greatest traffic flow of all stations. The removal of traffic and parking problems should add to the enjoyment of

Prospective view of the concourse level of Edmonton's Central Transit Station.

citizens attending Klondike Days festivities and other special events.

The fifth L.R.T. station will be the end of the present line. The Belvedere Transit Station (129 Avenue and Fort Road), like the Clarke Stadium and Exhibition Stations, will be a transfer point between the Light Rail Transit line and the surface bus fleet.

Both the physical location and operating schedules of the buses and Light Rail Transit trains will be carefully co-ordinated to make public transit an efficient, pleasant alternative to the automobile.

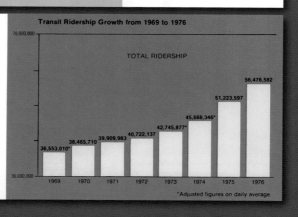

Passenger comfort is a major consideration in the selection of cars for Edmonton's Light Rail Transit system. When the system starts operation, Edmontonians will ride in trains that are clean, quiet and roomy.

All of us can look forward to L.R.T. — commuters, who will use the system to travel to work — shoppers, students, sports fans, theatre goers, even motorists will find relief from their daily traffic aggravations.

For many of us, Light Rail Transit will mean more convenient and comfortable day-to-day transportation. For others, it's a solution to the traffic problems usually associated with public events. Faced with rising automobile costs, price increases in fuel, insurance and parking, Edmontonians will continue to find public transit an economic and efficient alternative.

Exterior view of the Stadium Transit Station showing the interphase between Light Rail Transit and the surface bus fleet.

How Does LRT Work?

The Light Rail Vehicle is powered by electricity drawn from an overhead wire. The power is fed from four Edmonton Power substations adjacent to the LRT line which transform and rectify the 13.8 KV to 600 volts direct current.

The Light Rail vehicle works on much the same principals as a trolley bus but instead of two current collectors, it requires only one, called a pantograph. The rail provides the return path.

The installation of the LRT's catenary suspension electrical system was done by City of Edmonton personnel. Expertise and innovation combined to complete this unique project.

How Was The LRT Constructed?

Central Transit Station, located under downtown Edmonton's busiest street corner, was the first phase of construction. Using a method known as tangent-pile construction, traffic flow was restored to normal in a record four months.

The tangent-pile method involved drilling holes for cast-in-place concrete support piles, excavating between the piles, covering the hole and resurfacing.

The rest of the work was then completed underground. The same construction method was used for the Churchill Transit Station.

The two rail tunnels connecting the Central and Churchill

Transit Stations were bored with a 22-and-a-half-foot wide excavating machine known as a mechanical mole. The rest of the construction was completed using the conventional cut and cover method.

The stations were designed with safety in mind. Dark corners were eliminated through the use of high ceilings, light colors, and large open areas with a minimum of physical obstructions.

A closed circuit television system scans all stations 24 hours a day. A radio system enables the console operator watching the T.V. monitors to dispatch security people to any problem areas.

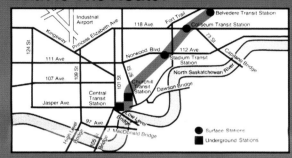

What Is The Route?

Edmonton's Northeast LRT Line starts at Central Transit Station (101st Street and Jasper Avenue.). It travels 1.5 kilometres under the city's business and shopping core. The remaining 5.7 kilometres of track are built on the surface and share the right-of-way with Canadian National Railway to the present terminus at Belvedere Transit Station (60th Street and 129th Avenue.)

The line has five stations, two of which are underground. Central Transit Station has connections at the mezzanine level to many buildings between 101st Street and 100th Street along Jasper Avenue.

Churchill Transit Station (99th Street and 102nd Avenue) gives convenient access to the art gallery, library, Citadel Theatre, Sir Winston Churchill Square and City Hall.

Central and Churchill Transit Stations are divided into two levels, mezzanine and platform. The mezzanine provides an area for circulation and access to surrounding facilities, ticketing, turnstiles, service rooms, control and station agent kiosk and retail outlets.

Two of the surface stations are located at major public facilities, Commonwealth Stadium (11000 Stadium Road) and the Coliseum (75th Street and 118th Avenue.) These transit stations have covered waiting areas at track level.

Belvedere Transit Station is also on the surface and has been upgraded to provide an enclosed entrance and heated passenger waiting area.

Where Did The Cars Come From?

Edmonton's light rail cars are manufactured in Germany by Siemens/DuWag; firms which have proven their reliability in Europe for years. About 35 per cent of the cars' components were made in Edmonton. Each car is about 24.3 m long and 2.65 m wide and has a flexible, jointed section in the middle to allow for sharp cornering. The lightweight body is made of welded steel and the articulated section is covered by reinforced plastic parts, to ensure safe passage from one end of the car to the other. Passengers can stand in the articulated section even when going around a sharp corner.

Noise-absorbing layers on the inside of the side walls, resilient wheels and rubber padded suspension make the ride quieter than that of a conventional bus.

The cars are heated in the winter and force-ventilated in the summer. Doors open individually by a passenger push-button which must be first released by the operator. Sensitive edges and a photo-electric cell ensure the doors from trapping patrons.

Wheel-spinning or sliding is prevented by electronic controls. Solenoid-operated, heated sanders automatically spread sand onto slippery tracks in snowy or rainy conditions.

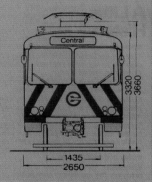

Are Any Future Extensions Planned?

Work is underway on a 2.2 kilometre extension which will take the Northeast Line to the Clareview subdivision. Service will be extended to this area by mid-April 1981.

Edmonton City Council has approved a $100 million dollar extension of the line to Government Centre which is expected to be in service mid-year 1984. This line will have three new stations. It will continue from Central Transit Station underground west down Jasper Avenue as far as 108th Street before curving and heading south along the Canadian Pacific Railway right-of-way parallel to 109th Street.

The line will eventually cross to Edmonton's South Side over the High Level Bridge and continue to the University of Alberta and the Millwoods subdivision.

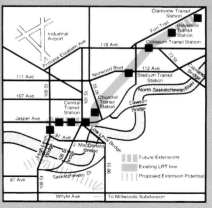

How Does LRT Fit In With The Rest Of Edmonton Transit?

Light Rail Transit service is just one component of Edmonton Transit. LRT Route 101 is treated the same as any main line route in the transit network. Only the hardware is different. The regular fare and monthly passes with free transfers between routes all apply to LRT.

With the fleet of buses, which has been carefully scheduled for passenger ease of transfer, the LRT provides fast, direct service for all its riders. It is an integral part of the entire public transit system in Edmonton.

THE CITY OF Edmonton

Editorial cartoons speculated on what the Northeast LRT line would add to life in Edmonton. *(Edmonton Sun, 17 April 1978, ETS Collection)*

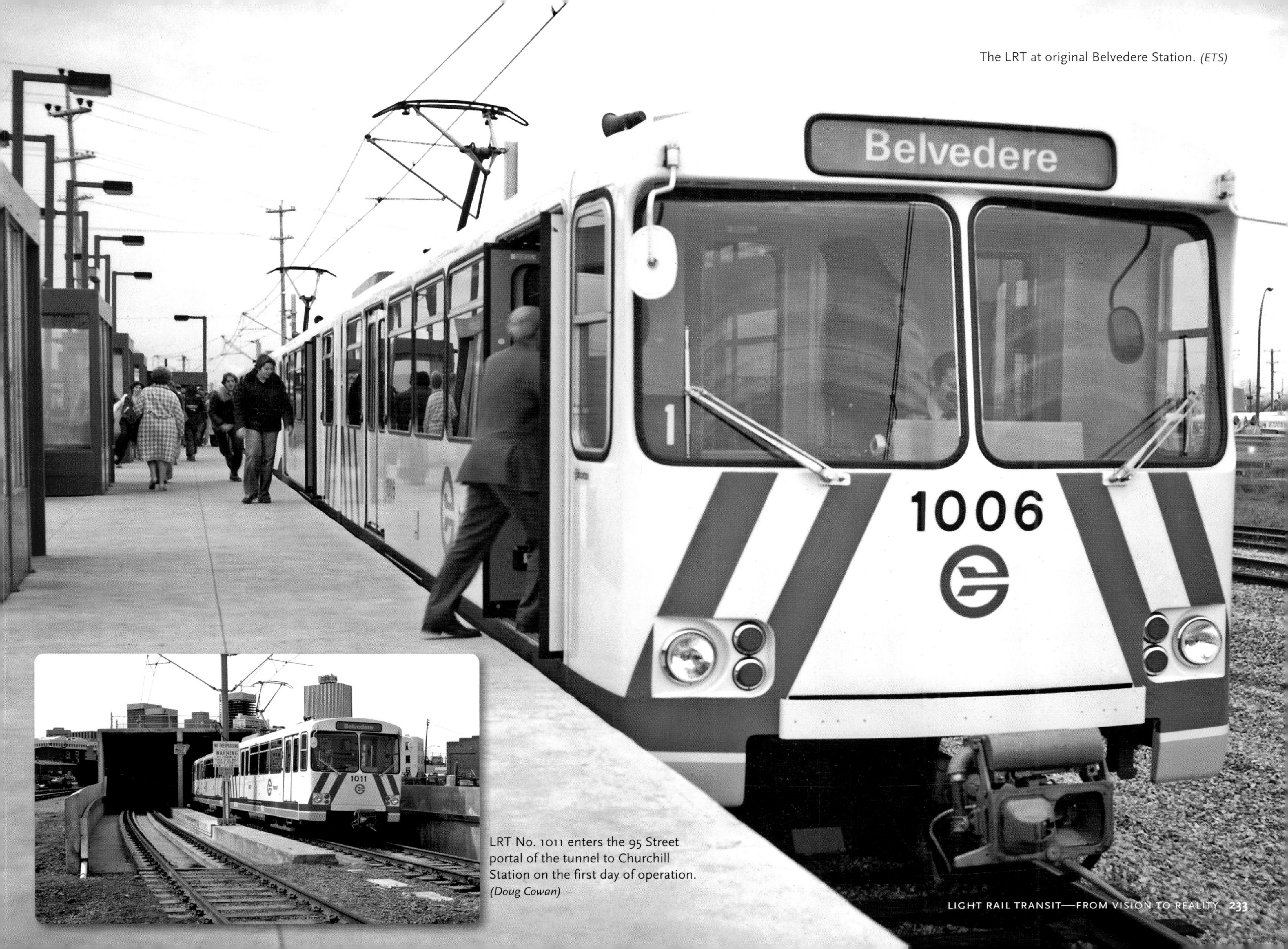

Belvedere

1

1006

LRT No. 1011 enters the 95 Street portal of the tunnel to Churchill Station on the first day of operation. *(Doug Cowan)*

Stadium Station during the Commonwealth Games. *(ERRS)*

Edmonton Journal

XI Commonwealth Games
Edmonton 1978

20 CENTS   FINAL   TUESDAY, APRIL 18, 1978

What an exhi-LRT-ing ride . . . for public!

By DON THOMAS

Edmonton Transit has a winner.

The Northeast Light Rail Transit (LRT) line opened today to the public with free rides and shortly after station doors opened at 9 a.m. long lineups began forming.

The people stood patiently for a chance to crowd into the cars where most of them had to stand for the 30-minute round trip.

At some of the surface stations, such as Coliseum and Stadium, the people could only stand and look as jam-packed cars eased in and out without any room for them.

So far the problems with the system seem minor.

A few times cars came to a shuddering halt as novice drivers went a bit too fast in some sections, causing the car's braking systems to slam on automatically.

At the Coliseum Station one car had to be pulled out of service when a door wouldn't close properly.

Through the delays people waited patiently as slightly-harried Edmonton Transit officials fiddled with controls and called in other cars on their radio system.

People generally seemed pleased with the cars which ride smoothly and have open, spacious interiors with huge windows.

"I'm impressed," said Doug Cowan, who calls himself a transit fanatic and brought his 27 Grade 3 and Grade 4 pupils out from McLeod Elementary School.

The school children are all from northeast Edmonton and will be using the LRT from the Belvedere Station.

For this trip, the students were carrying special quiz papers to note all the signs and information labels on the trains and stations.

"The cars are attractive, bright, have good vision, and ride smoothly."

"I hope they don't stop here. The system should be extended into south Edmonton to really work."

Yoka Groenendyk and Mike Kostek, teachers at

Policeman looks over car that failed to stop at crossing bar

PHOTO BY KEN ORR

Braemar Elementary School, had taken their Grade 5 classes through the LRT station downtown in February.

Now they were back to ride the system and the students hopped up and down with excitement at Coliseum Station waiting for an empty car.

Seats in the cars face each other, promoting conversation and conviviality not generally seen on the buses.

Passengers in the cars are separated from the drivers who sit in an enclosed compartment at the end of the coach.

To guard against vandalism and possible rowdyism, security guards will periodically ride the trains. Some guards were evident in the cars today.

Work at all five stations is still in progress with the

Belvedere Station furthest from completion.

It still doesn't have railway gates to protect 129th Avenue so a security guard had to be posted there to hold autos back when the LRT cars came in.

On the first trip out from Central Station the car came to a shuddering halt as the driver exceeded the speed

More LRT Page A3

The *Edmonton Journal* reported on the enthusiastic public reception to the free rides and to the rapid adjustments made when "too many people [were] trying to crowd on—and taking too long in the doors to look at the wonderful new cars!" *(Edmonton Journal, ETS collection)*

Edmonton Journal

XI Commonwealth Games
Edmonton 1978

20 CENTS   FINAL   MONDAY, APRIL 24, 1978

LRT off to a good start

A few kinks . . . then right on track

By DON THOMAS

Scores of people were late for work this morning as northeast Edmonton residents adjusted to the quirks of the new Light Rail Transit (LRT) system.

A faulty door held up a train in the Churchill Station at about 7:15 a.m. and passengers at Coliseum Station complained they had to wait nearly 25 minutes before seeing a train.

That appeared to be the major problem on the first day of revenue service for LRT and trains appeared to be running on time for most of the morning rush hour.

John Reid, co-ordinator of LRT for Edmonton Transit, said "we thought it went very well this morning all in all."

The delay at Coliseum Station was because of "one of

those little bugs that has to be expected when you're putting a new line into service." The problem was caused because a door wouldn't open properly. A crew of electro-mechanics was used to repair the door.

A crowd of perhaps 150 to 200 people was waiting in the Coliseum Station and when a train finally came in from the north at 7:40 a.m. It was already full.

Only a handful of those waiting on the platform at Coliseum were able to get on the train. Most had to wait for the next train.

Trains were riding almost empty at about 7 a.m. and by 8:45 a.m. crowds had again thinned out and there was no problem getting a seat.

Today was a day of adjustment for most riders. Many

bus routes in northeast Edmonton have been adjusted to terminate at an LRT station instead of going downtown.

For many people who had been used to taking one bus downtown, it meant taking a bus to the LRT station, riding LRT to a downtown station, then boarding another bus.

Many people said the combined bus-train ride took longer while others said they were able to save time.

Mr. Reid says passengers could save time on the LRT by not "dawdling" at the doors which have to be opened manually by the passengers.

Today many people appeared to be confused about whether the doors would open for them or whether they had to press a button.

He said that Sunday — when nearly 100,000 people were carried on the last day of free LRT rides — children playing with the doors caused problems.

The doors have an electric eye to prevent the door closing on someone and children playing with the eye held up the trains which won't move as long as a door is open.

There appeared to be few problems today with LRT cars holding up traffic at railway crossings.

There were only short traffic lineups behind the gates which are controlled by electronic devices and co-ordinated with the passage of LRT cars.

At the Belvedere Station where 400 spaces are available

More TRAINS Page A3

Picture Page B1

COMMONWEALTH GAMES TRANSIT SERVICE

*Edmonton Transit is dedicated in providing Edmontonians with fast, safe and convenient public transportation to the various Games venues.
We'd like to remind spectators that automobile parking will be extremely limited at most Games sites.
IN THE AREA OF THE COMMONWEALTH STADIUM, THERE WILL BE NO PARKING FOR AUTOMOBILES.
Edmonton Transit will be providing a comprehensive transit service for the Games. This includes increased Regular Service on many routes, Special Services, Park 'N' Ride and L.R.T. service. Complete service details will be well advertised before the Games.*

1978 COMMONWEALTH GAMES TRANSIT INFORMATION

FARE STRUCTURE
All Commonwealth Games Transit Services (e.g. Regular Service, Park 'N' Ride, Special Services and L.R.T.) will be provided at REGULAR FARE.
Adults .... 40c · EXACT COIN FARE
Children (15 years and under) ... 25c · EXACT COIN FARE.
Transfers, Monthly Transit Passes and Courtesy Passes are valid.
Park 'N' Ride Parking Fee $1.00

TRANSFERS
Will be issued only at the time the initial fare is paid.
Transfers are valid for one (1) hour from time of issue and good for travel in any direction.

LIGHT RAIL TRANSIT (L.R.T.)
Same Fare Structure as noted above. Transfers between bus service and L.R.T. service totally compatible.

DOWNTOWN TRANSIT INFORMATION CENTRE
Visit our Transit Information Centre, Jasper Avenue and 100 A Street for any transit related material you may require; schedules, route maps, etc.
Hours of Operation* Monday - Saturday 9:30 a.m. - 5:30 p.m.
* These hours may be adjusted for the duration of the Commonwealth Games.
A temporary Transit Information Kiosk will be located on the Mezzanine Level of Churchill Transit Station for the duration of the Commonwealth Games. Hours of operation will be the same as noted above.

TRANSIT TELEPHONE INFORMATION
For specific route and schedule information call Transit Information at 432-1234.
Hours of Operation
Monday-Saturday .... 6:30 a.m. - 11:00 p.m.
Sunday .... 8:00 a.m. - 11:00 p.m.

LOST & FOUND
Edmonton Transit's Lost and Found Depot is located at Churchill Transit Station, Concourse level. Most convenient entrance is 99 St./102A Ave. Telephone 428-3514
Hours of Operation
Monday-Friday .... 8:30 a.m. - 4:30 p.m.

AUGUST 1978 ADULT TRANSIT PASS
Edmonton Transit is dedicated to providing Edmontonians and visitors to our City with fast, safe and convenient public transportation to the various Commonwealth Games venues.
To make your transit trips with the least bit of inconvenience, may we suggest you purchase an August, 1978 Transit Pass for $15.00 from any one of over 150 outlets throughout the City of Edmonton.
The August Transit Pass can become your Transportation ticket' to the Commonwealth Games and the rest of Edmonton as well as a souvenir of the 1978 Commonwealth Games.

Your Official Commonwealth Games Transit Information and Event Tickets

Edmonton Transit prepared the public for parking limitations and encouraged the use of the excellent services provided by Edmonton Transit. The message obviously resonated with the public, as Edmonton Transit was the major provider of transportation to the Games.

Brochures featured the distinctive Commonwealth Games logo and provided detailed information about the Games and using the services of ETS to attend events. *(ETS)*

TRANSIT SERVICE BY SPORT AND VENUE

Edmonton Transit will provide a comprehensive transit service for the 1978 Commonwealth Games. This includes increased Regular Service on many routes, Special Services, Park'n Ride and L.R.T. Service.
Listed below is a complete schedule of Edmonton Transit's public transportation service to and from the various Commonwealth Games Venue Sites.
EXTRA SERVICE WILL BE ADDED TO ALL ROUTES AND SERVICES, WHERE REQUIRED, APPROXIMATELY 2 HOURS PRIOR TO COMPETITION TIME. This expanded level of transit service will also be in operation after the completion of each event.
THERE WILL BE NO AUTOMOBILE PARKING AVAILABLE IN THE VICINITY OF THE COMMONWEALTH STADIUM OR COMMONWEALTH AQUATIC CENTRE. PARKING AT OTHER VENUE SITES IS EXTREMELY LIMITED. THE COMMONWEALTH GAMES FOUNDATION SUGGESTS YOU USE PUBLIC TRANSIT TO GET TO AND FROM THE VARIOUS VENUES.

OPENING CEREMONIES - AUGUST 3
CLOSING CEREMONIES - AUGUST 12
COMMONWEALTH STADIUM

Routes 1, 7°, 11, 32†, L.R.T. 101
Special Service from: 87 Ave./115 St. E.B.; 91 Ave./Walterdale Hill Rd. N.B.; 96 Ave./Rossdale Rd. N.B.; 99 Ave./Bellamy Hill Rd. N.B.; 101 St./Jasper Ave. N.B. *every 15 min.*

Park 'N'Ride Service from: Airway Park 110 St./111 Ave. N.B.; Park Plaza 118 Ave./103 St. E.B.;N.A.I.T. 106A St./118 Ave. S.B.; Beechmount 125 Ave./west of 97 St. E.B.; Rossdale North Lot 103 St./Rossdale Rd. E.B.

Additional Park 'N' Ride Service for Opening and Closing Ceremonies: Renfrew Lot 103 St./96 Ave. W.B.; Coliseum 73 St./119 Ave. S.B.; Exhibition Ground Parking Lot.

ATHLETICS - AUGUST 6, 7, 8, 10, 11, 12
COMMONWEALTH STADIUM
Same service as noted above with the deletion of the additional Park 'N' Ride locations that are only in effect for the Opening and Closing Ceremonies.

BADMINTON-AUGUST 4, 5, 6, 8, 9, 10, 11
UNIVERSITY OF ALBERTA, ICE ARENA
Routes 8, 19†, 32†, 36†, 37, 38†, 39†, 40, 46, 56†, 63, 64, 69, 73°†??
Special Service from: Commonwealth Stadium Bus Bay; 101 St./Jasper Ave. S.B.; 99 Ave./Bellamy Hill Rd. S.B.; 96 Ave./104 St. S.B.; Aquatic Centre: *every 15 min.*

BOWLS - AUGUST 4, 5, 6, 7, 8, 9, 10, 11
CORONATION PARK
Routes 4§, 5, 11, 17, 21, 22, 37, 94†, 96§
St. Albert - 60 min. service plus extras
Special Service from: Westmount Transit Centre; 135 St./112 Ave. S.B.; 135 St./115 Ave. S.B.: *every 15 min.*

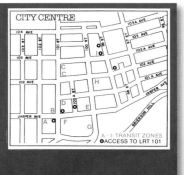

NORTHEAST LIGHT RAIL TRANSIT LINE

LRT 101

CITY CENTRE

A - 1: TRANSIT ZONES
◆ ACCESS TO LRT 101

BOXING - AUGUST 4, 5, 6, 7, 8, 9, 11
EDMONTON GARDENS
Routes 5, 6† 11, 18, 20†, 23, 28†, 66, 75, 80, L.R.T. 101
Special Service from: 98 Ave./56 St. W.B.; 136 Ave./93 St. S.B.:*every 10 min. for Boxing & Gymnastics only*

CYCLING - AUGUST 4, 5, 6, 7, 8, 9, 10
VELODROME
Route 8, 44, 45†, 47, 48†, 53, 67§, 75, 76, 81†, 93§
Special Service from:83 St./82 Ave. W.B: *every 15 min.*

GYMNASTICS - AUGUST 6, 7, 8, 9,
EDMONTON COLISEUM
Same Service as Boxing

SHOOTING - AUGUST 5, 6, 7, 8, 9
STRATHCONA RANGE
Same Service as Cycling
Special Service from: 83 St./82 Ave. W.B.:*every 30 min.*

SWIMMING, DIVING - AUGUST 4, 5, 6, 7, 8, 9
COMMONWEALTH AQUATIC CENTRE
Routes 9, 32†, 41, 42, 46, 49†,52§,61§,62§64, 73°? 77
Special Service from: 96 Ave./101 St.W.B.:*every 10 min.* from: Commonwealth Stadium Bus Bay, 101 St./Jasper Ave. S.B.; 99 Ave./Bellamy Hill Rd. S.B., 96 Ave./104 St. S.B.; 87 Ave./115 St. E.B.: *every 15 min.*

WEIGHTLIFTING - AUGUST 4, 5, 6, 7, 8
JUBILEE AUDITORIUM
Same Service as Badminton.

WRESTLING - AUGUST 9, 10, 11
UNIVERSITY OF ALBERTA, MAIN GYM
Same Service as Badminton.

LACROSSE - AUGUST 10, 11
EDMONTON COLISEUM
Same Service as Gymnastics.

■ 30 minute Service - Call Transit Information for Service Details
※ No Night Service
† No Night or Sunday Service
§ Peak Hours Service only
° Nights, Sunday & Holiday only

CITY CENTRE KEY BOARDING POINTS FOR GAMES VENUES

Listed below, in alphabetical order, are the Commonwealth Games Venue Sites. Appropriate transit zone boarding locations are indexed to the various Venues.

VENUE	TRANSIT ZONE LOCATION	ROUTES
Argyll Velodrome	G, I	47, 76
Commonwealth Aquatic Centre	A	9, 32, 41, 42, 49
		52, 61, 62, 64,
		73, Special Service
	I	49, 52, 61, 62
Commonwealth Stadium	D	Special Service
	F	1, 32
	H	
Coronation Park	B	5, 21
	C	4, 17, 22
	E	4, 5
Edmonton Gardens/ Coliseum	F	5, 6
Edmonton-Strath- cona Range (Transfer Required)	G	45, 48, 53, 67
		81, 84
University of Alberta (Ice Arena, Main Gym, and Jubilee Auditorium)	A	32, 64, 73, Special Service
	B	40, 56
	E	32, 40, 56
	G	46
	I	64

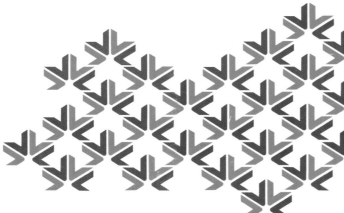

Inspector J. Elniski assisting riders at Commonwealth Stadium during the Commonwealth Games. The dedication of Edmonton Transit employees helped ensure a resounding success for Edmonton in an event that would be foundational to the City's future bids to host other events. *(ERRS)*

The first phase of Edmonton's Light Rail Transit was completed after two decades of intensive planning and construction. To this point, the LRT had cost $64.9 million, $45 million of which had been provided by the Province of Alberta. Great expectations seemed to have been realized, but by 1982 financial and political barriers had emerged to threaten future expectations for system expansion. It took longer than hoped, but the LRT forged ahead, continuing to develop within the broader transit system to meet the challenges of the coming years.

Works Cited

Buck, George H. *A Technological History of Municipally Owned Public Transportation In Edmonton:* 1893–1981. Edmonton, Alberta: University of Alberta Thesis, 1985, pp. 601–02; 607; 610; 612.

Burck, Glibert. "How to Unchoke Our Cities," reprinted in *Report on the Present Operating Conditions of the Edmonton Transit System With a View to Determining a Policy for the Future Operation of the System,* City of Edmonton Transit, Mitchell Division, HI-HE 4211 1961 TR.

Canadian Transportation. February 1960, cited in Buck, George H. *A Technological History of Municipally Owned Public Transportation In Edmonton:* 1893–1981. Edmonton, Alberta: University of Alberta Thesis, 1985, p. 600.

City of Edmonton. Transportation Planning Branch. *South Corridor LRT Functional Design Study, Final Report, July* 1979.

Edmonton Journal. 13 June 1975; 18 April 1978; 24 April 1978.

Edmonton Transit News. June 1975.

Edmonton Transit System, *Annual Report,* 1978, p. 6.

Geake, Dave. ETS Centennial Interviews, 2007–08. Edmonton, Alberta: ETS Archives.

Hatcher, Colin, *Edmonton's light Rail Transit: The First 25 Years,* 1978–2003. Edmonton, Alberta: Edmonton Transit System, 2003, p. 10.

Lawrence, Llew A. "The Marketing of L.R.T. and the Integration with Bus Routes and Services." Paper presented at the Case History and Conference on LRT in Edmonton, Faculty of Extension, University of Alberta, 2 June 1978.

Purves, Cec. ETS Centennial Interviews, 2007–08. Edmonton, Alberta: ETS Archives.

Rail Travel News. Vol, 7, No. 21, First Issue, December 1977.

Reid, J. ETS Centennial Interviews, 2007–08. Edmonton, Alberta: ETS Archives.

www.edmonton.ca/transportation/transit/LRT Brochure_2007. pdf (Accessed 14 December 2008)

Despite economic downturns, the LRT would continue to be a vital force in transit in Edmonton. Here, LRT vehicle No 1005 heads north through the tunnel. *(ETS)*

Chapter 14
The LRT—Keeping on Track

1979–99

The long road Edmonton Transit travelled from the planning to the launching of the first stage of light rail transit ended with the successful launch of the first LRT service during the 1978 Commonwealth Games. But many challenges remained, some anticipated and others imposed by political and economic variables that could not be foreseen. Although the dream of expanding light rail transit service survived, after the first successful stage was implemented many felt that the dream had been abandoned, and widespread frustration was voiced because of the slow extension of LRT lines into new neighbourhoods that already felt they had waited too long for that service.

Rick Millican, General Manager of the City's Transportation Department, summed up the problem as it extended into the early 1990s: "The lack of money was the real concern at the time. Edmonton was deep in a recession. Grants were non-existent; the province wasn't giving us any money. All around, there was less money for transit capital. The recession negatively affected transit's ability to modernize itself. We were fighting to get the people and resources to expand, but all throughout the early 1990s, the city experienced service cutbacks. We struggled just to hold service levels to current standards" (Millican).

Incremental progress did occur despite the funding roadblocks. City Council approved a 2.2-kilometre extension from Belvedere on the Northeast line in 1979, and Clareview Station opened in 1981. The Corona and Bay Stations opened downtown

Even under economic constraints, the LRT stations were impressive. The vaulted ceiling of the Bay Station was the kind of unique feature that added to the sense of eye-catching space and public art at LRT stations. *(ETS)*

in 1983 (the same year that D.L. MacDonald Garage and Yard was opened), Grandin Station would follow in 1989, and the University Station in 1992. The University Station served as the terminus of LRT for longer than many riders had hoped, but LRT showed signs of life again when service began to a new and more elegant Belvedere Station in 1998. Finally in January 2006, the provincial centennial year, the opening of the Health Sciences Station proved that the LRT was nearing the end of its difficult passage through the University of Alberta campus, and that rapid transit might realistically be anticipated to make further southward progress before much longer.

Regular service began in April 1978, with each train consisting of two coupled cars; three car configurations were sometimes used during peak passenger hours. With the Clareview extension, Edmonton Transit ordered three additional RTE1s to maintain service. These (Nos. 1015 through 1017) arrived in August 1979, were assembled at the Cromdale Garage and placed in service even before the completion of the Clareview line. Twenty more cars (Nos. 1018 through 1037) were built during 1981 and 1982, and all were in service by the following year. Sixteen of these had to be assembled in the new Anderson LRT Shops in Calgary because of space restrictions in Edmonton. Canron Railgroup Company also produced a service car for the LRT line, powered by a GMC 453 diesel engine, which could move on roads as well as tracks under its own power (No. 3850). The Kal-Trac heavy-duty road/rail vehicle, as it was called, was painted bright yellow (Buck).

Mayor Cec Purves officially opened the Clareview Station on 21 April 1981 at a ribbon-cutting ceremony that was followed by a jaunt for invited guests on the first train to officially roll into the station. Clareview was the first integrated LRT-bus facility operated by Edmonton Transit, and the Proof of Payment area was first introduced for both LRT trains and buses at that station. Belvedere and Clareview were built as temporary facilities. In fact, Clareview was constructed of modules that could be dismantled and relocated as part of a planned Clareview Town Centre complex (*Transit News*).

Keeping Edmonton Transit fares part of a unified system, even as new and improved services were offered, was a concern. LRT fares were planned to integrate completely with the existing Edmonton Transit fee structure to enable and encourage cross usage among riders. Fares were 40 cents for adults, 25 cents for children, and $15 for adult monthly passes in 1978. At first riders paid fare agents directly or presented them with bus passes or transfers at fare booths located in every station. Turnstiles preceded the Ticfak machine, and the system soon evolved to further improve customer service as Ticfak machines and Proof of Payment (POP) areas came into use. The POP system began on 19 November 1980, and was widely promoted. Riders soon became familiar with the turnstiles that replaced the old fare booths. Once in a POP area, riders were required to provide proof of payment if they were requested to do so by an Edmonton Transit fare agent, and could be fined if they had entered the area without paying. POP seemed to quickly ease the bottlenecks at loading and unloading areas throughout the LRT system. New Cubic Western ticket vending machines came into operation in 2004. In 2008 the smart card pilot project was initiated (Hatcher; Geake).

John Reid, who wrote the first operating rules for the LRT, noted

The ETS Pipes and Drums perform at the 1981 opening ceremony of the Clareview LRT Station. Mayor Purves is in the foreground. *(ETS)*

Little Poppers

Children riding the LRT will still be eligible for child's fare. However, they must press a special button on the turnstile after depositing fare. This button is well-marked and should pose no problem for young passengers.

Exiting

Patrons leaving the paid areas will exit through either the exit gates or the pass-and-transfer turnstiles, which rotate in both directions.

Special Events

To accommodate large crowds during events at the Commonwealth Stadium and Coliseum, exit gates will become entrance gates with Fare Agents handing out POP receipts as passengers deposit their fares in a special box.

Why Pop?

POP offers several advantages for passengers. Entering "paid" areas will be faster as all passengers will not have to line up at a single fare booth.

There will be better crowd control during rush hours and following events at the Coliseum and Commonwealth Stadium.

Entrances at both ends of the stations will be open whenever the LRT is operating. Riders will be able to enter and leave from whichever end of the station is most convenient.

So, come November 19,

DON'T FORGET TO GET POPPING.

THE CITY OF Edmonton

Edmonton transit

INTRODUCING POP*

The New LRT
*Proof of Payment
Way to Pay Your Fare

Starting November 19

Proof of Payment area in Central Station, with the Ticfak fare machine in the foreground. *(ETS)*

The POP campaign involved considerable work and advertising to make the system user-friendly.

These checks will be made on a random basis throughout the paid area, including the trains, station platforms and at exits. Watch for them at exits, and have your Proof of Payment ready.

Fare Agents are authorized to ask for identification and to issue citations for fines between $25 and $100 to anyone not carrying Proof of Payment.

So keep your transfer or POP receipt for your entire trip. Your POP receipt will also serve as a transfer if you continue your trip by bus.

POP RECEIPT OUT
COINS IN

Entering The LRT

There are now two kinds of turnstiles. The newest equipment is the coin-operated machines which will provide POP receipts after exact coin fare is dropped in.

So pop the money in and out pops the receipt. Then you can proceed through the turnstiles.

The other turnstiles are for passengers with passes or transfers from buses. These turnstiles will be free-wheeling. Passengers using these turnstiles will have to show either a pass or transfer if asked by a Fare Agent. The POP receipt must be produced by passengers without passes or transfers if questioned by the Fare Agent anywhere in the paid area of the LRT system.

A POP receipt will look like this:

Be sure to have exact fare with you when you enter the station. Coin-operated turnstiles will not give change.

Passengers Unable To Use Turnstiles

Swing-gates and special POP receipt dispensers will be provided for anyone unable to use the coin turnstiles. The dispensers will be located at:
- the east end of Central Transit Station
- the south end of Churchill and Stadium Transit Stations
- the north end of Coliseum and Belvedere Transit Stations

A passenger stamps her ticket as she enters the Proof of Payment area in the Central LRT Station. *(ETS)*

Let's Get Popping

Over the last month you may have noticed some construction going on inside the LRT stations. Workmen have been installing new turnstiles for the Proof of Payment (POP) fare collection system. Starting November 19, POP will be in full operation.

What Is Pop?

It's really very simple. Once the system is in operation, all LRT passengers, on the "paid" side of the turnstiles will be required to have some form of Proof of Payment.

This can be the regular monthly transit pass, a courtesy pass, a bus transfer or a Proof of Payment (POP) receipt from the new coin-operated turnstiles.

Our Fare Agents (we were going to call them Fair Agents because they're really nice people) will be able to ask passengers to produce their Proofs of Payment.

LRT Car No. 1010 after accident. *(ETS)*

The original LRT control room. *(ETS)*

that scrutiny by the federal Board of Transport was intense at the start of light rail transit in Edmonton. As this was the first such system in Canada, the Board was required and ready to exercise its jurisdiction over the LRT if necessary. Reid, who came from Canadian National Railway (CNR), used the rough draft prepared by his supervisor, Bob Clarke, which in turn was based on the legally proven CNR Uniform Code of Operating Rules. However, both the manual and the drivers who used it proved to be well up to safety standards when it came to the test of actual operation (Reid). Another reason for the close scrutiny was that the LRT operated between the CN tracks, and all crossings were regulated by the Board of Transport.

Accidents have been a fascinating, albeit expensive, part of the transit story from the first days of the Edmonton Radial Railway. These were always a comparatively costly problem for the transit system, and the enormous increase in disruption and cost in more recent times is graphically illustrated by the first significant accident on the LRT system that occurred early in its history. On 18 September 1981, a car crashed through the traffic barrier at 66 Street into the side of LRT cars 1004 and 1010 as they were crossing the intersection. Repairs totalled over $1 million, and 1010 had to be sent to Calgary for repairs by Siemens–Duewag. (Hatcher).

LRT vehicles have built-in safety features that largely ensure the safe movement of the cars. LRT

Operator Ken Taylor at the controls of a light rail vehicle. *(ETS)*

vehicles are governed by a wayside block signal system, in which signal lights are installed at stations and strategic points along the track to provide direction to onboard operators. LRT trains must stop at all red-light signals; failing this the train is automatically brought to a stop. If a red light is violated the operator can only move the train by receiving permission by radio from central control. As the LRT train moves past a green signal, the light reverts to red, making certain that another train does not enter that control block until the first one has left it. Operators who exceed the speed limit find that their train is automatically shut down (Hatcher).

One year after completion of the first section of LRT track in 1978, another 0.8-kilometre underground extension from Central Station westward beneath Jasper Avenue to two new stations was approved, with construction beginning in 1980. The Bay Station was located near the Hudson's Bay Company department store between 103 and 104 Streets, and the Corona Station was located near the temporary terminus of the line between 106 and 107 Streets. Mayor Cec Purves signalled the beginning of construction in October 1980 by driving the new LRT Locomotive (No. 2001) through a ceremonial banner in Central Station.

Years of construction on the Bay and

Locomotive 2001, driven by Mayor Cec Purves, breaks the banner to signal the extension of the LRT from Central Station in October 1980 beneath Jasper Avenue to 107 Street. No. 2001 is a 1912 Alco Steeplejack shunting locomotive used to move freight on the Vancouver docks. ETS rescued it from a warehouse in Burnaby and retrofitted it to haul the tunnel spoil away during LRT construction. *(ETS)*

Fred Singer wearing his "I DIG IT" T-shirt in 1981. *(ETS)*

Corona Stations along the Jasper Avenue corridor would again disrupt business in downtown Edmonton. Dave Geake was in close contact with the DART committee during these years and recalls some of the headaches associated with the prolonged construction work:

"Part of my job on the Corona project was to be in touch with the businesses along Jasper and try to resolve their issues. My favourites were dealing with Henry and Fred Singer, Ed Snyder, the owner of Laura Lee, a shoe store next door, and Burlington Art. We constructed bridges across excavations into their facilities, they ran the 'dirty shirt' sale and were always willing to give you an earful about how their business was going broke, the construction was unbearable, and what a difficult bunch we were to deal with.

"Some issues really were serious. I got a call from a small sandwich shop next to Waterloo Motors that his facility was being hit with shrapnel and it was killing his lunch business. I hustled down to find the station contractor was merrily jack-hammering concrete on the road surface to repair it and was indeed showering the front of the business with concrete chips. We got the work stopped and they rescheduled it at a better time" (Geake).

"Transplan," the Transportation System Plan, was received as information by City Council 11 May 1982. The Recommended Strategy was used as the basis for development of the Transportation System Bylaw 6707 required by the Province's City Transportation Act 1970, and was also used for amendments to the General Municipal Plan Bylaw 6000. (ETS)

Construction along Jasper Avenue in the early 1980s looking west from 103 Street. (ETS)

LEGEND
.... City Boundary prior to 1982 01 01
— — — City Boundary 1982 01 01

———————— Those LRT facilities existing and under construction

▪▪▪▪▪▪▪▪ Those LRT facilities proposed, where location is to be determined.

NOTE: Prior to City Council approval of an improvement shown in either category, a detailed functional planning study will be completed.

RECOMMENDED STRATEGY
TRANSIT NETWORK

EXHIBIT 3.9

A view of the Corona Station chandelier from the mezzanine level. There were some grumblings from the public and media at the time about the perceived extravagence of the chandeliers, and a member of the project team joked they should hang a trouble light and long extension cord instead. *(ETS)*

Passengers await the LRT under the chandelier in the Corona Station. *(ETS)*

Mayor Cec Purves at the opening ceremony for Corona LRT Station in 1983. *(ETS)*

The Bay Station, Corona Station and the connecting trackage finally were completed, and Mayor Cec Purves and Hon. Marvin Moore, Minister of Transportation, officiated at the official opening of the new extension on 21 June 1983. The striking Corona Station boasted chandeliers that descended from the mezzanine ceiling to the platform, while the shorter Bay Station featured an impressive vaulted ceiling. The stylish new stations featured Ticfak fare machines and barrier-free entrances that permitted free downtown riding beginning in November 1983 (between rush hours) and on Saturdays, in an effort to promote off-hours use, especially for downtown shopping.

With the LRT construction now moving so quickly, and expensively, an outside review of the South Light Rail Transit (SLRT) plan was authorized by City Council in October 1981. The review panel included Dr. Herbert Felz, Director of Planning and Development, Üstra, Hannover. (Üstra was originally the abbreviation for Überlandwerke und Straßenbahnen Hannover AG. The company also provided electricity to private customers as well as operating bus and tram services in Hannover. In 1960, the company changed its name to Hannoversche Verkehrsbetriebe (ÜSTRA) AG, then to ÜSTRA Hannoversche Verkehrsbetriebe AG in 1980, changing the word üstra to lowercase in 1996.) Other panel members were David F. Howard, Director of Planning,

The tunnel-boring machine in operation in the northbound tunnel from the north portal to Grandin Station. *(ETS)*

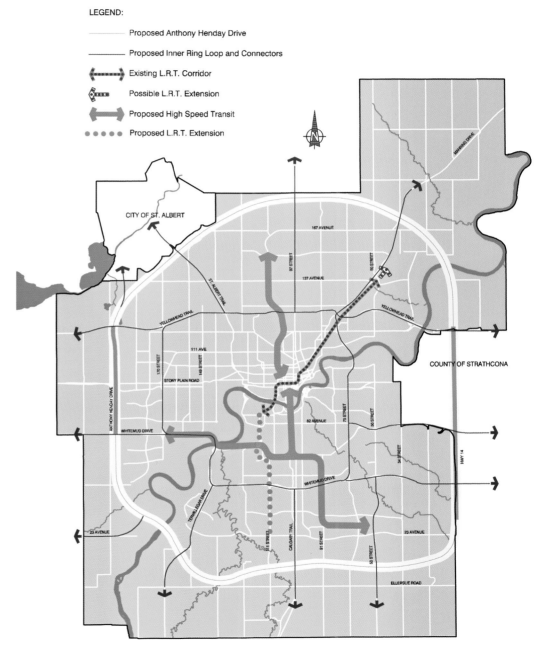

MAP 5 - THE TRANSPORTATION MASTER PLAN CONCEPT

LEGEND:

Proposed Anthony Henday Drive

Proposed Inner Ring Loop and Connectors

Existing L.R.T. Corridor

Possible L.R.T. Extension

Proposed High Speed Transit

Proposed L.R.T. Extension

The D.L. MacDonald Shops and Yard

As the LRT grew, so did the need for maintenance facilities. The D.L. MacDonald Shops and Yard replaced the venerable old Cromdale Garage in December 1983 at a cost of $28.2 million. Because the new shop was designed specifically to meet the operational and maintenance requirements of the LRT, it was fitting that it be named in honour of the ETS manager who played a leading role in bringing the light rail concept to the city. The shop complex consists of four sections dedicated to daily LRT operations.

Donald "Don" Lyon MacDonald was born and raised in Edmonton, beginning his civic career in 1946. He served two decades as General Superintendent of the Edmonton Transit System, the longest tenure ever in that position. Among his many achievements was overseeing the first computerized control system, but his greatest contribution was as champion of the LRT system for Edmonton. When he retired in 1977, he went to work for the City of Portland, Oregon, as project director for their light rapid transit system (*Transit News*).

Dumping dirt removed from LRT tunnelling operations on the construction site of the D.L. MacDonald Yard. *(ETS)*

The D.L. MacDonald Yard under construction. *(ETS)*

Edmonton Journal article about the contribution of native Edmontonian D.L. (Don) MacDonald, to the City and to ETS. *(Edmonton Journal)*

E.T.S. Superintendent Native Edmontonian

In 1952, when Mr. T. Ferrier retired from the post of E.T.S. Superintendent, it was not neccessary to go far afield to find a capable successor, he was already in the E.T.S. as assistant superintendent, and was a native Edmontonian to boot, none other than D. L. (Don) MacDonald.

D. L. (DON) MacDONALD

Born in Edmonton 38 years ago, Mr. MacDonald received his education at McCauley Public, and Victoria High Schools. His capabilities were evident early in life, and he won his first recognition by winning the Gyro Scholarship for attaining the highest scholastic standing in the city, when he graduated from grade eight at McCauley, to grade nine at Victoria High.

After completing high school, Mr. MacDonald entered the U. of A. from which he graduated in 1944 with his B.Sc. in electrical engineering. While attending university, Mr. MacDonald took University Naval Training Course, and in the summer of 1943, served on convoy duty in the North Atlantic. After graduation, the Navy became a full time job, and from 1944 until the spring of 1946 Mr. MacDonald served as Engineering Officer aboard H.M.C.S. Huron on overseas active duty.

In the spring of 1946, upon coming out of the navy, he joined the E.T.S., where his talents were immediately used on the conversion work required to complete the change-over from street cars to trolley and motor buses. With this out of the way for the time being, the development of other studies relative to the ever-expanding requirements of the Transit System became full time work, serving as a design engineer, technical assistant, and finally as assistant to Superintendent T. Ferrier, which position he held till 1952, when Mr. Ferrier retired. Today after nine years as superintendent, Mr. MacDonald has met and is meeting the challenges presented by our rapidly expanding and sprawling city and its transit problems.

Mr. MacDonald is a registered professional engineer in Alberta, and holds membership in the following technical associations: Engineering Institute of Canada, Society of Automotive Engineers, American Institute of Electrical Engineering, Institute of Radio Engineering, and recently completed a one year term as president of the Canadian Transit Association (1959-1960).

In 1948 Mr. MacDonald married Miss Irene Tomlinson of Edmonton, and today with their family of three boys and one girl they play an active part in community life, and are members of Robertson United Church.

An active Rotarian, Mr. MacDonald also finds time to pursue his hobbies of skiing and swimming. Reading plays an important role in his life as he keeps up with many demands and answers to the problems peculiar to the ever expanding transit systems throughout the world.

In 1960, the Canadian Manufacturers Association in conjunction with the Alberta Research Council sponsored the formation of the Alberta Productivity Council, whose aim is to develop more efficient methods (by case studies) of improving productivity in existing industries in the province. The council's first president, Mr. L. L. MacDonald.

Tyne and Wear Passenger Transport, Newcastle Upon Tyne; and Dr. Vukan R. Vuchic, Professor of Civil and Urban Engineering, Transportation, University of Philadelphia. Its report—*South Edmonton Light Rail Transit*—was completed in April 1982. Among its six recommendations was a plan to take the LRT line south from the University of Alberta to Southgate and Heritage areas, then to branch into the rapidly developing Mill Woods. This report also recommended a separate bridge to accommodate the river crossing, judging the High Level Bridge (completed in 1913) to have too limited a remaining lifespan at that point. Both these recommendations would prove persuasive, although this vision would not be fully realized until 2010, almost three decades after the plan was laid out and approved.

By 1983 the LRT was poised to cross the North Saskatchewan River and open up service to the south side. City Council gave approval in principle to the next two phases of LRT development in August 1983, including pre-engineering and design for the route from Corona Station to Government Centre, and then from the Legislature district across the river to the University of Alberta. Bylaw 6707 (September 1983), making the LRT eligible for provincial grants, was crucial to the project at the time. Mayor Laurence Decore and Al Adair, Alberta Minister of Transportation, officially launched the first phase of this south-side connection, known as the Grandin Extension, on 12 September 1986. This proved to be the most demanding section for tunnelling because of the postglacial sand through which it had to be driven. Drilling conditions resulted in the failure of the main bearing in the mole's cutting wheel. Also, community concerns for heritage green ash trees along the construction corridor had to be mitigated by a change in the location of the Grandin Station. Building the route

to Grandin–Government Centre would prove an extremely demanding task from virtually every angle ("South LRT is Coming Your Way").

Grandin Station opened on 31 August 1989, with Mayor Terry Cavanagh and Transportation Minister Al Adair officiating. The most ambitious and enthusiastic celebrations yet heralded the completion of what had proven to be perhaps the most controversial and difficult section of the LRT.

Interior construction on the D.L. MacDonald facility. *(ETS)*

Construction of the D.L. MacDonald Yard in 1983. *(ETS Archives)*

Grandin Station with the heritage trees that were saved during construction. *(ETS)*

Two new high-tech Light Rail Transit vehicles were officially unveiled on 6 July 1988 at the D.L. MacDonald Transit Yards, the final result of a joint agreement between the Province of Alberta, Siemens Electric Limited, the City of Calgary and the City of Edmonton. The Province, as part of their economic diversification initiative, purchased from Siemens a technology transfer agreement that would see the manufacturing of these high tech LRV propulsion systems in Edmonton. As part of this arrangement, the Alberta government requested the assistance of Edmonton and Calgary in their development and testing (*Transit News*).

The next phase of LRT construction to the south side would take the rails across a new, dedicated transit bridge, through the heart of old Walterdale, west of where the first ferry crossings were made before bridges were constructed, and then underground into the University of Alberta campus, where the new transit centre and University Station opened on 28 August 1992.

The interior of the Grandin Station with murals depicting the history behind the name and neighbourhood. *(ETS)*

One of the two cars that would be powered by a Siemens alternating current propulsion system. Colin Hatcher, in *LRT 25th*, noted that these demonstrator units were eventually sold to Calgary because Edmonton's fleet was big enough to meet the system needs at the time. *(ETS)*

The Dudley B. Menzies Bridge

The Dudley B. Menzies Bridge crossed the North Saskatchewan River just upstream from the High Level Bridge, and was the first bridge in western Canada to use the box girder system of construction. It was designed for multiple uses, accommodating a shared pedestrian and cyclist deck below the dedicated LRT deck. The bridge has six concrete piers, supporting 216 concrete box girders; each box girder had to be built specifically to accommodate the subtle curvature of the bridge. It was the first segmental post-tensioned bridge constructed in Western Canada. When it was constructed it contained the longest span for a post-tension bridge in North America. The Alberta Chapter American Concrete Industry presented this project its award for excellence in design in May 1991. Dudley B. Menzies, for whom the bridge was named, was the longest serving City Commissioner in Edmonton history, serving as Public Works Commissioner from 1945 to 1970. Menzies also served as a City Alderman from 1971 to 1974. (http://www.edmonton.ca/tranportation/transit/LRT_Brochure_2007)

Piers being erected across the North Saskatchewan River to carry the new Dudley B. Menzies Bridge. *(ETS)*

Close-up view of the box girders that formed the bridge constructed on the south bank of the river. *(Doug Cowan)*

Box girders during installation. The girders were individually fabricated to accommodate the curvature of the bridge. *(Doug Cowan)*

Girders being placed on piers. *(ETS)*

The LRT running across the completed bridge, towards the north side, with the Edmonton Radial Railway Society streetcar operating on the High Level Bridge. *(ETS)*

The renovated Belvedere Station.
(ETS)

The Verne MacKenzie Story

The LRT has its stories, as did the streetcars and trolleys in their day—from citizen reliance on the newest and fastest form of transit, to citizen frustration at tie-ups caused by construction, to driver experiences. The Belvedere Station is central to one of these reminiscences. Former operator Verne MacKenzie recalled one of these:

"Carl was on the locomotive and Jack was on control. Carl says, 'Well, am I clear to go back to D.L MacDonald?'

"D.L. had just opened and Jack said, 'Sure, why don't you use the northbound track through Belvedere?'

"Well everybody forgot that the northbound track platform was built out six inches wider [with a temporary wall on the platform edge], so when Carl hit it the whole thing came down. He saved a lot of money for the City of Edmonton because they didn't have to do a new demolition; it was already done" (Hatcher).

The LRT was successfully extended southward during 1992, terminating at the attractive new University LRT Station and Transit Centre. The Dudley B. Menzies multi-use LRT Bridge was completed after some funding difficulties. The LRT system now was 12.3 kilometres in length, with six underground, and four surface stations.

Mayor Jan Reimer, Hon. Al Adair, and University President Paul Davenport officially opened the University Station on 23 August 1992. The opening marked the completion of the LRT project to the end of that phase. Benefits from the new line were felt immediately. The many bus routes previously clogging the university campus now were less necessary for the efficient operation of Edmonton Transit. The new LRT line also would generate more rides in the coming decade, rising from 23,400 daily in 1990 to 36,000 daily by 2000.

The Northeast line also received some attention, even though this was a period of short funding and general restraint in the LRT plan. A new station was opened at Belvedere in August 1998.

The upgraded Belvedere Station opened on 23 September 1998, as a covered facility with a grade-separated passenger access and a platform now long enough to accommodate a five-car LRT train. Its stained glass windows added to the ambience. The attractive new Belvedere facility won the Award of Excellence from the Masonry Contractors Association of Alberta, and the Canadian Institute of Steel Construction, Alberta Steel Design Award for the most innovative use of structural steel.

Clareview Station was similarly upgraded during the spring of 2001, to more closely complement the designs of the Stadium and the Coliseum Stations. Sepia print transfers, funded by the Edmonton Arts Council, were added to the site design.

Allan Bolstad, City Councillor from 1992 until 2004, was a vigorous LRT supporter from the beginning of his time in office. "Just by standing on my block and watching the traffic build up on St. Albert Trail. That's one of the reasons I ran for City Council in 1992. I was looking at that and thinking, 'My God. What's going to happen here? There's no room to expand the road.' This route goes down through Groat Ravine and was constricted by existing neighbourhoods at that time, and was just on the brink then of attracting huge traffic volumes.

A bus outside the Hub Mall entrance to the University LRT Station. While citizens waited for the LRT to be completed, buses still provided an efficient and well-used service. *(ETS)*

ETS motorman, Olav (Ole) Larsen, brings in the first LRT car at the opening of the University Station with Acting Mayor Sheila McKay shaking hands with Mr. Justice William Stephenson. *(ETS)*

Stained glass panels in the upgraded Belvedere Station. *(ETS)*

New window art at the Clareview Station. *(ETS)*

Edmonton Transit worked with the Edmonton Arts Council and the "Art and Design in Public Places" program fostered by The Works International Visual Arts Society to enhance the atmosphere of its LRT stations. Transit Officer Tracy DeGraves stands in front of her likeness in the mural created by Mariann Sinkovics at the LRT Central Station to mark the 20th Anniversary of the LRT. *(ETS Archives)*

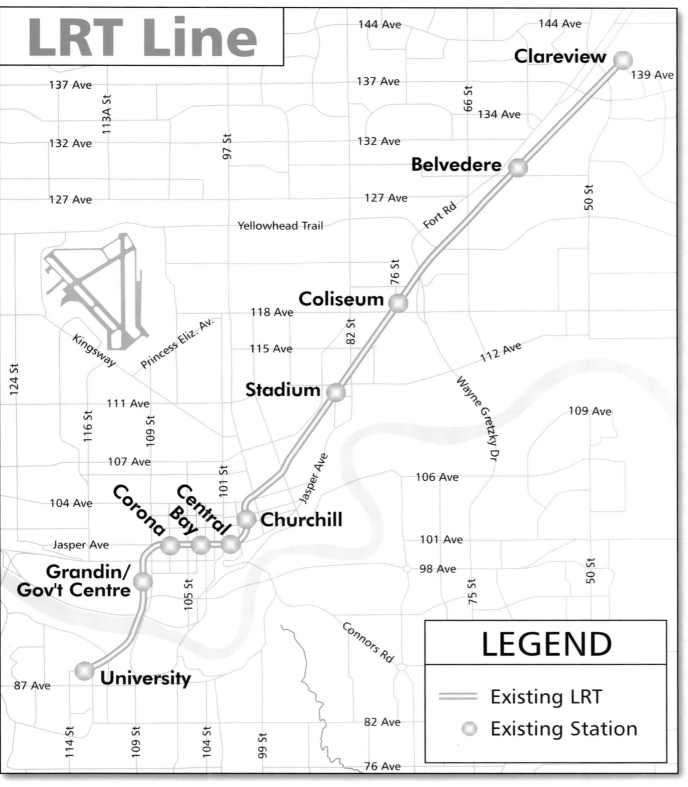

LRT Line

144 Ave

144 Ave

Clareview

139 Ave

137 Ave

137 Ave

66 St

134 Ave

113A St

132 Ave

132 Ave

Belvedere

97 St

127 Ave

127 Ave

Fort Rd

50 St

Yellowhead Trail

76 St

Coliseum

118 Ave

82 St

115 Ave

112 Ave

124 St

Kingsway

Princess Eliz. Av.

Stadium

Wayne Gretzky Dr

109 Ave

111 Ave

116 St

109 St

107 Ave

101 St

Jasper Ave

106 Ave

Corona

Central Bay

Churchill

104 Ave

101 Ave

50 St

Jasper Ave

98 Ave

75 St

Grandin/ Gov't Centre

105 St

University

87 Ave

Connors Rd

LEGEND

—— Existing LRT

⬤ Existing Station

114 St

109 St

104 St

99 St

82 Ave

76 Ave

One of Bolstad's first initiatives as City Councillor was the promotion of rapid transit planning for the northwest. "I took a lot of criticism for that. When I first came out with that in 1992 people thought I was 'dreaming in Technicolor. . . .'" That was the headline in one of the newspaper stories. People thought that was pretty outlandish. So it was a long struggle through some difficult times in the first years I was on Council because of the finances. . . ."

Today Bolstad marvels at the planning for the South Light Rail Transit (SLRT) and North Light Rail Transit (NLRT). In the mid-1990s building two lines simultaneously would have been impossible, he says. While sprawl has kept the ETS struggling, LRT today remains ETS's "star player. . . ."

Councillor Bolstad recalled during the ETS centennial year that things changed "quite dramatically" from the time when he was first elected to City Council to the present day. "They [the Provincial government] eliminated a $5 million annual transit grant in the blink of an eye," he said, snapping his fingers. "There was no phasing it out. . . . It just went. That money went to help us keep fares low. . . . Our transportation grant was cut dramatically as well to fund capital projects. That was cut from $70 per capita to $25 per capita over a three-year period [that is, phased in over three years]. That cut our funding to a third of what we had before. That's what really spelled the end of LRT in about 1994 or so. When those cuts began to come into effect it became crystal clear to us that there was just no point in trying to continue with LRT by ourselves" (Bolstad).

The line completed by 1992 continued to be the extent of LRT service for 10 more years. (ETS)

Two ex-mayors also voiced concerns about provincial funding. Cec Purves noted that "part of the problem was that [the Progressive Conservative cabinet] didn't understand cities, even though a lot of them lived in cities. Terry Cavanagh also attributed the stalling of the LRT project to "[Premier Ralph] Klein cutbacks and the general decline in the economy" (Purves; Cavanagh).

Public sentiment at the time supported cutbacks and staff layoffs so that tax increases could be held to zero for six years in a row. "Those were dark days," Bolstad concludes. This policy certainly proved to be shortsighted where transit development was concerned (Bolstad).

Edmonton Transit System neared the end of the 1990s with its Light Rail Transit service well established despite a long period of economic problems. It provided rides to 36,000 Edmontonians on any given weekday over a trunk line 12.3km in length—4.7 kilometres underground, including the Dudley B. Menzies Bridge, and the remaining 7.6 kilometres above ground. Its 37 sleek vehicles were a familiar and fondly regarded part of city life. Ten stations were strung along the line, connecting the northeast with the south side via downtown Edmonton. To this point the system had cost $344.7 million, and most felt that it had been a good investment in the future life of their city. If anything, the only question for many seemed to be, "When will we get LRT service in our neighbourhood?"

Works Cited

Bolstad, Allan. ETS Centennial Interviews, 2007–08. Edmonton, Alberta: ETS Archives.

Buck, George H. *A Technological History of Municipally Owned Public Transportation In Edmonton: 1893–1981.* Edmonton, Alberta: University of Alberta Thesis, 1985, pp. 600–59.

Cavanagh, Terry. ETS Centennial Interviews, 2007–08. Edmonton, Alberta: ETS Archives.

Hatcher, Colin. *Edmonton's light Rail Transit: The First 25 Years, 1978–2003.* Edmonton, Alberta: Edmonton Transit System, 2003, p. 23; 25; 33.

Geake, Dave. ETS Centennial Interviews, 2007–08. Edmonton, Alberta: ETS Archives http://www.edmonton.ca/tranportation/transit/LRT_Brochure_2007 (Accessed 14 December 2008).

Millican, Rick, ETS Centennial Interviews, 2007–08. Edmonton, Alberta: ETS Archives.

Purves, Cec. ETS Centennial Interviews, 2007–08. Edmonton, Alberta: ETS Archives.

Reid, John. ETS Centennial Interviews, 2007–08. Edmonton, Alberta: ETS Archives.

"South LRT is Coming Your Way," City of Edmonton Archives, MS 420, Llew Lawrence Fonds, Box 1, 1985.

Transit News, Vol. 8, No. 2, May 1981, p. 10; Vol. 10, No. 1, Spring 1983, p. 20; Vol. 15, No. 3, Summer 1988, p.14.

CHAPTER 15

Edmonton Transit Rolls On

1980–89

Edmonton artist Peter Lewis kicked off the exuberant decade of the 1980s by installing the Great Divide Waterfall on the High Level Bridge. Now operated on special occasions in summer, it is the largest manmade waterfall in the world. Constructed to celebrate Alberta's 75th Anniversary, the waterfall was an ironic emblem of a decade of mixed blessings during which Edmonton rode the highs of excesses and the lows of downturns in a pattern now very familiar to the province's resource-driven economy.

In the downtown core, the demolition of heritage buildings continued throughout the 1980s. The Rialto Theatre, the beautiful Art Moderne Eaton's store, and the Woolworth's and Tegler buildings all fell to the wrecking ball, but the City also forged ahead with worthy new architectural landmarks. In 1976 Peter Hemingway's striking Muttart Conservatory, characterized by its pyramid pavilions, became a distinctive part of the river valley in Cloverdale. The futuristic Edmonton Space Sciences Centre, designed by renowned Alberta architect Douglas Cardinal, opened at Coronation Park on Canada Day 1984. Mayor Terry Cavanagh proclaimed the old City Hall closed on 28 February 1989, and Edmonton architect Gene Dub was awarded the design contract for the new City Hall that anchors Churchill Square. Phase I of the West Edmonton Mall opened its doors in September 1981 with Phases II through IV opening in 1983, 1985 and 1999. Boasting nearly 502,000 square metres of space, including the

257

The waterfall created on the High Level Bridge in Edmonton by Peter Lewis is 7.3 metres higher than Niagara Falls. *(City of Edmonton Archives EA-340-1113)*

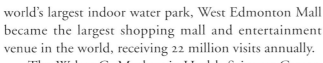

world's largest indoor water park, West Edmonton Mall became the largest shopping mall and entertainment venue in the world, receiving 22 million visits annually.

The Walter C. Mackenzie Health Sciences Centre, dedicated to the pursuit of research and health care, opened in September 1986, a sign of the position the City and Province was taking at the forefront of medical research. By the 1980s, the University of Alberta hospitals were renowned for their work in heart and kidney transplants. Each new development shifted transit dynamics and created challenges for the Edmonton Transit System.

Edmonton's multicultural roots were celebrated with enthusiasm during the 1980s with events such as the Heritage Festival that signalled an increasingly cosmopolitan outlook. Edmonton earned the distinction of Canada's Festival City. The first Fringe Theatre project, inspired by the great Edinburgh Fringe, was launched early in the decade and grew to become the largest in North America. It became a foundation upon which subsequent festivals would build. The Fringe, the Edmonton Folk Music Festival and other events presented seasonal challenges in ridership to ETS, where the personnel roster reflected the growing multi-ethnic reality. Things had come a long way since the days when men with the "wrong names" found it hard to secure employment with the City of Edmonton.

The Edmonton Folk Music Festival. *(ETS)*

Sports continued to bring Edmonton fame as the City of Champions during the decade. The Edmonton Oilers won five Stanley Cups in 1984, 1985, 1987, 1988 and 1990. The Edmonton Eskimos dynasty won the Grey Cup again in 1987, adding to an impressive record of playoff berths that no North American sports franchise has equalled.

The XII World Universiade Games held 1–11 July 1983 galvanized citizens' renowned spirit of volunteerism as Edmonton hosted the first World University Games held in North America. Churchill Square rang to the sounds of international entertainers as athletes competed in venues around the city. The Games' legacy included the Edmonton Convention Centre.

Edmonton Transit played a major role in transporting spectators to the games. Unfortunately, a crush of over 40,000 passengers bound for the official opening on Canada Day threw the entire system into chaos, and hundreds arrived late for the ceremony. One rider claimed the ride from the new Corona Station to the Commonwealth Stadium took over an hour because the new Ticfak fare machines could not handle the crowds (*Transit News Canada*).

The Pipes and Drums of Edmonton Transit performed at the World Universiade Games, as at so many other prestigious events and venues in Edmonton and elsewhere. Ernie Bastide recalls how a group once "got to play with the Ghurkhas [and] met Prince Charles and Princess Di. . . ." The Pipes and Drums Band was formed in the summer of 1964 by a group of ETS operators interested in Scottish bagpipe music. Early financial support by the union local was later supplanted by ETS, which subsequently purchased the band uniforms. Mayor Stephen Mandel declared the group the official City of Edmonton band in November 2005. During the Games, Edmonton Transit used No. 9 route to run its Gallery in Transit, where the work of many prominent Edmonton photographers replaced the advertising normally on display (Bastide, Paul).

Edmonton Transit and Sports Fans

Edmonton Transit has played a special role in providing service to patrons of Clarke Stadium and Commonwealth Stadium for over four decades. Special transit services to major events at Clarke Stadium were first introduced in 1966, and the scale of the service grew from a 1975 ridership of 32,000 to well over 80,000 in 1983 (statistics prior to 1975 are not available). Annual costs increased from $67,000 to an estimated cost of $495,000 during that period.

Having adopted the Clarke Field Development Scheme Bylaw in 1975, the City assumed responsibility for ensuring that the impact of events at Commonwealth Stadium on adjacent neighbourhoods would be minimized. The requirements for neighbourhood parking restrictions and special transit services to major events remain an important responsibility. A later innovative response has been to provide free access to transit services for game days for all ticket holders.

By 1983 special transit services (Park and Ride, and shuttle buses) were provided for events with an expected attendance of over 16,000, with Edmonton Transit to recover 50 percent of the cost of providing these special transit services. According to the Transit Strategy Review in 1983, Edmonton Transit was to provide transportation for 50 percent of event patrons by means of Park and Ride, shuttle buses, LRT and regular transit services (City of Edmonton, *Transit Strategy Review*).

Buses and the LRT provide major event transportation at the Clarke Stadium/ Commonwealth Stadium site. *(ETS)*

A bus provides park and ride services prior to 1976. *(ETS #8.3 S203)*

The official opening of the World Universiade Games on 1 July 1983. Edmonton Transit transported crowds to Commonwealth Stadium.
(City of Edmonton Archives EA-340-2034)

JAPAN

The Ellis Burk Story

Edmonton Transit employees remained committed to public service despite the disappointments of events such as the strike in the early 1980s. The *Edmonton Journal* reported one ETS employee doing what members of the service routinely have done since the start of public transit in the city—looking out for their fellow citizens.

EYES ON EDMONTON

"ETS employees have frequently served as the ears and eyes of the community as they go about their business.

"Early on a Monday morning in the spring of 1986, Rick Rakowski, his wife and two children were sleeping peacefully. The Rakowski family was awakened abruptly by someone banging on their front door. Ellis Burk, a neighbour and ETS inspector who was on his way to work that morning of 12 May 1986, had noticed smoke billowing from the garage behind the Rakowski house, just as it spread to the roof of their residence.

"After rousing the other neighbours, Burk continued on to work *(Edmonton Journal).*"

The Pipes and Drums Band wearing the early red uniforms. *(ETS)*

Demands from newly annexed areas increased following the extension of municipal boundaries on 1 January 1982 that brought adjacent areas of Parkland County, Strathcona County and the Municipal District of Sturgeon into the city. A provincial report indicated that "the directions of growth represented by the boundary changes take account of a number of factors including . . .the need for rational planning, servicing and transportation . . ." (City of Edmonton, *Report and Decision Concerning the Edmonton Annexation Application*).

The booming 1970s came to an end with an economic slump following the failure of the Alsands project in 1982. The malaise grew following the Gainers Strike, the most violent in the city's history. Edmonton Transit endured its own very acrimonious strike in 1982. The rest of the decade would be marked by relatively slow economic progress in many sectors and labour unrest.

Having endured a bitter 44-day strike in 1982, lasting from February 15 to March 29, Edmonton Transit drivers returned to work feeling less than happy. They had won wage parity with Calgary (which would really only be achieved two years into the contract), but had lost the battle to keep all drivers as full-time employees. The City won the point on part-time drivers, committing to introduce this change slowly and to ensure that these drivers worked no more than 20 hours per week. This change was presented as saving costs for the system. Drivers already worked split shifts to accommodate system needs and feared the practice of hiring part-time workers would eventually impact the availability of full-time positions. One returning driver summed up the general feeling, saying to the *Edmonton Journal*, "We're getting almost the same wage as what we started and there's still the part-time. But we really didn't have an option, did we? A lot of us are starving" *(Edmonton Journal).*

The drivers' fears proved justified. Edmonton Transit, in a surprise reversal of its stated policy, announced plans to lay off up to 106 bus drivers and cut 4,200 operating hours from the coming summer schedule starting 17 July 1982. The original plan was to phase in cuts throughout July, September and November, but Bob David, head of the City's Transportation Management Department, favoured the single cut. Eighteen routes would be eliminated, while midday and evening weekend services would be reduced on 31 routes. Public reaction was immediate, with riders on three affected routes collecting over a thousand signatures on petitions.

The ETS Pipes and Drums Band playing at the 2005 opening of the LRT extension to the Health Sciences/Jubilee Station. The City purchased the new uniforms. *(ETS)*

ATU Local #569 supported the workers in the 1986 Gainers strike, remembering their own bitter struggle of 1982. *(ETS Archives)*

POLICE/

MAKE THE RICH PAY !

ATU ELECTRICAL WORKERS LOCAL 424

A.T.U. LOCAL 569 SUPPORTS CHANGES TO THE LABOUR ACT

PUBLIC SERVICE ALLIANCE

LABOR UNITE OR FALL

BOYCOTT GAINERS

LETTER CARRIERS

LETTER CARRIERS

BOYCOTT GAINERS

Routes 23 (Kingsway–Montrose) and 32 (Windsor Park–Belvedere), scheduled for elimination, were partially restored. But maintaining existing service levels would cost an extra $1.5 million. Alderman Jan Reimer said that Edmonton Transit's administration was top-heavy and it, rather than service, should be cut. Morale among drivers, especially the most junior, was very low, with City and Union estimates of layoffs varying between 58 and 106. Eighteen of the least-senior drivers received layoff notices and were offered part-time work. Drivers fielded most complaints about the April service cuts and had to cope with overcrowded buses and impatient riders.

City Council voted 12 July 1982 to instruct Edmonton Transit to find up to $600,000 in its budget to meet demand for service. General Manager Bob David had warned that without an additional $800,000, this might not be possible, while the Public Affairs Committee had recommended that

$1.3 million be reallocated to maintain services. Only about $500,000 had been found. It took a motion of Aldermen Bette Hewes and Olivia Butti to allow service to be restored on the 31 routes that were due to be cut (*Transit News Canada*).

The transit fleet continued to grow rapidly in response to growing ridership. Major decisions had to be made about the best direction in which to expand the fleet in the future. The Canadian Car and Foundry trolley buses were being retired by the early 1980s, and the question of whether to retain trolley service was raised once again. The trend in other Canadian, American and European cities was to replace their trolleys with diesel buses. The City of Edmonton had hired Hu Harries and Associates in 1975 to assess the future requirements for transit. The *Harries Report* concluded that while trolleys were more expensive to purchase they had an optimum lifespan 10 years

One of 100 Brown Boveri/GMC trolleys purchased by Edmonton Transit in 1983. These trolleys ran until the discontinuation of the service in 2009. *(ETS)*

greater than motorbuses, 25 years opposed to 15. Harries additionally pointed out that trolleys produced less air pollution, were quieter, and required less maintenance than most motorbuses. An updated version of the *Harries Report* recommended two years later that Edmonton Transit acquire enough trolleys to ensure that at least 105 units for daily service. City Council approved the purchase of 100 new trolleys on 10 July 1979 (Nos. 100–199) (*Edmonton Journal*).

On 13 August 1980, City Council approved the Brown Boveri Canada trolley bid, presented by the Canadian subsidiary of the Swiss firm Brown Boveri and Company. Brown Boveri planned to install their electronic apparatus in GMC 5307 bus bodies. Although the company did not submit the lowest bid, their equipment had a very high reputation, and the City had a long relationship with Brown Boveri dating back to the first mercury arc rectifier purchased for the ERR in 1929, which was manufactured by Brown Boveri. The rectifier remained in service until the late 1970s. As well, the GMC 5307 was well known to ETS personnel since Edmonton operated nearly 400 T6H-5307 GMC diesels by this time.

The bodies for the new trolleys were manufactured at the GMC Quebec plant and were similar to the T6H-5307 diesels then in use. Because GMC was a subcontractor to Brown Boveri, the GMC insignia on the front of the bus was replaced with the letters *BBC* representing the Brown Boveri Company. The new units were known as chopper trolley buses because a single compound-wound motor was mounted longitudinally at the rear of the trolley and controlled by a solid-state unit called a chopper. The chopper trolleys seated only 42, but this conformed to Edmonton Transit specifications intended to allow more standees, thought to benefit high-density routes at the time. The Brown Boveri Company supplied the main motor and the control apparatus. The solid-state apparatus, as well as a redesigned air compressor, made the new trolley buses quite efficient and virtually maintenance free (Buck; Paul).

Bennett and Emmott assembled the BBC trolleys in Edmonton, and they were placed in service in 1981–82. With these additions to the fleet, Edmonton Transit operated more trolleys than at any other time in its history. Despite oil shocks and moves toward more environmentally friendly public transit, the energy efficient trolleys would remain controversial in local politics until their final end was decided in 2008.

The Mitchell Garage

As the Edmonton Transit fleet continued to grow with demand, so did the need for storage and maintenance facilities. The Mitchell Garage, Edmonton Transit's newest garage, became operational in February 1981 and was officially opened on 7 April by Mayor Cec Purves. The facility, enclosing two hectares under one roof, was constructed under the direction of the Real Estate and Housing Department. Special guests at the opening were Bob Mitchell and his wife, Betty, the son and daughter-in-law of Frederick John Mitchell, in whose honour the garage was named.

Frederick John Mitchell served as Alderman on City Council from 1941 through 1964. His was the longest term of civic office held in the history of Edmonton and included a brief stint as mayor when William Hawrelak resigned on 9 September 1959. Following civic elections on 19 October 1959, Mitchell returned to his former position as alderman. At the time he was elected mayor, Mitchell was serving on the interim Development Appeal Board, the Amalgamation Committee, and the Edmonton District Planning Commission. Born 4 December 1893 in Stratford, Ontario, Mitchell attended the Berlin [Kitchener] Collegiate and Technical Institute. He died in Edmonton on 25 December 1979 (*Transit News*).

Mitchell Garage became home to 145 transit vehicles, stored and serviced there daily as it became home base for about 225 operators. Trolley bus operation began at Mitchell Garage in 1983. It directly serviced transit needs to Jasper Place, and buses travelling to St. Albert also originated from the new facility. "Mitchell Garage is strategically located to provide more direct service to Edmonton's northwest communities. We anticipate future growth in the City's west end in the next several years, and this new facility will handle any anticipated upsurge of transit requirements for our citizens," said General Manager Don Miller (Paul).

The Mitchell Garage opened in 1981. *(ETS)*

The interior of the Mitchell Garage under construction. *(ETS)*

A Brown Boveri Company trolley runs east on 102 Avenue under the Chinatown Gate in downtown Edmonton. *(ETS)*

In the spring of 1985, two mercury-arc rectifiers and the DC switch-gear were replaced at 360s trolley substation (105 Avenue and 104 Street), which supplied most of the trolley traction power to the downtown core. Colin Harke, Electrical Plant Engineer, coordinated the project. The original equipment at 360s was approximately 30 years old and was no longer considered reliable. System reliability was ensured by replacing the mercury arc rectifiers with solid-state rectifiers, and replacing the DC switchgear with a much safer version (*Transit News*).

By the spring of 1985, the Transportation Department also was conducting a review of Edmonton Transit's trolley bus operation despite the substantial investment made five years earlier in the trolleys. The future of trolley service looked bleak. Only 60—and sometimes as few as 30—of the 100 new BBC/GM trolleys were in service at any given time. Also, only one or two of the 37 Flyer E-800s—by this time about 10 years old—were in operation. The Flyer trolleys were intended simply to supplement the BBC/GM fleet, but when they proved unreliable, they were removed from service and subsequently sold to Mexico City in 1986.

The trolley controversy became concentrated on a Transportation Department study that contradicted the Harries' report by claiming that trolleys cost more to operate than diesel buses, after the high "diesel standby" cost (the diesel buses required to replace trolleys when the roadways of the major trolley routes were being torn up) were considered. The report also concluded the vaunted longer design life of trolleys was not borne out in practice. The new BBC's were now depreciated over 15 years, the same as diesel buses, instead of over 22 years like the old Brills. Commentators opposing the new report insisted that there had not been any diesel standby fleet until Edmonton Transit discovered that it had too many diesel buses, and the editor of *Transit News Canada* concluded that "the oldest of [the trolleys] actually lasted 31 years, vs. 23 years for the oldest diesel" (*Transit News Canada*; Paul).

Transportation Department official John Schnablegger supported some claims made by critics, who termed the study a "quickie." He noted that Edmonton had spent $800 million upgrading its trolley overhead network since about 1982, including a second set of wires on 102 Avenue from 128 Street to 156 Street to allow express trolley service to West Jasper Place. The installation cost $800,000, but the route was never converted to trolleys. Schnablegger ordered an operational audit of trolleys and diesels to verify the study's claims.

Llew Lawrence, always a spirited advocate for trolleys, argued that trolleys were quieter, cleaner, more comfortable, and smoother than their alternatives in a 1982 speech to a trolley bus workshop in Seattle. He also turned the trolley's supposed disadvantage of inflexibility due to fixed routes into an advantage. People always know where the trolley is coming from and where it is going, he pointed out. Trolleys benefit Edmonton Power as much as diesels benefit oil companies, he continued. In 1984 Edmonton Power sold $230,000 worth of electricity to Edmonton Transit, which also paid $850,000 for construction and maintenance of overhead lines. Lawrence estimated that Edmonton Transit construction provided work for 15 Edmonton Power employees (*Transit News Canada*).

While the trolley controversy raged, Edmonton Transit continued to evaluate articulated buses as a means of expanding carrying capacity. Edmonton Transit conducted two articulated vehicle demonstration projects during the summer of 1982 involving the Crown Ikarus 286 and the GMC New Look diesel models.

The steering committee responsible for testing articulated buses already had decided to lease and evaluate two West German M.A.N. and one Swedish Volvo articulated diesel bus during 1977–79. While this trial was generally very successful, the Province felt it was desirable to gain further experience with other articulated vehicles, and the 1980s brought further tests. In August 1981, representatives from Edmonton Transit, Calgary Transit, and Alberta Economic Development visited the Crown Coach Corporation in Los Angeles to view the final assembly of the Crown-Ikarus bus, carry out a preliminary assessment of its mechanical and structural features, and prepare for a future demonstration in Alberta. On 24 March 1982, the Department's Executive Management Committee approved a formal proposal for an in-service demonstration of a Crown-Ikarus articulated diesel over a four-week period commencing 7 June 1982. At the same time as arrangements were made with Crown Coach Corporation, Edmonton Transit contacted the Diesel Division of General Motors of Canada to arrange a demonstration of their New Look 60-foot articulated bus.

The M.A.N. articulated test bus, one of the prototypes tested in the late 1970s. *(ETS Archives)*

Crown-Icarus Portland Tri-Met #781 on loan for demonstration outside the Westwood Garage.
(Mike Dasher, www.barp.ca/bus/ets)

The GM model TA 60102N, Mississauga #5001, demonstration bus on Route 9, in Edmonton in August 1982.
(www.barp.ca/bus/ets, Peter Cox)

The Crown-Ikarus 286 was manufactured by Ikarus, a Hungarian manufacturer and the largest articulated bus-maker in the world, in cooperation with Crown Coach Corporation of Los Angeles. It incorporated many American features like a Cummins diesel engine and an Allison transmission. During the test, some passengers complained of the noise levels and elevated seats, while drivers found their compartment difficult to enter and exist. Otherwise it met with general approval.

The GMC New Look 60-foot articulated diesel bus was manufactured by its Diesel Division, one of the most reputable North American companies. This model was introduced in Canada in 1981 after nearly four years of design and testing. The model was based on the existing 35- and 40-foot New Look platforms already in use in Edmonton. It was a pusher type using the rear axle to drive the vehicle, unlike the European design that used the centre axle as the drive unit. Its Detroit Diesel 8V71 engine and Allison transmission were placed in the familiar rear cradle in the same configuration as that of the existing GM diesel bus (Paul).

Extensive vehicle evaluations—including passengers', operators' and mechanics' views—were carried out on the articulated models, coordinated by the Projects and Engineering Section. Route 9 was chosen for the tests during the summer of 1983 because it was a major route on the mainline network with a heavy service schedule; it also operated over Bellamy Hill, one of the steepest grades in Edmonton. Edmonton Transit was confident that winter conditions would not be a problem because of a special traction feature that automatically cut power to any wheel that began to spin. The "accordion buses," as the media dubbed them, turned more easily than feared, but some drivers, like Brian Mason, who after his transit career became a City Councillor and then an MLA, never fully adjusted to the fact that the rear end was out of sight on tight turns. The test buses seated 157 passengers, rather than the standard 107. Despite relatively good reviews, articulated buses did not become a major part of the fleet until 2001 when New Flyer low floor models were purchased (Keshwani; *Edmonton Journal;* Mason).

A significant reorganization occurred in late 1983, when a new Transportation Department was created from Edmonton Transit, Engineering, and Transportation Management departments. (The consolidation and formation of the Engineering and Transportation Department occurred in 1971. In late 1979, the Transportation Planning Branch of the Planning Department changed to the Transportation Systems Design Department which later morphed to the Transportation Management Department; this latter department was created with the mandate of strategic planning, and the Engineering Department and Edmonton Transit were operationally and tactically focussed.) Barry Temple, Manager of Operations and Development for Edmonton Transit, provided some context: "There is a general pattern in business of consolidating functions during economic downturns and then decentralizing to handle rapid growth. The groundwork for our growth in the mid-1970s was laid in the old consolidated department, so there are advantages to each approach" (*Transit News*). Greg Latham, who joined the City in 1973, was acting manager for the Transportation Department in 1988–89. He recalled the reorganizations of Edmonton Transit as focused on standardizing how changes were made and ensuring that all employees could excel:

"I started out with major in-house interviews, looking for issues that needed to be focused on. And I worked closely with the transportation manager. We started things out with a workplace action team process to address specific issues. We standardized the process for making changes and met every quarter to determine how things were progressing. We wanted the best performance from our people and wanted to create an environment that they could reach that potential. This meant working alongside union management, too."

This focus on responsiveness made it possible to respond promptly to concerns for customer service and innovation. Thus, in April 1983, City Council directed the Transportation Management Department to study possible paratransit options. Edmonton Transit moved swiftly to update a 1978 study conducted in Clareview, Hermitage, Beverly, Duggan, Westbrook, Petrolia and Kaskitayo, which proved too costly at that time. This system harked back to the old hail-cabs and jitneys of the early twentieth century. Elsewhere, Dial-a-Bus, a more comprehensive system, was developed in the United States during the 1960s, and demand-responsive systems soon were being experimented with throughout North America. Many of these failed (*Transit News*).

In November 1983, Edmonton Transit began its experiment with Dial-a-Bus in Riverbend that replaced regular service on two routes on evenings, Sundays and holidays. The new twist saw riders calling their drivers directly rather than the dispatch office. Another innovation saw the LRT line between Churchill and Corona stations become a free-ride zone in off-peak hours to promote downtown shopping. Ridership soared for a while, especially during the Christmas season in 1983 (*Transit News Canada*).

While Edmonton Transit moved ahead with new initiatives, it still took time to celebrate its history when its 75th Anniversary occurred on 9 November 1983. Alderman Julian Kiniski unveiled a plaque commemorating the event near the intersection of 95 Street and 118 Avenue, the northern terminus of the first streetcar line in 1908. The Edmonton Transit Pipes and Drums Band played at the ceremony, and dignitaries later took a ride over the old route in No. 432, a restored 1958 GM coach. This bus became part of the Edmonton Transit heritage fleet, a permanent legacy for the citizens of Edmonton.

On Canada Day 1985, all 1,050 Edmonton Transit drivers and inspectors donned a new uniform. The old uniform, described as a leisure-suit style, was replaced with a sports-jacket style, blue like the previous uniform, with solid navy blue ties, except for one band of the Edmonton Transit white-and-gold. The former ties had a blue-white-and-gold pattern on the entire tie. Each driver received a new uniform each year (*Transit News Canada*). That same year, Edmonton Transit began to enforce the same no-smoking regulations on its drivers that had been in force for decades with passengers. Drivers would now have to step off the bus at their layover point to light up, due to "the aggressiveness of anti-smoking groups, and the increasing number of complaints from riders" (*Transit News Canada*).

Len Erickson shows off the new uniform introduced in 1985. *(ETS Archives)*

The first two so-called superbuses also appeared on city streets a year later. The innovation, which clad the entire bus in advertising, was proposed to Transit Manager Geoff Atkins in February 1986 by Trans Ad, the contractor, which then was directed to sell the idea to Edmonton businesses. Edmonton Transit became the first transit system in Canada to have superbuses operating on regular service runs. The Equipment Section added the graphics, and the first two buses were painted in transit facilities. The radio station CISN bus and the Remax Real Estate bus were done completely in-house (*Transit News*).

The restored 1958 GM coach used at the 75th Anniversary ceremony. *(ETS)*

The hand-painted Remax and CISN buses. *(ETS)*

ETS designed this painted bus to promote the express service from Heritage Transit Centre.
(ETS and Doug Cowan)

ETS took up the advertising challenge with designs like this one promoting Earth Day (with Mayor Jan Reimer posing beside the bus).
(ETS and Doug Cowan)

THINK GREEN, THINK CLEAN.

Celebrate EARTH DAY
April 22, 1990

Edmonton transit

What will you do?

96K-LITE
FM STEREO LiteRock LessTalk

Don't Pull the Shade on our Environment

158

9

With the increase in high-rise development, even the top of the "super-wrap" bus carried advertising. Starting in the mid-90s, bus wrap advertising covered a wide range of subects from this promotion of horse-racing . . .
(ETS and Doug Cowan)

252

... to entertainment in the city,
such as visiting Fort Edmonton Park) ...
(ETS and Doug Cowan)

. . . to promoting
shopping at malls
such as Heritage.
(ETS and Doug Cowan)

On 31 July 1987, a powerful tornado cut a swath of destruction as it ploughed through south and east Edmonton and across the North Saskatchewan River, leaving 29 Edmontonians dead. As a result, the Edmonton Emergency Relief Agency was organized, and sophisticated Doppler technology was installed to forecast severe inclement weather more accurately.

Edmonton Transit's emergency call-out and operation plan went into action at 4:00 PM on Black Friday and already was in place when the City declared an emergency and established its Disaster Operations Centre at City Hall.

Edmonton Transit's Plant and Electrical Systems worked tirelessly between 4:00 PM Friday and 4:45 PM Sunday afternoon repairing damage caused by the tornado. A major sewer collapse in northeast Edmonton overloaded the storm sewer in the area of the LRT tunnel at 66 Street. The resulting water backup caused manhole covers to pop, washing out over a hundred feet of track bed. (The tunnel area was lower than the storm sewer and filled quickly with two metres of water.) Track Crew Foreman Albert Luethe arranged for pumping equipment and immediately organized crews to repair the track. All Edmonton Transit staff turned out and struggled against the adverse conditions to lend assistance, many cutting short their vacations.

It was impossible to keep bus services on schedule because of flooded underpasses and streets, and downed power lines caused traffic light failures and memorable traffic jams. Edmonton Transit's Control Centre and inspectors became involved in many emergency activities, including operating shuttle bus services between the Disaster Command Centres for Evergreen Mobile Home Park and the southeast industrial area. Don MacDougal distinguished himself as liaison with Police Inspector Frank Topp in northeast Edmonton. Edmonton Transit also aided the City Hall Operations Centre with communication and field requirements such as hot meals and new injury reception areas.

The tornado hits Edmonton on 31 July 1987. *(ETS)*

Shelter and plant crews assisted the LRT track crew to move equipment and ballast trains throughout the weekend while repairing broken equipment and installing pumps and hoses. Even LRT inspectors and Control personnel helped by moving work trains and equipment to the work site. Through such Herculean efforts, limited LRT service was restored by four o'clock on Saturday afternoon, just in time for the football game service. By the same time the following day, full LRT service had returned by 4:45 on Sunday afternoon and full scheduled service was back by Monday morning (*Transit News*).

Rain pounding the city caused flooding and disruption to many services during the 1987 tornado. Here, commuters huddle in shelters and run for cover. *(ETS)*

While Edmonton Transit was losing some of its important innovators such as Llew Lawrence in 1988, others were working to preserve the memory of the old system. Old No. 99, a Canada Car Brill (Model 36), which trundled down Edmonton streets between 1946 and 1967, was restored to working order and became a part of the Edmonton Transit heritage fleet. These buses have been used for special events since the late 1980s (*Transit News*).

Brill No. 99 restored and used in parades after 1988. *(ETS)*

Greater public involvement, enhanced cooperative planning and commitment to growing the service grid marked the start of the final decade of the century. The 1980s confirmed Edmonton as a city of champions and festivals, and civic pride was buoyed by the achievements of its sportsmen and sportswomen, and cultural events. The city, as always, looked to the future, laying the groundwork for the progress that it hoped would come in the 1990s.

The Llew Lawrence Story

Llew Lawrence at his retirement in 1988. *(ETS)*

Llew Lawrence retired in April 1988. Lawrence was a prime example of the man who works his way up the ladder of success. Young Llew came to Canada from England in May 1953, first working on an Ontario dairy farm, then moving west to continue working on farms and other jobs around Paradise Valley and Edmonton. He applied for an operator's position with the Edmonton Transit System and was accepted on 4 November 1954, became a Relief Dispatcher in 1956, then permanent Dispatcher in July 1957. (Llew was the dispatcher who opened Westwood Garage in 1961.) He was a Night Shift Supervisor between 1962 and 1965.

Superintendent D.L. MacDonald seconded Lawrence as a Special Projects Officer to the Personnel Department in 1965. For a while, Lawrence also completed assignments for Edmonton Power, Edmonton Telephones, and the Personnel and Parks Departments in classification, organization, salary review and planning. In November 1968, MacDonald brought him back to Edmonton Transit as his Special Projects Officer. It was during this period that he assisted MacDonald to build the Rapid Transit Planning team, did special studies for the Commission Board and the Parks and Recreation Departments, and laid the groundwork for the formation of the Engineering and Transportation Department that was launched in 1972–73.

Lawrence was promoted to Director of Marketing for Edmonton Transit in November 1972, and in January 1982, he became the Director of Operations. He started the program of visiting communities to "talk transit" to people and to see that Transit plans were acceptable and workable. In 1984 Lawrence was named Director of Studies and Special Projects *(Transit News)*.

The Edmonton Radial Railway Society

The City's 75th Anniversary in 1979 focused civic pride on the importance of Edmonton's past. One group with close ties to ETS had a leading role in this renewal of interest in the city's deep history. The Edmonton Radial Railway Society (ERRS) set about restoring Street Car No. 1 for use in city celebrations. Using the railway tracks and towing a generator, No. 1 rolled across the High Level Bridge on Thanksgiving Weekend in 1979. This event sparked the dreams of the ERRS, and the group struck an agreement with the Fort Edmonton Park Foundation to restore and run streetcars as one of the main transportation modes in the park.

Streetcar barn under construction at Fort Edmonton Park. The facility provided space for the extensive restorations of streetcars by the ERRS. *(ERRS)*

Car No. 80, seen here when it was new, was one of five steel construction cars built by the Ottawa Car Company for delivery to Edmonton in 1930. *(ETS)*

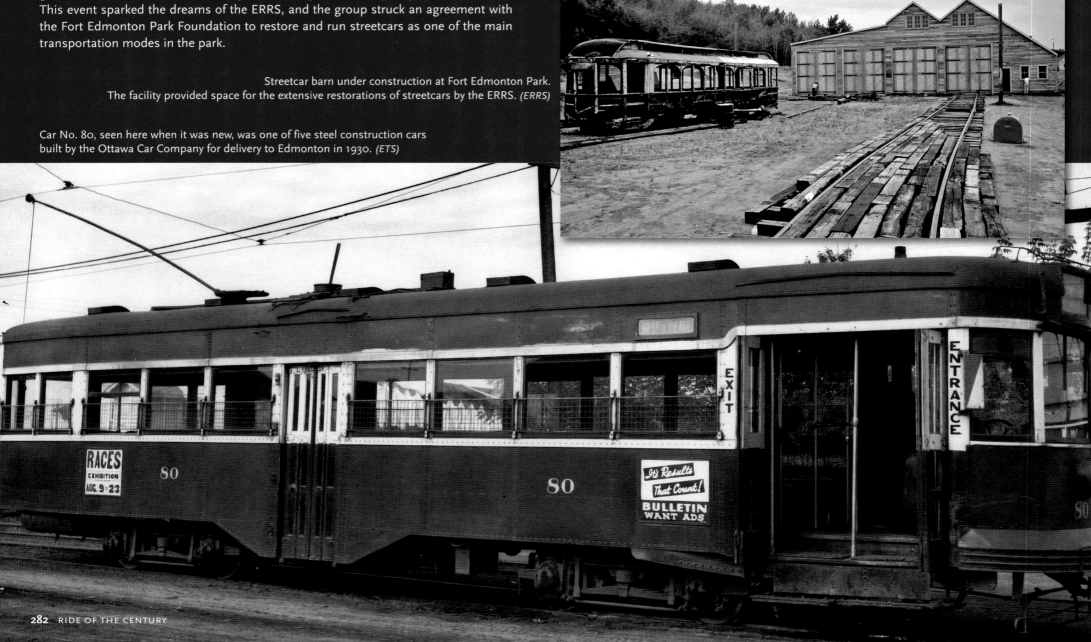

Streetcar Nos. 1, 42 and 80 are part of the ERRS fleet at Fort Edmonton. All required extensive restoration and all were significant in Edmonton's streetcar history. No. 1, as the first car was an obvious choice. No. 42 has the distinction of becoming a mobile maternity ward when Peter Budnyk was born on 19 June 1914. It survived as a cottage at Sylvan Lake until the ERRS rehabilitated it shortly after getting No. 1 in running order. No. 80, built by the Ottawa Car Manufacturing Company with all steel construction, is an example of the most modern streetcars to see service in Edmonton. It is the only one of five delivered in 1930 that survives. Turned into a roadside diner in Dawson Creek, and later a farm building in Fort St. John, it needed 20 years of dedicated work by ERRS members to bring it back to operation.

Streetcars No. 1 and 42 on the regular service run at Fort Edmonton Park. *(ERRS)*

ERRS member Bill Keith staples an edge of the new roof canvas on a restored streetcar as Don Bearham prepares to remove air bubbles between the canvas and the mastic applied to the subroof to get a good seal. Other members apply mastic at the front of the roof. *(High Iron Photos)*

Streetcar No. 80 is delivered to Fort Edmonton Park after years of use as a diner and a farm building in British Columbia. *(ERRS and Don Bearham)*

Streetcar No. 80 restored and back in regular service at Fort Edmonton Park.
(Doug Cowan)

As ERRS members restored streetcars, they hatched a plan to provide service on the High Level Bridge for special events. The dream became a reality when a restored Japanese street-car, originally purchased for spare parts, ferried passengers from 104 Street to the former railway tunnel near the Granite Curling Club during the 1995 Fringe Theatre events. When rais-ing power lines across the High Level Bridge proved too costly, ERRS members took on the job themselves using the poles fortunately left in place from the original streetcar lines. In the fall of 1996, OSAKA Car No. 247 rolled over the bridge for the first time under its own power. In 1997 service over the line from Strathcona to Grandin commenced. The ERRS continues to add cars and service. A museum was opened to celebrate Edmonton Transit's 100th Anniversary in 2008, and plans to extend the service and increase the use of cars original to Edmonton continue to be realized.

The Japanese streetcar, originally purchased for parts, was used to reintroduce historic streetcar rides over the High Level Bridge. In this photo, the lines have been reconstructed, and the generator no longer has to be towed behind. (ERRS)

The contributions of public transportation to life in Edmonton would continue to grow and be celebrated, as evident in this "bus wrap" seen here at Commonwealth Stadium, reminding citizens of the chance to experience their past through the work of the Edmonton Radial Railway Society. *(ETS)*

Works Cited

Bastide, Ernie. ETS Centennial Interviews, 2007–08. Edmonton, Alberta: ETS Archives.

Buck, George H. *A Technological History of Municipally Owned Public Transportation In Edmonton: 1893–1981.* Edmonton, Alberta: University of Alberta Thesis, 1985, Buck, pp. 594–95.

City of Edmonton, Transportation Management. *Transit Strategy Review Part IV: Major Event Special Transit Service Strategies*, November 1983.

Edmonton Journal. 11 July 1979; 29 March 1982; 13 May 1986; 19 June 2001.

Keshwani, Salim. "Articulated Bus Demonstration Project," *Transit News*, Vol. 10, No. 1, Spring 1983, pp. 14–16.

Latham, Greg. ETS Centennial Interviews. Edmonton, Alberta: ETS Archives.

Mason, Brian. ETS Centennial Interviews, 2007–08. Edmonton, Alberta: ETS Archives.

Paul, Rick. ETS Centennial Interviews, 2007–08. Edmonton, Alberta: ETS Archives.

Province of Alberta. *Report and Decision Concerning the Edmonton Annexation Application*, June 1981, p. 6.

Transit News. Spring 1983, p. 19; Fall 1983; December 1983, p. 10; Fall 1986, p. 12; Summer 1987, p. 13; Spring 1988, p. 5, 12.

Transit News Canada. August 1983, p. 7, 9; May 1981, pp. 8–9; Winter 1985, p. 7; April 1985, p. 6; August 1985, p. 8.

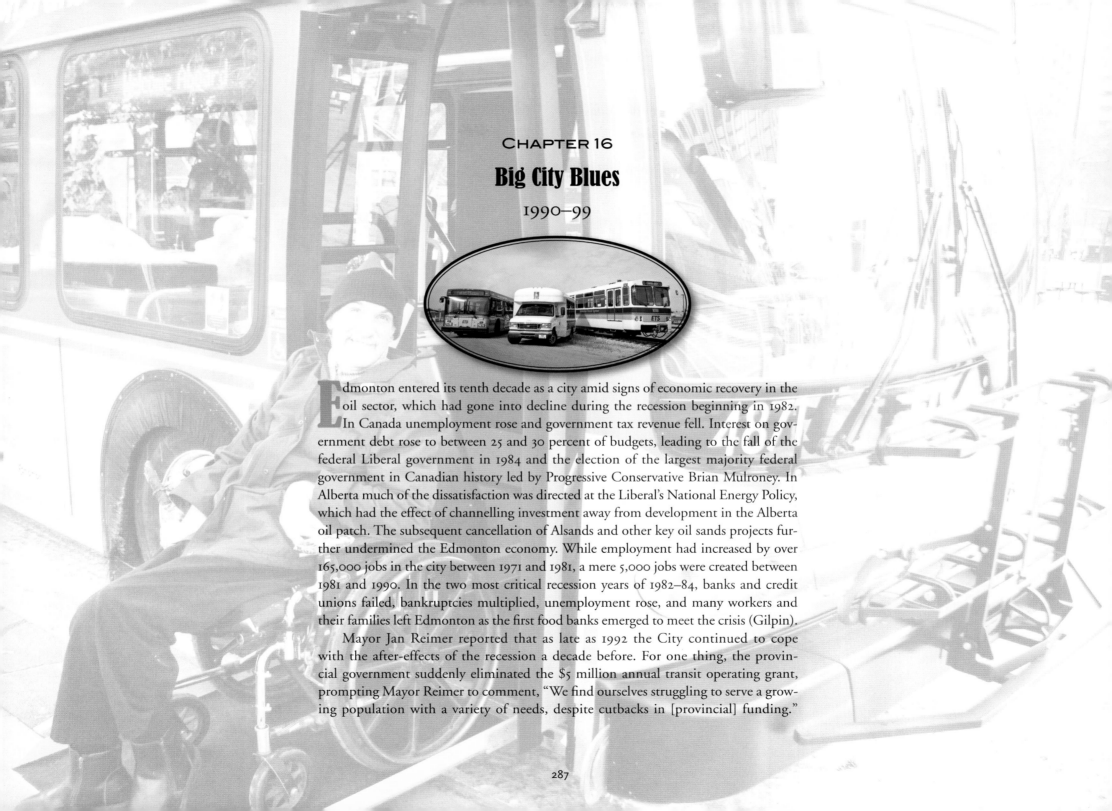

CHAPTER 16

Big City Blues

1990–99

Edmonton entered its tenth decade as a city amid signs of economic recovery in the oil sector, which had gone into decline during the recession beginning in 1982. In Canada unemployment rose and government tax revenue fell. Interest on government debt rose to between 25 and 30 percent of budgets, leading to the fall of the federal Liberal government in 1984 and the election of the largest majority federal government in Canadian history led by Progressive Conservative Brian Mulroney. In Alberta much of the dissatisfaction was directed at the Liberal's National Energy Policy, which had the effect of channelling investment away from development in the Alberta oil patch. The subsequent cancellation of Alsands and other key oil sands projects further undermined the Edmonton economy. While employment had increased by over 165,000 jobs in the city between 1971 and 1981, a mere 5,000 jobs were created between 1981 and 1990. In the two most critical recession years of 1982–84, banks and credit unions failed, bankruptcies multiplied, unemployment rose, and many workers and their families left Edmonton as the first food banks emerged to meet the crisis (Gilpin).

Mayor Jan Reimer reported that as late as 1992 the City continued to cope with the after-effects of the recession a decade before. For one thing, the provincial government suddenly eliminated the $5 million annual transit operating grant, prompting Mayor Reimer to comment, "We find ourselves struggling to serve a growing population with a variety of needs, despite cutbacks in [provincial] funding."

Mayor Jan Reimer in the front plaza of
City Hall, which opened in 1993. *(ETS)*

The transportation capital grant was cut to $25 per capita from $75 over a three-year period. Of course, these constraints also limited other aspects of ETS service.

As the City began preparing for the 1995 Biennial Celebration of the original Fort Edmonton, the outlook finally began to improve. Four years earlier, the superbly restored Macdonald Hotel had reopened. The Mac, which dominated the river valley skyline for many years, was once again the pre-eminent hotel in the city and the place to meet visiting dignitaries from prime ministers to rock stars like the Rolling Stones. The northern focal point of Churchill Square began to take its final form in 1993 when the magnificent new City Hall opened. The new Square would be completed in time for the City Centennial in 2004. Another important addition to cultural activity around the square was the opening of the Winspear Centre for Music in 1997. Francis Winspear, an Edmonton philanthropist, made the project possible through a $6 million donation, the largest single private donation in Canadian history at the time.

In the northeast, Canadian Forces Base Namao expanded during the decade. The renamed Canadian Forces Base Edmonton eventually became the largest base in western Canada. The growth of the base would have a lasting effect on subsequent development of Edmonton Transit, further increasing the demand for the northeast extension of the LRT system.

During the 1990s, Edmonton strengthened its identity as Canada's Festival City. The Heritage Festival, established in 1976, was recognized in 1999 by the American Business Association as one of the hundred foremost events in North America. Edmonton Transit played a central role in making this phenomenally popular event possible as it handled the logistics of carrying the happy hordes of celebrants to and from Hawrelak Park. Other events including the Jazz City International Music Festival, the Symphony Under the Sky, the Edmonton Folk Music Festival, the Fringe Theatre event, and other festivals filled the city's streets from spring to fall. Just as in the early days of the Edmonton Exhibition when the streetcar fleet was marshalled to carry the surge in ridership, Edmonton Transit employed low-floor buses, DATS service and LRT trains with the goal that more Edmontonians could participate in events during the brief, hectic summer months. Edmonton Transit was keeping pace and preparing for the even more demanding blitz of international events that would flood into Edmonton in the new millennium.

Edmonton Transit's effort to provide transit service to Edmonton's burgeoning festival life coincided with efforts to ensure that service was extended to all Edmontonians, whatever their needs. In 1992, in response to the widespread public awareness generated by Rick Hansen's Wheels in Motion world tour, the Province launched three demonstration projects—accessible taxis in Edmonton, low-floor buses in St. Albert and paratransit scheduling in Calgary—to improve access to public transit for those with limited physical mobility. Perhaps the most visible example was the emergence of the low-floor bus (LFB) that accommodated wheelchairs and walkers.

Edmonton Transit's commitment to provide access for all citizens shaped decisions on the purchase of new rolling stock and was reinforced by the provincial government's restriction of funding to only handicapped-accessible buses. So, when it came time to renew the fleet in 1993, Edmonton Transit purchased 43 New Flyer Industries D40DL low-floor buses, which, in the following decade, would become the staple of the fleet.

An articulated bus is on display at the Old Strathcona Silly Summer Parade in 2001. ETS played a role in many city events not just by providing transit service, but also by being part of events. *(ETS)*

New Flyer Industries low-floor bus. *(ETS)*

Another 16 low-floor models were added the following year, while 80 more were added in August 1998, and another 49 in 1999. The New Flyer LFBs purchased in 1998 were built to specifications overseen by Dave Geake, then Edmonton Transit Director of Plant and Equipment. He introduced significant enhancements required for the Edmonton climate, including the first warm-wall heating system for LFBs, auxiliary engine heaters, and a change from Detroit Diesel to Cummins engines. LED electronic signs also were introduced to the Edmonton Transit fleet at this time (Geake).

The D40LF, produced by Winnipeg's New Flyer Industries, was developed in Europe in 1988 from the B85 model built by Den Oudsten Bussen BV. In 1989 the D40LF was introduced as the first 40-foot low-floor bus in North America, and New Flyer Industries started selling the model two years later. The D40LF was constructed with a raised rear section that was accessed by steps within the bus, setting the standard for future low-floor design in North America. The remainder of the cabin and exterior entrances had no steps. The new design was meant to facilitate easy boarding of mobility aids such as wheelchairs and walkers through a hydraulically operated ramp and a kneeling feature that allowed the entire bus to be lowered on its air suspension system to a more accessible level. Two wheelchair spaces were included in the New Flyers.

Edmonton became one of the first major cities in North America to adopt the New Flyer low-floor bus rather than the lift-equipped buses more

A LFB, a dedicated DATS vehicle, and an LRT train demonstrate new models of rolling stock introduced into the ETS fleet in the 1990s. *(ETS)*

common in the United States. Edmonton Transit's Wayne Mandryk worked with engineer Jan den Odsten of New Flyer Industries, who was inducted into the American Public Transportation Association Hall of Fame in 2004 for this as well as other innovations. Simultaneously, Edmonton Transit worked with the LRT manufacturer Siemens to develop ramps that, under the lead of the LRT's Dave Pagett, set another industry standard in improving service in a system where the LRT stations already were characterized by accessible features such as elevators and automatic door openers (Latham).

A ramp replaced the front steps to the LF community bus, allowing easy access for those with limited mobility. (ETS)

Edmonton Transit customer Michael Johner used the controls to deploy the ramp on an LRT car to allow wheelchair access. (ETS)

A New Flyer low-floor bus in front of City Hall. (ETS)

Shelter from the Storm

Given Edmonton's harsh winters and occasional blistering summers, transit shelters have been an understandable preoccupation for both passengers and the transit system since the first days of the Edmonton Radial Railway. But it was not until 1957 that the Bellevue Community League constructed the first passenger shelter, a simple structure on the north side of 112 Avenue at 73 Street that could accommodate four to five people. (The only other shelter had been built some time previously by the Alberta government at the University of Alberta Hospital.) Subsequently, Edmonton Bus Shelter Advertising Ltd. began installing about 20 small open steel shelters in the town of Jasper Place in the summer of 1963 (*Edmonton Journal*).

More than a decade later, a prototype shelter described by the *Edmonton Journal* as "elaborate" was installed on 111 Street and 57 Avenue with the assistance of the federal Local Initiative Program. Designed by Hoffman and Associates, the shelter was the first of a series planned to hold up to 25 people in the new Malmo community. However, the Transportation Planning Branch declared this very stylish prototype "over-designed" and suspended its further use.

A futuristic shelter design from the 1960–77 period located in downtown Edmonton. *(ETS)*

The true shape of shelter design for the future was finally declared at the new Westmount Bus Station, which opened during the summer of 1977 at the ETS terminal just west of the Westmount Shopping Centre. Another shelter of this design soon followed at Southgate Shopping Centre in January 1980. Plans to incorporate the station into the mall had been rejected by its tenants, so it was built across the parking lot at the west side of the shopping centre (*Edmonton Journal*).

In 1982 Edmonton Transit developed a new flexible module shelter to accommodate requirements for expandable, less expensive shelter facilities. The Real Estate and Supply Services Department was commissioned to engage consultants and architects to develop the concept. The component shelter developed under their cooperative efforts evolved into a simple, expandable structure that was economical to build and, very importantly, economical to repair and maintain under the onslaught of vandalism. Special attention was given to using materials that were very difficult to damage (such a steel structural frames), or could easily be repaired or replaced (such as small tempered glass panes).

An old-style bus shelter typical of the earliest designs. *(ETS Archives)*

A pre-1976 shelter. *(ETS Archives)*

The Westmount Shopping Centre Terminal, which opened in 1977, featured the new "Pacman" ETS logo. *(ETS Archives)*

Another prototype structure opened at West Jasper Place Transit Centre in November 1984. The Edmonton Transit Division and the Engineering Division of the Transportation Department cooperated with the Real Estate and Supply Services Department and Maltby Prins Architects on this innovative project. When the Northgate Transit Centre opened on 16 January 1987, the terminal won an architectural award for its design and function at the Second Annual Edmonton Architectural Awards Competition. It also received an honourable mention for excellence presented at the National Architect Competition held by the Royal Architectural Institute of Canada *(Transit News)*. New design specifications established a standard for all future bus terminal facilities, while at the same time reinforcing the identity of Edmonton Transit. Shelters at transit centres would now include an infrared heated public waiting area as well as an unheated shelter.

Despite efforts to develop more robust structures, shelters were plagued by vandalism. Especially hard hit was the considerable amount of glass required in shelters to provide visual access for passenger security. By 1978 the 370 shelters located in Edmonton required a staff of 13 to provide daily maintenance. Llew Lawrence estimated that as many as 10 shelters were damaged each day, and approximately 25 glass panes were replaced daily.

Perhaps the most spectacular case of vandalism occurred behind Abbottsfield Mall in September 1982 when a pipe bomb ripped a shelter apart late on a Friday night. At the time, such improvised bombs were being used to destroy newspaper boxes as well. Six years later, in late June, another pipe bomb destroyed a shelter at 137 Avenue and 24 Street during another rash of pipe bomb incidents *(Edmonton Journal)*.

Lawrence urged the public to help reduce vandalism costs to little avail. Unfortunately, vandalism of ETS shelters, the most vulnerable part of the system, did not disappear. During 1999, 723 shelters were vandalized in 1,591 individual incidents, causing over $200,000 damage.

Public demand for accessible, safe and comfortable bus stop facilities resulted in the development of the current iteration of shelter design featured at Heritage Mall and Mills Woods Town Centre. The large new centres opened in 2000 at a total cost of $4 million and were specifically designed to be open, inviting, functional and safe. The *Edmonton Journal* reported:

"Newly renovated stations opened at Heritage Mall and Mill Woods Town Centre in September 2000, both designed by Cohos Evamy Partners, a prominent Edmonton architectural firm. Robert Swart, the lead architect, cited European stations as his inspiration. 'Their use of inverted roofs and lightweight platform protection really stuck with me. These are great designs, very functional and yet there's a sense of welcome to them.'

"In particular, the V-roof design mitigated runoff, a distinctive Edmonton problem. The new Mill Woods Transit Centre on 25 Avenue at Hewes Way began operation about the same time" *(Edmonton Journal)*.

Shelter cleaning contributed to maintenance costs. Routine cleaning was sometimes performed to maintain a pleasing streetscape, as in the view of shelter cleaning in the Old Strathcona area. Other times more drastic measures were called for, and high-pressure washing was required. *(ETS)*

The transit centre shelter at Northgate was designed to allow high visibility for passengers while using small panes of glass to allow easy and more economical replacement. *(ETS)*

The front upper body of the early D40LF was ridged, and the area around the headlights protruded. In 1994 the front ridge area around the headlights was smoothed out, giving it the look that came to characterize the Edmonton Transit fleet. The D40LF and its variants became the foremost transit bus in North America, accounting for 36 percent of the market in 2006.

For all their advantages, the early New Flyers gave their share of grief to Edmonton Transit maintenance crews over the years, but ET veteran Bernie Budney remembers the models arriving in the late 1990s as much more satisfactory than earlier versions. By then the bodies were built much stronger, although they still had some "design issues." Many improvements were suggested by Edmonton Transit and other transit systems, and New Flyer proved responsive to these ideas. The New Flyers improved and became more popular with each year, often through the efforts of operational personnel (Budney).

Edmonton Transit had taken its message to Edmontonians from the first days of streetcars with advertising and information directed at existing and potential riders. Through most of the first century of operation, advertising in daily newspapers was augmented with system maps, ride guides and route brochures. At first these were fairly straightforward examples of the advertising art, but a customer-driven rather than an operationally-centred approach to marketing resulted in more sophisticated marketing initiatives emerging the 1990s. A strategic marketing plan and complementary communications plan developed in 1990 integrated customer research, and route and service planning with operator training, advertising and promotions.

Rider and transit guides from the 1980s typical of ETS information services. *(ETS)*

Efforts by Edmonton Transit to become more responsive to customers' needs and build strong community ties were reflected in the establishment of the Edmonton Transit System Advisory Board (ETSAB) in September 1994. ETSAB advised City Council, the Transportation and Streets Department, and Edmonton Transit on improving public transit. ETSAB consisted of 12 members with one additional ex-officio associate. The original ETSAB mission remains integral to its present operation: "to provide a safe, effective, efficient, and environmentally preferred mode of transportation." Its goals include "a family of services which allows all people in Edmonton equal and fair opportunity to access public transit."

Edmonton Transit desired not only community feedback, but also opportunities to become more involved in the community and give back to those who supported public transit. One 1995 initiative involved Christmas Lights Tours that departed from City Hall on a tour that included Candy Cane Lane and the beautifully lit Provincial Legislature grounds, where participants enjoyed carolling and a hot chocolate in the Legislature following their tour of the grounds. A tour through the Chamber of Commerce's Bright Lights Festival at Hawrelak Park was added in later years. The tours were fully subscribed each year and were made possible through ET staff volunteering as drivers and hosts.

The strong volunteerism of Edmonton Transit staff has also played an important part in Edmonton Transit's sponsorship of the Stuff-a-Bus campaign along with its media partners, Save-on-Foods and the Edmonton Food Bank. Each late November or early December since 1995, ET buses visit Save-On-Foods' locations to collect non-perishable food donations from the public for the Edmonton Food Bank. The campaign has grown from a one-day event to six days. Between its inception and the end of 2008, the Stuff-a-Bus campaign has collected 216,902 kilograms of food and $280,521 in cash donations to help feed Edmontonians in need. Some 30,600 kilograms of food were collected in 2008 alone.

Another charitable initiative, the Donate-a-Ride program, was the brainchild of City Councillor Allan Bolstad and later headed up by Councillors Kim Krushell and Bryan Anderson. Farebox donations from the public throughout January and donations throughout the year from corporate sponsors provide Edmonton Transit tickets to over 50 Edmonton social service agencies that assist clients in crisis situations. Launched over the Christmas and New Year's holidays in 1996, the program has become one

ETS personnel volunteer at the Stuff-a-Bus campaign in 2006. The Edmonton Food Bank benefits from the Christmas event each year. *(ETS)*

of the more successful ETS community initiatives. Bolstad recalled, "We just sort of stumbled on [the Donate-a-Ride] in a way. . . . The real key was to work through social agencies to identify people who need this and to supply tickets." No abuse of the system occurred because no money was used, and today other communities look to Edmonton as a model for this type of program. Bolstad further notes that Donate-a-Ride was simply "a reaction to the need that was there. It started from scratch at the beginning with leftover ticket stubs from other promotions . . . leftover little envelopes, and we just wrote on them with a pen, 'Donate-a-Ride.' Today all the city centre agencies use this program" (Bolstad).

The fourth annual Donate-a-Ride drive raised $25,000 in January 2000, a tenfold increase over the first annual drive and enough to aid over 10,000 adults and children when distributed through eight city agencies. The program received $2,500 from the ATU Local 569 alone. Ernie Bastide, president of the local, stated that ETS drivers saw "the direct ramifications" of the program on a daily basis as they met users on their buses (*Edmonton Journal*). A Donate-a-Ride website (www.donatearide.ab.ca) was launched in December 2001. In 2007, 57 agencies administered through the United Way benefited from Donate-a-Ride. The program has raised $928,200 since inception.

As Edmonton and the transit system that served it grew in size and complexity, riders needed more timely information to make the best

use of ETS. BusLink, an automated telephone information service providing riders with route and schedule information, was first introduced for Mill Woods residents in 1994. Many other Edmonton neighbourhoods were benefiting from BusLink by April 1995, and by 1999 transit users could make use of the BusLink to access a range of transit information including special events, accessible service and the Bikes-on-Buses program. Additional system information also was made available on a local bulletin board system (BBS) in 1994, and in May 1995 on Edmonton FreeNet. In January 1996, ETS was on the Internet, beginning a commitment to digital information services that have become more extensive with each passing year.

In the early 1990s, ETS developed a number of innovative services, events and promotions in a widening effort to attract people to public transit in the wake of declining ridership. During the mid-1990s, ExpressLink, the super-express route from Heritage Transit Centre, was introduced, as was the Bikes-on-Buses program championed by City Councillor Tooker Gomberg. An active voice for urban ecology policy on Edmonton City Council from 1992–95, Gomberg, the first City Councillor to sit on the ETSAB, supported a number of Edmonton Transit initiatives, even donating part of his councillor's salary to purchase the first bicycle racks to outfit Route 9. Previously, Gomberg had served as the Executive Director of the Edmonton Bicycle Commuters and a co-founder of the EcoCity Society.

Donate a Ride

Give someone in need a lift.

The logo for the Donate-a-Ride program launched in 1996. *(ETS)*

She's a cool operator...

They tell me she knows all there is to know about getting around town, so naturally I have to talk to her. I find her in the ED TEL White Pages, page 49, and call her up. Right away she asks for my BusLink number. I tell her and, sure she tells me when the next bus is coming. But I want more. Say, kid, how about the weekend schedule? She tells me! I ask if she's busy next week. She's coy, but take it from me, she's there for me 24 hours a day. She's one cool operator.

 **496-1600**
24 hour bus schedule information.

Edmonton Transit System

The Alternative Mode

Billboards, pamphlets and a half-wrap on the side of a bus illustrate the various ways in which BusLink was publicized. *(ETS)*

Transit Time Hotline
496-1600
Edmonton Transit System
Owned and Operated by The City of Edmonton

ExpressLink
Shoot downtown in 23 minutes!
Street Smart
Edmonton Transit System

Advertising for Edmonton Transit's new Express Route service that promised quicker, more direct service from a major southside Transit Centre to the downtown core.

By 2009 bike racks were fitted on buses on the Routes 1, 4 and 9, including the articulated buses on the Route 9. It is estimated that loading and unloading a bike takes only about 20 seconds, and instructions are printed on each rack. The racks hold two bicycles each with space available on a first-come, first-served basis. Regular ETS fares are charged while the bike rides free.

Bicycles on the LRT

It's as Easy as 1, 2, 3 !

You and your bicycle can also travel on the LRT. Bicycle travel is allowed on all LRT trips except between 7:30 - 9:00 AM and 4:00 - 5:30 PM Monday through Friday. There are no hourly restrictions for bicycles on Saturday, Sunday and statutory holidays.

Please remember that you and your bike are sharing space with other ETS customers, so the conditions for travelling on the LRT are different than those for buses.

1. Please walk your bike in LRT stations and vehicles. You may use stairs, escalators or elevators (except where noted) providing you yield to the right-of-way of others. Hold onto your bike at all times when using stairs, escalators or elevators.

2. You pay the regular ETS fare while your bike rides free!

3. Please enter and exit through the middle doors of the LRT vehicle. The bent poles at the doors allow for easier access. Please allow other passengers to exit and enter the LRT first. Green signs are posted on the LRT doors to show which ones to use.

Remember to...
Please stay with your bicycle at all times while in LRT stations and vehicles. Stand beside your bike and hold onto it while riding the LRT. Do not straddle or sit on your bike or prop it against a seat, door or any place else that might cause damage or injury. Bicycles are not to be chained to poles, seats or other equipment in an LRT station or vehicle. Please ensure no mud or grease drops from your bicycle onto LRT stations, vehicles or other passengers.

ETS may, at any time, refuse entrance to cyclists due to crowded trains or platforms, or unsafe conditions (e.g. before or after a concert or sporting event). Regulations for bicycle travel on the LRT are governed by a City of Edmonton - Conduct of Transit Passengers - Bylaw No. 8353. ETS is not responsible for damages incurred or caused by or to bicycles on ETS property.

BIKES ON ETS

Bicycle Parking at ETS Facilities

Bicycle parking areas are available, free of charge at many Transit Centres and LRT Stations. You are responsible for securely locking your bicycle in the rack. The following Transit Centres and LRT Stations have bike racks.

Millgate Transit Centre

Westmount Transit Centre

Heritage Transit Centre

Southgate Transit Centre

Belvedere Transit Centre

Belvedere LRT Station

Clareview LRT Station

Coliseum LRT Station

Stadium LRT Station

Grandin LRT Station

ETS is not responsible for damages incurred or caused by or to bicycles on ETS property.

Further Information

For further information call Transit Information at 496-1611, BusLink, our 24 hour automated information system at 496-1600, or check *www.takeETS.com.*

ETS
Edmonton Transit System
Owned and Operated by The City of Edmonton

Wherever life takes you...
ETS
we'll get you there!

Promotional literature for Bikes-on-Buses, which continues to be a major ETS initiative. (ETS)

Ken Thomas exiting a low-floor bus with ramp access at front door and bike racks on front. *(ETS)*

Bike racks in use on an ETS Bus.
(Norm Corness)

Priority Seating
For persons with reduced mobility.

The front seating on all Edmonton Transit buses is designated as priority seating for persons with mobility difficulties. *(ETS)*

The Mobility Choices Travel Training program represented another initiative to make the transit system more accessible. The first such initiative in Canada, this award-winning customer service program educates individuals with mobility challenges on how to make the best use of travel options offered by ETS. The idea of training clients—particularly those using DATS—to use regular transit service was first raised in one of the 1993 DATS audit recommendations that noted the importance of establishing a stronger link between DATS and the other services provided by ETS. The concept was fully developed in the 1994 DATS strategic plan and implemented in 1995 when training was first offered to DATS customers able to use the new enhanced-access low-floor buses. The program included instruction for trainers and agency representatives, a video for customers, group and individual training sessions, and support with other transit materials. By the end of 2008, over 1,500 customers per year were participating in the training program.

Edmonton Transit's fleet of low-floor buses has grown yearly in concert with new routes targeted at the needs of seniors and those with mobility challenges. The position of Accessible Transit Coordinator was formalized in 2003, with a dedicated staff member in Community Relations overseeing accessibility programs, including Mobility Choices. The training program has continued to provide information and instruction to existing and potential customers, and new tools were developed to enhance the transit experience for customers through the introduction of Mobility Cards, Bus Hailer Kits and Customer Communication Cards. With the added services and enhancements such as priority seating in buses and LRT trains, community bus routes targeted specifically at meeting senior's needs, electric ramps in LRT vehicles, the Stop Request program and the introduction in 2007 of the Seniors on the Go program (a summer program providing a

A hydraulic ramp allows access to individuals using mobility aids such as walkers. *(ETS)*

The Seniors-on-the-Go program provides special charters and information and training sessions for seniors during the summer months. *(ETS)*

Ride Free

No fuss, no muss, just climb on the LRT or bus, and enjoy Family Day on us.

Take the entire family to any one of a number of Family Day events around the city free of charge on ETS. There are lots of activities to choose from. Let Edmonton Transit take you there. Travel anywhere, as often as you like, all day long, for free, on ETS.

ETS routes will operate on regular Sunday schedules except for Route 10 on Family Day, Monday, February 20.

At the Sunday service level, buses run every 30 or 60 minutes all day. There is no peak hour service.

Route 10 West Jasper Place to Downtown.
Route 10 buses will run every 7-8 minutes between West Jasper Place - Downtown from 11 a.m. to 6 p.m.

For more information call Transit Information at 496-1611.

DATS Service

DATS will operate on a holiday schedule (Booking Office closed) Monday, February 20. Vehicles will be running as usual, but all subscription bookings will be cancelled for that day. If you still require your regular subscription trip for February 20, please call 496-4567. Bookings for Tuesday, February 21 will be accepted starting Friday, February 17. Bookings for Wednesday, February 22 will be accepted starting Sunday, February 19. Due to the high cost of providing the service, DATS service is not free on Family Day. DATS users are welcome to travel free on low floor buses where available.

Edmonton Transit System
Owned and operated by the City of Edmonton

On Family Day 1995, free ETS rides were advertised in the *Edmonton Journal*. (ETS)

free charter and onboard travel training to help seniors feel safe and confident using Edmonton Transit), ETS positioned itself as a barrier-free, accessible service for Edmontonians.

Over the years, Edmonton Transit's accessibility programs and services have been recognized in the many accolades and awards received from the ETS Nice Going Awards, the Advisory Board on Services for Persons with Disabilities, Diversity Leadership, and the Community Five-Star Awards (Dorey).

The 1990s brought many other promotions targeted at the general public. Following the lead of other North American cities, Edmonton sponsored its first Ride-Free Day on Remembrance Day 1994. Ride-Free days were extended to other holidays when lower system ridership was the norm. Starting in the late 1990s, special family fares were offered in conjunction with holidays and special events such as Family Day and for the Downtown Business Association's Santa Parade. On these days family groups could ride for a single adult fare.

The popular Splash-and-Ride promotion was launched in 1995 to encourage youth under 17 to make more extensive use of swimming and fitness facilities during July and August. Edmonton Transit and Community Services co-sponsored the promotion with the aim of introducing city services to youth and retaining them as life-long customers.

Transit vehicles have played more than a purely routine transportation role in many special events in Edmonton. The old streetcar Observation Car, for example, was very popular in its day, and today the Christmas Lights Tour continues the tradition. In the late 1970s, Edmonton Transit launched a program to restore and maintain a fleet of vintage vehicles for use

during commemorative festivities and to display at major events. During the 1980s, the volunteers of the Edmonton Transit Historical Society coordinated the display of these vehicles, including the 75th ETS anniversary celebrations in 1983. Edmonton Transit continued to store the vintage transit vehicles following the demise of the historical group. In 1999, during the celebration of the 60th Anniversary of trolleys in Edmonton, a Brill trolley was used to provide a short-loop tour leaving from the Provincial Museum. The tours proved so popular that Edmonton Transit initiated a program of historical tours in subsequent summers. Vintage buses were used to take passengers on historical tours of Edmonton with commentary provided by volunteer historical interpreters.

While Edmonton Transit has organized some heritage programming and maintained a small collection of artefacts and vintage buses, the real work of preserving the early history of Edmonton Transit has been undertaken by the dedicated members of the Edmonton Radial Railway Society (ERRS). The society began operating the High Level Bridge Streetcar on a regular basis during the summer months in 1997, and its popularity has made it a regular feature of the summer scene thereafter. The ERRS also provides streetcar transportation around Fort Edmonton Park.

While Edmontonians in the late 1990s witnessed vintage special events buses on their streets once more, the current fleet was undergoing a major facelift when the ETS brand and its fleet livery started to look dated. The ETS logo and graphic design at the time had been developed in the 1970s and the "Flying E" style of its logo was sometimes referred to as "Pacman." Focus groups conducted by Edmonton Transit in the mid-1990s indicated that public of recognition of the ETS brand was very low. A new look and colours were rolled out in 1998, and the name officially returned to the more widely used "Edmonton Transit System" designation. Operators, too, wore new livery adopted in 1997. The sporty blue-grey uniforms were a departure from the white with blue-yellow stripes uniform of the previous years.

Transit vehicles and facilities have generated advertising revenue since the very early days of the Edmonton Radial Railway. While the Edmonton Transit System was getting a new look in the 1990s, vinyl bus-wraps were also transforming the appearance of the ETS fleet in innovative but controversial ways.

Brill Trolley 99 has been restored for use in historical tours. *(Doug Cowan)*

ETS instructors, Margo Ottecher and Paul Parmar, in the new blue-grey uniforms, which included sweaters and had a sportier style than earlier uniforms. *(ETS)*

ETS dispatchers, Sherri Laing-Knarr and Dan Cormier, wear the new blue-grey uniforms of 1997. *(ETS)*

Distinctive vinyl-wrap buses
were introduced in 1995. This
line of buses at Commonwealth
Stadium demonstrates the range of
advertising the buses carried. *(ETS)*

Computer-generated vinyl wraps transformed buses into large rolling billboards. *(ETS)*

NOT IN SERVICE

241

241

ETS

WE PUT YOU IN THE MOVIES

At the same time, Edmonton Transit turned to the city's visual arts community to enrich passengers' experience of public transit spaces. ETS entered into a cooperative agreement with the Edmonton Arts Council, and the Art and Design in Public Places program fostered by The Works International Visual Arts Society.

The new look at the ETS coincided with major organizational changes taking place during the late 1990s. Greg Latham noted that 1992–93 customer satisfaction surveys of all City departments consistently ranked ETS employees highest.

"I was fortunate to work with them," said Latham. "We had a receptive, willing-to-trust and capable work force. This was a place where I wanted individuals to know that they counted and that we were willing to take the time to find their perspectives. It was a place where they could grow, where people cared. We strived to make it a family oriented workplace. If you win people's hearts, when you jump, they'll be with you. We had 'good going' awards, where customers and staff could nominate candidates. It was recognition for a job well done. We also had a service pin program for honouring staff who'd been on the job for so many years.

"And the Union talked and walked the same. The Union President and I looked at the first Union agreement from 1908 together. It called for a fair day's pay for a fair day's work, and that's what we still believed in. I felt that we were enabling people to recognize that they were good at what they were doing. We created an environment to let people make recommendations and if it worked, we'd do it.

"When I left, it was crunch time in the city. I could see the writing on the wall—the city was going into a depression again" (Latham).

As Latham predicted, financial restraint once again forced change on the ETS. Bruce Thom, City Manager from 1996-2000, undertook the far-reaching and fundamental reorganization of municipal departments as part of the City '97 Plan. The Transportation Department was reorganized and renamed the Transportation and Streets Department in 1997, while corporate restructuring, including Edmonton Transit, also took place. Transit fleet maintenance was transferred to Mobile Equipment Services. The Commendations and Concerns Telephone Information System (CACTIS)

also was implemented in late March of that year to strengthen ties with the public and provide a voice for those with concerns.

John Sirovyak recalls how ETS performed its own maintenance before the City '97 restructuring. He concluded that the new shared-services concept was "empowering" because "senior management could have better control and centralization" leading to better corporate enterprise. For example, hundreds of different computer systems could then be streamlined and integrated.

That said, Sirovyak also recognized that reorganization had some negative side effects. "We were force-fed all into one box" after 1997. Some of the uniqueness and historical character [of Edmonton Transit] was diminished. Recognition programs for driving and attendance became more standardized after this time. It may have become more difficult to accommodate the unique problems for transit operators." Sirovyak suggests that so-called poor attendance, for example, may simply reflect the rigors of shift work, constant exposure to germs, stress (resulting from 4:00 AM starts), weekend work, or poor lifestyle and eating habits encouraged by the job (Sirovyak).

The early to mid-1990s were far from halcyon days for Edmonton Transit. ETS suffered from reduced ridership as a residual effect of the 1982 strike and the lingering effect of the recession. The provincial government's emphasis on eliminating the province's debt resulted in steep cuts to grants and subsidies to municipal services. City Council responded with directives to reduce services and increase user fees to meet budget guidelines. The public reacted as expected to the prospect of paying more for less even as suburban sprawl continued largely unabated, changing travel patterns as it spread. Contributing to the general malaise was a 1994 scandal in which an employee was convicted with theft over $1,000 for appropriating over $2 million in monies from transit fare collection boxes. The story even made the pages of the supermarket tabloid *The National Enquirer*.

Still, as the decade progressed, Edmonton Transit looked ahead to the new century. The Horizon 2000 Service Plan came into being in 1996 to envision comprehensive service restructuring that included basic network routes supplemented by flexible community routes. By 1998 ridership began to increase in a trend that would continue into the new millennium.

As ETS looked toward its centennial year, it could reflect on ten hectic decades of service to the people of Edmonton, Strathcona and surrounding metropolitan districts. It had worked hard to meet its many challenges, and was beginning to be rewarded by improved service and rider satisfaction. There were many bright spots. Track construction had commenced from the Grandin Station to the University LRT Station. The Horizon 2000 project was generating more customer-service orientation, consistent routes and a simplified fare structure. The purchase of 100 new low floor and eight smaller accessible buses had been approved. However, it was clear that the challenges were not about to disappear and that the coming decade would provide its own trials. ETS responded to the prospect of these future challenges by hosting its first Community Conference in 1999. The conferences are now an annual event, with transit users, providers and community stakeholders coming together to improve the already high standard of public transit provided by ETS.

The Community Conference reflects the ETS's commitment to continued service improvements. *(ETS Archives)*

Works Cited

Bolstad, Allan. ETS Centennial Interviews, 2007–08. Edmonton, Alberta: ETS Archives.

Budney, Bernie. ETS Centennial Interviews, 2007–08. Edmonton, Alberta: ETS Archives.

Dorey, Margaret. Communication to Ken Tingley, 2008. Edmonton, Alberta: ETS Archives.

Edmonton Journal. 14 December 1957; 10 July 1963; 10 January 1973; 29 August 1977; 13 September 1978; 9 January 1980; 11 September 1982; June 1986; 1 January 2000; 10 March 2000; 5 September 2000; 7 September 2000.

Fung, Henry. "Hello Northgate Transit Centre!" *Transit News*, Vol. 14, No. 1, January–February 1987, p. 7.

Geake, Dave. ETS Centennial Interviews, 2007–08. Edmonton, Alberta: ETS Archives.

Gilpin, John. *Responsible Enterprise: A History of Edmonton Real Estate and the Edmonton Real Estate Board.* Edmonton: Edmonton Real Estate Board, 1997.

Latham, Greg. ETS Centennial Interviews, 2007–08. Edmonton, Alberta: ETS Archives.

Nowicki, Dennis. Communication to Ken Tingley, 2008. Edmonton, Alberta: ETS Archives.

Paul, Rick. Communication to Ken Tingley, 2008. Edmonton, Alberta: ETS Archives.

Sirovyak, John. ETS Centennial Interviews, 2007–08. Edmonton, Alberta: ETS Archives.

Stewart, Lorna. Communication to Ken Tingley, 2008. Edmonton, Alberta: ETS Archives.

CHAPTER 17

A New Millennium and a New Vision

2000 ONWARD

The Edmonton Transit System entered the new millennium as a continuing barometer by which to gauge Edmonton's swings of fortune. The system had shared the recurrent economic cycles of the preceding ten decades and had worked hard to meet the needs of its owners and clients, the citizens of Edmonton. As it celebrated its centennial during 2008, it could look back with pride on its accomplishments, while looking forward to renewing the spirit of innovation that had sustained it through the years.

The transit system of the first decade of the new millennium was anchored on the well-established model of an integrated light rail and bus system. A long hiatus from LRT construction had occurred during the 1980s and 1990s, primarily because of funding insufficiency, but earnest support for light rail transit technology in Edmonton was once again on the rise. Rapid transit was soon to get back on track as an important component in the solution to emerging long-term transit problems. Municipal, provincial and federal politicians also were increasingly supportive of the LRT concept, and the federal government was willing to supply greater financial support. At the same time, the public began to embrace light rail transit as an environmentally friendly and more convenient means to commute. Serious planning for the South Light Rail Transit (SLRT) was in the works, and the main trunk line resumed its southward course at last.

The Transportation and Streets Department was directed to draft a brief to the Alberta government in the spring of 1999 to project city infrastructure construction plans for the next four years and beyond. Brice Stephenson, head of planning for this committee, reported that LRT was at the top of the municipal wish list, along with the Anthony Henday ring road and several smaller projects. An LRT line from the University of Alberta campus to Heritage Mall was planned at a cost of $425 million. City Council subsequently voted to spend $550 million in the coming decade to complete this project, after rejecting transitional plans for high-speed bus lanes (Bus Rapid Transit).

City Council made an historic commitment to Light Rail Transit, though former Mayor Bill Smith conceded that the motion he brought forward in May 1999 and later saw passed had a caveat attached to it. "That was: When federal and provincial funds were available. What I wanted to do was to get it started," Smith recalled. "Get it so the administration knew that Council was supporting this. And reflection on the motion would show it said, 'When funds are available.' But I knew if you got both feet in the water it would go." Smith had three meetings with Finance Minister Paul Martin during which he obtained support in principle for the initiative. Smith identified the "young engineers" of the time—Rick Millican and Brice Stephenson, "an exceptional thinker"—as instrumental in launching the renewed vision of public transit at the beginning of the decade (*Edmonton Sun*; Smith).

"Public transit develops as a spectrum," Rick Millican observed. "At first a small community will have 12-passenger buses. As the population increases, they may go to 30-passenger buses, and then 40-passenger buses or articulated buses, then on to a bus rapid transit of some type. From there you get into light rail transit. Beyond that, there is the heavy rail that you see in Toronto and other larger centres. This is all related to size and demand" (Millican).

Mayor Bill Smith made transportation a priority during his tenure, with light rail transit one of the keys to solving the problems of Edmonton's growth. Smith negotiated with all levels of government to secure the necessary funding and support. In March 2002, he visited Calgary to forge a renewed commitment with other levels of government to revive a 2000 agreement to fund the Edmonton LRT and Calgary C-Train. "I brought forward the idea of the five-cents-per-litre fuel tax. Al Duerr and myself took

that to the federal government. We subsequently took it to the provincial government . . . and the mayor of Calgary, who now was David Bronconnier. We were successful, the two mayors, in getting five cents per litre for the gasoline consumed within our cities. This provided at that time about $85 million for Edmonton, about $120 million for Calgary. . . . That was the way to start financing transit and roads. [We were] the only municipalities in Canada to get that at that time." Edmonton's LRT system celebrated 25 years of service on 22 April 2003, just in time for the beginning of its second significant growth phase and a fitting way to celebrate a birthday (Smith).

Dave Geake had started work at Edmonton Transit as a junior project engineer on the original LRT start-up project in May 1975. He and Larry McLachlan were virtually the entire LRT Equipment Section in those early days, overseeing vehicles, electrification and signals. Geake would fill many positions with the LRT before leaving after the Corona Station opened in 1984. When he returned to the ETS in the mid-1990s, little had changed with LRT. He felt as though he had taken a holiday and returned to Edmonton to find things exactly where they had been when he left a decade before. "We never had the political support we needed," he concluded. "That has been the fundamental change. This Council and the previous Council have been very supportive of LRT and see the merit of having that as the backbone for the system." Geake feels that another factor in the resurgence of LRT interest is the simple fact that the Edmonton road network is becoming more congested now, creating an urgent demand for public transit (Geake).

Bob Boutilier, who recently spent 11 years with the Toronto Transit Commission (TTC), took over as Transportation General Manager in September 2007 to launch a new phase of planning and development. Boutilier feels that previous experience with Calgary Transit prepared him for his new duties with ETS. For one thing, he feels that "Edmonton and Calgary are unique in the sense that there aren't many places where you find Transit as part of the Transportation Department." (The Toronto Transit Commission is separate from Transportation, while many systems in the United States are regionally administered.) "I think having an understanding of how Alberta works [was helpful since] it's quite different from Toronto . . . where there was a culture of transit." In 2001, while visiting in Calgary, he concluded that the "culture in Alberta tended to be automobile and roadway, and not particularly high on transit. . . . So I came back [to Alberta] knowing full well that there would be a challenge in Edmonton to bring public transportation to the forefront and to face the challenges of trying to match public transit with the roadway system" (Boutilier).

Boutilier was surprised by the "lack of extent of the LRT system." He had visited Edmonton once several years previously, but had not ridden the LRT system. "When I got [to Edmonton] and actually saw what it carried, I was a bit disappointed," he admits. "Yes, it was good for ball games and hockey games, but that's not good enough for a transit system. I was disappointed to see the Churchill Station usage. I came in one morning and compared [it] to Toronto, where you couldn't move in Yonge Station, or Yonge and Bloor, [but at Churchill Station] was nobody there. Here was a modern system, and it just sort of stopped in time.

"I was in Calgary in the mid-90s, and I had heard the stories about how Edmonton had gone underground and Calgary had gone above ground. Also, the fact that Calgary had attempted to build from the outside in, sort of forcing the issue that when money ran out, there still had to be more money to at least make the linkage. At the time, it seemed to make a lot of sense that going above ground would get you the distance, but now that I've been in Edmonton and I've seen how going underground affects the downtown core. It's beginning to look like a very wise decision, the reason being [that] in Calgary, the C-Train obviously has an impact on the traffic in the city core. The area that should have developed [along the] C-Train . . . corridor . . . is not particularly fashionable, whereas in the City of Edmonton, the downtown core has

retained its character. The streets are free to drive through, the businesses are thriving. It makes sense to have the city core sitting on top of the LRT station. So I think in hindsight it was a pretty good decision" (Boutilier).

Reinvigorating LRT expansion and introducing alternative vehicles like hybrids into the transit fleet with the associated decline of the trolley represented the main transformation to occur within ETS between 2000 and 2008. As transportation planning began to gather steam once again, different options for expanding the transit system were examined. By 2003, for example, Bus Rapid Transit (BRT) had emerged as a transitional concept to meet the immediate strain on the system. BRT, a mode of high-speed transit delivery, was fiercely debated between 2003 and 2007 before being rejected.

A municipal study was undertaken in June 2003 after several City Councillors complained that all attention seemed to be focused on the LRT extension to Heritage Mall to the neglect of other forms of high-speed transit servicing other wards. The resulting study raised three options for improved transportation service in Edmonton: increased bus service based on dedicated road lanes; a more basic bus service with priority signals and other efficiency features; and more LRT lines, the option that would finally win the day. Councillor Stephen Mandel, who represented a west-end ward, felt at the time that "the reality is that putting in an LRT throughout the whole city is prohibitive at this stage" (*Edmonton Journal*).

The Transportation Department presented the *West High-Speed Transit Planning Study* to City Council's Transportation and Public Works Committee on 6 April 2004. The report favoured a transitional Bus Rapid Transit step to bridge the gap between current pressing demand the eventual LRT system. The BRT

A nearly empty Churchill LRT station, as Bob Boutilier observed. *(ETS)*

Edmonton Journal article explaining the working of the mole used to tunnel from the University Station to the Health Sciences Centre. The project started in April 2003 and was anticipated to cost $100 million. (Edmonton Journal)

concept envisioned an integrated network of designated high-speed bus routes feeding into the LRT system as it emerged. The Northern Alberta Institute of Technology (NAIT) campus was the most immediate and vital link in the planned north LRT route. NAIT President Sam Shaw stated that in NAIT's expansion plans "[we've] maintained the 106 Street corridor for the LRT. We're very cognizant that in the future we hope it will be here" (*Edmonton Journal*).

The proposed BRT network seems to have been modelled on OCTranspo in the Ottawa and Gatineau National Capital Region with its dedicated high-speed bus-only lanes. Ken Koropeski, ETS Director of Service Development, argued that Edmonton's geographically dispersed population centres were unlike Ottawa's concentrated high-tech and government workforces. Meanwhile, Brice Stephenson, Manager of Transportation Planning, warned City Council that every effort should be made to secure the high-speed route from Churchill Station to NAIT for LRT development. "The area between 105 and 107 Avenue west of 101 Street is under a lot of redevelopment pressure," he reported. "We need to look in this area at what our options are fairly quickly or we'll lose out on right of way" (*Edmonton Journal*).

Groups like the West End Business Association (WEBA) criticized the West High-Speed Transit Planning Study for its shortcomings, citing west-enders' demand for better transit access to the industrial areas west of 170 Street and north of Stony Plain Road. BRT would be slowed by signal delays and traffic congestion, unlike the LRT. After spirited debate, City Council finally rejected the BRT plan in December 2007. "Few tears will be shed at the sudden demise of the proposed bus rapid transit system to Edmonton's west end," an editorial in the *Edmonton Journal* concluded (*Edmonton Journal*).

LRT also was slated for extension on the north side of the river. The North Light Rail Transit (NLRT) route planned stops at Grant MacEwan Community College (now Grant MacEwan University), the Royal Alexandra Hospital, and a joint station for NAIT and Kingsway Garden Mall. A revised NLRT route from downtown to NAIT was released on 5 December 2007, showing the Kingsway Transit Centre moved from its site south of the mall to a site located between Kingsway and 111 Avenues. The existing transit centre was becoming too small, argued Brad Smid, Project Manager for the NAIT LRT route. The new centre was proposed to accommodate buses and an LRT station serving the mall and hospital. The new line would go underground north from the Churchill LRT Station to surface near 105 Avenue, along which it would travel before heading north on 105 Street, "jogging east one block for the hospital

---

LRT sees daylight

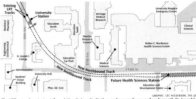

Existing LRT Tracks / University Station / Education North / New Northbound Track / New Southbound Track / Future Health Sciences Centre

GRAPHIC: CEC NICKERSON, THE JOURNAL

The LRT extension starts at the existing University Station and proceeds upward underneath St. Joseph's College and the Education Building Car Park, exiting in front of the Walter J. MacKenzie Health Centre. The New Health Sciences Station will be located on the east side of the Jubilee Auditorium parking lot.

Work finally starts on ambitious expansion 25 years after line opened

SARAH O'DONNELL
Civic Affairs Writer
EDMONTON

The sound of earth rippers on the University of Alberta campus is trumpeting the start of one of Edmonton's most ambitious construction projects in a decade.

After a dozen years of dreaming, political squabbling and precise planning, Edmonton's 25-year-old light rail system is on the verge of seeing daylight on the city's south side.

Construction crews are digging an open pit before starting work on a pair of tunnels to be carved through almost eight storeys of dirt to reach the University station, the LRT's most southerly stop deep beneath HUB mall.

The $100-million project will add only 640 metres to the city's LRT line, and about 380-metres of that is underground. But the work will open the door to less costly extensions to the south in the future.

Setting this project apart from the hundreds of kilometres of varied-sized tunnels snaking beneath Edmonton are the soil conditions.

"They're wicked," south LRT project co-ordinator Brad Griffith said. "We have a couple of metres of clay on the top and then five to seven metres of sand."

Sand is the enemy of tunnel engineers everywhere. But for Edmonton's LRT engineers, the fine-grained sand deposits near the North Saskatchewan River are a familiar nemesis. Delays and tunnel collapses plagued the LRT extension to Grandin station, near the legislature, slowing the giant tunnelling machine to a crawl for several months in 1987.

Engineers say tunnelling technology has improved a lot since then, but the soil conditions are always the biggest question marks.

"That's why we had to put so much effort into the geotechnical investigation," Griffith said.

That's also why the tunnel contractor, PCL Maxam, a Joint Venture, is having "the mole" shipped here from Singapore.

The massive tunnel-boring machine weighs as much as 81 adult elephants. It has a round, tunnelling head that's six metres wide and extends 67 metres — the length of the Skyreach ice surface.

Work on the southbound LRT tunnel starts in April.

The mechanical mole will

chew through the ground, spitting the soil onto a conveyor belt and on to a series of muck cars to be hauled to the surface. Every metre or so, the mole will stop while an arm on the machine secures together a ring of pre-cast tunnel liners around the freshly cut earth.

"We want to do four linear metres a day once we get going," PCL Maxam project manager Jeff Willan said.

At that rate, the southbound tunnel will reach the University station by August, he said.

The boring machine will then be lifted out of the ground through a 24-metre vertical shaft because the tunnel liner makes it impossible for the mole to back up. The mole will then to moved to the 12-metre deep trench next to the Jubilee auditorium parking lot and repeat the earth-chewing process to dig the northbound tunnel.

By the time the mole's excavating work is done in the summer of 2004, it will have quarried enough dirt to fill 4,000 dump trucks — that's enough to cover the Skyreach Centre's entire ice surface under 25 metres of soil.

Deciding how and where to bring the LRT above the ground was a lot like threading an embroidery needle. Winding the two six-metre-wide tunnels to the surface under the university campus buildings, buried power lines and water mains will be an exercise in precision.

To avoid the utility corridor buried in the path of the LRT extension, the tunnel will angle at a six-per-cent grade — the slope of Groat Road as it runs beside Hawrelak Park. The grade is the steepest of any slope on the LRT line. And the city had to spend $7 million to retrofit trains' brakes so cars could handle the grade.

But that's cheaper than the estimated $20 million it would cost to move the underground utilities.

On paper, the 240-metre radius curve makes the tunnel look like a corkscrew.

Complicated? Yes. Big? For Edmonton, absolutely.

But compared with excavations around the world — the Channel Tunnel, for example — the south LRT extension is small potatoes.

Planners, contractors and engineers think they've considered every possibility in building the new extension to the LRT.

"You're never out of total, total danger when you tunnel, but I think we've done a very good job of doing everything we can," Griffith said.

sodonnell@thejournal.canwest.com

"They're wicked. We have a couple of metres of clay on the top and then five to seven metres of sand."

South LRT project co-ordinator Brad Griffith, on soil conditions for project

Crews broke ground last month.

BRIAN GAVRILOFF, THE JOURNAL

Preparing to sink a form for one of the stabilizing pilings.

BRIAN GAVRILOFF, THE JOURNAL

The business end of the TBM (tunnel boring machine)

CITY OF EDMONTON, SUPPLIED

The Vibro Hammer in action

BRIAN GAVRILOFF, THE JOURNAL

St. Joseph's College / Education Car Park / 87th / PORTAL / CLAY / SAND / 24m / CLAY (TILL) / University Station / UTILIDOR / 83rd Ave. / Aberhart Building / SAND / UTILIDOR / CLAY (TILL) / University Avenue / SAND

GRAPHIC: CEC NICKERSON, THE JOURNAL

The extension starts nearly eight storeys underground and must be driven through variable soil conditions.

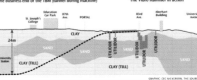

Rendering of the Health Sciences Station

CITY OF EDMONTON, SUPPLIED

How the tunnel exit may look.

CITY OF EDMONTON, SUPPLIED

LRT 2
JUST THE FACTS

TUNNELS
- Twin Tunnels (Southbound tunnel and Northbound tunnel)
- Diameter of tunnel:
  Outside: 6.55 m
  Inside: 5.8 m
- Length of tunnels: 300 m each tunnel, approx. 600 m total.
- Length of cut and cover: 80 m
- Length of retaining wall: 115 m
- Length of Future Health Sciences Station: 125 m
- Length of Pedestrian Walkway (two at 10 m each): 20 m
- Length of total extension: 640 m
- Deepest part of portal or depth: 12 m
- Estimated excavation volumes:
  Portal: 23,000 m³
  Tunnel section at 600m (both): 17,000 m³
  Total: 40,000 m³
- In perspective: you can fill the hockey rink at Skyreach Centre with the total excavated dirt (40,000 m³) to a height of 25 m
- Concrete to be placed on retaining wall section: 4,000 m³

THE PRICE OF PROGRESS
- Tunnel construction: $30 million
- Tracks and Signals: $9.4 million
- Roadwork and Utilities: $5.9 million
- Catenary (overhead power): $1.6 million
- Health Sciences Station: $7.4 million
- Engineering: $16 million
- Land: $2.54 million
- Insurance: $2.5 million
- GST: $3 million
- Updated braking system: $7 million
- Lighting and fire protection: $3 million
- Landscaping: $1 million
- Contingency funds: $11 million
- Engineering and land for extension to Neil Crawford Centre: $8 million

TUNNEL LINERS (SEGMENTS)
- Average length: 1.2 m
- Thickness: 250 mm
- Number of panels: 7 pieces
- Type of Connection: Bolted
- Inside diameter (assembled): 5.8 m
- Outside diameter (assembled): 6.3 m

TUNNEL BORING MACHINE
- Tunnel Boring Machine (TBM) coming from Singapore
- Left Singapore on February 17, 2003 to Edmonton
- Tentative arrival will be mid- to late April 2003
- There are 17 crates — some to be shipped to Toronto for refurbished work — the rest direct to Edmonton
- TBM Head Length: 9 m
- TBM Back-up Length: 67 m
- TBM outside diameter: 6.3 m
- Weight (TBM): 442 tonnes
- Weight (TBM and back-up): 676 tonnes
- Productivity rate: 6 m per day

COMPARISONS OF SCALE
- The Skyreach hockey rink:
  Size: 61 m x 26 m
  Area: 1,586 m² x 1 m thick
  Volume: 1,586 m³
- Earth to remove: 40,000 m³
- Using 10 m³ capacity trucks: 4,000 truckloads of earth will be hauled away.

TRACKS AND TUNNELS: EDMONTON'S LRT CONSTRUCTION HISTORY

April 1978
- First 6.9-kilometre piece of Edmonton's LRT line opens
- Connects two underground stations and three surface platforms: Central, Churchill, Stadium, Coliseum and Belvedere
- Price: $64.9 million, plus $6.3 million in upgrades to Belvedere station in 1998

April 1981
- First northeast extension adds 2.2 kilometres of track to line
- Connects Clareview station to system
- Price: $9.5 million, plus $11.5 million in upgrades to Clareview station in 2001

June 1983
- Newest underground extension opens after 0.8 kilometres of tunnelling westward
- Bay and Corona stations open to passengers
- Price: $89.6 million

September 1989
- The LRT turns south as the city digs out another 0.8-kilometre extension
- Grandin Station, the last stop north of the river, opens
- Price: $67.1 million

August 1992
- In a massive bout of tunnelling, the city moves the LRT across the river and opens a station on the University of Alberta campus
- The Dudley B. Menzies bridge opens next to the High Level bridge so trains can shuttle across the river from one tunnel to another
- Price: $79.1 million

February 2003
- Construction finally begins on the newest south LRT extension
- Trains will surface across the street from the University Hospital
- Anticipated price: $100 million

Source: Edmonton Transportation and Streets department

MOLE MATTERS Bore diameter: 6.3m Length overall: 67m Weight: 442 tonnes Cutterhead: rotates up to 4rpm Min. tunnel curvature: 150m Lining: precast concrete segments, 0.25m thick and 1m long. Seven pieces and 1 key per complete ring

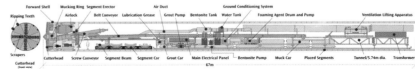

Forward Shell / Mucking Ring / Segment Erector / Air Duct / Ground Conditioning System / Ripping Teeth / Airlock / Belt Conveyor / Lubrication Grease / Grout Pump / Bentonite Tank / Water Tank / Foaming Agent Drum and Pump / Ventilation Lifting Apparatus / Scrapers / Cutterhead (front view) / Cutterhead / Screw Conveyor / Segment Beam / Segment Car / Grout Car / Main Electrical Panel / Bentonite Pump / Muck Car / Placed Segments / Tunnel/5.74m dia. / Transformer / 67m

station," then back west toward Kingsway Mall (*Edmonton Journal*). Dave Geake notes that the connection to the existing line was made possible by the tunnel design created in 1975 when the LRT system was at the planning stage.

Paula Simons, an Edmonton newspaper columnist, wrote in the spring of 2004: "[After] decades of missteps and missed opportunities, we have a truncated little LRT line that serves only a sliver of the city. Its progress has been painfully slow. Finally, finally, the train is preparing to poke its head above ground at the University Hospital" (*Edmonton Journal*).

Rick Millican, General Manager at the time, recalls the issues:

"When I started as General Manager of the Transportation Department in the early 1990s, transit was stalled in the context that the city was in a recession. . . . The LRT was stalled at the University. . . . We did everything we could to get out of the hole at University Station. It was a huge expense to get the LRT to the surface, but people wanted Council to commit to getting it out of the ground. Council's policy on debt meant that the funds for such a large project were not available. I maintained that as soon as it was out of the ground, [LRT] is cheap, and so is going above grade to south Edmonton. We broke the overall project of LRT to the south into smaller works that could be funded" (*Edmonton Journal*; Millican).

What seemed to many Edmontonians as a long hiatus in realizing the next phase of LRT extension came to an end in 2005 when the new Health Sciences Station just west of the Mackenzie Health Sciences Centre was completed on the university campus. The official opening took place on 3 January 2006. It also was noted that covering the 640 metres to the University Station had cost just over $100 million. Part of the problem, of course, was that much of the intervening planning and tunnelling had taken place out of the public eye. With the new station and line above ground, the LRT was once again before the public and in their thoughts, which would not always be charitable as surface construction once again began to intrude on their daily commute and residential existence (*Edmonton Journal*).

The first LRT vehicle coming through to the Health Sciences/ Jubilee LRT Station. *(ETS)*

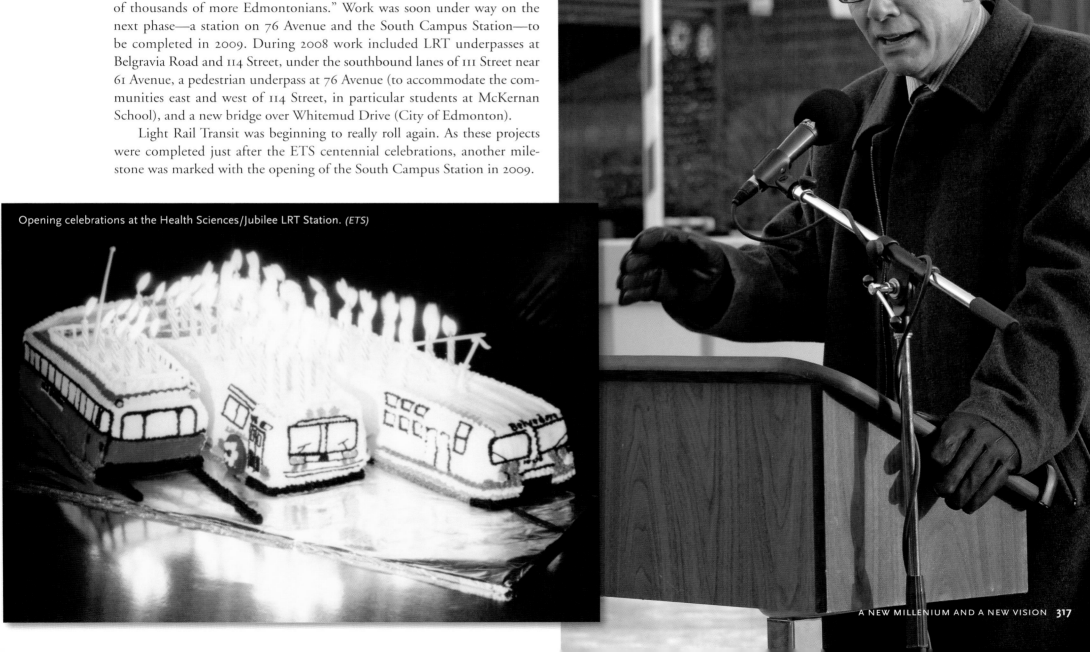

Mayor Steven Mandel opening the
Health Sciences/Jubilee LRT Station.
(ETS)

Mayor Stephen Mandel, elected in October 2004, stated that the new station represented "a benchmark step in our plans to fast-track the south leg of the system, which will make LRT an attractive travel option for tens of thousands of more Edmontonians." Work was soon under way on the next phase—a station on 76 Avenue and the South Campus Station—to be completed in 2009. During 2008 work included LRT underpasses at Belgravia Road and 114 Street, under the southbound lanes of 111 Street near 61 Avenue, a pedestrian underpass at 76 Avenue (to accommodate the communities east and west of 114 Street, in particular students at McKernan School), and a new bridge over Whitemud Drive (City of Edmonton).

Light Rail Transit was beginning to really roll again. As these projects were completed just after the ETS centennial celebrations, another milestone was marked with the opening of the South Campus Station in 2009.

Opening celebrations at the Health Sciences/Jubilee LRT Station. *(ETS)*

The Marion Robinson Story

The Edmonton Transit System has been closely linked with the lives of many Edmontonians, sometimes for decades and generations. The story of Marion Robinson, whom ETS invited to be in the VIP car and help unveil the plaque at the South Campus opening, is one example. She tells the story in her own words:

"My parents were on a soldier settlement farm in Entwistle in 1921. On March 20, a neighbour shot and killed my father over a pitchfork that belonged to my father. My father had fought for four years in World War One.

"Two weeks later, my mother lost her eighteen-month-old daughter to pneumonia. The Red Cross moved my mother and her children to Edmonton. They put them up in the Ritz Hotel on 97 Street. Five weeks later, on April 27, I was born. Old Dr. Baker delivered me.

"We moved to Norwood and lived there for three years. By this time, the older children moved out to work. Sometimes my mother and I would ride the streetcar from Norwood to Whyte Avenue, then walk a mile or two up the dirt road to 53 Avenue to visit my father's grave at Mount Pleasant Cemetery. Imagine doing that with a three- or four-year-old! Other times we'd take the streetcar to North Edmonton, where Swift's Packing House was. We'd walk from the streetcar to Fort Road, past the Transit Hotel to a grocery store and pick up my mother's order.

"My mother and I moved to McKernan. Mrs. Manning had a rooming house, and we rented a room for three dollars a month. My mother had a ten-dollar-a-month mothers' allowance. In about 1933, my mother traded her sewing machine for a twelve-foot by fourteen-foot wall tent. It was put up in the bush on a shiplap floor and a three-foot shiplap wall. We had no stove, only a round heater [that] was used to heat and cook. We lived there in 40 degree below weather for six years. When it stormed in summer, we ran the half block to Mrs. Manning's barn and slept with the sow. There were no others living in tents, heavens no! No one else was that stupid. Mother didn't go for relief—food and clothing vouchers. She had Norwegian stubbornness.

"I used to ride the Toonerville Trolley. It travelled along 104 Street from 82 Avenue, went to 76 Avenue, turned right down 76 to 106 Street on the north side of 76 Avenue, then crossed over to the south side of 76 Avenue to 110 Street, then back over to the north side to 116 Street. There were just quagmire roads, and when it rained they were gumbo. Sure as shooting, that trolley would come off the tracks where McKernan Lake used to be. At the end of the line, the conductor would reverse the trolley and take the controls to the other end and go back the same way. It was either old Scotty Macintosh or the deaf one, Montgomery, who drove. Adult tickets were five for 25 cents; children's were ten for 25 cents.

"I couldn't afford to ride every day, but occasionally I would ride over town, transfer to the red and white, and go downtown to Woodward's or Eaton's. I didn't have to pay to transfer, but no one could ride back home on the same ticket. The trolley crossed the High Level Bridge on the outside lanes, and drivers would get it swaying side to side. Some people were terrified, but I thought it was a big joke. When it was very late coming home, there was so much bush that the driver would let me off in front of Fred and Mary Knight's house at 11426–76 Avenue, the only house between 112 Street and 116 Street. The Knights saved my life.

"I married Fred Robinson in 1939. We met when I worked on the Stannard's farm east of Edmonton; he worked on the farm across the street. We came into the city after two or three months, and then he joined the army. We lived near the old Rutherford School, and my children would ride the streetcar to a show every Saturday afternoon at the Strand Theatre. When my daughter Jeannie was 12 years old, a family from Scotland moved to the street, and she invited our new neighbours' three kids to go the theatre, too. Their mother saw them off on the streetcar but stood out there waiting and waiting when each streetcar came around for them to return. They did, of course, at the end of the day. Soon they just rode the streetcar by themselves and never thought anything about it.

"Fred, my oldest son, worked as a mechanic for Edmonton Transit in the Ferrier shops. He retired as the head mechanic after 31 years. And my daughter Sue has been a driver with ETS for 15 years. She met the love of her life there, too, Mark Day, who has driven for over 30 years. Sue and Mark arranged for me to go to the grand opening of the South Campus LRT station in April this year. Fred had taken his children to the grand opening of the LRT

Mrs. Marion Robinson (fourth from left) unveiling the commemorative plaque for the official opening of the South Campus LRT Station. Others are (left to right) Debbie Bok, Susan Robinson, Mark Day, Rona Ambrose, and Indira Samarasekera. *(ETS)*

in 1978. I met Mayor Mandel and Ann-Marie Thivierge, the president of the McKernan Community League. It was a wonderful day riding the train from one end to the other.

"One day I'm going to take my walker up the ramp and take a lovely ride on the LRT by myself. I won't tell my kids until after. I'm a sneaky old thing! I take DATS now. I wouldn't get out otherwise, but I'd give my eyeteeth to jump on a bus and go wherever I want to go. I used to go out every day with my seniors' pass to go shopping or to visit friends. It was a wonderful way to get around" (Robinson).

The unveiling of the commemorative plaque at the official opening of the South Campus LRT Station. *(ETS)* Participants included (left to right) Gene Zwozdesky, MLA for Edmonton Mill Creek and Deputy Government House Leader; Stephen Mandel, Mayor of Edmonton); Indira Samarasekera, President of the University of Alberta; Don Hickey, University of Alberta Vice President, Facilities and Operations; unidentified woman; Rona Ambrose (obscured); Marion Robinson; unidentified gentleman. *(ETS)*

Route changes in the decade following 1998. *(ETS)*

Blue - 1998 Routes
Red - 2008 Routes

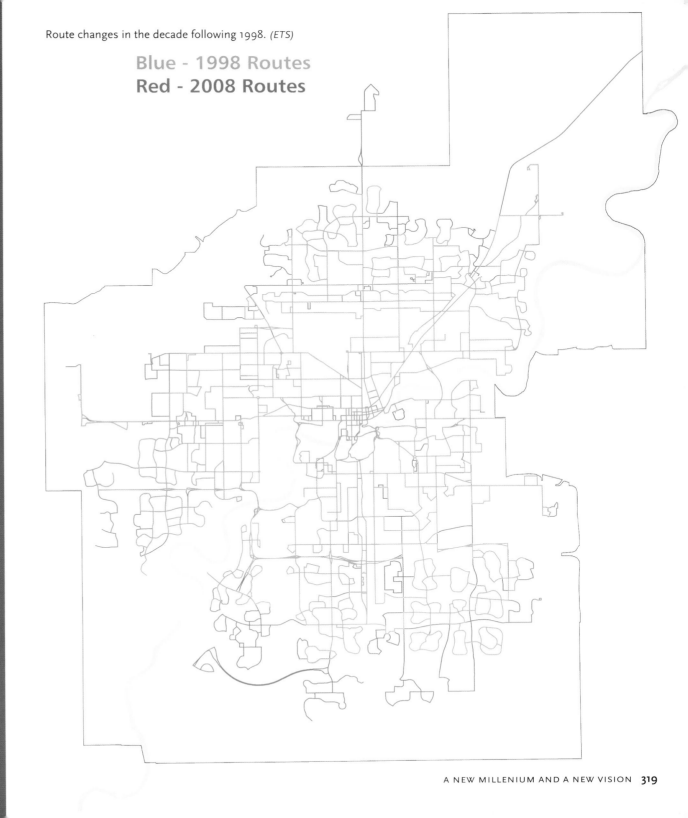

Much of the LRT rolling stock had been operational since the inauguration of light rail transit service in Edmonton in 1978. The fleet sorely needed to be renewed and brought up to date in every aspect from technology to livery. An overhaul contract was awarded to Bombardier to retrofit and refurbish the original 37 U2 LRVs. It was felt that this would add another 15 years to their life. The fleet was doubled with 37 new SD160 vehicles from Siemens to serve the ridership increases and the SLRT extensions.

ETS planned to make the fleet totally accessible by 2012, but was able to meet the goal by the end of 2009. This was accomplished partly through the elimination of the electric trolley buses earlier than anticipated, due mainly to the sudden stringent annual municipal budgeting during 2008 following the international financial crisis. The remaining GMC buses also were decommissioned in November 2009. With the older buses decommissioned, the new fleet now met the desired accessibility standards.

An expanding public transit system requires constant additions of new rolling stock, and during 2001 ETS received 66 New Flyer low-floor buses, and six articulated buses. Fifty-three new low-floor buses were added to the ETS fleet in 2002. New priority seating decals were installed at the front of each bus, emphasizing the special service provided to a growing part of the transit ridership and the ETS's commitment to improved accessibility. The ETS added another 50 low-floor buses and seven articulated buses to the fleet in 2003. In 2005 the fleet was further expanded when 85 New Flyer low-floor buses were purchased; in 2007 a further 231 low-emission low-floor buses were purchased, the largest single purchase of New Flyers ever. The ETS also purchased 12 low-floor ELF community-service buses in 2005, and another 13 Glaval community buses in 2007.

Greg Latham recalls that the ETS "took bold steps in the design of the first low-floor bus in Edmonton. A task group was assigned to work alongside the designers . . . to customize the entire spectrum of the bus. Several other transit systems ordered our specifications after we were done." (Latham). This early initiative would pay off in the 2000s as low-floor buses came to dominate the ETS fleet.

DATS celebrated its twenty-fifth anniversary in 2000. In July 2005, DATS implemented a new business model approved by City Council in 2002 following a City Manager's Review. Under the new plan, the City purchased 91 lift vans that would be operated by unionized drivers. At the same time, DATS installed Mobile Data Terminals (MDTs), also known as onboard computers, equipped with an automatic vehicle locator (AVL) and software to display an electronic manifest of client trips for a given day.

The last trolley in service enters the Westwood Garage on 2 May 2009. *(ETS)*

An ETS historical trolley helps commemorate the last day of service for trolley buses in Edmonton. *(ETS)*

The small Glaval bus runs in neighbourhoods with narrow streets and tight corners. *(ETS)*

An ELF, one model of small community bus, stops near a senior's complex. *(ETS)*

If dispatch is unable to contact a driver by radio for any reason, it can use the AVL to locate the vehicle. In addition, the MDTs offer text messaging for dispatchers and drivers to communicate more effectively.

The City-operated lift van service was supplemented with a contracted ambulatory service. Architect Ron Wickman, son of former City Councillor and MLA Percy Wickman, dedicated the new Percy Wickman Garage in May 2006. Located in the City's Davies civic precinct, the facility became

Sarbjit Mann, DATS driver, using the Mobile Data Terminal (MDT) in the DATS lift-equipped van. *(ETS)*

the home of the newly expanded City-operated DATS service. In May 2007, DATS implemented a call-ahead feature using interactive voice response (IVR) technology. Drivers activate an automated call via the IVR when they are about five to 10 minutes away from a pick-up address so the client can be ready when the vehicle arrives. This new technology reduces the uncertainty for both rider and driver.

DATS implemented a new computer system from Trapeze Group with a "go live" date of 23 November 2008. This new system offered DATS automated scheduling capability, a feature that was lacking in the old in-house system. DATS users can now call booking agents to schedule their ride directly onto a run for the next day. Schedulers review the runs generated with the automated scheduling function and ensure that the routing is logical and efficient for both the rider and the driver. On the day of service, dispatchers take over and monitor the delivery of service, helping drivers stay on schedule and manage incidents that arise. In 2008 DATS delivered 916,488 trips to Edmontonians with disabilities (Nowicki; Stewart).

The trolley debate became more animated in the years after City Council directed that ETS continue operation of its fleet of trolley buses. At the same time, Council also authorized the administration to test new hybrid bus and trolley technology, and to report on their relative merits. On 27 July 2004, City Council passed motions that Edmonton Transit continue to operate trolleys until 2008, that the administration arrange to have a demonstration of low-floor trolley and hybrid buses to be utilized within the system for information gathering, that expansion of the trolley fleet to Northgate be considered in the 2006 budget and that a report be provided to Council in 2008 regarding continuation of trolleys based on service levels, environmental concerns contingent upon demonstration of low-floor trolley, hybrid buses and other options, and that the administration continue to look at ways to maximize the cost benefit of the existing trolleys.

In January 2006, the ETS announced its intention to purchase three new types of hybrid diesel–electric buses to replace the aging diesels or perhaps even replace the trolleys whose fate was becoming more heatedly debated in Council Chambers and on the street. The new hybrids required an expensive roof-mounted battery pack requiring replacement every six to eight years. Although their engine and brake life seemed superior to conventional buses, the relative cost efficiency could not be known until tests could be conducted under local conditions (*Edmonton Journal*; Paul).

Just before Christmas 2006, two new diesel–electric hybrid buses made their appearance on Route 106, connecting Lessard, West Edmonton Mall, the University of Alberta campus and Capilano. The ETS was sceptical of

the manufacturer's claim of fuel savings of up to 50 percent. After all, New York City's hybrid buses had realized savings closer to 20 percent. Given the cost of $700,000 per vehicle—up to 70 percent more than comparable diesel buses—testing was crucial to verifying fuel and maintenance savings. The City developed a plan to do this.

Amid the renewed LRT initiative and greater emphasis on system efficiency and special services, Edmonton Transit's vehicle procurement process had to finally deal with the long-standing issue of the electric trolleys in 2008. Trolleys were environmentally friendly and believed to be less expensive to operate than diesel buses. But trolleys were expensive to buy, required extensive and expensive infrastructure, and were inflexible in meeting operational requirements. Nostalgia was on the side of the trolleys that had trundled through city streets for almost 70 years. The future was on the side of light rail transit and the emerging diesel–electric hybrid bus technology. The two sides squared off, though few in the debate did not feel mixed emotions. Former Mayor Terry Cavanagh recalls that a motion during his term to retain the trolleys

A hybrid New Flyer with the battery pack visible on the roof. *(ETS)*

A hybrid Orion bus. *(ETS)*

"came up in Council, and I supported that, and a motion passed that [rolling stock] stay as is until 2000. . . . But we haven't bought more [trolleys]. Some are 30 years old. . . " (Cavanagh). Former Mayor Bill Smith said, "People are saying [trolleys] are more environmentally friendly, and they are." Still, he had to concede that "There was really a move at that point to get rid of the trolleys, and it made a lot of sense." The trolleys had become "an insignificant part" of the system as a whole. (Smith).

City administration purchased six hybrid buses from two different manufacturers, involving three different types of technology. Two Orion VII/BAE hybrid LFBs, two New Flyer/Allison hybrid LFBs and two New Flyer ISE hybrid LFBs were to be tested against a new trolley bus leased from Coast Mountain Bus Company in Vancouver (TransLink). ETS had briefly tested an Orion in 2003. The Orion and one of the New Flyers are "power-blending" with all traction power supplied by onboard batteries. The other New Flyer is a parallel design that couples the internal combustion engine to the final drive through an electro-mechanical transmission. Electric motors blend in and out with the engine throughout the speed range.

The bus-test units represented three types of transit vehicle technology: electric trolley, "clean diesel" and hybrid. Trolley buses would continue to use an electric propulsion system with power delivered through overhead trolley line infrastructure. "Clean diesel," the preferred term for recent diesel engine technology, became the standard in the ETS and other transit fleets in North America. The new "clean diesel" engines comply with 2007 Transport Canada standards and those set by the United States Environmental Protection Act. Lower emissions are obtained by the use of ultra-low-sulphur fuel, and post-combustion converter technology to capture some of the emissions before they leave the tailpipe (*Edmonton Journal*).

City Council commissioned *The Transit Vehicle (Trolley) Technology Review (2008)* to study the many issues concerning trolleys. Consultants played a crucial role in evaluating the future of ETS trolleys in relation to clean diesel and hybrid buses. Dr. David Checkel of the University of Alberta, a recognized authority in the field of vehicle fuel and emission technologies, conducted "micro" vehicle technical evaluation, including noise testing, and assessed the results of emissions tests carried out independently by Environment Canada. Booz Allen Hamilton Consultants, one of the largest international technology and management consulting firms, and specialists in urban mass transportation with special expertise in bus technology, conducted a "macro" fleet-wide analysis and reviewed data from other transit systems as well as published technical information.

The consultant's cost–benefit report, *Transit Vehicle Technology Review*, concluded that the continued operation of trolleys was the most expensive option. The consultants' report indicated that energy costs of trolley buses

One of the environmentally friendly New Flyer hybrids. *(ETS)*

would be approximately 50 percent less than diesel buses, while the hybrid would probably use 15–20 percent less fuel than diesels. "While the energy costs for a trolley bus itself are substantially below those of either the clean diesel or the hybrid," the report acknowledged, "when you add the costs of annually maintaining the overhead system and substations, the cost of running a trolley bus is approximately double those of the other two technologies."

On the matter of purchase cost, the trolley came up short again. The estimated capital cost to purchase clean diesel buses was $425,000; hybrid, $650,000; trolley, $950,000. Purchasing 47 new hybrid buses would cost $14.1 million less than trolleys. In addition, the estimated capital cost to upgrade the overhead system and substations for the estimated 18-year life of the trolley buses was $66.3 million. The review estimated that replacing trolley buses with hybrids would avoid costs of $99.7 million.

While purchasing and operating costs were important considerations, environmental concerns dominated the debate. The ETS is governed by the City's Environmental Policy (C512) that emphasizes the prevention of pollution, continual improvement in emissions reductions, and meeting or exceeding regulatory and voluntary emissions regulations. Edmonton also is a member of the Federation of Canadian Municipalities (FCM) Partners for Climate Protection (PCP) program that requires greenhouse gases produced in the generation of electrical power for municipal use be included in any city greenhouse gas emissions inventory.

The analysis of emissions was therefore extensive and undertaken from both micro and macro perspectives. Micro tests were conducted on each of the three vehicles tested locally. Estimates were developed from those measurements to represent emissions generated by the extraction of the base fuel and its manufacture. Macro estimates of emissions were generated through 2027 utilizing industry (EPCOR) numbers for the different vehicles under consideration. "The trolley bus itself does not have any emissions," noted the consultants. "From a route perspective these vehicles are emission-free. However, from a regional perspective the fuel (coal burning) ultimately results in emission levels that . . . are higher than hybrids or clean diesels. And if the emissions (well to wheel) associated with getting the feedstock out of the ground and to the refinery or generating plant are included, total

emissions associated with use of trolley buses [are] higher in all categories. The hybrid bus offers the best overall emission reduction opportunity."

Finally, noise tests indicted that the older diesel buses produced the highest noise levels, while the trolley bus had the lowest noise levels, "although only marginally less than the hybrid bus."

The consultants also concluded that hybrid or clean diesel buses would provide more opportunity to introduce "service efficiencies through changes to route designs since the restriction of the overhead infrastructure will be gone. Hybrids would likely be assigned to those routes for which they are best suited (i.e. congested routes with a lot of stop and go traffic)."

The results of public consultation indicated that 62 percent of the general public supported purchasing hybrid buses. Sixty-six percent of ETS operators preferred diesel buses, with hybrids second and the trolley a distant third.

The 2008 review concluded that the existing trolley system was "outdated and expensive to maintain and operate." Hybrid buses "best meet all of the City's criteria, functionally, operationally, financially and environmentally to replace the existing trolley system." The report bowed to the inevitable in recommending that trolleys be phased out of operation during 2009–10 along with the decommissioning of the remaining trolley infrastructure. It also recommended that the purchase of 47 new hybrid buses be approved with funding identified in the 2009–11 capital budget process.

After a long and animated debate in City Council and the media, the decision to terminate trolley service was finally made on 18 June 2008. Before the summer of 2008 was over, trolleys began to disappear from some routes, their overhead wires soon to follow (Stolte and Sirovyak).

During City Council's 2009 Budget deliberations held in December 2008, a motion was approved to replace the purchase of the 47 diesel hybrid buses with 66 "clean diesel" buses. This amendment to the capital budget resulted in additional transit buses brought into service to serve the community during a time of fiscal restraint.

Closing the city's chapter on trolleys, City Council voted on 28 April 2009 to move forward the decommissioning of the trolley operations in Edmonton as one of the cost-saving measures intended to address a citywide budget deficit. The last day of trolley bus operations in Edmonton was May 2, 2009.

Doug Cowan Remembers the Trolleys

Doug Cowan, now retired from a teaching and educational administration career in Edmonton, provided many of the photographs of the trolleys used in *Ride of the Century*. "I've always been interested in the transit system," he says. "I grew up on a trolley line, you see, and we never had a car in our family, so riding the bus . . . was a treat. I would often go on outings by bus with my parents. As a little boy, I really enjoyed riding downtown. The bus went up 101 Street, and there were five-and-ten-cent stores along there, as well as Woodward's and Eaton's. The Bay was a little off the way. There weren't malls like there are today, so all our shopping was done downtown. When I was ten, I was allowed to go downtown on my own, and I'd go to get my hair cut at Mohler's barber school near the old Dreamland Theatre.

"I was fascinated by the trolleys—the lights blinking when the bus went over a switch, the variety of models of trolleys . . . everything. I remember riding the 1939

English trolleys, the Mack trolleys—there were only three of them, the Pullmans—they were an American bus, and the Brills that came in around 1946 and 1947. There were other vehicles in transit, but I just followed the trolley buses."

Doug Cowan's photographic collection has become a significant historical resource that transcends transit history. His photographs always seem to contain historical context that place his subjects firmly in their time frame. "I got into photography when I left high school. I started serious photography in the early 1960s. It wasn't only buses—I took pictures of buildings downtown, billboards, neon signs . . . a lot of things," he says.

"I first worked with Edmonton Transit in 1999 when they were celebrating the Sixtieth Anniversary of trolleys in Edmonton. Kevin Brown and I were both on the committee, and [the ETS] was very receptive to our suggestions. Then they asked us both to be more involved with historic transit tours. I guess I had helped ETS prior to that with displays at the exhibitions. When they displayed vintage vehicles, I allowed them to use my photographs, and I was there to interpret for the public. I began working on the school programmes after I retired about eight years ago. We cover everything from the early streetcars, trolleys and streetscapes with the use of my photos."

Brill No. 202, the last Brill ever manufactured in Canada.
(Doug Cowan)

"Somehow these vehicles should not be sent to the scrap yard," he recalls feeling when the Pullmans were to be scrapped in 1966. "I wrote to City Council to encourage them to preserve the buses. I still have the letter they sent in reply. Unfortunately, they had no money to restore them. They did have some heritage vehicles, but they didn't have any trolleys saved at the time. In fact, Edmonton's Brill trolley, Number 202, was the last Brill ever manufactured in Canada. We need to keep them here and exhibit them, or ideally operate them."

"The Brills were first purchased in 1947, but the last one was bought in 1954. Twelve years later when you need parts, what do you do? ETS strived to keep the trolley system running. Many cities were phasing trolleys from their fleet. ETS wanted to buy parts and heard that Regina was retiring their trolley fleet. They told Regina what they needed, but Regina said it cost more to cannibalize their buses and send the pieces. Why not just take the whole bus? ETS bought ten Brills for $700 each. When they got here and were inspected, they were judged to be in better condition than the ones waiting here to be overhauled,

Doug Cowan, on right, leading an ETS Historical Transit Tour. Operator Dan Linder is on the left. *(ETS Archives)*

so they put these replacement buses in service instead. There were no hills in Regina and the vehicles probably didn't have the strain or miles on them that our buses faced. They were numbered 121 to 130 and they ran these until 1978 when all the Brills were retired. They were darn good vehicles" (Cowan).

Brill No. 156, one of 47 Brill trolleys purchased by Edmonton Transit in 1947, heading west on Jasper Avenue at the corner of 97 Street. *(Doug Cowan)*

ETS has launched many special services to meet individual and group needs for some time, but with the arrival of the new millennium such efforts became more concerted and imaginative in their delivery. One noticeable example was the introduction of digital messaging on the South Light Rail Transit (SLRT) station platforms to indicate the next train time. Other special services introduced since 2000 included a new, improved version of the Mobility Card for persons with disabilities and a subsidized monthly transit pass for Assured Income for the Severely Handicapped (AISH) recipients. BusLink hit a new record on 5 September 2006 when the system handled 15,224 calls (an average of one call every six seconds). Bus Hailer Kits, Customer Communication Cards, the Seniors-on-the-Go program, the expansion of the Mobility Choices travel training program, and a pilot program for travel training for newcomers and new immigrants were further indications of ETS's recognition of the diverse needs of the riding public.

As the city's population began to age, senior riders became an increasingly vocal and numerous part of the ETS's clientele. When the Transportation and Streets Department recommended in 2002 the elimination of both the low-income annual bus pass and the regular annual seniors bus pass, seniors spoke out. Irl Miller, President of the Edmonton Seniors One Voice Association, informed City Council that seniors' income was rapidly declining. "Their income has been eroded by serious drops in interest rates, the lack of pensions in many cases, and therefore a small increase in fares means a loss of income for other purposes, including food," he said.

Wayne Mandryk, Manager of Edmonton Transit, held that the department wanted to eliminate the annual seniors transit passes because they were seen as unfair by other riders, and the change would be consistent with the principles in the ETS Fare Strategy Review. Other low-income groups wanted to be treated equitably. Mandryk felt that the recommendation was consistent with the principle of fairness, while also simplifying the fare structure by reducing fare products. In fact, Edmonton was one of the few cities to continue with an annual pass. The main objective, according to Mandryk, was to introduce a monthly pass. Councillor Allan Bolstad argued that the administration's recommendation made little sense since the City was encouraging seniors to remain active and healthy. "Transportation is a key part of that,

particularly for elderly people who are in their homes and aren't able to drive anymore," he concluded (*Edmonton Journal*).

It was estimated that the proposal would have increased City revenue by about $1.8 million over two years, but also would have reduced the number of trips by an estimated 260,000 a year. The Transportation and Public Works Committee responded to the public protest and City Council concern by recommending retention of the annual passes for seniors. The administration was directed to look further into the introduction of monthly seniors' passes that would be available in addition to the annual passes for those who did not use transit year round. These new passes became available in April 2003. Councillor Bolstad concluded that "we came up with a good compromise" (*Edmonton Journal*).

The senior's bus pass for August 2008. *(ETS)*

Students represent another group with a strong interest in bus passes. University of Alberta Student Transit Passes were first sold in 1962. A recent development targeting post-secondary students is the U Pass. The pass allows students access to the Edmonton, St. Albert and Strathcona County transit systems was introduced in 2007. It was an instant success.

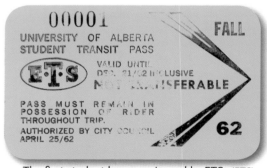

The first student bus pass issued by ETS. *(ETS)*

With the coming of a new century, the city continued to build on its international reputation as a host of prestigious sporting events, and the ETS provided services essential to ensure success. The BG World Triathlon came to the city on 22 July 2001, the first event in a busy series

The U-Pass endorsement on a 2008 University of Alberta student card. *(ETS)*

U-Pass advertising in the first year of the initiative in 2007. *(ETS)*

of events followed immediately by the Eighth International Amateur Athletic Federation (IAAF) World Championships in Athletics on 3–12 August. Commonwealth Stadium once again rang to the cheers of an international crowd as 1,677 athletes competed in 46 events. The Edmonton IAAF competition was the first held in North America. The IAAF, obviously satisfied with the spirit of civic support, returned to Edmonton for its World Half Marathon Championships on Saturday, 1 October 2005.

Wayne Mandryk, Manager of Edmonton Transit, was present at the IAAF competition and recalls the event:

"We had great plans to get people out of [Commonwealth Stadium]. We were going to take all the athletes on buses from the Commonwealth Stadium out Stadium Road. It was such a great evening that the organizers decided that the athletes shouldn't have to leave. They should be able to stay and watch the events. So, of course, all the buses on Stadium Road never moved. And then, when it was over, the whole crowd broke at once.

Team Canada marches at the World Championships in Athletics, August 2001. *(ETS)*

"So what we had was all the athletes coming out to the buses, and you couldn't move a bus because Stadium Road was plugged with buses. And we had a thunderstorm coming in from the west, and it was just going to get really, really ugly. We almost had a riot out there.

"The inspectors really did handle it well. We had operators and inspectors directing traffic, playing policeman. I thought we were on the edge of a riot. I was in the parking lot at the time trying to help. . . . Unfortunately, one of my friends . . . had come out there and said, 'Hey, there's the Transit Manager. Ask him.'

"The next thing I knew I had about a hundred people around me. I think they wanted to string me up because they were waiting in the Park-and-Ride lot. I had to have some of my inspectors help me out of the Park-and-Ride lot. As it turned out, the storm just hit along the edge. . . . You've got to be a little bit lucky as well" (Mandryk).

The World Championships in Athletics, Commonwealth Stadium, August 2001. *(ETS)*

Chris Williams and Me

Though hosting international events involves long hours and stress, ETS personnel have a reputation for making athletes feel at home. Operator Dean Kulhavy recalled the World Championships in Athletics with special fondness. "One of the highlights of my driving career happened back in the summer of 2001, where I worked a night run charter for the athletes' village out of the Delta Inn for the World Track and Field Championship. Memories and stories involving handing out Canada pins to the athletes and dignitaries, collecting autographs and meeting the President of Qata still bring a smile to my face every time I reminisce.

"One story begins on a Monday when Chris Williams boarded at the Delta Inn with his coach in tow. They were both pretty quiet, so I offered them a Canada pin in exchange for Chris's autograph, to which he was too humble to take and Chris respectfully asked if he could sign the book later [in the] week. . . .

"We started talking, and I found out that Chris was competing in the 200-metre event for Jamaica. His coach was continually giving his athlete words of advice and encouragement. As we were getting closer to Commonwealth Stadium, I too started chiming in with his coach and began encouraging Chris and pumping him up for the practices and heats to follow. It soon became a ritual as each day they would wait patiently at the Delta Inn so they could specifically board my bus to take them to Commonwealth Stadium. As the week progressed, I continued encouraging Chris and watched as he continued to advance through his heats, each time gaining more confidence. By Friday he eventually made it past the semi-finals and then advanced to the finals.

"On the evening of the finals, Chris and his coach boarded my bus, and I could tell they were nervous and focusing hard on what needed to be done. They were both quiet, so I in turn also kept quiet. When we arrived, Chris came up to me and said, 'Well, aren't you going to say anything to me?'

"I replied, 'Here, take this good-luck Canada pin with you and when you win, you're going to sign my autograph book, right?'

"He took my pin, smiled and alighted from the bus.

"Later that night, I was waiting at Clarke Stadium to take some athletes back to the Delta Inn. I saw Chris and his coach off in the distance, walking towards the staging area. I then heard his coach yelling from across the field, 'Dean, we got silver! We got silver!'

"I ran past the security guards and inspectors to congratulate Chris on the field, only to be picked up and shaken by his coach and have Chris put his silver medal around my neck. After some high fives and handshakes, Chris boarded my bus and said, 'Thanks for your help. Now I will sign your book.'

"P.S. He also let me wear his medal back to the Delta Inn" (Kulhavy).

RIDE OF THE CENTURY

ETS also transported thousands to Commonwealth Stadium for the 2002 Grey Cup game, as it had for Grey Cups in 1984 and 1997. The FIFA U-19 Women's World Championship also was held in Edmonton in 2002, when the crowds once again streamed through the Stadium Station to watch the final match of the inaugural championship. Again, one success led to another, and the FIFA U-20 World Cup returned to the city in 2007. In 2003 the Heritage Classic, the first regular season outdoor hockey game, also drew over 60,000 fans to the Commonwealth Stadium many arriving by LRT and special event park and ride.

ETS personnel provided extra service on Friday, 8 October 2004 for Edmonton's Centennial celebrations. The following year, ETS also offered special services to support the Royal Visit that May during the Alberta Centennial Year. In 2005 ETS also played a major role in providing an extensive Park 'n' Ride service for the inaugural West Edmonton Mall Grand Prix, which was repeated after 2006 as the Rexall Edmonton Indy. ETS provided many essential special services for the Alberta Centennial celebrations in September 2005, just a year after the demanding city centennial celebrations. Among other logistically challenging events hosted that year were the World Masters Games, the largest multi-sport event in the world, held from 22–31 July. Thousands of local, national and international participants from 100 countries gathering to compete in 27 events. Other special events included concerts, the annual exhibition at Northlands, Heritage Days, the Folk Festival, First Night celebrations, and many more.

With the new century, ETS continued the pursuit of a fresh new look in the way it presented its services. In 2000, Pattison Outdoor Group was awarded a 10-year advertising contract that included vehicles, benches and shelters and that resulted in a noticeable change in the ETS street presence. The ETS website also got a new look in conjunction with the City of Edmonton's virtual redevelopment, with the new ETS website, www.takeETS.com, launched the following year. The BusLink menu changed in September 2001 with a new Route

Edmonton Transit provides services to special events such as the firework display held outside City Hall that marked Edmonton's Centennial as a city. *(ETS)*

Crowds gather to use ETS service to attend the 2005 Champ Car Race, first Grand Prix held in Edmonton. *(ETS)*

Schedule Search feature added in the spring of 2004. A new Trip Planner was introduced on www.takeETS.com in 2004, and a Bus Stop Schedule Search also was launched. In January 2005 an address and intersection search feature was added to online tools to make it easier for passengers to find the location of bus stops. A mapping feature was added to the Trip Planner in March 2007. Another refreshed look for the ETS website was launched in March 2007 to highlight all of the new online trip planning tools.

Enhanced service extended to the ETS Customer Services Centre when the Churchill LRT Station was renovated in 2000. In partnership with Telus, ETS also installed public TTY payphones in all LRT stations that year. The greening of ETS continued as the Bikes-on-Buses program was expanded to Routes 1 and 4 in September 2002, thanks to a donation of bike racks from the Edmonton Bicycle Commuters Society. Edmonton Transit became the first major city department to transfer its information line into the new 311 Call Centre at the end of January 2008. Residents could now call to obtain information on city services and programs 24/7.

Several new transit centres opened to fulfil service mandates as the system expanded. A new Heritage Transit Centre replaced the existing one in 2000, the same year that ETS opened the Mill Woods Transit Centre, the third Mill Woods location. The newly renovated Clareview LRT Station went into service in March 2001, and was officially opened in September. Construction on

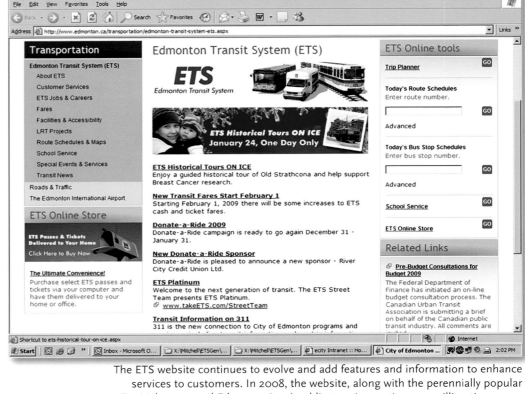

The ETS website continues to evolve and add features and information to enhance services to customers. In 2008, the website, along with the perennially popular BusLink, answered Edmontonians' public transit questions 5.5 million times—an average of a contact every six seconds of every day of the year. *(ETS)*

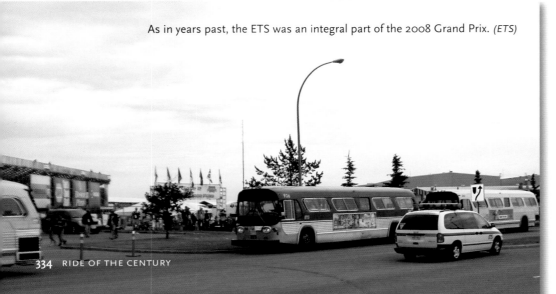

As in years past, the ETS was an integral part of the 2008 Grand Prix. *(ETS)*

the upgrades to the Kingsway and Castle Downs Transit Centres also began in September 2001, and were completed in February 2002. That August also brought the unveiling of ETS's first graffiti art mural in the LRT system. In 2005 ETS began operating a commuter service to Fort Saskatchewan and the newly expanded "Superbase" at Edmonton Garrison. Finally, the Health Sciences LRT Station opened on 3 January 2006, completing 12.9 kilometres of serviced track.

With renewed growth throughout the decade, security became an overarching concern for ETS. In the past, the few criminal incidents reported could be handled by the inspectors, operators and public. That changed in December 2003 when Edmontonians were shocked to learn that two men had been charged with the sexual assault of five women in and around the Clareview LRT Station. Reported criminal incidents on the transit system had increased from 410 in 2001 to 454 in 2002 with weapons offences more than doubling and assaults on the rise as well. The public expressed increasing concern about its safety on the buses and LRT, especially at night. Concern for public and employee safety led City Council to order an internal investigation of security in late 2003 (*Edmonton Journal*).

Edmonton Transit System security officers were checking for proof of payment in Churchill Station on the morning of 11 May 2004 when they stopped a man who had not paid his fare. While waiting for Edmonton Police Service personnel to arrive, the man attempted to escape, knocking down and breaking the collarbone of an ETS officer. Wayne Mandryk, then ETS Manager, reported that such episodes were now

A graffiti wall was added to the ETS collection of public art in August, 2002.
(ETS)

occurring about three or four times every year. Confrontations with aggressive groups and suspected drug users also were on the rise. Although patrols were carried out in pairs for safety, security officers worked alone because there were only 32.5 fulltime positions in 2004. A former Edmonton Police Service officer taught ETS officers a basic restraint course, but clearly more training was required to deal with more serious incidents. While other large Canadian cities like Toronto and Vancouver allowed their security personnel to carry pepper spray and batons, Edmonton security officers were limited to handcuffs and personal protection gear such as slash-proof gloves and protective vests. Wayne Mandryk concluded regretfully that the city might have to issue pepper spray and batons to security officers. "I believe that is where we're going to end up," he said (*Edmonton Journal*).

The ETS security report presented on 16 July 2004 concluded that Transit Security should constitute a special constabulary modelled on forces in Calgary, Toronto and Vancouver that had the power to arrest and use pepper spray and batons to enforce security. It recommended that personnel be increased to 46, including an increase in the number of special constables from 19 to 24. Manager Wayne Mandryk rejected the $32 million price tag for implementation of all the report's recommendations, but set in motion several new initiatives after "identifying funding and an implementation plan, followed by a restructuring process that led to a significantly more effective and highly trained security force as seen today." The Amalgamated Transit Union Local supported the change. On 24 August 2004, this report was tabled with the Transportation and Public Works Committee (*Edmonton Journal*).

ETS security personnel were sworn in as peace officers beginning in March 2006; Darren Taitinger in photo. *(ETS)*

Security officers work with drivers to ensure safety on the transit system. Richard Florian talking with Teresa Kukara.. *(ETS)*

ETS security procedures include surveillance. James (Jiggs) Haiden is shown in Control Centre. *(ETS)*

Pranksters and Operators

Children's pranks on the transit system have sometimes been viewed by operators as a thorn in their side. But usually a mutual respect prevails. The following story from former Operator Gord Dykstra suggests how this can happen in unlikely circumstances:

"In high school, my record with transit was less than polished. I spent much of my time with a group that relished tormenting our bus driver. Repeatedly ringing the bell unnecessarily was only one approach used. On one occasion the whole situation escalated. The Operator turned the bell off, and one of my friends then lifted his entire weight using the bell cord, breaking the cord. Thinking this was still a joke, he tried to pass the cord out the window and then tie it to a bus-stop pole. Unknown to him, the operator had contacted police.

"The Edmonton Police met our bus at the last stop through our neighbourhood when the bus was empty except for one other student and me. Given the generic blond 'feathered' hairstyle I was sporting at the time, we were taken into custody instead of the actual culprits and whisked off to the police station. The only thing that saved me from further punishment was that our separate stories lined up under further interrogation. I was very relieved to bring a happy ending home to my parents.

"Four years later, I stepped onto a bus for my first day of on-the-road training. You can imagine my shock and surprise when a huge ex-military man with a white-haired buzz cut bellowed out, 'Hey, I know you! The police pulled you off my bus!'

"It was my new Auxiliary Instructor, Harold White, the same driver who had arranged for my arrest several years before!" (Dykstra)

Fred Leblanc had been working as an ETS security officer for 28 years when the new status of Special Constable was conferred on him. He expressed relief, saying that the job had never been as dangerous with 300 violent incidents occurring on the transit system yearly. On 20 March 2006, Fred Leblanc was one of 32 new Special Constables sworn in to fulfil their increased duties following an intensive three-week training course (*Edmonton Journal*).

In 2005 attention turned to the 350 property crimes and 1,600 drug- and alcohol-related incidents occurring on the transit system. Within the context of about 50 million annual rides, the numbers were not overwhelming, but they nevertheless signalled a disturbing trend. Inspector Mike Derbyshire was seconded from Edmonton Police Service to reorganize the ETS security department along an "intelligence-led, needs-based deployment model" that seeks to anticipate problems with the assistance of computer analysis. "We call it fishing with a fish finder," he notes. "We have to go in where the problems are going to be, not where they were" (*Edmonton Journal*).

Security on ETS was further enhanced in November 2006 when Edmonton received $2.2 million in federal funds to improve anti-terrorism safety on the system. Some of this money was directed at increased surveillance. However, Bill Chahal, President of ATU Local #569, also called for greater criminal penalties for those who assault transit drivers. The Local petitioned for penalties more in line with those for criminals who attack pilots and sea captains, which under the Criminal Code could result in a life sentence for the offender (*Edmonton Journal*).

Former Mayor Bill Smith, looking back, observes that there "was a period of time when the Police Service and the Transit Security people did not work closely together. . . . There were some bad feelings, and it did not work" (Smith, ETS Centennial Interview). Today, security arrangements encourage a high degree of cooperation between transit security personnel and Edmonton City Police.

In 2008 the Edmonton Transit System celebrated a milestone with its centennial. During the year, the ambitious extension of South Light Rail Transit (SLRT) could be witnessed daily by Edmontonians as trenches and excavations progressed steadily southward to fulfil the longstanding vision of a light rail transit system connecting the downtown core and other urban nodes with more distant residential communities within Edmonton's municipal boundaries.

Leading off the celebratory year, Edmonton Transit hosted the Canadian Urban Transit Association Annual Conference in May 24-28, 2008. Transit professionals from across Canada and other countries helped make this event a very successful kick-off for the centennial.

ETS held a homecoming on 21 June at Fort Edmonton Park. Over 1,000 employees, past and present, and their families attended. A highlight of the event was the chance to ride on Streetcar No. 1 operated by the Edmonton Radial Railway Society for the event. The streetcar barns also were open for tours. Rides on several heritage streetcars and buses, a performance by the ETS marching band, centennial cake and a night of dancing ensured that all had a great time.

The venerable Leyland No. 5 restored for heritage operation. *(ETS)*

Streetcar No. 1, restored and running at Fort Edmonton Park for the 21 June 2008 ETS Homecoming. *(ETS)*

The Edmonton Radial Railway Society Streetcar
No. 80 passes the ETS Heritage Fleet Leyland
Bus No. 5 and Brill Trolley No. 202. *(ETS)*

The ETS Pipes and Drums Band performs for participants during the homecoming celebration. *(ETS)*

Transit Centennial Week, held 11–20 September 2008 in Churchill Square, was the highpoint in the celebrations hosted by ETS. The week was launched at City Hall, where Gord Oleschuk, who had driven streetcars and every transit vehicle since, presented a moving speech focussing on the importance of history. The debate in City Hall that led to establishment of the Edmonton Radial Railway was re-enacted for the public. The Edmonton Transit Pipes and Drums Band then led an official procession to Churchill Square, which was packed with displays and vehicles from the ETS Heritage Fleet. More than 100 vintage vehicles would be on display for the public before the week ended. A crowd of excited transit enthusiasts followed, and over 40,000 attendees participated in garage open houses, historical bus tours, live performances, movies-on-the-square and other activities. Many ETS retirees were present wearing period uniforms to add a nostalgic atmosphere to the festivities. The beautifully restored Streetcar No. 1 was proudly displayed outside City Hall. Many purchased centennial souvenirs such as calendars, commemorative pin sets and centennial prints at the Shop on the Square.

From left to right, Hans Ryffel, president of the Edmonton Radial Railway Society, and retirees Andy Eistew, Gordon Oleschuk, Sigard (Sig) Schoenleber and Walter Newman proudly display their uniforms. (ETS)

The ETS heritage fleet on display in Churchill Square during Transit Centennial Week, with City Hall and CN Tower in the background.. Streetcar No. 1 forms the centrepiece. *(ETS)*

Charles Stolte (left) and Hans Ryffel (right) watch Gord Oleschuk (centre left) and Councillor Dave Thiele, City Council's representative on CUTA, cut the official Centennial cake. (ETS)

ERRS members Richard McLoughlin (left) and Gord Oleschuk stand in front of Streetcar No. 1 on display during Transit Centennial Week. The ERRS played a huge role in the Centennial celebrations. *(ETS)*

Charles Stolte, Manager of Edmonton Transit, stands in front of the oldest and the newest: Street Car No. 1, the first vehicle in the transit fleet, with one of the newest, a New Flyer hybrid, parked behind it. *(ETS)*

Doug Cowan shares his wealth of knowledge with school children during Transit Centennial Week at Churchill Square.
(ETS)

The culmination of centennial events occurred with the Very Important Transit event held on 8 November 2008 in the Shaw Conference Centre. The public was invited to view extensive displays on ETS history and heritage buses. The event featured the Edmonton Transit Pipes and Drums Band, Rapid Fire Theatre, information kiosks and family-oriented fun—building with Lego—and of course, a transit bus shaped cake.

Ernie Bastide worked on the school historical tours both as a driver and as a guide for students in the Transit Museum that was set up in Churchill Square for the centennial event. (ETS)

The Pipes and Drums of Edmonton Transit led by Drum Major
Chuck Van Deel Piepers at the VIT (Very Important Transit) event,
Shaw Conference Centre, 8 November 2008. *(ETS)*

Display at the VIT (Very Important Transit) event,
Shaw Conference Centre, 8 November 2008. *(ETS)*

During the centennial year, ETS Manager Charles Stolte awarded a certificate to Rodney Newell as the one-hundredth operator hired during the year. The year also saw the ETS attending the nuptials of Bobby and Emily Kuhl, who chartered a bus to provide limo service for their wedding party. The tradition of ETS service gained timely attention when a woman, feeling unwell after leaving a funeral service at Holy Rosary Church, began to faint. Her friend was not strong enough to support her, but a passing ETS operator stopped to lend assistance, preventing a serious fall down the church steps (*Transit News*).

As the ETS centennial year concluded, the city reflected on the first 100 years of public transit. "Plus ça change, plus c'est la même chose," the French say. "The more things change, the more they stay the same." Just as the fledgling Edmonton Radial Railway struggled to supply streetcar service to Highlands, the Edmonton Transit System remains behind the eight ball trying to maintain customer service at a high level as the city expands. Nevertheless, the centennial year marked a change that promises to reverse the long-standing trend. Rick Millican cites the redevelopment of the areas around 66 Street and Fort

Rapid Fire Theatre Improv Group performing at the VIT (Very Important Transit) event, Shaw Conference Centre, 8 November 2008. *(ETS)*

Road, and the old Heritage Mall site as examples of the City starting to use the LRT as a focus for development. Once again, Edmonton was a leader in this venture (Millican).

The first transit-oriented development (TOD) occurred in Edmonton in 1976 with the original development of the LRT. "The northeast line ran through an industrial corridor," Armin Preiksaitis points out. "And how do you intensify the area around transit? There wasn't anything to compare this to. It was a North American phenomenon—even California was auto-oriented. There were study towns in . . . German cities, as Siemens was the leader in transit technologies, but at that time the focus was on engineering rather than land use" (Preiksaitis). Armin A. Preiksaitis and Associates, James KM Cheng Architects, and Bunt and Associates in concert with Urban Planning and Community Consultation and Transportation Planning designed and developed the Century Park plan for the Heritage area. Heritage Mall operated for just under two decades before it was closed in 2000. Century Park Developments Ltd. purchased the site in November 2003. The plan was consistent with City initiatives such as *Plan Edmonton* and *Smart Choices,* and was closely coordinated with the City of Edmonton Planning and Development Department. Preiksaitis cites the development of LRT with significant changes in urban design:

"1976 gave us the first opportunities for city shaping. They called the northeast LRT "The Line That Gretzky Built." It connected Stadium to Coliseum and ran through an industrial corridor. The Northeast LRT Land Use Plan proposed higher density residential development around LRT stations. And now we have Station Point in the Belvedere area, a transit-oriented development where once a cluster of meat packing plants saw their day.

"When you look at the history of development in Edmonton and at the development of transit, you have a better appreciation that land patterns are influenced by transportation. We are recognizing that sustainable development is vital, as are physical and social environmental sustainability and reducing our carbon footprint. And now we have a rebirth of transit. With international pressure for long-term sustainability in Europe, Asia and the States. . . . It really is the golden age of transit.

"Transit-oriented development optimizes synergies between transit and land use to support transit ridership. The key elements include increased density within 400 metres walking distance to transit and mixed-use development—and that can be within a single building or single area and connected employment centres. We see that here with the U of A, Walter Mackenzie Health Sciences Centre and South Campus. Increasing density [makes possible] walkability, connectivity [and] moving away from park-and-ride facilities. Mixed-use development encourages reverse ridership by connecting at least main transit stations with institutional centres like the university and major recreation centres. It also includes street-oriented retail development that is attractive to pedestrian traffic.

Aerial view and model for Century Park, which received an Award of Merit from the Alberta Association, Canadian Institute of Planners, in 2005. *(Armin Preiksaitis)*

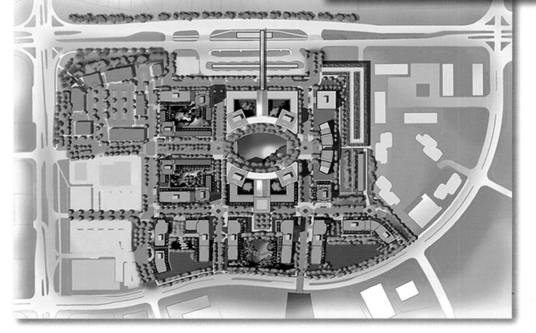

"Century Park is the best illustration of this. We're re-envisioning the city. It is greyfield land—economically obsolete real estate. The old shopping centre has seen its day. And it wasn't even that old (built in 1981), but [it] succumbed to changing retail patterns and the development of South Edmonton Common. What we've got in Century Park is a transit-oriented, mixed-use urban village created with the resident in mind. This is different than the town-centre model, which was shaped around a commercial centre.

"As far as connectivity to transit, there's a pedway to the Century Park LRT that the developer committed to paying for. This incorporated sustainability with green roofs, the recycling of storm water and encouragement of car sharing. Century Park has now become the benchmark for other large-scale infill sites.

"When City Council approved the rezoning for Century Park on 3 February 2005 there was not yet a firm commitment to extend the South Light Rail Transit.

"Was Century Park the catalyst for extending the LRT? The stars aligned. We are conscious of environmental issues: sustainability and global warming, and this only became forefront in the last 10 years. Our environmental footprint matters. Then there are psychographics: Edmonton grew up. We had a sort of Red Deer-on-steroids philosophy. We are in an auto-oriented province and have a need to keep energy costs low. Now, with immigration from other places in Canada and overseas, we have various ethnic groups used to increased density living. All of these coalesced to be where we are at now with Century Park" (Preiksaitis).

Today there may be young visionaries like Armin Preiksaitis dreaming of future transit systems for the City of Edmonton. With a nod to that time yet to come, the ETS invited young students to share their visions of the future during the centennial year. Their colourful and imaginative art captured the spirit of expectation and innovation that has characterized the first 100 years of public transit in Edmonton. When the bicentennial rolls round in the year 2108, who knows which of these flights of fancy may look very familiar to Edmontonians?

The plan for the South LRT announced in the summer of 2005 took the LRT line out to the Century Park area, adding momentum to the residential development on the site. *(ETS)*

Join the **Ride** of the **Century**

www.takeETS.com

ETS

Leo

Join the **Ride** of the **Century**

Present   Futuer

ETS AIR

www.takeETS.com   Rhian.

Bus

Join the **Ride** of the **Century**

Trolley

Fire Engine

Edmonton Transit
1908 100 ys. 2008
Catherine L.   Sept. 12, 2008
www.takeETS.com

Join the **Ride** of the **Century**

DESIGNERS Name: Lalie Busname: Sky Runer

In The Future

Buses will run on
Pollutants

(and conductors
will where
top Hats!)

Sky
Runer

Har-
Plac

www.takeETS.com   **ETS**
Edmonton Transit System

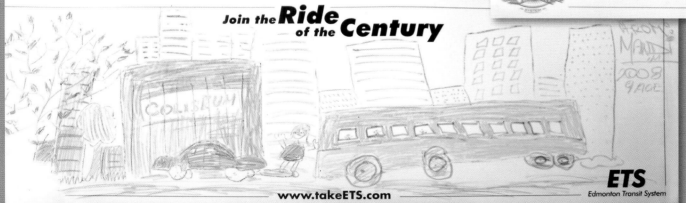

Works Cited

Boutilier, Bob. ETS Centennial Interviews, 2007–08. Edmonton, Alberta: ETS Archives.

Cavanagh, Terry. Communication to Ken Tingley, 2009. Edmonton, Alberta: ETS Archives.

Cavanagh, Terry. ETS Centennial Interviews, 2007–08. Edmonton, Alberta: ETS Archives.

City of Edmonton. *Transit Vehicle (Trolley) Technology Review*, 2008.

City of Edmonton. *Transportation Master Plan*, 1974.

Cowan, Doug. ETS Centennial Interviews, 2007–09. Edmonton, Alberta: ETS Archives.

Dykstra, Gord. *ETS Centennial* 2008, Issue 3, September 2008.

Edmonton Journal. 21 August 2002; 14 March 2003; 12 September 2003; 6 April 2004; 7 April 2004; 28 April 2004; 13 May 2004; 17 July 2004; 31 December 2005; 7 January 2006; 21 March 2006; 25 March 2006; 15 November 2006; 27 July 2007; 6 December 2007; 14 December 2007; 2005, 2006, 2007.

Edmonton Sun. 14 May 1999.

Geake, Dave. Communication to Ken Tingley, 2008. Edmonton, Alberta: ETS Archives.

Kulhavy, Dean. Communication to Ken Tingley, 2008. Edmonton, Alberta: ETS Archives.

Latham, Greg. ETS Centennial Interviews, 2007–09. Edmonton, Alberta: ETS Archives.

Mandryk, Wayne. ETS Centennial Interviews, 2007–08. Edmonton, Alberta: ETS Archives.

Millican, Rick. ETS Centennial Interviews, 2007–09. Edmonton, Alberta: ETS Archives.

Nowicki, Dennis. Communication to Ken Tingley, 2009–10. Edmonton, Alberta: ETS Archives.

Paul, Rick. ETS Centennial Interviews, 2007–09. Edmonton, Alberta: ETS Archives.

Preiksaitis, Armin. ETS Centennial Interviews, 2007–09. Edmonton, Alberta: ETS Archives.

Robinson, Marion. ETS Centennial Interviews, 2007–09. Edmonton, Alberta: ETS Archives.

Smith, Bill. ETS Centennial Interviews, 2007–08. Edmonton, Alberta: ETS Archives.

Stewart, Jim. Communication to Ken Tingley, 2009. Edmonton, Alberta: ETS Archives.

Stolte, Charles and John Sirovyak, *Transit Vehicle (Trolley) Technology Review*, 7 May 2008.

Transit News. August 2008.

Afterword

Stories are in abundance when reflecting on the active role of public transit in Edmonton's history and development. This book highlights many of the accomplishments and challenges in the 100-year history of Edmonton Transit. From four streetcars serving a population of 18,500 in 1908 to a fleet of over 1,000 vehicles in a city of 782,500 at the end of 2009, Edmonton Transit has evolved from being a groundbreaker in providing public transit to a small prairie city to being an industry leader in the new millennium. The ETS fleet at the end of 2009 was comprised of 891 40-foot low-floor buses, 13 articulated low-floor buses, 45 low-floor community buses, 70 light rail vehicles, and 98 lift-equipped DATS vans.

In the year since our centennial celebrations concluded, the innovation, imagination and improvement in ETS has continued at a pace unparalleled since the introduction of public transit in Edmonton. Heading up a long list of major investments in our public transit infrastructure were the light rail transit projects. In April the newest extension to the South LRT line opened with the commencement of service to McKernan/Belgravia and South Campus stations on April 26, 2009. Mayor Stephen Mandel noted at the opening event how "The City's strategic plan has an awful lot to do with transportation, moving people, but with environmental sensitivity and being creative in the way we move people in the 21st Century. Development of LRT is a key strategy to achieve our City Vision. For Edmonton to remain one of Canada's most livable and sustainable cities, we need to become more compact, and move people safely and efficiently."

Track work continued on the final two stages of the South LRT extension to Southgate and Century Park, and construction began for Lewis Farms and Meadows Transit Centres. Design work also commenced for Lewis Farms Phase II and Eaux Claires Transit Centres. Park 'n' Ride facilities are being built in conjunction with Century Park, Meadows, Lewis Farms and Eaux Claires transit facilities.

In late 2009, a new Park and Ride facility at Belvedere LRT station was completed to replace the former site. In November the Jasper Place Transit Centre was demolished to make way for construction of a brand new facility. Work also continued with the construction of our new Centennial Garage located in the southwest part of Edmonton. This is our first new facility since the 1981 opening of Mitchell Garage

and the 2005 start-up of the new DATS business model in the renovated Percy Wickman Garage. Work also commenced to fully enclose the unheated part of Wickman Garage.

Trolley bus service ended in May 2009 with the decommissioning of all remaining trolley vehicles followed by the start of the overhead wire removal program. GMC (high floor) buses were decommissioned in December 2009. Upon the decommissioning of the GMC "Jimmy" buses, Edmonton Transit's fleet became 100 percent accessible, a milestone event achieved only by a few transit systems in Canada.

The last of the 37 new light rail vehicles were commissioned and commenced service in the spring, incorporating new technology and a sleek new design to serve customers throughout the expanded light rail network. One hundred and twenty-one 40-foot buses also were purchased throughout the year, while an additional seventeen 30-foot community buses were added to the fleet, to fulfil the 2009–10 vehicle replacement and growth requirements. All new 40-foot buses are equipped with bus camera systems and bike racks.

Ridership growth continued in 2009 with a total of almost 68.5 million regular transit and 923,000 DATS rides. This growth, even in a time of economic slowdown, can be attributed to the major capital investments made throughout the system and programming and services offered to customers including the expansion of the ETS@Work employee pass program, introduction of Transit on Google Maps, making transit data and schedules available (or open) for the public to develop new applications, extension of the very popular U-Pass program, introduction of Air Miles for redemption and collection of travel miles for monthly adult passes and expansion of the Bikes On Buses program from four to eleven routes. In May ETS began testing smartcard technology with a pilot project involving staff from the University of Alberta travelling on the LRT.

The new TraXSafe LRT safety program was initiated in March to educate customers, vehicle drivers, school children and community residents about pedestrian and traffic safety along the new LRT line in south Edmonton. Also on the safety front, the new ETS Control Centre Intergraph dispatch software was implemented in 2009.

A busy year? You bet! We continue to plan for the future. In the short-term, planning has begun for the official opening

of the two new LRT stations scheduled for April 2010 and two new transit centres opening in April and August. Our Community Fair is once again scheduled to coincide with the LRT grand openings. The newest transit garage, Centennial, is also anticipated to be in operation by the spring of 2010.

Looking longer term, City Council approved the Transportation Master Plan on September 14, 2009. Entitled *The Way We Move,* this long-range plan calls for public transportation to be a cornerstone of a sustainable, liveable city, where more people use transit as a preferred travel choice. The Capital Region's Regional Transportation initiative continued to gather steam with discussions on providing public transit service to the International Airport and coordinating regional specialized transportation services such as DATS.

Public consultations and planning commenced for proposed plans for public transit services as well as new LRT alignments to North Edmonton past MacEwan University and NAIT, the southeast to Mill Woods, west to West Edmonton Mall and Lewis Estates, and to Gorman in the northeast. With spirited community discussions strongly reminiscent of those in the early 1900s regarding the original alignments and viability of the proposed streetcar services, the future LRT alignments have citizens once again contemplating public transit's critical relationship with land use development and liveable community planning.

I'm proud to be part of the revitalization of Edmonton Transit, and I look forward to working with employees and the community as we chart the course for our second century!

–**Charles Stolte**
Manager of
Edmonton
Transit
2010

357

Fleet List

Year Acquired	Year Withdrawn	Vehicle type	Road #	Colours	Manufacturer	Model	Quan.	Capacity	Notes
STREETCARS									
1908	1927	Streetcar	7	Green, wood trim, gold letters	Ottawa Car Company Ltd.	Double ended	1	32	Most streetcars repainted brown, yellow and white between 1916 and 1926; then red, ivory and black after 1926
1908	1947 to 1951 [#2: 1918]	Streetcar	1 to 6	Green, wood trim, gold letters	Ottawa Car Company Ltd.	Originally double ended; Rebuilt as single end cars	7	40	Most streetcars repainted brown, yellow and white between 1916 and 1926; then red, ivory and black after 1926
1909	1938 to 1948	Streetcar	10, 12, 14, 16	Green, red and white	Preston Car and Coach Company, Preston, Ontario	Originally double ended; Rebuilt as single end cars; Pay As You Enter	4	40	Most streetcars repainted brown, yellow and white between 1916 and 1926; then red, ivory and black after 1926
1910	1948 to 1950 [#21: 1919]	Streetcar	15, 17 to 21	Green, red and black	Ottawa Car Company Ltd.	Originally double ended; Rebuilt as single end cars; Pay As You Enter	6	32	Most streetcars repainted brown, yellow and white between 1916 and 1926; then red, ivory and black after 1926
1911	1948 to 1951	Streetcar	24 to 27	Green, red and black	Ottawa Car Company Ltd.	Single end; Pay As You Enter	4	41	Most streetcars repainted brown, yellow and white between 1916 and 1926; then red, ivory and black after 1926
1911	1948 to 1951	Streetcar	28 to 31	Green, red and black	Preston Car and Coach Company, Preston, Ontario	Single end; Pay As You Enter	4	41	Most streetcars repainted brown, yellow and white between 1916 and 1926; then red, ivory and black after 1926
1911	1948 [#22: 1917; #23: 1913]	Streetcar	8, 9, 11, 13, 22, 23	Green, red and black	Ottawa Car Company Ltd.	Single end; Pay As You Enter	6	37	Most streetcars repainted brown, yellow and white between 1916 and 1926; then red, ivory and black after 1926
1912	1949 to 191	Streetcar	32 to 46	Green, red and black, with a gold stripe	St. Louis Car Company, St. Louis, Missouri	Originally double ended; Rebuilt as single end cars; Pay As You Enter	15	36	
1913	1948 to 1951 [#50, 58: 1918]	Streetcar	47 to 74	Green, red and black, with a gold stripe	Preston Car and Coach Company, Preston, Ontario	Single end; Pay As You Enter	28	44	Most streetcars repainted brown, yellow and white between 1916 and 1926; then red, ivory and black after 1926
1914	1951 [#80, 81: 1917]	Streetcar	75 to 81	Green, red and black, with a gold stripe	Preston Car and Coach Company, Preston, Ontario	Single end; Pay As You Enter	7	44	Most streetcars repainted brown, yellow and white between 1916 and 1926; then red, ivory and black after 1926
1920	1929	Streetcar	Observation Car	White and gold, with red trim	Edmonton Radial Railway		1	42	Originally streetcar #22, repaired to service tourists
1930	1951	Streetcar	80 [2nd], 81 [2nd], 82 to 84	Red, ivory and black	Ottawa Car Manufacturing Company Ltd.	All steel constuction; Front entrance, centre exit	5	51	
1941	1949	Streetcar	Library Car	Blue and ivory	Edmonton Radial Railway		1	[none]	Originally streetcar #14, refurbished in 1941
TROLLEYS									
1939	1950 to 1951	Trolley coach	101 to 103	Red and ivory, with an orange band and black stripes	Associated Equipment Co./ English Electric Co.		3	38	

Year Acquired	Year Withdrawn	Vehicle type	Road #	Colours	Manufacturer	Model	Quan.	Capacity	Notes
1939	1950 to 1951	Trolley coach	104 to 106	Red and ivory, with an orange band and black stripes	Leyland Motors, UK/ Park Royal Coach		3	38	
1942	1951	Trolley coach	107 to 109	Red and ivory, with an orange band and black stripes	Leyland Motors, UK/ Park Royal Coach		3	39	
1943	1962	Trolley coach	110 to 112	Red and ivory	Mack Manufacturing, Pennsylvania		3	40	
1944	1964 to 1966	Trolley coach	113 to 120	Red and ivory, with black stripes	Pullman-Standard		8	44	Bus 116 renumbered 113 in 1966
1945	1964 to 1966	Trolley coach	121 to 128	Red and ivory, with black stripes	Pullman-Standard		8	44	
1945	1966	Trolley coach	129 to 130	Red and ivory	American Car and Foundry-Brill	TC-44	2	44	
1947	1973 to 1978	Trolley coach	131 to 177	Red and ivory	Canadian Car and Foundry Company Ltd.-Brill	T-44	47	44	
1948	1974 to 1978	Trolley coach	178 to 187	Red and ivory	Canadian Car and Foundry Company Ltd.-Brill	T-44	10	44	
1949	1973 to 1978	Trolley coach	188 to 192	Red and ivory	Canadian Car and Foundary Company Ltd.-Brill	T-44	5	44	
1952	1975 to 1978	Trolley coach	193 to 196	Red and ivory	Canadian Car and Foundary Company Ltd.-Brill	T-48A	4	48	
1954	1978	Trolley coach	197 to 202	Red and ivory	Canadian Car and Foundary Company Ltd.-Brill	T-48A	6	42	
1962	1974 to 1978	Trolley coach	203 to 212	Red and ivory	Canadian Car and Foundary Company Ltd.-Brill	T-44	10	44	Built in 1947, acquired from Vancouver in 1962
1966	1974 to 1978	Trolley coach	121 [2nd] to 130 [2nd]	Red and ivory	Canadian Car and Foundary Company Ltd.-Brill	T-44	10	44	Built in 1949, acquired from Regina in 1966
1974	1982	Trolley coach	213	Red and ivory	Flyer Industries Ltd.	E10240	1	49	
1975	1982	Trolley coach	214 to 237	Red and ivory	Flyer Industries Ltd.	E10240	24	49	
1976	n/a	Trolley coach	238 to 249	Red and ivory	Flyer Industries Ltd.	E10240	12	49	
1981	n/a	Trolley coach	100	Off-white, with blue and yellow striping	Brown Boveri/GMC	5307N	1	42	
1982	Currently in service (2008)	Trolley coach	101 [2nd] to 112 [2nd]; 113 [3rd]; 113 [2nd] to 199 [2nd]	Off-white, with blue and yellow striping	Brown Boveri/GMC	5307N	99	42	
2006	Currently in service (2008)	Trolley coach	6000		New Flyer		1		Short term lease
MOTOR BUS									
1932	1944	Motor bus [gasoline]	1	Red, ivory and black	Leyland Motors	Cub	1	21	Converted to diesel in 1937.
1932	1944	Motor bus [gasoline]	3	Red, ivory and black	GMC		1	25	Converted to diesel in 1937.
1932	1947	Motor bus [gasoline]	2	Red, ivory and black	White Truck Co.	613	1	21	
1938	1941	Motor bus [gasoline]	n/a	n/a	GMC		2	21	Leased from Bus Universal Supply Ltd.
1939	1947	Motor bus [gasoline]	4	Red and ivory, with an orange band and black stripes	Leyland Motors	Lioness	1	27	Bookmobile from 1951; Mobile command post for emergency services
1939	1954	Motor bus [diesel]	5	Red and ivory, with an orange band and black stripes	Leyland Motors	Cub	1	23	Converted to gasoline in 1949.

Year Acquired	Year Withdrawn	Vehicle type	Road #	Colours	Manufacturer	Model	Quan.	Capacity	Notes
1940	1951	Motor bus [diesel]	6	Red and ivory, with an orange band and black stripes	Leyland Motors	Cub	1	23	Converted to gasoline in 1949; Bookmobile from 1951
1940	1954	Motor bus [diesel]	7	Red and ivory, with an orange band and black stripes	Leyland Motors	Lioness	1	27	Converted to gasoline in 1949.
1941	1954	Motor bus [diesel]	8 to 10	Red and ivory, with an orange band and black stripes	Leyland Motors	Tiger	3	30	Converted to gasoline in 1949.
1943	1954	Motor bus [gasoline]	11 to 13	Red and ivory	Ford	Victory	3	27	
1944	1951 to 1954	Motor bus [gasoline]	14 to 16	Red and ivory	Ford	Victory	3	27	Bus 14 converted to propane in 1949
1946	1947	Motor bus [gasoline]	n/a	n/a	Ford		1	n/a	Leased from McMullen and Noullett
1946	1959 to 1969	Motor bus [gasoline]	17 to 28	Red and ivory	Canadian Car and Foundary Company Ltd.-Brill	C-36	12	36	First buses with the ETS logo: 'ETS' in yellow, surrounded by a black oval.
1947	1957 to 1968	Motor bus [gasoline]	29 to 35	Red and ivory	Canadian Car and Foundary Company Ltd.-Brill	C-36	7	36	
1948	1967 to 1969	Motor bus [gasoline]	36 to 45	Red and ivory	Canadian Car and Foundary Company Ltd.-Brill	C-36	10	36	Bus 43 renumbered 99
1950	1969 to 1971	Motor bus [gasoline]	46 to 53	Red and ivory	Canadian Car and Foundary Company Ltd.-Brill	C-36	8	36	
1950	1971 to 1975	Motor bus [propane]	60 to 69	Red and ivory	Twin Coach	45-S	10	44	First two-way radios on Canadian municipal transit installed on some of these buses in 1952. All buses received two-way radios and a telephone handset in the 1970s in conjunction with the LRT system.
1950	1972 to 1975	Motor bus [gasoline]	54 to 58	Red and ivory	Twin Coach	44-S	5	44	
1950	1975	Motor bus [propane]	59	Red and ivory	Twin Coach	44-S	1	44	First two-way radios on Canadian municipal transit installed on some of these buses in 1952.
1951	1952	Motor bus [gasoline]	M132 to M139	n/a	Twin Coach	41-S	8	41	Leased from B.C. Electric, Vancouver
1951	1962 to 1969	Motor bus [gasoline]	83 to 93	Red and ivory	Canadian Car and Foundary Company Ltd.-Brill	C-36	11	36	Purchased used from Saint John, New Brunswick Power Co.
1951	1963 to 1964	Motor bus [diesel]	94 to 99	Red and ivory	Mack Truck Company, Pennsylvania	C-37DT	6	37	
1951	1972 to 1975	Motor bus [propane]	70 to 82	Red and ivory	Twin Coach	45-S	13	45	
1952	1963 to 1967	Motor bus [propane]	401 to 408	Red and ivory	Twin Coach	FLP-40	8	52	
1955	1978	Motor bus [diesel]	409 to 433	Red and ivory, with a black stripe	GMC	TDH-5105	25	52	
1960	1984	Motor bus [diesel]	434 to 438	Red and ivory	GMC	TDH-5301	5	51	Large aluminum side panels led to ETS personnel calling these buses "silversides"
1962	1965 to 1967	Motor bus [gasoline]	511 to 520	Red and ivory	Twin Coach	38-S	10	38	Purchased used from Winnipeg; Buses 512, 513, 516 and 519 renumbered buses 11, 12, 13 and 14 [2nds] in 1966
1962	1966 to 1968	Motor bus [gasoline]	501 to 510	Red and ivory	Twin Coach	41-S	10	51	Purchased used from Winnipeg; Buses 501 to 509 renumbered in 1966 to buses 1 to 9; First buses with cast aluminum ETS crest in stylized script
1962	1984	Motor bus [diesel]	439 to 443	Red and ivory	GMC	TDH-5301C	5	51	
1963	1971	Motor bus [gasoline]	854	Red and ivory	Bluebird		1	67	Modified school bus for regular transit service
1963	n/a [#445: 1963]	Motor bus [diesel]	444 to 473	Red and ivory	GMC	TDH-5301C	30	51	
1964	1971	Motor bus [diesel]	10 [2nd]	Special version of red and ivory	Mitsubishi-Fuso	MAR750L	1	51	Renumbered 600 in 1968
1964	1973	Motor bus [diesel]	601 to 603	Red and ivory	Nissan	6LRA110-K2	3	48	

Year Acquired	Year Withdrawn	Vehicle type	Road #	Colours	Manufacturer	Model	Quan.	Capacity	Notes
1964	n/a	Motor bus [diesel]	474 to 493	Red and ivory	GMC	TDH-5303	20	52	
1964	1977	Motor bus [gasoline]	855 to 868	Red and ivory	Bluebird		14	45	Modified school bus for regular transit service
1966	n/a	Motor bus [diesel]	494 to 500; 501 [2nd] to 510 [2nd]	Red and ivory	GMC	TDH-5303	17	52	
1966	1973	Motor bus [diesel]	701 to 703	Red and ivory	Daimler	SRC6 Roadliner	3	44	Prototype
1966	1974	Motor bus [diesel]	604 to 613	Red and ivory	Nissan	6LRA110-K2	10	46	
1967	n/a	Motor bus [diesel]	511 [2nd] to 520 [2nd]; 521 to 535	Red and ivory	GMC	TDH-5303	25	52	
1967	1973 to 1974	Motor bus [diesel]	704 to 728	Red and ivory	Daimler	SRC6 Roadliner	25	44	#707 refurbished as Infobus
1968	n/a	Motor bus [diesel]	1 [3rd] to 10 [3rd]	Red and ivory	GMC	T6H-4521	10	45	
1969	n/a	Motor bus [diesel]	11 [3rd] to 14 [3rd]	Red and ivory	GMC	T6H-4521	4	45	
1969	n/a	Motor bus [diesel]	15 [2nd] to 25 [2nd]	Red and ivory	GMC	T6H-4521	11	45	
1972	n/a	Motor bus [diesel]	700	Winnipeg transit colours	Western Flyer Company	D700A	1	51	Renumbered 800 in 1977
1972	n/a	Motor bus [diesel]	536 to 569	Red and ivory	GMC	T6H-5307N	34	49	
1973	n/a	Motor bus [diesel]	26 [2nd] to 35 [2nd]	Red and ivory	GMC	T6H-4523N	10	45	
1973	n/a	Motor bus [diesel]	570 to 590	Red and ivory	GMC	T6H-5307N	21	49	
1974	n/a	Motor bus [diesel]	301 to 321	Red and ivory	GMC	T6H-5307N	21	49	
1974	n/a	Motor bus [diesel]	591 to 599, 600 [2nd]	Red and ivory	GMC	T6H-5307N	10	49	
1974	n/a	Motor bus [diesel]	731 to 740	Red and ivory	Flyer Industries Ltd.	D800	10	49	Renumbered 831 to 840 in 1977
1975	n/a	Motor bus [diesel]	322 to 371	Red and ivory	GMC	T6H-5307N	50	49	
1975	n/a	Motor bus [diesel]	372 to 396	Red and ivory	GMC	T6H-5307N	25	47	
1976	n/a	Motor bus [diesel]	1 to 10 [special]	St. Albert colours	GMC	T6H-5307N	10	49	St. Albert service, renumbered 811-820 in 1977
1976	n/a	Motor bus [diesel]	397 to 399	Off-white, with blue and yellow striping	GMC	T6H-5307N	3	47	First buses with the new Edmonton Transit logo: a blue stylized 'E' decal, followed by the word 'Transit' in black
1976	n/a	Motor bus [diesel]	601 [2nd] to 613 [2nd]; 614 to 697	Red and ivory	GMC	T6H-5307N	97	47	
1977	n/a	Motor bus [diesel]	821	St. Albert colours	GMC	T6H-5307N	1	49	St. Albert service only
1977	n/a	Motor bus [diesel]	698 to 699; 700 [2nd] to 728 [2nd]; 729 to 767	Off-white, with blue and yellow striping	GMC	T6H-5307N	70	47	
1977	n/a	Motor bus [diesel]	841 to 858	Off-white, with blue and yellow striping	Flyer Industries Ltd.	D800	18	49	
1977	n/a	Motor bus [diesel]	859 [2nd] to 868 [2nd]	Off-white, with blue and yellow striping	GMC	T6H-5307N	10	49	
1978	n/a	Motor bus [diesel]	900 to 925	Off-white, with blue and yellow striping	GMC	T6H-5307N	26	47	
1979	n/a	Motor bus [diesel]	822 to 824	St. Albert colours	GMC	T6H-5307N	3	[47]	St. Albert service only
1980	n/a	Motor bus [diesel]	825 to 827	Off-white, with blue and yellow striping	GMC	T6H-5307N	3	[47]	St. Albert service only
1980	n/a	Motor bus [diesel]	926 to 955	Off-white, with blue and yellow striping	GMC	T6H-5307N	30	49	First buses with electronic signs and cloth upholstry
1980	n/a	Motor bus [diesel]	956 to 995	Off-white, with blue and yellow striping	GMC	T6H-5307N	30	47	
1982	Not in service	Motor bus	4001-4045	Blue and Gray	GMC	T6H-5307N	46	49	
1993	Currently in service	Motor bus	200-242	Blue and Gray	New Flyer	40' low floor	43	37	First purchase of accessible, low floor buses

Year Acquired	Year Withdrawn	Vehicle type	Road #	Colours	Manufacturer	Model	Quan.	Capacity	Notes
1994	Currently in service	Motor bus	243-258	Blue and Gray	New Flyer	40' low floor	16	37	
1998	Currently in service	Motor bus	4046-4125	Blue and Gray	New Flyer	40' low floor	80	37	
1999	Currently in service	Motor bus	4126-4174	Blue and Gray	New Flyer	40' low floor	49	37	
2000	Currently in service	Motor bus	4175-4233	Blue and Gray	New Flyer	40' low floor	60	37	
2001	Currently in service	Articulated Bus	4900-4905	Blue and Gray	New Flyer	60' low floor, articulated	6	57	
2001	Currently in service	Motor bus	4234-4299	Blue and Gray	New Flyer	40' low floor	66	37	
2002	Currently in service	Motor bus	4300-4352	Blue and Gray	New Flyer	40' low floor	53	37	
2003	Currently in service	Motor bus	4353-4402	Blue and Gray	New Flyer	40' low floor	50	37	
2003	Currently in service	Articulated Bus	4906-4912	Blue and Gray	New Flyer	60' low floor, articulated	7	57	
2004	Currently in service	Motor bus	4403-4437	Blue and Gray	New Flyer	40' low floor	35	37	
2005	Currently in service	Motor bus	4438-4477	Blue and Gray	New Flyer	40' low floor	39	37	
2006	Currently in service	Motor bus	4478-4522	Blue and Gray	New Flyer	40' low floor	45	37	
2006	Currently in service	Hybrid	6005-6006	Blue and Gray	Orion VII/BAE	40' low floor, hybrid	2	37	
2007	Currently in service	Hybrid	6001-6002	Blue and Gray	New Flyer/Allison	40' low floor, hybrid	2	37	
2007	Currently in service	Hybrid	6003-6004	Blue and Gray	New Flyer/ISE	40' low floor, hybrid	2	37	
2007	Currently in service	Motor bus	4523-4753	Blue and Gray	New Flyer	40' low floor, low emission	231	37	
COMMUNITY BUS									
1991	Not in service	Elf CSB	50		Ford	30' low floor community service buses	1	21	
1993	Not in service	Elf CSB	51-53		Ford	30' low floor community service buses	3	21	
1994	Currently in service	Elf CSB	54	Blue and Gray	Ford	30' low floor community service buses	1	21	
1996	Currently in service	Elf CSB	55-58	Blue and Gray	Ford	30' low floor community service buses	4	21	
1997	Currently in service	Elf CSB	59-64	Blue and Gray	Ford	30' low floor community service buses	5	21	
1998	Currently in service	Elf CSB	65-66	Blue and Gray	Ford	30' low floor community service buses	2	21	

Year Acquired	Year Withdrawn	Vehicle type	Road #	Colours	Manufacturer	Model	Quan.	Capacity	Notes
1999	Currently in service	Elf CSB	67-71	Blue and Gray	Ford	30' low floor community service buses	5	21	
2001	Currently in service	Elf CSB	72-79	Blue and Gray	Ford	30' low floor community service buses	8	21	
2005	Currently in service	Elf CSB	80-91	Blue and Gray	Ford	30' low floor community service buses	12	21	
2007	Currently in service	Glaval CSB	1-13	Blue and Gray	Glaval	30' Easy-On low floor community service buses	13	21	
DATS VEHICLES – CITY OWNED AND OPERATED									
2000	Currently in service	DATS GOSHEN BUS 9 PASS	5001	White	FORD / GOSHEN	E350 / GCII #806	1	9 PASS	4 passengers 5 wheelchair position
2003	Currently in service	DATS BUS 9 PASS	5002-5004	White	FORD	E350	3	9 PASS	4 passengers 5 wheelchair position. 5003 caught on fire at Percy Wickman garage and was a total loss.
2003	Currently in service	DATS BUS 9 PASS	5005-5010	White	FORD	E450	6	9 PASS	4 passengers 5 wheelchair position
2005	Currently in service	DATS BUS 9 PASS	5011-5091	White	FORD	E450	81	9 PASS	4 passengers 5 wheelchair position
2006	Currently in service	DATS BUS 9 PASS	5097	White	FORD	E450	1	9 PASS	5 passengers 5 wheelchair position. 5097 was replacement for unit 5003.
2008	Currently in service	DATS BUS 9 PASS	5098-5104	White	FORD	E450	7	9 PASS	6 passengers 5 wheelchair position
LRT									
1977	Currently in service	LRT	1001-1014	Off-white, with blue and yellow striping	Waggonfabrik Uerdingen AG Werk, Dusseldorf, West Germany	U2	14	64 plus 97 standing	
1979	Currently in service	LRT	1015-1017	Off-white, with blue and yellow striping	Waggonfabrik Uerdingen AG Werk, Dusseldorf, West Germany	U2	3	64 plus 97 standing	
1982	Currently in service	LRT	1018-1021	Off-white, with blue and yellow striping	Waggonfabrik Uerdingen AG Werk, Dusseldorf, West Germany	U2	4	64 plus 97 standing	
1983	Currently in service	LRT	1022-1037	Off-white, with blue and yellow striping	Waggonfabrik Uerdingen AG Werk, Dusseldorf, West Germany	U2	16	64 plus 97 standing	
2005	Currently in service	LRT	1038-1063	White and blue	Siemens Canada Ltd	SD-160	26	60 plus 100 standing	
2007	Currently in service	LRT	1064-1074	White and blue	Siemens Canada Ltd	SD-160	11	60 plus 100 standing	
OTHER									
1909	1951	Service car: Baggage-sweeper	1		McGuire-Cummings Manufacturing Company, Chicago, Illinois		1		

Year Acquired	Year Withdrawn	Vehicle type	Road #	Colours	Manufacturer	Model	Quan.	Capacity	Notes
1909	1921	Service car: Sprinkler	S-1		Preston Car and Coach Company, Preston, Ontario		1		
1910		Service car: Horse-drawn tower wagon (non-rail)	1		Ottawa Car Company Ltd.		1		
1911	1915	Service car: Sand car	[S-3?]		Ottawa Car Company Ltd.		1		
1912	1951	Service car: Flat car	S-4		McGuire-Cummings Manufacturing Company, Chicago, Illinois		1		
1913	1918	Service car: Differential dump car	S-5		Canadian Car and Foundary Company Ltd.		1		
1913	1924	Service car: Sprinkler	S-2		McGuire-Cummings Manufacturing Company, Chicago, Illinois		1		
1913	1951	Service car: Line car	L-1		Edmonton Radial Railway		1		Renumbered S-5
1914	1922	Service car: Flat car	[S-6?]		Edmonton Radial Railway	Unmotorized unit	1		
1915	1918	Service car: Line car	[S-3?]		Ottawa Car Company Ltd.		1		
1918	1951	Service car: Sweeper	2 [2nd]		Edmonton Radial Railway		1		Originally streetcar #2
1918	1949	Service car: Sweeper	2		Ottawa Car Company Ltd.		1		Renumbered 3 in 1928
1922	1951	Service car: Ballast spreader	5		Edmonton Radial Railway		1		
1925	1951	Service car: Wrecker	6		Edmonton Radial Railway		1		Originally service car #S-2
1928	1937	Service car: Weed killer	n/a		Edmonton Radial Railway		1		Originally streetcar #7
1937	1951	Service car: Rail grinder	n/a		Edmonton Radial Railway		1		Originally Service Car (weed killer)
1961	1963 to 1966	School bus [gasoline]	801 to 803	Yellow	Oneida		3	48	
1961	1966 to 1968	School bus [gasoline]	804 to 805	Yellow	Carpenter		2	54	
1962	1969	School bus [gasoline]	834	Yellow	Superior		1	72	
1962	n/a	School bus [gasoline]	830 to 833	Yellow?	Bluebird		4	72	
1962	1970 to 1975	School bus [gasoline]	835 to 844	Yellow	Carpenter		10	72	
1963	n/a	School bus [gasoline]	845 to 849	Yellow	Carpenter		5	72	
1963	1975	School bus [gasoline]	850 to 853	Upper portion ivory; red, grey and ivory below the windows	Bluebird		4	67	
1964	1975	School bus [gasoline]	869 to 874	Yellow	Bluebird		6	67	
1975	1981	School bus [gasoline]	801 [2nd] to 805 [2nd]; 806 to 810	Yellow	Bluebird	FC 3400	10	72	
1977	n/a	LRT service equipment: Kal-Trac heavy duty land/rail vehicle	3850	Yellow	Canron Railgroup Co.		1		
1980	n/a	LRT service equipment: 32' Flat car	2101	Olive green	Edmonton Transit, Cromdale Shop		1		Originally Northern Alberta Railway box car
1980	n/a [#2301: 1981; #2304: 1980]	LRT service equipment: Differential dump car	2301 to 2310	Olive green	K.M.L. Custom Fabricators Ltd., Edmonton		10		Originally Northern Alberta Railway cars
1980	n/a	LRT service equipment: 40' Flat car	2102 to 2103	Olive green	Edmonton Transit, Cromdale Shop		2		Originally Northern Alberta Railway idler car
1980	n/a	LRT service equipment: Centre-cab electric locomotive	2001	Off-white, with blue and yellow striping	American Locomotive Company		1		Built in 1912
1981	n/a	LRT service equipment: Depressed centre flat car	2201	Olive green	K.M.L. Custom Fabricators Ltd., Edmonton		1		Originally Northern Alberta Railway plow car

Index

One Hundred Years...And Counting

In 2008, Edmonton Transit celebrated its One Hundredth Anniversary. I am proud to say that we, the Union, have been associated with Edmonton Transit for ninety eight of them.

Under the title of the Amalgamated Association of Streetcar and Electric Railway Employees of America, we agreed to our first Collective Agreement with the City in August 1911. The rate for an operator back then was 27.5 cents per hour. How things have changed.

Many other things have changed over the years, such as equipment, routes, and schedules; however one thing has remained the same. That is, the commitment both the city and union have given the citizens of Edmonton to provide a transit system that is the envy of the country.

I am sure most of you are aware of the direction Edmonton Transit is heading with the expansion of the LRT, new garages, equipment and improved security. Edmonton Transit is striving to continue its commitment to give Edmontonian's the transit system they demand.

Hopefully all of you have heard of The Working Relationship Agreement with the City of Edmonton. A one of a kind document ATU Local 569 is proud to be a part of. It's an agreement endorsed by Union / Association Leaders and Senior Management Team on behalf of all civic employees. We believe collaborative relations between management of the City of Edmonton (Edmonton Transit) and the unions and associations representing City employees can serve the long term interests of all parties. In no way does this diminish the right and responsibility of ATU Local 569 to represent the best interests of our members.

As President of this Local, I am very proud to serve my members. I can also say that for the last twenty plus years, I was proud to say I worked for Edmonton Transit.

The Union looks forward to what the future holds, we look forward to working together, and we look forward to participating with Edmonton Transit in developing the best transit system in the country.

On behalf of the full time officers, Executive Board, and members of Amalgamated Transit Union Local 569, I would like to offer our sincerest congratulations to Edmonton Transit on its 100th Anniversary.

Sincerely,
Stu Litwinowich, *PRESIDENT*
Claude Doucette, *FINANCIAL SECRETARY TREASURER*
Daniel Revega, *VICE PRESIDENT/MAINTENANCE*
The Executive Board
And all members of Amalgamated Transit Union Local 569

Each operator, mechanic, engineer and active/previous member of your organization has played an important role to make this centennial a possibility. We congratulate you on reaching your 100-year anniversary, and to the future successes that lay ahead.

We are proud to support your organization, which is a major part of our success as well as focus for our company, and look forward to continuing to provide to you the best possible engines and support to keep Edmonton moving.

Best wishes from the management and staff of Cummins Western Canada.

Congratulations Edmonton Transit System on your Centennial

www.westerncanada.cummins.com

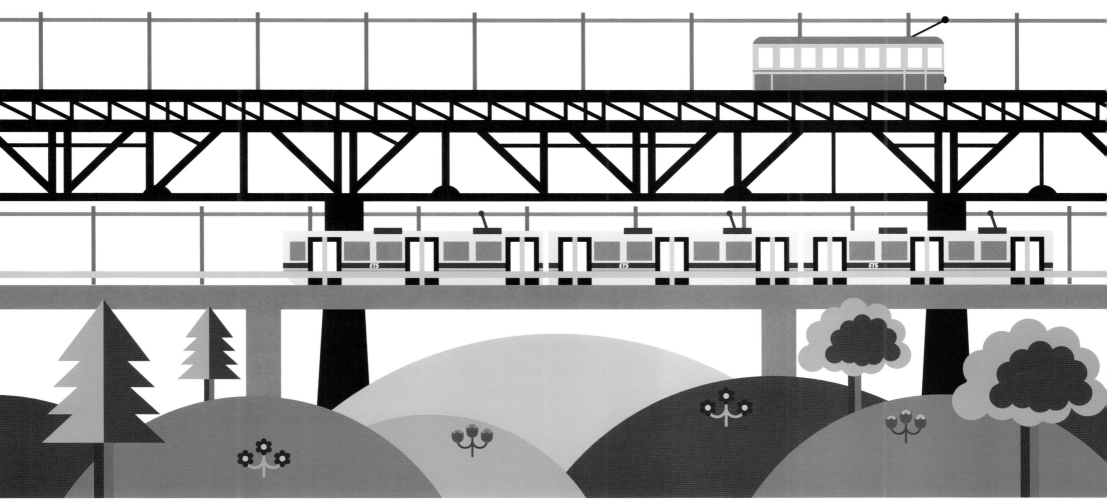

CONNECTING ONE CENTURY TO ANOTHER.

EPCOR happily congratulates the Edmonton Transit System on their 100-year milestone! ETS' commitment to people and service makes us proud to have powered its streetcars, trolleys and LRTs for the last century. We look forward to the next 100 years.

epcor.ca

PROVIDING MORE

NEW FLYER

New Flyer congratulates Edmonton Transit System for one hundred years of service and contribution to the success of the city and its citizens.

Our relationship with ETS began in 1971 with the delivery of one D700A model – a high-floor diesel vehicle with a four-window windshield for improved visibility. Our more recent deliveries include a DE40LFR model with a prototype low-profile enclosure for the hybrid drive system.

Like ETS, New Flyer's long history included dealing with the harsh conditions in Western Canada. Our company's namesake was the Western Flyer model, and, as its name seemed to imply, this region provided unique challenges to the transportation industry. Back then, the concerns were with rugged terrain, dust in the engine, heat and cold. Today the challenges are traffic congestion, accessibility and reduced emissions.

New Flyer and ETS have been through it all by embracing change and by engaging innovative strategies. We are proud to be associated with ETS and look forward to another century of its continued success.

"Congratulations to Edmonton Transit System for a century of providing mobility to the people of the city where they live, work, and play."

—*Marco Jungbeker, Vice President Mobility Division, Siemens Canada Limited*

Siemens is proud to support Edmonton Transit System and their mission of providing "customer focused, safe, reliable and affordable public transit services that link people and places." We look forward to enhancing our relationship through innovation and respect. Together we can build a sustainable and environmentally friendly future of Light Rail Transit in Edmonton and highspeed rail in the Province of Alberta.

Answers for Canada.

SIEMENS

ETS ANNIVERSARY

Connecting People, Connecting Communities

YELLOW CAB Prestige Transportation

Edmonton is a city on the move. Everyday, thousands of Edmontonians travel around our great city using public transportation provided by Edmonton Transit System (ETS). They travel to stay connected. They travel to make connections. And as they travel, they help connect communities along the way. As Edmonton's premier taxi-service provider and a Gold sponsor, Yellow Cab is pleased to congratulate Edmonton Transit System on its 100 years of dedicated and unwavering transportation service. Being a local transportation provider, we realize that connecting people in a bustling city on any given day is a monumental task, but to achieve this for a century with consistent skill and efficiency is a remarkable feat.

In recent years, Yellow Cab has been proud to connect with ETS on a partnership level. Both companies continue to collaborate on innovative projects designed to connect Edmontonians and city visitors with the best transportation service possible. Our sister company, Prestige Transportation has been offering DATS ambulatory transportation service under various contracts and business models for 24 continuous years. Disabled and handicapped clients are able to arrange for a comfortable, safe ride in one of Prestige's approximately 70 DATS vehicles. Furthermore, to help keep communities connected, Yellow Cab offers services that can be paired up with regular ETS service. For Edmontonians who must travel farther to reach a major "transportation hub," Yellow Cab's service connects them to these "hubs," after which they can use public transportation for the rest of their trip.

Now that Edmonton has become a major hub in Alberta, with its quickly growing population, ETS is committed to the future and to making transit an effortless part of everyday life in Edmonton. LRT extensions, Customer Care Centres, and other programs such as Donate-a-Ride are examples of how ETS is constantly adapting and improving its service. After 100 years of experience, ETS has become a leader in transit service, safety, and accessibility.

Congratulations again, ETS! We're proud to help you celebrate this "road" marker and look forward to making more connections through partnership!

FGI
FORT GARRY INDUSTRIES

Heavy-Duty Parts, Service & Equipment

Congratulations Edmonton Transit System
on **100 years** of public transportation!

EDMONTON   Phone: 780-447-4422
16230 118th Ave NW   Fax: 780-447-3289

CALGARY	Phone: 403-236-9712
RED DEER	Phone: 403-343-1383
GRANDE PRAIRIE	Phone: 780-402-9864
LETHBRIDGE	Phone: 403-331-6315
LLOYDMINSTER	Phone: 780-875-9115
SURREY	Phone: 604-888-5522
SASKATOON	Phone: 306-242-3465
REGINA	Phone: 306-757-5606
WINNIPEG	Phone: 204-632-8269
BRANDON	Phone: 204-571-5980
THUNDER BAY	Phone: 807-577-5724
MISSISSAUGA	Phone: 905-564-5404

www.fgiltd.com

EDMONTON TRANSIT
1908 **100** 2008
SYSTEM

1908-2008

ETS celebrates **100** years

Design by Shelby Briggs